KU-517-386

Ac

FROM
THE LIBRARY
UNIVERSITY OF
WINCHESTER

KA 0005522 0

THE SOCIOLOGY OF PROTESTANTISM

ROGER MEHL

THE SOCIOLOGY OF PROTESTANTISM

SCM PRESS LTD

Translated by James H. Farley
from the French
Traité de sociologie du protestantisme
published 1965 by Delachaux & Niestlé
Neuchâtel, Switzerland

KING ALFRED'S COLLEGE

280.4
MEH   80630

334 01558 8
First published in English 1970
by SCM Press Ltd
56 Bloomsbury Street London WC1
Translation © SCM Press Ltd 1970
Printed in Great Britain by
Western Printing Services Ltd Bristol

CONTENTS

PRINCIPAL ABBREVIATIONS

ASR	*Archives de sociologie des religions*
CIS	*Cahiers internationaux de sociologie*
CS	*Christianisme social*
ETR	*Etudes théologiques et religieuses*
FV	*Foi et Vie*
MNC	*Le Monde non chrétien*
PUF	Presses Universitaires de France
RHPR	*Revue d'Histoire et de Philosophie religieuses*
RHR	*Revue de l'Histoire des religions*

TRANSLATOR'S INTRODUCTION

In *History and Truth*, Paul Ricoeur states that in our time a complete answer to the problem of the meaning of history would require the abilities of the historian, the sociologist, and the theologian. It is interesting that Ricoeur dedicates his book to Roger Mehl, for few scholars have taken such a lively and informed interest in the "inter-disciplinary" approach to the problem of the meaning of history. To the degree that the elucidation of the meaning of history is the first and most important step in the elucidation of the human condition, our present human situation cannot be fully comprehended without the serious, critical, and sometimes difficult type of reflection carried out by Mehl in *The Sociology of Protestantism*. In *De l'autorité des valeurs*, an important yet curiously neglected work published in 1957, Mehl begins by saying that human thought is enclosed in the dialectic of essence and existence, a dialectic that illuminates the stages of philosophy. Once again we are in a period of history where existence is in rebellion against essence. The whole phraseology of the Now Generation reflects an assault on essential values and the structures based on those values. Such an assault creates manifold problems, the most important of which is the unexpected emphasizing of the precariousness of ungrounded existence. Few people have the courage of the "ideal existentialist", who accepts the anxiety implicit in his freedom. Thus the search for new values begins. On a philosophical level, Mehl has provided a valuable reflection on the authority of values in *De l'autorité des valeurs*. In *The Sociology of Protestantism*, he approaches the subject of the dialectic of essence and existence from a sociological perspective, that is, he treats the subject of the dialectic of event and institution. With great sympathy for the existential analysis of life, yet at the same time realizing that there must be some organization of the structures of existence, Mehl provides a wide-ranging study of the religious bases of Western civilization. Implicit in his study is the belief that values have authority in themselves, but that this authority is a "charismatic" one. Values, in Mehl's view, cannot be assimilated to essences. Nevertheless, values do have an objectivity. The values of Christianity are given to it in the kerygma of the primitive church. That is, the charismatic values of Christianity are given in the Christ-*event*, in the self-revelation of God to the Christian community. But in any human situation, there is always the danger that the charisma will not out-last the event. Thus we have the growth of institutions. In Mehl's view, it is this dialectic of event and institution that marks the distinctive nature of Protestantism. A proper understanding – sociological as well as theological – of the historical nature of Protestantism will help to keep the necessary institution from being "the trap of the event". *The Sociology of Protestant-ism* will provide much-needed insight and historico-sociological under-standing to the contemporary Christian concern with the theme of *presence in the world*. The pendulum is swinging back from institution to event, and if Protestantism is true to its nature it will take its place in the centre of the events of our time.

The translator would like to express his gratitude and affection to his wife, Nancy Farley, for her assistance and good-natured patience in awaiting the completion of the translation, and to Roger Mehl, for his abiding friendship and inspiration.

New Hope, Pennsylvania   JAMES H. FARLEY
Christmas, 1969

PREFACE

It is indeed a risky venture, at the present time, to attempt to write a sociology of Protestantism. Although the sociological examination of "religion" began as early as the nineteenth century, the attempt at methodical investigation freed of philosophical *a priori* is only a few decades old. Furthermore, it should be emphasized that Protestantism is somewhat behind in this respect in relation to Roman Catholicism. In undertaking this venture, we are fully aware that our work is quite incomplete and tentative. We offer it to scholarly criticism knowing full well that we shall not be dealt with tenderly.

We have resolved to run this risk because, in our opinion, the variety of current empirical research calls for an attempt at synthesis. Without such a synthesis, the trees will hide the forest from us.

This book has been rewritten several times. The first drafts were prior to 1950 and the present form of the text has little in common with these first manuscripts. Indeed, numerous works have been published during the past fifteen years. Religious sociology has begun to take its rightful place among the churches. All this research has enabled us to give a less theoretical aspect to our book.

Nevertheless, many sections of the book still remain purely provisional. The views presented in these sections, rather than being thoroughly grounded, are simply illustrated by examples and do not claim to be conclusive. We have had to forgo including systematic bibliographies,[1] since the present state of research does not yet permit this. This book is intended simply to provoke discussion among scholars concerning the orientation and direction of their research, and to propose some general hypotheses that may aid in co-ordinating so many valuable individual studies.

Obviously, we shall be concerned primarily with Protestantism. Yet, in certain respects, Protestantism cannot be isolated from the diverse Christian families with which it lives, which it meets face to face, with which it co-operates. As a sociological reality, Protestantism often has a broad common denominator with Roman Catholicism and Orthodoxy. This is why we have not hesitated to borrow our examples from other Christian communities. What is more, the comparative method is often quite illuminating as we attempt to grasp the specific sociological characteristics of the churches issuing from the Reformation. Thus it would not be surprising to find ourselves frequently going beyond the framework of Protestantism.

One of our basic hypotheses is that Christian communities, much more than other religious communities, are societies whose life, practice, and type of organization are determined largely by doctrinal symbols, by convictions of faith, by the *depositum fidei*. This is why we have so often felt it possible to appeal to doctrine in order to account for a sociological reality. It would be absurd to view our parishes and congregations as communities which regulate themselves only according to a doctrinal model (although they often claim to do so). Yet, at the same time, it would distort the ecclesial reality if we were not to take account of the fact that their structures have a doctrinal starting-point. Protestantism was born of a movement of doctrinal reform, which was carried out by theologians. Moreover, the *regulum fidei* (Scripture, confession of faith) enjoys a particular authority (theoretically sovereign) in Protestantism. Thus Protestantism undoubtedly is one of the forms of Christianity where sociological inquiry can least dispense with a recourse to theology. We are convinced that a dialogue between theologians and sociologists is indispensable to the advancement of sociology. We have said many times (and hope to have followed the rule) that a society cannot be studied without considering the values to which it gives allegiance, even though these values may be only imperfectly realized. That such allegiance is given is enough to inform the society's structures.

The attention of the sociologist is not directed primarily to doctrine in its essence. Rather, he is concerned with doctrine in so far as it determines social structures, collective behaviour, a style of piety and of life, and response to the surrounding society.

It is our firm hope that we have finally and definitively left that unfortunate period in which sociology had the pretension of teaching the believer the true object of his faith and the true meaning of that object.

Strasbourg, September 1965

1. Hervé Carrier and Emile Pin have published a bibliography in which Protestantism is given a large place: *Sociologie du Christianisme; bibliographie internationale* (Rome: Presses de l'Université grégorienne, 1964).

I

The Possibility and Limits of a
Sociology of Christianity

It is not necessary to hold to a particular theory of the origin or significance of religion to feel authorized to undertake a sociology of religions. Whatever one thinks of a religion, it is incontestable that it is a social phenomenon from the sole fact that it is lived and practised by a community and that the community which lives and practises it receives an imprint and various characteristics from it. Of course, it is true that certain philosophical beliefs having God as object and eliciting a contemplation of God and of human destiny, because of their content, are sometimes difficult to distinguish from properly religious beliefs. The true criterion of distinction between them is of a sociological nature: the philosophical beliefs, even when shared by a great number of individuals, and even if these individuals constitute a *school*, do not give birth to any common practice. They do not manifest themselves in that specific moment of the life of a community which we call worship. They are the object of a personal reflection, but they do not give rise to any dogmas having constraining value for a social group. Thus it is clear that religion can become the object of a sociological investigation, even though the investigation will not claim to exhaust all the aspects of religion. Indeed, sociology can study only the visible, objectively-ascertainable aspects of religion.

Analysis reaches only the external acts; it is incapable of apprehending the motivations of these acts which alone give the acts their true meaning.[1]

Perhaps it is possible to assume that sociological analysis can go further and that, by exploring the form, the regularity, and the intensity of practice it will hold some hope of arriving at certain motivations, of grasping the intentional aims which underlie the practices. Yet it is true none the less that the secret dialogue of a soul with its God, especially when this dialogue is liberated from traditional forms and rises to the ineffable language of faith, is beyond the reach of sociological observation. Sociology has no right to assume that it reaches religion in its essence, and even less does it have the right to claim that it is in a position to furnish an exhaustive explanation of religion. It cannot reduce religion to the social, as Durkheim so rashly did. It must recognize its limits. Yet a wide field of investigation still remains open to it, a field encompassing the community congregated for worship, the rites which this congregation performs, the symbols utilized by the congregation or to which it refers and, beyond these symbols, the dogmas and the beliefs which give them their meaning and confer upon them their vitality while at the same time engendering a collective discipline and an ethic.

But is the recognition of these limits sufficient when sociology deals with Christianity? Is there not in this respect a new problem that could be formulated bluntly in these terms: is Christianity a religion? The history of religions has accustomed us to classifying Christianity among religions. Religious phenomenology, such as we find in van der Leeuw's work, encourages us certainly to see Christianity as a superior form of religion, but at the same time as a religion whose forms are in continuity with other religions. The same categories, for example, worship, prayer, sacrifice, and so on, are applicable to both.

It is possible that the sociologist will view the Christian's reticence in regard to the sociological enterprise as the expression of Christianity's straightforward claim to be recognized as an absolutely particular and original religion, owing nothing to the world of religions surrounding it. This claim, which has long since been mitigated by the historical study of primitive Christianity, can itself be considered as a sociological fact tied to the supremacy of the Christian West.

But perhaps things are not quite so simple. Should we not ask if Christianity's claim does not have some basis? Is the sociological characteristic of religion in general really applicable to Christianity? Durkheim asserts that religion comes into existence at the time when a distinction between sacred and profane appears in collective practices and symbols.[2] Indeed, it must be recognized that in the majority of religions stress is placed on the organization of relations between these two worlds, the sacred and the profane. Practices are inspired by the concern to "appropriate" the sacred without too much risk. Feasts are directed towards integrating the sacred into profane existences. Sacralization and desacralization are essential moments of the religious life. This sacred is localized in heaven, in a given region of the earth, or under the earth, and man does not enter the zone of the sacred without taking precautions. The priesthood is essentially a particular way of access into the sacred.

These characteristics are not foreign to Christianity, which also has its holy places, its days "set apart", its sacerdotal functions. One certainly can affirm that Christianity also is a religion. In its relations with other religions it is led to understand itself as a religion. The question, however, is of knowing if the term "religion" adequately expresses the essence of Christianity.

This can be doubted. In fact, the distinction between sacred and profane gives rise in Christianity to a double distinction which does not simply recapitulate the preceding distinction. On the one hand, there is the distinction between Creator and creature; on the other hand, there is the tinction between the holy God and sinful man. By virtue of the first distinction, all that is not God is creature of God. Thus the entire universe in so far as created is profane. God does not live in shrines made by men's hands. By virtue of the second distinction, the holy God's action on the creature does not consist in a sacralization or even in a divinization, but rather in a sanctification of the whole man and of all of man's action in creation. Although by virtue of the first distinction all that is not God is profane, by virtue of the second distinction nothing is profane by intended purpose and all can be sanctified. But this latter cannot be achieved by ritual practices. That is to say, the polarity between sacred and profane is constantly placed in question. Although Christianity has replaced other religions in a large part of the world (especially in the West), and, from this fact, has taken over the functions which these religions assumed in society, the sociologist must never neglect the fact that this situation is a sort of permanent temptation for Christianity (to which it often succumbs). To overlook this fact is to do injustice to the spirit of Christianity.[3]

Perhaps it will be objected that the sociologist is not supposed to concern himself with the purity and orthodoxy of the religions which he studies. Thus he will study Christianity as he finds it given historically, as it appears empirically, and consequently he will have the right to apply categories to it which he utilizes for other religions. Is it not true, in fact, that Roman Catholicism has its holy places, its pilgrimages, that its priests are cloaked with an indelible sacred character? Does not Protestantism itself conduct consecrations of church buildings and even of bells, and, all the while denying the priesthood, carry out ordinations of ministers which strongly remind one of sacerdotal consecrations? All this cannot be denied, and sociology makes no claim to be a normative science: it studies a religion as phenomenon.

There is certainly much that is true in such an attitude. However, social facts are not things (contrary to Durkheim's assertion[4]) nor are societies simple empirical realities – they can be understood only if one does not limit oneself to their institutions and practices alone but also takes account of the values which they profess through these institutions and practices, and sometimes in spite of them. Nor can a social group be isolated from the objectives at which its values aim. So in the same way can the Christian communities be understood only if one takes account of the reality to which they give allegiance, for this reality informs their existence, in their institutions and practices as well as in their reformations, their abortive endeavours, their regrets, and their guilty consciences.

In other terms, no sociology of Christianity could do without a socio-phenomenology of the specific religious object. Let it be well understood that sociology is not a substitute for theology. It does not describe the mystery of God or of the Trinity, but it must take account of the fact that God is given to the Christian community and received by it in a certain manner and that the way in which God manifests his action and his demands in the community has a basic importance for the fashion in which this community is organized, develops, reforms itself, becomes self-aware both of what it is and what it should be.

The sociology of religions, and especially that of Christianity, can contribute to the calling into question again of a sociologism which became prominent around the end of the nineteenth century and which modelled itself on the psychologism of that time. As psychologism[5] held that consciousness was nothing but the subjective states of consciousness and, joining up with idealism, enclosed consciousness within itself, so sociologism wished to know only social facts, social structures, collective representations. Psychologism did not pose the question of the intentionality of consciousness, of objectives of consciousness. In the same way, sociologism did not pose the question of the social group's aim towards an objective, around which it forms itself as a group and whose nature and demands explain the group's own structures. It was the influence of Husserlian phenomenology which broke the circle in which both psychology and sociology were enclosed.

Just as all thought is directed towards an object (on the reality and validity of which phenomenology makes no comment) and receives its content and its structure from this object, so does a human society exist only as it is grouped by an object which has enough power to effect social cohesion and to give this society its form and structure, to model the social relationships within the society. Just as the cohesion of a nation is explained by the way in which its members apprehend this reality – so difficult to define – which is called "the fatherland", just as the cohesion and the specific organs of action of a social class are explained by the way in which it relates to an ideal object (which can be, for example, social justice), so does a church derive its social and ecclesial density, its ceremonies, its hierarchy, its discipline, and its doctrinal symbols from the way in which it apprehends "the religious object",[6] God, from the way in which God is revealed to it, from the way in which it thinks that God makes himself present for it. Sociology, as such, does not need to pose the question of the real or fictitious, the objective or mythological nature of this object. It is sufficient for sociology to observe that this object, as it is apprehended by the religious community, acts with power on this community and orders its morphology, its institutions, its practices. To be sure, the determination of the group by the object to which it refers is not the sole component in sociological understanding. Other factors intervene: the size of the given society, the variations in this size, the geographical, historical, and social environment in which the group is situated, the action of other social groups, the phenomena of acculturation and of contamination, the structures of the global society in which the group is immersed. If we lay stress on the object, and in particular, on the religious object, it is because quite often sociology has neglected it. It seems impossible to us to undertake a sociology of the Christian churches without taking account of the fact that their sociological structures are at least partially determined by their ecclesiastical symbols and that the latter depend, in the final analysis, on the way in which the churches apprehend a revealed given. Thus sociology must have a phenomenological knowledge of this given as it appears in the consciousness of the religious community. This is why it will pay particular attention to the testimony of the faithful themselves, even more so when such testimonies are considered in the church as normative. A doctrinal symbol or a confession of faith has more value for the sociologist than an individual work of theology.

It must be remembered, of course, that sociology does not describe an ideal church. It describes the church in its empirical reality, which is not always in accord with the norms to which this church claims to refer. But every society, and the churches in particular, do indeed refer to norms and this effective reference is not without influence on their comportment.

These remarks permit us to escape from the difficulty in which we found ourselves, namely, is a sociology of Christianity possible and is it possible without reducing Christianity to a sort of common denominator, i.e. religion, which Christianity would challenge? Indeed yes, to the degree that sociology will not begin with the *a priori* according to which Christianity is nothing more than one of a thousand variations of the religion theme. It is often said that it would be unscientific to proceed in this way. The scholar does not postulate the unity of his various objects of study before investigation. By taking into consideration the religious object, we will be led to take into account the specific nature of each religious community, whereas a consideration only of the sociological factors relevant to social morphology will lead us to the general. The sociology of religions should be directed towards a religious typology. Thus the claim of Christianity that it is not to be considered as one religion among many should not offend the sociologist's sensitivities. Rather, it should inspire him to investigate whether there is a relationship between some particular characteristic of Christianity's religious object and its claim of uniqueness, which is a fact and which is expressed in the missionary zeal and in the exclusivism of Christianity (whereas ancient paganism admitted all possible gods into its Pantheon, while contemporary Judaism thinks that conversion to Judaism is not necessary for man's salvation, and the religions of the Far East are open to all sorts of syncretism). This claim should lead the sociologist to investigate whether it is effectively and objectively expressed in the forms of Christian practice and piety (for example, in prayer). If the classic dichotomy between sacred and profane does not apply, or applies only imperfectly, to Christianity, is it not because the religious object in Christianity is not able to be included in the general term "sacred"? In order to understand Christianity, must we not take into account this refusal of the sacred which so often is manifested in biblical religion?

The common error of the sociologist is that of thinking that he does not have to take doctrinal elements into consideration, because these elements would be the intellectual superstructures which only record a religion's effort to adapt to the cultural level in which it lives. Perhaps this is not a total error. Indeed, even in Christianity it would be easy to lay out in graphic detail the great effort to insert the Christian faith into the intellectual structures which came to it from Greek philosophy, especially from Aristotelianism. Biblical criticism, sometimes excessively (cf. the school of Reitzenstein), already had effected this work in regard to the canonical texts themselves, to the point that Johannine thought was presented to us as an essentially hellenized thought. But if this type of research is valid, who does not see that it also proceeds from the idea that the doctrinal element, the intelligible and rational element is always a sort of artificial veneer in a religion, that religion by itself is foreign to all ambitions of intelligibility? It may be that certain religions correspond to this criterion. But what right does one have to apply it to a religion which sees itself, as does biblical religion, as a religion of the Word, that is to say, as a religion in which the religious object itself is Word? . . . Word addressed to man, intelligible word, word whose *meaning* enlightens man's life, orients his conduct, determines his intellectual pathways.

If a sociology of Christianity must take account of this fact, a sociology of Protestantism has even more reason to bear it in mind. For Protestantism was born of a doctrinal reform which was effected by doctors of theology. This reform was raised against the omnipotence of practices, of forms of piety, of the elements of sociological morphology. It aspired to reform the visible communities of the church according to a doctrinally determined archetype. It had desired that the line going from Christology through ecclesiology to the organization of the parishes be as direct as possible. The question is not primarily one of knowing if the Reformation was perfectly successful in this enterprise and if "non-theological factors" intervened in the constitution of the church and of the parishes. The primary obligation of the sociologist who studies the Protestant church is that of taking account of this intention, of this essence of Protestantism, following which he can investigate the manner in which they have operated or not operated.

The Limits of a Sociology of Christianity

When sociology studies Christianity as social phenomenon and the Christian religion as "institutionalized",[7] it inevitably encounters the limits which arise from the one-sided nature of its point of view. It is easy to reach agreement on this in theory. But it is more difficult to locate these limits with exactitude. Some scholars readily extricate themselves from the difficulty by evoking the two complementary aspects of the church. The church is first of all the reality of the body of Christ, an invisible reality which rests on the invisible bonds of faith. As such, it escapes all sociological investigation. But it is also a visible, organized, structured, and hierarchical community, and it is as such that it can be made the subject of a scientific study.[8] The point of view is certainly not false, but only on condition that one be very conscious of the danger it involves. The danger is that of dissociating what is really united in Christian thought and intention, that is to say, of considering the visible church to be a reality distinct from the invisible church. For Roman Catholicism, the invisible church is *realized* in the visible church. For Protestantism, the invisible church appears and is *manifested* in the visible church (of all the Reformers Calvin gave the most consistency to the visible church; nevertheless, he maintained that the invisible church and the visible church were only one church). The visible church, for Protestantism, is the sign of the invisible church. It is important not to lose sight of this intention of Protestant thought; otherwise, belonging to the church would become identical with belonging to any spiritual, charitable, or philanthropic society whatever. Even in sociological surveys which are conducted by means of questionnaires, this particular, unique, and always ambiguous nature of the church must be taken into account in the questions asked. For example, one cannot limit oneself to asking: Do you contribute to the church; how many times do you attend worship? These are necessary questions, certainly. But it is also important to ask: Why do you consider it necessary to participate in worship and in the life of your parish? One cannot be satisfied with pure statistical data because such data give us information only on the state of a "church", which would be nothing more than one association among others.[9] The minutes of the general assemblies are of great interest for ordinary associations. For the church, which also has its general assemblies, such records are of only limited importance and give us scarcely any information except on that in which the church is not church. In the same way, the social appearance of the members of the parish, i.e., the role that they play in municipal and political life, etc., informs us only very indirectly about the religious vitality of the parish; whereas, for another group, the presence of many notable figures who are active in the life of society would be a good indication of the influence of this group.

In sum, that which authorizes the undertaking of a sociology of the church is the visible, institutional aspect of the church. But the sociologist must never consider this aspect for itself, without being concerned with the fact that this aspect is only the obverse of another aspect. The social forms which are established or predominate within an ecclesiastical group are nothing other than the reflection of the relationships which unite the members of this group to the Lord of the church. Not only should this be so, but the group *is aware* that it should be so.

In light of the foregoing remarks and cautions, it does not seem necessary to us to fix limits, as G. Le Bras does, to sociological investigation. In our opinion, it is not necessary to reserve a sort of holy of holies in the life of the church, a sort of taboo sanctuary to which sociology is forbidden entrance.

Obviously, sociology can freely study church membership and fluctuations in membership, participation in various acts of ecclesiastical and cultic life, the activities of the church and the movements which centre upon it, the interaction which is established between the ecclesial community and other communities, the institutions proper to the church, liturgies and disciplines, the participation of lay men in the ministry of the church, variations in the form of the pastoral ministry, trends towards the "High Church" style, towards liturgism, towards ecumenism. But sociology should also be able to study beliefs, dogmas, and doctrines themselves. Why, indeed, could there not be a sociology of dogmas and of confessions of faith? These formulations have a date, they have taken form at a certain time in history, in a certain social context, to answer certain needs felt by the community. Is it not true that the great doctrinal formulations of Christianity were undertaken at a time when intellectuals of Greek background had penetrated widely into the church and had brought with them their culture and their concern (which, moreover, was authentically Christian) to make known the Christian message to pagan cultural élites in a language that was accessible to them?

Even though it be granted that the doctrinal formulation can be the object of an historico-sociological study, it undoubtedly will be contended that this study can be directed with precision only to the form and never to the content, which, by its transcendent origin, escapes all sociological investigation. Once again, this assertion is only half true, for the form and the content can never be separated in any absolute way. When exegetes, who in their way also are sociologists, study the New Testament revelation, they emphasize how much this revelation is couched in categories inherited from Judaism, from prophetism, from late-Judaism, from apocalyptic and Essene sects, etc. At the same time, they underline the dogma of the unity of the Old and New Testaments. The biblical revelation is tied to a certain human group which has its own sociology and mentality. To want to separate the two, under the pretext of distinguishing the content from the form, would be to falsify this revelation itself. It would be to renew, perhaps under less flagrant but no less pernicious form, the attempt of the *Deutsche Christen* to dejudaize Christianity. In showing all of the theological concepts of the Old Testament, all of the ceremonies and laws of the Old Covenant to which Jesus referred in his words and deeds, the exegete is engaging in the sociology of dogmas. In showing how Jesus, in instituting the Lord's Supper, united the spirit of the old and that of the new within the framework of the Jewish passover, the exegete engages in sociology, and no one would think of reproaching him for his impiety.

One would be quite wrong from another point of view as well: that the

Word of God always comes to us in a given historical and sociological situation, not only by means of formulas but also through concepts and institutions dependent on certain sociological structures, should neither astonish nor offend the Christian to the degree that he believes God is Immanuel, God for man, God who comes to man, the Word made flesh. Jesus' statement that salvation comes from the Jews is both a theological datum and a sociological fact. Christianity declares that God reveals himself not in a non-temporal fashion but in history, that he makes himself known to a given group of men, to such-and-such a society. It teaches that this revelation is received (and always partially rejected also) through the categories of thought, the ideas, and the schemas which are the particular possession of a given society.

From that, we are justified in saying that not only does Christianity authorize a sociology of Christianity; in certain respects it calls for it. Perhaps one could not say the same for all religions, in so far as they claim to be bearers of a non-temporal revelation; at least in intention, they have declined to become involved in history. In fact, they also have become incarnate, but with a bad conscience; Christianity does it in all good conscience.

Do we therefore deny all limits to the sociology of Christianity? Assuredly not. Sociology can in no way establish the truth of Christianity. Is the history to which Christianity refers true history or myth? Sociology will not settle the question. Sociology can consider from its point of view the whole of Christianity, in its social structures as well as in its doctrinal statements. It can apply itself to this whole, including revelation – but always to the revelation as it is received by the community. What it lacks, what every other science also lacks, is the possibility of grasping this revelation as the act of God revealing himself.

NOTES

1. J. Binet, "Sociologie religieuse dans le Sud Cameroun", in *MNC*, 47–48 (July–December, 1958).

2. E. Durkheim, *The Elementary Forms of the Religious Life*, translated by Joseph W. Swain (r.p.; New York: The Free Press of Glencoe, 1965, and London: Collier-Macmillan, 1961).

3. For this invasion of Christianity by the category of the sacred, see André Dumas, "L'Eglise envahie par la distinction du profane et du sacré", *FV*, 50 (May–June, 1952).

4. E. Durkheim, *The Rules of Sociological Method*, translated by Sarah A. Solovay and John H. Mueller, and edited by George E. G. Catlin (8th ed.; New York: The Free Press of Glencoe and London: The Macmillan Company, 1964).

5. [Trans. note. That is, the "structuralism" or "introspectionism" of Wilhelm Wundt and his school.]

6. See Charles Hauter, *Essai sur l'objet religieux* (Paris: Alcan, 1928).

7. See Henry Duméry, *Phénoménologie et Religion* (Paris: PUF, 1958), ch. 1.

8. This is the point of view expressed by D. Goldschmidt, "Ansätze einer modernen Religionssoziologie", in *Stimme der Gemeinde*, 10 (1958), No. 8.

9. From the perspective of a simple phenomenological description, the specific nature of the Christian church can be elucidated. Thus G. van der Leeuw, alluding to the distinction established by F. Tönnies between community and society (*Gemeinschaft und Gesellschaft* [1887]), can write: ". . . we have observed that the church is a form of 'human-social-being' which unites the community and the association (or society). The 'sacred-communal' that lies at the base of this unity is the act of God in Christ. There exists only one example of this type of communion. There is no other religion which has produced a church. In the primitive and semi-primitive religions, the religious community and the communion as such are identical. This was the case in Greece and Rome. The same was true in Israel: there was only one *qahal*, the national assembly and the religious community. Islam knows only a shaky tie of doctrinaire agreement. In Buddhism, there is only the monastic community. Nowhere does one find anything comparable to the church. For that, it would be necessary for the body to have a head. In all the history of religions, only the so-called mystery religions of the Hellenistic period had anything which resembled the structure of the church: a history of salvation, the history of a god whose passion, death, and resurrection called forth the participation of man. However, they completely lacked the element of the *qahal*, of the people, of the basic principle. For this reason, they never were able to succeed in being churches and remained associations. Inversely, the Christian church very nearly became restricted to a mystery association. This is no doubt the end which the *disciplina arcana* of the early church had in view. But with the introduction of infant baptism, the church (in opposition to the sects) definitively became the church, that is to say, a people of believers. As such, it exists eschatologically: the people finds its strength only in the gift of the kingdom of God which Christ has given to it. But it remains none the less a people. This fact preserves word and spirit, vocation and faith, from the arbitrary decision of the individual" ("Description phénoménologique de l'Eglise", *MNC*, 17 [January–March, 1951]). [Trans. note. Tönnies' book has been published in the United States under the title *Community and Society* (*Gemeinschaft und Gesellschaft*), translated and edited by Charles P. Loomis (r.p.; New York: Harper Torch Books, 1963). In England, the title is *Community and Association* (London: Routledge and Kegan Paul, 1955). For further information on Tönnies' work, see Gerhard Lenski, *The Religious Factor; a sociologist's inquiry* (rev. ed.; Garden City: Doubleday Anchor Books and London: W. H. Allen, 1963), p. 20, n. 26.]

II

The Object and Method of the Sociology of Religion

Having specified in what direction and under what conditions a sociology of Christianity is conceivable and legitimate, and how it can constitute a branch of the sociology of religion in general, it now remains for us to specify the object and the method of the latter.

The term "sociology of religion" is to be preferred to the equally prevalent but ambiguous term "religious sociology". A sociology can be qualified scientifically only by its object; the term "religious sociology" would seem to indicate a non-scientific qualification of that discipline.

1. *A Critical History of the Sociology of Religion*

The sociology of religion is surely one of the oldest branches of sociology, but its development has long been hampered by a certain number of encumbrances which have weighed upon it. The sociology of religion was undertaken in the nineteenth century, with the premature idea of explaining religion in general. In order to do this, it proposed to *reduce* religious phenomena and religion itself to other less mysterious, more rational manifestations of human activity. The initial attempts of the sociology of religion were waylaid by the danger of failing to recognize the specific nature of religion and of religions.

For Auguste Comte, religion was located at the beginning of a three-stage evolutionary process which presumably embraces the whole history of mankind:

By studying the total development of human intelligence in its various spheres of activity, from its very first, simplest strivings to our day, I believe that I have discovered a great fundamental law, to which it is bound by an invariable necessity. It seems to me that this law can be solidly established, either by rational proofs furnished by the understanding of how we are constituted, or by historical verifications resulting from a careful examination of the past. This law consists in that each of our principal conceptions, each branch of our knowledge, passes successively through three different theoretical states: the theological or fictive state, the metaphysical or abstract state, and the scientific or positive state. In other terms, the human mind, by its nature, successively employs in its inquiries three methods of philosophizing; these methods are essentially different and even radically opposed in character: first the theological method, then the metaphysical method, and finally the positive method. From these result three types of philosophies or general systems of conceptions regarding the totality of phenomena, and these types are mutually exclusive. The first is the necessary point of departure of the human intelligence; the third is its final and definitive state; the second is destined to serve only as a state of transition.

The theological state is defined in the following way:

In the theological state, the human mind, directing its inquiries primarily toward the intimate nature of beings, the primary and final causes of all the effects which reach it, in short, toward absolute knowledge, imagines that phenomena are produced by the direct and continuous action of supernatural agents, which are more or less numerous and whose arbitrary intervention explains all the apparent anomalies of the universe.[1]

This *Law of the Three States* (a type of philosophy of history which the founder of sociology formulated) was bound to inspire the first inquiries of the sociology of religion. We can see that there is a reduction of religion to something other than itself: religion is presented to us as a system of knowledge aiming at the absolute knowledge of the universe. Religion constitutes a primary and necessary step for the human mind; without it, the human mind would not rise to the idea of a non-empirical causality. Yet religious causality is both fantastic and anthropomorphic. From this fact, the phenomenon of religion is considerably valorized in the past but by the same token, religion is considered to be definitively outmoded in the present. It has served its intellectual function and can only disappear. What remains of it thus represents a survival from another age.

We come across this same attitude again at the beginning of the twentieth century in the much more scientific work of Lucien Lévy-Bruhl, who endeavoured to study primitive religions in a concrete way. Lévy-Bruhl considered religion to be the manifestation *par excellence* of mythical or pre-logical thought, that is to say, of a thought which does not utilize logical categories and for which the principle of contradiction is not valid. The appearance of logical, that is, scientific thought resulted in making it impossible for this thought and prelogical thought to coexist. Thus religion can be only a survival. The impressive work[2] of Lévy-Bruhl, based on the data of ethnographers and missionaries (the author never had direct contact with the religions which he studied), tends primarily to demonstrate

the mechanism of prelogical thought and to show its complete incompatibility with scientific thought. Religion is reduced to myth.

However, under the influence of the analyses and research of Maurice
Leenhardt, who devoted most of his life to the study of Melanesian
peoples and religions, Lévy-Bruhl was led, with rare honesty, to call all of
his works into question. The posthumous *Carnets* are evidence of this. He
recognized that the idea of a prelogical mentality was an "unsound hypothesis", that although primitive peoples and civilized peoples do not manifest the same logical exigencies, it does not follow that an absolute barrier
exists between their mentality and ours. He recognized that the logical
structure of the human mind is everywhere the same and that "myth",
any more than religion, cannot be thrown back into some distant age of
mankind.[3]

Emile Durkheim, although he had a much more intimate knowledge of
Judaism, also immersed himself in the study of primitive religions. In his
work, we find another form of the reduction of the religious fact. He was
preoccupied with determining the social function of religion. This function seemed to him to be considerable. Not only do all categories of thought
have a social and religious origin, but it is in the cultus and the religious
feast that the group becomes aware of itself and reshapes its cohesion. The
group receives higher strengths in worship. But it is not necessarily the
case that the idea which the group has of supernatural reality effectively
corresponds to reality. It is the task of the scientific sociologist to explain
the true nature of this reality. Durkheim felt that he had demonstrated
that this reality is society itself, in so far as it is both empirical reality and
ideal reality:

> A society can neither create itself nor recreate itself without at the same time
> creating an ideal. This creation is not a sort of work of supererogation for it, by
> which it would complete itself, being already formed; it is the act by which it is
> periodically made and remade. Therefore when some oppose the ideal society
> to the real society, like two antagonists which would lead us in opposite direc-
> tions, they materialize and oppose abstractions. The ideal society is not outside
> of the real society; it is a part of it. Far from being divided between them as
> between two poles which mutually repel each other, we cannot hold to one with-
> out holding to the other.[4]

Durkheim saw very clearly that there is no society where there is no concern with values, and that these values, in so far as they are really aimed
at, are an integral part of society, even if they are not realized. It is this
ideal aspect of society, as concretely present, which is the object towards
which the religious movement carries. Contrary to what a superficial ex-

amination might lead one to imagine, religious enthusiasm is not devoid of meaning. It is the adoration of something real. It is participation in the ideal society, without which the empirical society could not survive. This is why Durkheim could define religion as "the eminent form and, as it were, the concentrated expression of the whole collective life".[5] Thus, in religion there is something of the eternal destined to survive the symbols in which the various religions are expressed. For Durkheim, then, the religious, the moral, and the civil are categories which become identical, which can be reduced one to another. He counts on the progress of societies to bring about this reduction effectively.

What essential difference is there between an assembly of Christians celebrating the principal dates of the life of Christ, or of Jews remembering the exodus from Egypt or the promulgation of the decalogue, and a reunion of citizens commemorating the promulgating of a new moral or legal system or some great event in the national life?[6]

Durkheim's first approach is to sacralize all society, while his second approach is to secularize all religion.[7]

This reduction of the religious to the social is facilitated in Durkheim by another reduction, that of the variety of religious forms to unity. Durkheim never took seriously the profound conflict of religions nor the conflict of Christianity with all other religions. For him there was one essence of religion. Just as all societies, according to him, issue from the repeating and compounding of a basic social element or social atom, *the horde* (whose existence is, however, hypothetical), so are the various religions only the complex results of elementary forms of the religious life such as they appear in the least developed, i.e., the simplest, societies. The elementary is the fundamental: this is why Durkheim did not feel it worthwhile to include higher religions in his study and why he believed that he had found the secret in the analysis of the totemic system in Australia. The explanation which he had found there seemed to him to be applicable to Christianity itself.[8]

It is this very idea of *reduction*, which we have seen at work in the thought of Comte, Lévy-Bruhl, and Durkheim, that is open to criticism. Science, of course, must proceed to the reduction of a given object in order to reduce it to another type of reality. Do we not see the physicist reduce electrical, light, and sound phenomena to oscillatory phenomena? Yet this operation is valid only on condition that it is not a preliminary operation and only if it is justified by a complete analysis of all the facts. Now the French school of sociology limited itself to the study of primitive religions. Yet it had only second-hand knowledge of these religions.

Moreover, should this reduction, which also claims to be an explication, be considered as an essential, basic step in sociological inquiry? Before saying, as Durkheim does, that the collective religious consciousness deludes itself concerning its object, it is necessary to begin with a phenomenological analysis of the various collective manifestations of religious life. It is necessary to take account of the intentionality of the religious understanding itself. What is the object to which the group refers in the different manifestations of its religious life (worship, practices, symbols, doctrines)? In so far as this object is really the focal point of the group and, consequently, informs the religious practices themselves, it is phenomenologically and, as concerns us, sociologically real. Once again we discover here the need for the sociology of religion to be first of all a socio-phenomenology. It goes beyond the bounds of science when it aspires to be something more. It must lay aside the question of the absolute reality and of the metaphysical validity of the object to which allegiance is given. For what would give it the right to pronounce on the reality and the validity of this object, unless it begins with a philosophical *a priori* or with an idea about the superiority of one religion in relation to another. Indeed, it has been observed that Comte had in view the creation of a new religion, the positivist cult, the religion of humanity, and that Durkheim himself, with less naïveté, expressed his wish to see a civic religion based on the idea of solidarity. In fact, it is always the idea of a natural religion inherited from the eighteenth century which lies behind all these theorizings and which sidetracks the analyses of these sociologists. Scientific sociology requires this criticism of these schools which we have considered.

The sociology of religion has also been undertaken from a completely different perspective, which also constitutes no less a type of reduction of its object. In this case, what is involved is either an *isolating* of the social elements of a religion (which presupposes that one already has a predetermined idea about the essence of religion), or a bringing out of the social implications (and sometimes the political and economic implications) of religion. This latter form of sociology has been developed pre-eminently by Max Weber, especially in his articles "Die protestantische Ethik und der Geist des Kapitalismus" (*Gesammelte Aufsätze zur Religionssoziologie*, 1920).[9]

Weber's general intention was, in his own words, to investigate "the influence of certain religious ideas on the development of an economic spirit, of the *ethos* of an economic system".[10] The thesis of the articles in question may be summarized in the following fashion: the Puritan (Weber established a line of filiation between Puritanism and Calvinism), never certain of his election and salvation (which depend solely on the free grace of God, on a predestination anterior to the creation of the world), seeks anxiously here below for signs of his salvation. Since he is convinced that nothing takes place in the world outside the will of God, he considers that the economic prosperity of his enterprise is the sign of God's good will towards him and brings him the assurance of his salvation. In order to assure the reality of his state of grace, the Puritan becomes bent on a constant control of himself and his conduct. In the process, he becomes the inventor of that ethical rationality and methodical asceticism which are in perfect harmony with the spirit of Western capitalism. Moreover, since his moral austerity prohibits him from resting, from living in idleness, or from using his wealth for luxury or pleasure, he must reinvest his money in the enterprise, which constitutes, according to the formula of Raymond Aron, "the formation of capital (which) takes place as a result of this ascetic obligation to save".[11] The Puritan's morality was bleak, but very much the master of itself. Since only steady work, rational calculation, and resistance to feelings and passion were in accord with such a morality, the Puritan would set the example of an extremely wise and prudent management and would play a considerable role in the concentration of capital in the West and in the birth of great modern industry. Thus a typically religious phenomenon and a well-defined religious doctrine were to have social consequences of considerable importance for the whole evolution of Western society. Today capitalism seems to us to be simply a given fact, an economic structure upon which our will has only a slight influence, a system which defines relationships of production and into which we enter whether we like it or not. Max Weber reminds us that it was at first the voluntary expression of a particularly lucid religious understanding.[12]

This is not the place to discuss the truth or falseness of this thesis, or if it adequately explains the development of Western capitalism.[13] We are concerned here only with evaluating the methodological point of view: do the works of Max Weber constitute a typical sample of what is meant by the sociology of religion? In our opinion, what we have in Weber's works is more an effort to restore religion within the context of a civilization, to uncover the interrelations (*Wechselwirkungen*) which can exist between religion, considered within the framework of the profoundly secularized Western world, and the global society. To do this, religion must be considered primarily in its doctrinal and ethical aspect (as the very title of Weber's essay bears witness). We shall qualify the idea of the sociology of religion expressed by him as *functionalist*, in the sense that it

seeks to determine the social function of religion. Furthermore, this functionalism is not a one-way street, for Weber endeavours to demonstrate the
reciprocity of influences which exist between religion and the global
society. Although in his study on the ethos of Western capitalism he
emphasized the decisive role of religion in economic life, in other studies
he showed the inverse relationship. This reciprocity of influences, moreover, enabled him to resist the lure of the Marxist interpretations of
religion. He emphatically rejected the thesis that

the characteristic feature of a religious attitude can be simply the function of the
social condition of the social stratum appearing as its representation; [and] that
this attitude would be only its "ideological" expression or a reflex of its material
or ideal interests.[14]

On this point we can say that Weber resisted all reduction of the religious
phenomena.

But does not his functionalism lead to *the placing side by side* of two great
phenomena: religion (or the types of religion) and society? Thus one can
wonder how this study, which is perfectly valid in itself, can be qualified
as the sociology of religion. It teaches us nothing on the sociology proper
of a religion. It instructs us only on the historical role which a given
religion has played in a given social context. It would seem that by refusing
to make religion an emanation of the social group, one is prohibited from
truly engaging in a sociology of religion. This difficulty has long weighed
(and undoubtedly still does) on the efforts of German sociologists of
religion, since Weber's influence remains strong and widespread in Germany.

Ernst Troeltsch was close to Weber in many respects. Yet his point of
view was more clearly sociological in that he asked the question of the role
of social factors in the historical development of a religion. In his *Soziallehren der christlichen Kirchen* (1912),[15] Troeltsch attempted to show that
present-day Christianity is not intelligible without these "social teachings"
and that although there is a theological development in the church (as
Harnack had shown), this development does not explain everything. The
social stage also must be taken into consideration; the church's social ethic
and the idea of community which the church holds also must be given their
just due. Troeltsch's study was undertaken in two directions:

1. In the first, he tried to show that the necessities tied to the life of the
cultic communities (the church, the sect, the mystical groups, that is, the
three sociological groups engendered by Christianity) explain the development of dogma. This was true especially concerning Trinitarian doctrine

and Christology, which Troeltsch did not consider to be inherent in the primitive evangelical deposit. Trinitarian dogma proceeded from the very nature of the cultic community of the church. It took a totally different form, much less objectivized and rationalized, in the sect and in mystical doctrine. Thus dogma, to a great degree, is the fruit of a sociological determining by the religious group. Religious doctrine is primarily the expression of the religious vitality of a community gathered in worship.[16]

2. In the second, he tried to demonstrate that in the course of the history of Christianity, the ethic proper to the church and to the sects acted on the surrounding society and determined the forms of its juridical, political, social, and economic organization. This action can be shown, in varying degrees, up to the end of the eighteenth century. Modern times, however, have been dominated by a science independent of theology, without contact with the church, and in the process of abandoning individualism in favour of collectivism. In short, the modern age is more and more secularized and will be increasingly less open to the influence of the Christian ethic. Troeltsch, for his part, admitted that he did not know what place the Christian ethic and the social philosophy of Christianity would be able to find in the modern world.[17] To be sure, during the ages when they acted upon the surrounding culture, they did not always succeed in retaining their absolute purity. Troeltsch indicates the various compromises which the different churches made with the world and how they borrowed elements from either the world's ideals or from its social structure. But in any case, the churches acted upon the social reality, whereas such action in the future remains problematical.

As one can see, Troeltsch's second line of research is similar to the sociology of Weber and gives rise to the same remarks. But his first approach is more original (we shall not discuss his statements in and of themselves) in that what he undertook was truly a sociology of dogma, revealing the role of the religious community in the formation and expression of doctrinal truth. Whereas the second approach tends only to uncover the social function fulfilled by a religion in the area of social ethics, the second tries to grasp an aspect of the vitality of the religious group itself, in its formative role. In the process it was necessary for Troeltsch to make some of the doctrines more precise (and on this point he undoubtedly fell prey to the excesses of the reigning liberalism). The only objection that can be raised is that Troeltsch devoted himself to only one aspect of the vitality of the religious group.

It was one of Weber's disciples, Joachim Wach, who has provided what is the most comprehensive, the most intelligible, and the most accurate definition of a sociology of religion. Of course, he was very much influenced by Weber's thought and utilized many formulas that are completely in the spirit of Weber. For example, "our purpose is to study the interrelation of religion and society and the forms of interaction which take place between them".[18] Such statements abound: "the manifold interrelations between religion and social phenomena" (as if the sociologist should not study religion itself as a social phenomenon); or again, "to contribute to a better appreciation of one function of religion" (here one goes back to Durkheim as much as to Weber); "to illustrate the cultural significance of religion".[19] The book's preface describes the sociology of religion as being useful in the understanding of "the vital importance and significance of religion as an integrating factor in human society" (which is pure Durkheim) and as helpful "in understanding its function in the contemporary crisis of civilization in East and West".[20] Thus Wach's theoretical position is open to the same reservations expressed in regard to that of Weber. It is not at all that they did not study real problems, but that both restricted the field of activity of the sociology of religion and that, perhaps, both were influenced by the concern (apologetic) of developing the social importance of religion during an age which was tempted to see in religion only a survival or deception. Of course, every sociology, even scientific, is a response to a question or a challenge of a society at a given moment in its development, and it is possible to have a sociology of sociologies.

But, *in actual fact*, Wach went beyond this theoretical position. He gives concrete evidence of this when he enumerates the objects of study of a sociology of religion. He lists three groups:

(*a*) the theoretical forms – myth, doctrine, or dogma;

(*b*) the practical expression of religion in cultus and forms of worship;

(*c*) the religious grouping itself, the specific forms of religious fellowship and association. And in regard to the third group, he adds what he calls "typology": "the individual, typological, and comparative study of which is the field of the sociology of religion".[21]

Wach described his own work as essentially a typology of religious and socio-religious groups:

Where the historian of religion follows developments, the sociologist is bound to discriminate between types which occur and reoccur in various places and at various times.[22]

And in similar vein:

Without the work of the historian of religion, the sociologist would be helpless. Yet neither can substitute for the other; whereas the former is interested in longitudinal lines of development, the latter tries to cut through these lines vertically.[23]

Of course, the establishment of a typology of religious groupings, to which Wach devoted his very patient study,[24] does not constitute the whole of sociology. But in the final analysis, the proper point of departure is the consideration of the religious group itself, whereas Weber and Troeltsch had considered the relations between religion and the global society. Wach's type of classification is the primary approach of all sociology. He no longer placed religion and society side by side; rather, he studied society in its religious aspect. Or, as he said so well himself, he studied the "types of religiously motivated groupings".[25]

At the end of this brief historical critique of the sociology of religion, we finally have a real point of departure. It now remains for us to make more precise the varieties of research which are possible in this vast field.

2. The Determination of the Different Levels of the Sociology of Religion

It is indeed from the following idea that we must start: there are societies which are motivated or informed by religion, in such a way that the structures and practices of these societies are religious in varying degrees. It is the study of such societies which constitutes the primary object of the sociology of religion. Thus the latter must not be confused with a general science or with an interpretation of religions, and thus also are we justified in undertaking a sociology of Christianity.

Obviously, this society which is informed by religion can be the global society itself. This is seen in the tribal societies studied by Durkheim, in ancient Israel, and, to a lesser degree, in contemporary Moslem society. But it can also be a society which is no longer coterminous with the global society, which is totally differentiated from this global society due to the process of secularization having affected the latter. In this case, problems of relationship between the social religious group and the secularized society will arise. These relationships can be of entirely different types: collaboration, hostility, benevolent neutrality, systematic ignorance. Although secularization is a phenomenon that has affected the entire Christian West since the end of the Middle Ages, it has not always followed the same tempo or occurred under the same forms.

The object of study of the sociology of religion, as we have delimited it, can be made more precise. Le Bras does so in the following fashion, in an article which serves as a manifesto and programme for the *Archives de Sociologie des Religions*:

> The sociology of religion aims at studying the structure and life of organized groups whose beginning and end is the sacred. That brief phrase implies three worlds: the cultic, or assembly of adherents; the supernatural, where hidden spirits reign; the civil, in the midst of which the company is established. Sociology is interested primarily in the first of these worlds. It describes and tries to explain the composition and coherence of this world, to measure its strengths and weaknesses, to understand its relationships to the other two worlds, to comprehend the image that it forms of them and of itself ... Consequently, the sociologist does not undertake to explore alone either the mystery of the supernatural or the intricacies of the terrestrial city. He works in conjunction with theologians and liturgists, canonists and legists to understand relationships, projections, languages. His function is one of discerning structures, of grasping the vitality of human groups, in the light of all the sciences of man.[26]

This strikes us as being a judicious delimitation of the object. The sociologist, focusing on the life and structure of religious groups, must be careful not to forget that these groups feel the pressure of the global society and are situated in a sociological context. But he must also bear in mind that they are not simply the reflection of this global society; they are also the projection of a supernatural world which Le Bras characterizes as the sacred. As far as Christianity is concerned, this term contains numerous ambiguities but may be retained with qualifications.

In this broad framework, it seems possible to specify various levels or steps of research:

1. *Sociography or descriptive sociology.*
It establishes memberships and determines the dimensions, volume, geographical density, and social density (the frequency and intensity of relationships on the interior of the group) of the religious society;

classifies members according to their degree of integration into the religious society. This degree of integration must not be confused with the degree of faith of the members, which is a reality that, as such, lies beyond the observation of the sociologist. Le Bras has proposed, for Catholicism, a classification that *mutatis mutandis* is valid also for Protestantism: the unattached, seasonal church-goers (Easter Christians), regular attenders at Sunday mass, the devout;

establishes the socio-professional composition of the religious group, the pyramid of ages, the distribution by sex, etc.;

measures the vitality of the group not only according to the comparative importance of the categories of members, but according to works, to the degree of morality, to the influence of the group on the whole of social life.

The ensemble of such research is based on history, statistics, inquiries, interviews, surveys of public opinion.[27]

2. *The typology of religious groups* is a classification that is based on the preceding analyses. It is a comparative science that endeavours to isolate the different types of religious organization. This typology will not consist solely of utilizing the official rosters of denominations (which maintain that they are distinct, separate, or in opposition). Such groups may very well have, beyond their divergences, similar structures: the episcopal structure creates analogies between confessions as diverse as Scandinavian Lutheranism, Anglicanism, Orthodoxy, and Roman Catholicism. There are also identical structures and behaviour on the part of churches which elsewhere are different and opposed, because they find themselves in the position of minority churches. There is an ensemble of characteristics that define the sect, be it Jewish, Essene, Christian, or Moslem. There can be communities of churches which are formed following a prolonged period of collaboration (for example, within the World Council of Churches), a collaboration which results in establishing a sort of osmosis between ecclesiastical types. Thus the typology is not at all set. The internal logic of a religion does not necessarily determine its typological development. A given denomination (Methodism, for example) which, in many countries of Europe, has the characteristics of a sect, loses such characteristics in America.[28]

3. *The internal relationships of a religion.* By this we mean the various relationships that are possible within a religion, between a certain number of set factors that, in more or less differentiated state, one encounters in most religions: cultic practices, myths, beliefs, dogmas, symbols. Here, indeed, it is necessary to get rid of certain intellectual prejudices which, for example, call for doctrines to inform and determine practices, for the form of worship to be determined by theology, for history unrelentingly to reject myth, etc. In fact, the theological development of Yahwism, for example, was determined to a great degree by the locating of places of worship, by the building of the temple of Jerusalem, etc.; mariology was engendered by popular devotion to Mary; and the historical nature of the Christian revelation has not entailed a radical demythologizing of holy history. Thus, in regard to each religion it is necessary to uncover the

internal relationships that are established between the various religious factors, because these relationships explain the configuration of the community and the expressions of its vitality (to the degree that such expressions are determined by its structure).

4. *The micro-sociology of religious groups.* The life of a religious group is expressed not only in the collective cultic acts or in the dominant ecclesiastical, social, cultural, and political attitudes; it is also expressed in the nature and quality of the relationships which are established between the members of the group and which are largely determined by their appurtenance to the group. Among these relationships it is necessary to consider those which have an obligatory character (for example, hierarchical-style relationships between clergy and laity) and those of a freer character (for example, between members of a given parish, such relationships being variously coloured by the nature of the religious group, its character as church or as sect, etc.). It would also be necessary to take account of the relationships which are established between the members and those outside. This is a problem that has played an important role in the history of primitive Christianity, in the relations between Christians and Jews, between Christians and Moslems, among Christian denominations (the problem of mixed marriages; a French Protestant tends to form his circle of friends primarily from his co-religionists).

5. *The socio-phenomenology of the religious object.* We have already stressed (chapter one) the necessity of taking into consideration this too-often ignored aspect of the sociology of religion. It is precisely the ignoring of this aspect that has led some sociologists to want to bring all religions down to a common denominator. Let us content ourselves here with showing how, in Christianity, the practice and activity of the different Christian confessions are influenced by the various ways in which they conceive of revelation (that is, *the object in action*).

In schematic fashion, we can say that for *Catholicism* this revelation resides in a sacred doctrinal deposit entrusted to a hierarchy which looks after its integrity, its teaching, and its explication; for *Protestantism* it resides in a living word which resounds from out the holy books of the Old and New Testaments, primarily when it is preached to the assembled community; for *Orthodoxy*, finally, it resides in a liturgy of the church which, because it is lived drama, abolishes the distance between the events of holy history and the present time, and thus integrates the faithful into sacred time.

From this derive the essentially different forms of religious behaviour. The primary concern of the Catholic church is to assure the continuity of the hierarchy (the foundation of the teaching church and of the validity of the sacramental acts) and the submission of all to the hierarchy (this primary concern has resulted, during certain periods, in a suspicion regarding the free usage of the Bible by the faithful).

The primary concern of the Protestant churches is to assure the preaching of God's word and the diffusion of the Holy Scriptures; the constitution of these churches gives clear indication of the will to dispose everything with a view to permitting, above all else, an unceasing preaching of Scripture, even more than to assuring the distribution of the sacrament: the translation of the Bible into the common tongues and its intensive diffusion is the point of all missionary activity. The spring of personal piety is to be found in the private reading of and meditation on Scripture. This also is the source of a constant preoccupation with elevating the cultural level of the faithful.

The primary concern of the Orthodox Church is to assure the celebration of the divine liturgy. This celebration takes the place of catechetical instruction. It is the imprint of the liturgy on the souls of believers which maintains them in the faith. Thus one sees the Russian Orthodox Church accepting with a certain facility the restrictions which the governments impose on its external activities and even on its teaching: the essential is safe as long as the church can celebrate its liturgy.

Along these same lines, until very recent times the various Orthodox churches have attached only minimal importance to the theological education of their priests, since the priest is primarily a celebrant.

It seems to us that by taking the religious object into consideration (for which, as Le Bras indicates, the assistance of the theologian is obviously indispensable to the sociologist), the sociology of religion will be able to move beyond the stage of the enumeration of factors and conditions, of the various types of the determination of some phenomena by others. It will be able to arrive at a true understanding of the religion under consideration, the understanding of the true *existential situation* of the members in relation to their God, since the structure of the community is the image, as it were, of this existential situation.

3. History of Religions and Sociology of Religion

Of all the auxiliary sciences of the sociology of religion, the history of religions is undoubtedly the most indispensable. Every religion has a past and valorizes this past in different ways in the present or projects it into the future.

It goes without saying that general sociology is important. This is true for several reasons: every religion, especially when it is differentiated from the global society, is situated in a certain social context; contemporary religions recruit their adherents from certain social classes rather than from others (it is a fact that the modern proletariat participates only to a limited degree in the life of the Christian churches); the political and ideological climate is capable of creating currents sympathetic to religion or, on the contrary, movements hostile to religion; the missionary activity takes varied forms according to the relations between continents and civilizations; in a general way, as Le Bras points out, "the capital fact of our time is the variety of contacts between societies of diverse types or beliefs"; and finally, to quote again from Le Bras, "the critical time for a religion is when it submits to the action of the civil society rather than inspires it".[29]

It is none the less true that the sociological interpretation of a religion must give an important and even decisive place to the history of the religion: every religion is characterized by a certain historical continuity (which differentiates it from philosophical schools) and must be studied in space and time. No sociography is complete which does not push its inquiry as far as possible in *time* and correlatively in *space*. For it is of the nature of a religion to be transmitted and diffused.

A religion is *transmitted* through quite diverse means: books, oral traditions, rites, initiation. In the transmission of Christianity, baptism has played a role as important and perhaps more important than the Bible itself. The Koran had no part in the transmission of Islam from the Middle East to Black Africa. By the sole fact of transmission, religion reveals one of its characteristics or one of its goals, namely that of transcending the generations, of maintaining itself within a perfect line, that of conserving itself pure and intact despite the course of time, of surviving individuals and of defying death. But in spite of this intention, it is never transmitted without at the same time developing within more or less strict limits. Even Christianity, which claims to have received an eternal and absolute revealed deposit, admits that it has a history. It admits, for example, that there is a *primitive* Christianity, characterized by a proliferation of *charismata*, by a direct action of the Holy Spirit on the life of the community, and by a minimum of organization (in Paul's letters, the list of *charismata* and the list of functions overlap and are never clearly differentiated). It admits that there is an *early* Christianity, characterized by a decline of *charismata* in favour of institutions, a correlative reduction of eschatological hope, and a fixing of doctrine (the formation of a canon, made necessary by the fight against heresies). Further, it admits that there is a *medieval* Christianity, characterized by the great theological syntheses, accompanied by a strengthening of pontifical authority, by the church's taking the whole of civilization in charge, etc.

The very line of development is typical for a religion. This transmission follows a logic proper to each religion and this logic plays a role as important as the external events. Why was the line of gnosticism finally broken in the development of Christianity? Why were the Judeo-Christian and judaizing tendencies, so powerful during Paul's age, finally overcome? Why does Protestantism remain faithful, through all its crises, to the principle of the return to the sources, whereas Catholicism is oriented towards attempts to explain primitive dogma and puts its trust in the living tradition? History alone calls forth such questions and they have need of being elucidated historically in order that sociology may grasp the profile of a religion.

Naturally, this transmission-development does not take place in isolation. Even when it is a question of religious communities that are quite exclusive, they are still sensible to the movement of general history, if not to all the events of this history, at least to the spirit of the age and to the history of customs and culture. And it is these non-religious factors which can lead to modifications of the group's religious sensitivity, of practices, of conceptual accounts of doctrinal formulations, of canonical and disciplinarian rules. It is possible for an internal development of religion to be joined with the action of external factors. An example would be the current purification of church buildings in Catholicism, and the decline of chaplets and rosaries in favour of the missal. Only history can enable us to understand the part played in this development by cultural factors.

A religion is *diffused* and this diffusion takes place following certain lines, in certain directions which are determined geographically and economically, and by the system of lines of communication. Paul's itineraries followed, in part, the great routes of navigation and travel of his age. But other factors intervened, namely, the widespread dissemination of Jewish proselytes and "God-fearers" throughout the Roman Empire, who constituted islands of particular receptivity for the good news. Religious and political factors intervene continuously in this diffusion of Christianity: it would not be difficult to show from the history of missions that the missionaries followed along the pathways opened by the traders and colonizers. Sometimes the missionaries pursued the same methods as the latter, that is to say, they contented themselves with christianizing the coastal areas in those places where the navigators and colonizers had not yet penetrated into the interior of the country. This same interplay of religious and political factors can be observed also at the time of decolonization: political autonomy can precede or follow the autonomy given to the younger churches. Only history permits us to understand how certain traits of religious communities derive from the mode of diffusion of the religion being considered, from the way in which it is established deeply or superficially.

Consciously or unconsciously, this transmission in time and this diffusion in space have a profound effect on the religion itself. At the same time, however, this effect is variable according to the type of religion being considered. For example, the following phenomena can be observed:

withdrawal into an orthodoxy, as a means of reacting against the destructive surrounding forces: such would be the case with African Christianity during the time of Saint Augustine;

syncretism which can go so far as to destroy the religious object itself: monotheistic Islam became fetishist in black Africa;

various forms of adaptation of a more subtle type: western Christianity slipped into the frameworks of the Roman empire and adopted its hierarchical structures.

Whether one considers a religion in its transmission or in its diffusion, only history can enable us to understand how these processes have shaped the religious communities and the understanding which they have of themselves.

But we should also emphasize the different attitudes which history and sociology take regarding these phenomena. History restricts itself to recording and describing the succession of stages and forms, in the attempt to see how they interact and condition one another, in the attempt to perceive the continuity between discontinuous epochs and to sort out the external and internal factors in the development.

Sociology must be in possession of this historical data, in order, first of all, to avoid constructing an *a priori* concept of the religion being considered. A conception of a religion cannot be based solely on doctrinal considerations such as they are presented to sociology by the religion's theologians. For example, sociology views Protestantism not simply as the reality defined by the theologian, be he conservative or liberal. For history teaches the sociologist that these two theological positions, both of which assume an absolute stance, have a history and are sometimes explained by events which the historian has had to integrate, assimilate, or reduce.

The sociologist has need of the historian, secondly, in order to be able to include certain suggestions into the idea of a given religion which are presented to him by the way in which the religion has developed and been diffused. In varying degrees, the history of a religion is part of its essence. We say "in varying degrees" because although Catholicism, due to its concept of tradition, quite easily integrates its entire history, Protestantism is continuously in the process of refining its own history.

But the objective of the sociologist is to construct religious types, types of religious communities, that are midway between the particular datum and the conceptual generalization. On the one hand, he will avoid limiting himself to the multitudinous facts, events, accidents, and misadventures, some of which indeed reveal the profound interpenetration between the life of the religious community and that of the surrounding society. On the other hand, he will avoid formulating, from the exalted perspective of a history of religions, a general idea of religion which would then be extrapolated, in the manner of Durkheim, to cover all religions. It is one thing to know, as historian, that the First Consul, under difficult and troubled conditions, made a concordat with the Catholic church in 1802; it is quite another thing to know (and this is one of the sociologist's tasks) that post-Constantine Christianity contains a constant tendency (which can, of course, be counteracted during certain periods) on the part of the church to regulate its relationships with the state and with the civil society on a concordat basis, that is to say, on the basis of a sharing of power. This second fact is important to the sociologist precisely because it represents a constant tendency, a permanent structure of the religion under consideration. He distinguishes another religious *type* in this tendency. An example of this would be biblical Israel, theocratic Israel, which did not conceive of a sharing of power and laid claim to the totality of power, on the religious level as well as on the political, juridical, military and international planes.

Georges Gurvitch writes:

The typological method proper to sociology constructs discontinuous types, but these types can recur at different stages. It generalizes to a certain degree, but only in order better to uncover the specific characteristics of the type. In constructing qualitatively different types, it individualizes to a certain degree, but only in order better to discover the frameworks which can be repeated.[30]

The sociologist always moves between empirical particularity, which history studies, and conceptual generality, which the physical sciences study. Actual societies develop in between these two perspectives.

We should add that this type constructed by sociology is always an *ideal type* (the meaning which we give to this expression is different from, although related to, the meaning which Max Weber gives to it[31]): it is ideal in the sense that it includes among its components the ideal values which the given society strives towards and partially lives. Not only does a society have its structures, an organization, certain practices and symbols – these realities also have a meaning, they are meant to signify something, they are directed towards something beyond themselves. The classic capitalistic societies of the nineteenth century attest in their organization and practice to the fact that they strove towards an ideal of happiness and social harmony. Perhaps the goal was utopian, yet it still acted effectively on these societies and explains the vigorous dynamism of the supporters of free enterprise.

Such ideal goals play an even greater part in a religious society. Such a society may even define itself formally as one characterized by the predominance of ideal goals, by a subordination (sought after, even if not effectively realized) of structures to the ideal values. It can happen, however, that the history lived by a religious community is a refutation of these ideal values. The history of Christianity is one of schisms, some of which were more or less resolved but others of which ended in manifold ruptures of Christian unity. The historian retraces these diverse accidents and explains them by a multitude of causes and circumstances. The sociologist cannot ignore these divisive occurrences. But neither can he define the Christianity-type as a religion which tends to split apart and crumble, even though Christianity has frequently furnished evidence of this. He must keep in view the persistence through this broken history of an ideal goal of unity, which is manifested in doctrine, liturgy, and piety. Sometimes, as in the century of ecumenism, this ideal goal is evidenced in the very policy of the Christian churches, even though this ecumenism remains an aspiration and has not yet resulted in any very spectacular achievements in regard to the unification of the great branches of Christianity. Despite its historical vicissitudes, Christianity claims to be and wants to be one and universal. Each Christian confession lays claim to catholicity.

The same is true of the missionary effort of Christianity, even though this effort has been impeded by different causes in different epochs of history. (Protestantism did not really become aware of its missionary vocation until the end of the eighteenth century.) Typologically speaking, Christianity (as opposed to Judaism for example) is in essence a missionary religion. Whatever be its deficiencies, renunciations, and failures in this respect over the centuries, Christianity is a missionary religion because it views itself not as a doctrine to be taught to the élite cadres of the western world, but as a good news to be proclaimed to every human being.[32]

This ideal, which thus includes actual components and ideal components in close association, makes it possible to distinguish between the normal and the pathological, between authentic religious forms and degenerate or aberrant forms (in relation to an ideal type). We would say, for example, that the fetishist Islam of black Africa is degenerate in relation to Koranic Islam (in the diversity of its traditions and schools of thought) precisely because monotheism is an essential and even central component of this type of religion. In regard to Christianity, it is the ideal type of a Christian confession which enables us to decide if a given sect belongs to it or not: in Catholic countries – France, for example – there is a tendency to attach any sect to Protestantism that makes use, in varying degrees, of the Bible (Jehovah's Witnesses, Christian Science, even Mormonism). Such procedure is definitely misguided, not only because the majority of the sect's members do not come from Protestantism but for an even more profound reason: these sects attach themselves to an ideal type that is completely different from the Protestant type. On the other hand, one is perfectly justified in attaching to Protestantism such groups as the Methodists, the Baptists, the Pentecostalists, and the Darbyites, even though some of these denominations recruit their adherents primarily from among Catholicism.

Thus, this concern to construct a typology is the primary distinction between sociology of religion and history of religions, which follows developments in their continuity and in the indefinite sequence of their forms.

Of course, the boundary that we have traced between these two disciplines is not always hard and fast. It shifts according to the degree that history ceases to be purely a history of events and becomes attached to the structural and permanent elements of a given society. For example, when history becomes the history of a civilization and applies itself to disengaging the basic characteristics, the configuration of a civilization, and the spirit of the society which bears it, then the boundary between history and sociology begins to waver. This is what Jean Baruzi is pointing to when he wonders whether Jacob Burckhardt's synthesis devoted to the Greek spirit was a matter of religious history or of sociology.[33] The same question could be asked concerning the work of Montesquieu, to the degree that events interest him less than the spirit of laws. It could be asked of

Toynbee, in so far as that which interests him is the manner in which a civilization constitutes a response to a challenge of history.

Moreover, it is the case that sociology was born of a history of civilizations and of a reflection on the life and death of civilizations. And if the history of civilizations can sometimes include sociology of religion, it is simply because no civilization could be understood without taking into consideration the values which it holds, values that obviously include religious values.

It remains, however, that the structural refers to an event which only history knows.[34] But this proposition is not equally valid for every religion. It is true of Christianity, whose worship, practice, and very organization refer directly or indirectly to the events in the life and passion of Christ (and to his resurrection, even if the objective historicity of this event cannot be established). But other religions have reference to mythical events, to a-historical events. These events are situated in a primordial time, anterior and superior to historical time, *in illo tempore*. This primordial time is no longer the time in which events unfold.[35] Let us recognize that there are diverse forms of events, that there is also a typology of events, and that the concept of historical event such as it has been forged in the Judeo-Christian climate of western thought does not exhaust the idea of event. Let us also recognize that the tie which a religious society establishes between its practices and the historical event is more or less clear: according to Lohmeyer, the Mandaean sect related itself to John the Baptist by a real historical filiation, but it itself does not include any precise reference to the figure of John the Baptist, to the "John the Baptist event". The tradition is maintained solely by the rite of baptism.

Thus sociology is not the negation of history, although it proceeds in a different manner from history. Sociology refers to history and ultimately to historical events. But this reference which effectively operates in the life of groups takes very diverse forms.

In any case, a sociology of Christianity could not forget the fact that in this religion there is an explicit, constant, and deliberate reference to that which took place under Pontius Pilate.

4. *Concerning Explication in the Sociology of Religion*

Since the sociology of religion has freed itself from a certain imitation of the physical sciences (moreover, from the nineteenth century) and from certain philosophical *a priori* which led it to reduce religion to something other than what it is, and since it has set itself to the concrete study of religious groups, it has had the tendency to restrict itself unpretentiously to descriptive and sociographical analyses. This being so, it has infrequently posed the question of explication, which took form in the last century as that of the study of sociological laws.

Furthermore, sociology in general has undertaken a critique of the very concept of law. This concept was naïvely borrowed by Durkheim's sociology from classical physics. It led him, contrary to his profound intuition of the value-positing nature of every social group, to claim that social facts are things and must be treated as such. Sociographic and statistical methods have undoubtedly proved that it is possible to trace certain curves, to establish concomitant variations, and to indicate in what direction a development is likely to move. But is this a matter of laws in the proper sense of the word? Georges Gurvitch proposes more modestly that we speak of "tendential regularities". The sociology of religion provides many examples of such "regularities": the sect has a tendency always to take identical attitudes *vis-à-vis* the church, for example, denunciation of the corruption of the church, of its hypocrisy, of its institutional, official nature, etc. This is true of the schismatic movements of the second century as well as of contemporary sects. In the same way, H. Desroche has traced the constant liaison in religious groups between messianism, moral rigorism, and communitarian socialism. But the idea of a law in the physical sense of the word is not applicable in this domain. For in this domain the given is always fluctuating and complex, the boundary between fact and aspiration cannot be traced, the real is always valorized, and the components of the given can never be isolated in their purity. On the other hand, it is possible to speak of stable liaisons between *structures* and *behaviours*, without making precise whether the behaviours determine the structures or vice versa.

In no case, as we are reminded by G. Le Bras,[36] would it be a matter of a "global explication" of the religious phenomenon or of religion itself. Would it, then, be a question of following the rule formulated by Durkheim,[37] namely, that of the explication of the social by the social, of a homogeneous explication in which, for example, the psychical would never be invoked to explain the social? Indeed yes, if we bear in mind that the social is not fixed in some sort of "*en soi*" category which would exclude every reference to any other reality. Of course, the religious society is a society informed by the religious, by the sacred. And science can make no pronouncements on the nature of this sacred. Yet this sacred, in so far as it is apprehended in a certain fashion by a social group, is also, phenomenologically, a social reality.

If the explication cannot be global without risking becoming a reduction of the Durkheimian (or possibly Marxist) type, this means that the modes of explication must be diversified according to the levels of sociological research, following the different aspects of the religious group. In the article referred to, Le Bras utilizes a distinction that he has presented under various forms: he proposes that we consider in the religious community three inter-related communities, namely, an autonomous community, which is differentiated from the global society; a social body in relation with other social bodies; a supernatural community. These are scientific abstractions; in reality, the three worlds intermix and form a whole. But it is valid to consider separately the group in so far as, conscious of its originality, it isolates itself; the group as it forms relationships with the surrounding society; and finally, the group as it seeks its ground in a communion with the supernatural.

In considering the autonomous community, it would be a question of explaining how it is constituted, separates itself from the world, recruits its members, maintains itself through time, and is diffused. And here the explications can be of a great variety: baptism, imitation, initiation, instruction, discipline, group authority or prestige, the power of tradition. Not all these factors are necessarily of a religious nature. Factors of a geographical and historical nature can intervene, the degree of isolation or the degree of contact between the group under consideration and the surrounding society. Thus is explained, for example, certain anomalies in the map of religious practice in the Vendean region of France:

In the north, 80 to 95 per cent (of practice); in the south, 15 to 5 per cent. In the fifteenth century there was unanimity throughout the region. Here we have the problem which I would call the subtraction of obedience. The solution begins to appear when we cast a glance at the southern advance of Protestantism in the sixteenth century, of Encyclopedianism in the eighteenth century, and finally, of the ideas of the Revolution; and when we consider in the north the Catholic resistance, the missions of Père de Montfort, the recruitment and the memories of the *Chouannerie*.[38]

This explication could be made even more precise by showing, for example, that the Protestant advance in the southern part of the Vendée, not having been able to maintain itself due to repression, had nevertheless been sufficient to destroy the old structures and traditions, thereby leaving behind it a void. This void was filled by libertarian ideas. Obviously, this explication is not exhaustive. One has to be content with clarifying a process, with rendering it less mysterious, more comprehensible.

In considering the group as it is immersed in the social body, it is necessary to study the repercussions of the social movements of the whole on the religious group. It will perhaps also be necessary to study the reciprocal action; for example, the segregation of French Protestants in certain limited areas (generally poor, agricultural regions) explains why the Protestant regions have been more affected by the great rural exodus of recent times. The Protestant body is ejected, as it were, from its reserves and diffused throughout the body of the nation. The action of the social body on the religious group thus is matched against the repercussions of the socio-professional composition of the latter. This socio-professional composition is a religiously neutral factor, but its religious repercussions can be profound. It is thus that French Protestantism, on leaving its "underground", has been reduced essentially, in the cities, to a social élite (liberal, commercial, industrial, and banking professions). Only this élite has had the reserves and the supports sufficient to resist. Now, the Organic Articles accord a preponderant part in the direction of the church to this élite. This explains why the church as a whole will be open to liberal and rationalist middle-class ideologies. This explains why the theology of French Protestantism will be more liberal than conservative.

But inverse examples can be given that show how the thought of the churches can radiate out into the social body as a whole. Thus in the nineteenth century the influence of the Protestant social employers of Mulhouse[39] and of social Catholicism effectively awakened the attention of numerous circles to the worker-problem and led the *bourgeoisie* to reject socialist solutions by orienting it towards social paternalism. Evidently, it was because the society as a whole was still Christian in the nineteenth century that the social doctrine of the church could resound there so profoundly.

In considering the "supernatural community", the society which the religious group forms with its God and its saints, one touches more easily on a properly religious causality. As Denis de Rougemont has shown,[40] the doctrine of Chalcedon has not been without an influence on the concern for the person so characteristic of western civilization. It was to safeguard a strongly contested trinitarian doctrine and to hinder it from developing outside the bounds of monotheism that the Greek and Latin Fathers forged this concept of person which had not been bequeathed to them by Hellenism and which was to have decisive import for theology as well as anthropology. As de Rougemont says, there is "a theological genesis of the person".

It was the theological concept of Christian liberty, so strongly emphasized by Luther, that was to influence the organization of the Protestant churches in a democratic direction that was neither foreseen nor wished by Luther.

There is indeed a properly religious causality which must have its part in the explication.

As is evident, it is nearly impossible to formulate a general doctrine of explication in religious sociology. In any case, it would be impossible to set up *a priori* the factors which would be considered as explicative. These factors are numerous, and it is not possible to reduce them to unity. Certain of them are extra-religious, others are theological. The explication will attempt to go back from external causality to internal causality, for the latter alone gives us a *comprehension* of the phenomena. That is to say, it enables us to grasp an organic necessity which explains a given development, a given evolution. The explication must tend towards the establishment of a relation between the nature of the religious object and the different aspects of the religious group. Yet, once again, it cannot claim an exclusive privilege.

The idea of arriving at a general socio-phenomenology of religion must not be abandoned *a priori*. But this socio-phenomenology must remain prudent. It can undoubtedly bring out certain structures that are repeated in a great number of religions, and which consequently will appear as permanent structures of religion, for example, the distinction between clergy and laity or the phenomenon of monasticism. But it must be attentive to the fact that these phenomena do not have the same meaning everywhere and do not express the same religious intention, and this is because they do not refer to the same type of religious object. It seems impossible to group under the term "sacred", as we have specified it, the diverse types of religious object.

As far as the idea goes of introducing into sociological explication a strict determinism such as Durkheim conceived it (to explain the social only by the social), it withers away in the perspective of a socio-phenomenology in which the focusing of the object has a decisive character. The sociologist can circumscribe this object in so far as it produces behaviours, attitudes, social structures, institutions. He cannot account for it. When he appeals, as is his perfect right, to explicative factors borrowed from the sociology of the surrounding society or from the particular sociology of the religious group being considered, he indeed establishes a sociological conditioning of the religious life. But this is not a global determinism. The insertion of a value at a determined epoch of history and in particular socio-economic conditions takes nothing away from the validity of this value:

Does the teaching of an Isaiah or a Luther, [asks Wach] even if "explained" sociologically, really lose any of its validity? It does not seem so. Even if it could be shown that economic or general social conditions in a given society have prompted a desire for deliverance, the ideas of redemption that may be included in a religious message are not invalidated by an inquiry into their social "background", provided we do not conceive of the relation in deterministic terms but consider conditions as a framework which may include a variety of contents.[41]

This last remark seems essential: like all the humane sciences, sociology of religion establishes functional relations, without ever being able to decide that it has isolated all these relations nor that the ensemble of these relations represents a causal explication. Moreover, it would be paradoxical, even on the scientific plane, for a reality bearing a meaning and a value to be explained by elements which would bear neither this meaning nor this value or which would not even have meaning or value. The last word, the last wisdom of all the humane sciences, is that meaning and value appear in a conditioning that one can afterwards study and define, but that the appearing itself retains its indelible mark as event.

NOTES

1. *Cours de philosophie positive*, 6 vols. (Paris: Bachelier, 1830–1842), first lesson.
2. L. Lévy-Bruhl, *How Natives Think*, translated by Lilian A. Clare (New York and London: Alfred A. Knopf, 1926); *Primitive Mentality*, translated by Lilian A. Clare (New York and London: The Macmillan Company, 1923); *Primitives and the Supernatural*, translated by Lilian A. Clare (New York: E. P. Dutton & Company, 1935 and London: George Allen & Unwin Ltd., 1936); *The Soul of the Primitive* (1928).
3. *Les carnets de Lucien Lévy-Bruhl*, published by Maurice Leenhardt (Paris: PUF, 1949).
4. Durkheim, *Elementary Forms*, p. 422.
5. ibid., p. 419.
6. ibid., p. 427.
7. Durkheim thus shows his dependence on the philosophical idealism characteristic of the beginning of the twentieth century which sought the basis of all religion in the area of values. We have shown the equivocal nature of such an attempt in our *De l'autorité des valeurs* (Paris: PUF, 1957).
8. In the work of E. Dupréel, we find a similar form of reduction. It tries to explain religion without minimizing the objective nature of religion, and gives this objectivity a psycho-sociological interpretation: "... what is the primary qualification for a belief that cannot be verified and to which the facts lend no support? *It is necessary that one not have invented it oneself.* Now, all verification is a type of renewed invention, since it is substituted for the primary information, of which one no longer has any need. The mystery, in order for it to be believed, must be *objective*: it must be *independent of us*, as the real elements were at the beginning, observables upon which technics operate ... This objectivity which, in the mystery, could not result from experience, is obtained by virtue of the fact that belief is communicated by others. The multiplicity and diversity

of minds is the creator of objectivity. An agreement between Peter and Paul is a fact for James, a determination of things which he experiences on occasion as a force. Tradition, also, is a fact, something objective for the person who receives it; that which it inculcates remains in him as a nature independent of his imagination" (*Sociologie générale* [Paris: PUF, 1948], p. 227). The history of the Christian churches, and especially of Roman Catholicism, is abundant proof that tradition can accredit the objectivity of certain facts. Has not Vincent of Lerins defined the truth – the objective – as that which the Fathers "have been able to hold in unity of thought and feeling" (Migne, *Patrologiae cursus completus,* Latin series, vol. 50, col. 675)? The *traditum* defines that which must be believed as true. But the whole question is one of knowing if tradition itself is not focused on a reality whose objectivity remains independent of it and which cannot be reduced by the psycho-sociological analysis of the formation of this tradition itself.

9. Max Weber, *The Protestant Ethic and the Spirit of Capitalism,* translated by Talcott Parsons (London: George Allen & Unwin, Ltd., 1930 and New York: Charles Scribner's Sons, 1948; p.b. reissue, 1958). [Trans. note. See also Weber's *Sociology of Religion,* translated by Ephraim Fischoff (Boston: Beacon Press, Inc., 1963).]

10. *Protestant Ethic,* p. 27.

11. Raymond Aron, *German Sociology,* translated by Mary and Thomas Bottomore (New York: The Free Press of Glencoe, 1964 and London: Collier-Macmillan, 1965), p. 94.

12. Cf. M. Merleau-Ponty, *Les aventures de la dialectique* (Paris: Gallimard, 1955), p. 23.

13. Weber himself, moreover, did not present this thesis as a complete interpretation of the phenomenon, as a spiritualistic interpretation placed over against the materialistic and Marxist interpretation of capitalism. For a discussion of this thesis, see especially, R. H. Tawney, *Religion and the Rise of Capitalism* (New York: Harcourt, Brace and Company, 1926, and London: Penguin Books); also, H. Luthy, "Calvinisme et capitalisme", in *Preuves,* 164 (July, 1964).

14. Quoted in Joachim Wach, *Sociology of Religion* (p.b. ed.; Chicago: University of Chicago Press "Phoenix Books", 1962), p. 12.

15. Ernst Troeltsch, *The Social Teaching of the Christian Churches,* 2 vols., translated by Olive Wyon (London: George Allen & Unwin, Ltd. and New York: The Macmillan Company, 1931).

16. *Social Teaching,* vol. 2, p. 995.

17. ibid., p. 992.

18. Wach, *Sociology,* p. 11.

19. ibid., p. 5.

20. ibid., p. v.

21. ibid., p. 2.

22. ibid., p. 351.

23. ibid., p. 2. For further details on Wach's method, see the Wach memorial issue, *ASR,* 1 (January–June 1956), especially H. Desroche's study, "Sociologie et théologie dans la typologie religieuse de Joachim Wach".

24. See his book, *Types of Religious Experience* (Chicago: University of Chicago Press, 1951).

25. Wach, *Sociology,* p. 10.

26. "Sociologie religeuse et sciences des religions", *ASR,* 1 (January–June, 1965), 6–7.

27. One of the dangers in current sociological research is that of becoming satisfied with this level. This is probably done for the sake of prudence. Such prudence is fine, but it should not prohibit the opening-up of wider perspectives for the future. Le Bras

is conscious of this. H. Desroche, in outlining the philosophy of Le Bras' work, writes: "The statistical distribution between the groups defined by these external indices (practices) has been and remains (for Le Bras) the preliminary prerequisite of all precise procedure. But such statistical distribution is not sufficient by itself for discerning if such phenomena, in equivalent percentages, are ascribable to a religion which has become sociological by constraint or, on the other hand, to a society which has become religious by conviction. Nor is it sufficient for discerning the part played by social constraint and the part played by personal conviction, and even more profoundly, for discerning the part of the profane and the part of the sacred in this synthetic and pervasive force which is beyond juridical definitions, namely, the popular and living transmission of that unknown quantity, custom" ("Domaines et méthodes de la sociologie religieuse dans l'oeuvre de G. Le Bras", *RHPR*, 34 [1954], 146). This distinction between a religion become sociological by constraint and a society become religious by conviction is indispensable if one wishes to understand a phenomenon like the Reformation, and if one wishes to understand the shift of a large part of the population of the major European countries to a new form of the church and of the faith (despite the dangers that such a passage entails).

28. The constructing of a typology necessarily implies a sociology of religious institutions, which could also be considered as a separate chapter.

29. "Sociologie religieuse et science des religions", *ASR*, 1 (January–June, 1956).

30. Georges Gurvitch, *Vocation de la Sociologie* (2nd ed.; Paris: PUF, 1957), p. 10.

31. On Weber's concept of the "ideal type", see Raymond Aron, *German Sociology*, pp. 71–75.

32. On the attitude of sociology of religion in regard to ideal values, see J. Labbens, *La sociologie religieuse* (Paris: A. Fayrard, 1959), p. 9.

33. J. Baruzi, *Problèmes d'histoire des religions* (Paris: Alcan, 1935), pp. 3–4.

34. See our study, "Le dialogue de l'Histoire et de la Sociologie", *CIS*, 3 (1947).

35. Cf. Mircea Eliade, *Cosmos and History; The myth of the eternal return*, translated by William R. Trask (New York: Harper Torch Books, 1959 and London: Routledge and Kegan Paul).

36. "L'explication en sociologie religieuse", *CIS*, 21 (1956), 68.

37. Durkheim, *Sociological Method*.

38. Le Bras, art. cit., 70–71. [Trans. note. The *Chouannerie* was the insurrection of Vendeans in 1791, which was provoked by the decree (*Constitution civile du clergé*) of July 12, 1790 declaring the French clergy independent of the Holy See.]

39. [Trans. note. For further information on the social patronate of the Mulhousian Protestants, see the author's *Society and Love*, translated by James H. Farley (Philadelphia: The Westminster Press, 1964 and London: Hodder & Stoughton, 1965), p. 20 and p. 213, n. 3. A phenomenon similar to the Mulhousian paternalism was found in the "coal camp" of Appalachia, where the mining company provided (for a token price) everything that management thought the miner and his family might need; cf., for example, Jack E. Weller, *Yesterday's People; life in contemporary Appalachia* (Lexington, Ky.: University of Kentucky Press "Kentucky Paperbacks", 1966), esp. pp. 92–93.]

40. D. de Rougemont, *Man's Western Quest* (New York: Harper's, 1957).

41. In the collective volume edited by G. D. Gurvitch and W. F. Moore, *Twentieth Century Sociology* (New York: Philosophical Library, 1945), p. 420.

III

The Specific Nature of the Sociology of Protestantism[1]

The expanding research being undertaken by ecclesiastical and religious sociology is not always viewed without uneasiness or scepticism by the church, parishes, and the faithful. Sociology has not yet won full acceptance within Protestantism.[2] Parishioners wonder why they are taken as objects of study and what utility such research can have for the church. Protestant piety contains a certain modesty which is annoyed by the prying of the sociologist.[3] But rather than be disturbed by this incomprehension, we must return to the base of the problem and examine the meaning, the possibilities, and the limits of a sociology of Protestantism. The more successful we are in clarifying these problems, the better we shall be able to respond to criticisms and misgivings.

A sociology of Christianity in general and of Protestantism in particular is made possible by a very explicit theological and sociological fact, and this same fact explains why this sociology has a specific nature and is not simply one variety of religious sociology. We are referring to the fact that from the beginning, the intention and actual effect of Christian preaching, of the apostolic *kerygma*, was to create particular communities whose practice, life, and organization would be informed and structured by this apostolic *kerygma* and by the revelation to which it pointed. We are not speaking here simply of the general influence of religion on society (which is a problem that has rightly occupied the attention of Max Weber, Troeltsch, Mensching, and many others); rather, we are speaking of the creation, growing out of the preaching of the gospel, of original *communities*, which were formed to receive and transmit this same gospel.

To be sure, we know of other cases where the preaching and teaching of a doctrine led to the formation of a society that was differentiated from the global society. This was the case, for example, with the Essene sect at the time of Jesus. But the particularity of the Christian community lay in the fact that although it undoubtedly was constituted as a differentiated group it was not a closed society. It was not of the world, but it was indeed in the world. For as long as possible, it maintained ties with the synagogue and with the circles of Jewish proselytes; but at the same time it was oriented entirely towards mission. These characteristics are completely opposed to those of a closed society, as the Qumran sect seems to have been.[4]

A sociology of Christianity is possible and valid because the objective of the apostolic preaching was the formation of communities structured by the Christian message, differentiated from the surrounding society, yet not segregated from it. The specific nature of this sociology is based on this historical and theological fact. Obviously, we do not intend to deny that a sociology of Hinduism or of Islam is possible. However, the communities studied by such sociologies would be much less differentiated from the global society. The social impact of religious doctrine would be much less marked in the society. In fact, these communities have the same limits and the same structure as the ethnic group itself. The sociology of these religions would be at one and the same time the sociology of ethnic, racial, political, and cultural groups. When Joachim Wach considers "the religious grouping, religious fellowship and association [and] the individual, typological, and comparative study" of each of these groups to be one of the basic aspects of sociological research, and when he states that therein lies "the field of the sociology of religion",[5] his definition fits the sociology of Christianity perfectly. This is because the latter is characterized by the concern to build religious communities without considering ethnic origin or cultural level, communities which are informed essentially by doctrine itself.

The nature of Christian churches as differentiated groups has been sometimes more marked, sometimes less marked over the course of history. In the West, during the ages of "Christendom", it has been attenuated when the religious society and the civil society tended to coincide, when the parish and the "commune" overlapped. With secularization, which has introduced a growing distance between the two societies, this differentiation has been accentuated. But it has not been created solely by secularization. The church, from its very foundation, took its place as a community distinct from the surrounding society (even during the course of the Constantinian age, when it sought to impose its laws on society) and as a community whose principles and norms of internal organization were found in the message which was proclaimed to it and which it proclaimed. Of course, this doctrinal determinism was not the only factor that played a role in the organization of the church. A large part was also played by many other social, political, and cultural factors, by many phenomena of acculturation (already discernible on the doctrinal level).[6] But however important these might have been, we cannot overlook the original and never entirely veiled fact that the content of the preaching determined the forms of community life, of worship, of discipline, and even forms of sociability. Did not the missionary structure of the primitive church grow out of the very nature of a gospel which, as good news, was to be proclaimed to all men?

From a sociological point of view, it can be said that the Reformation, which took place precisely at a time when secularization began to make its effects felt, represented an effort to re-establish communities where this doctrinal determination could assert itself. The church, such as it has been progressively constituted since Constantine, had become a universal type of institution covering the whole of men's lives. This development had reached its apogee between the twelfth and fourteenth centuries. The Reformation never explicitly repudiated this heritage of Christendom. Yet by the sole fact of defining the church as the congregation of the faithful assembled by the preaching of the Word and the administration of the sacraments,[7] the Reformation removed the emphasis from the universal institution (characterized by its hierarchy) and placed it on to the communities effectively gathered to receive Word and sacrament, that is to say, on to the parish. Protestantism is characterized by the fact of the parochial community. Thus a sociology of Protestantism, because of the direct incidence of ecclesiology on sociological structures, would have the parish group as its primary object of study. The parish is a differentiated society in relation to the global society, and attempts to exert, with varied success, an influence on the latter. Naturally, this idea of parish should not be given a purely traditional, i.e., geographical meaning. The parish is the group that attempts to assemble Christians according to laws of human proximity: such proximity can be socio-professional as well as purely spatial.

Thus we shall define the sociology of Protestantism as the sociology of these parochial groups, in which the ecclesiology appertaining to the Reformation is expressed. Of course, this sociology of Protestantism will utilize other branches of sociology, to the degree that these parish groups undergo determinations other than the ecclesiastical-doctrinal one, to the degree, for example, that they are groups characterized by the predominance of a certain social class. But the heart of the research of the sociology of Protestantism will be the life, the practices, the institutions, the vitality, the missionary strength of this specific group that we have just defined.

It should not be objected that we have defined an ideal group and that sociology, as an empirical science, studies only realities which are concretely given to it in history. There is no doubt at all that the Protestant parish has never conformed *entirely* to the ideal norm defined by Protestant ecclesiology. Without any doubt, it is *something even more* than the congregation of forgiven sinners assembled by the preaching of the Word and the administration of the sacraments, through the working of the hidden power of the Holy Spirit. It is also, of course, a group sustained by a certain local, regional, or national tradition; it is a society of mutual assistance limited by the boundaries of social class; it is a means of personal identification for the individuals which it brings together; it is the group that stands over against the Catholic church, or perhaps the minority that defends itself against the majority of another denomination. All of these aspects are real and must be taken into account. But they must not make us lose sight of the fact that the parish is primarily (in intention if not in fact) this congregation that we have described. For, in a collective consciousness, intention carries weight even if it is not fulfilled. It orients behaviour and gives life to organizations. It maintains a tension within groups which prevents them from yielding to other determinations. In a general way, sociology is a science which, without pretending to be normative, integrates the consideration of values into the collective consciousness, in so far as these values are truly living (even as ideals).

If such is really the object of the sociology of Protestantism, this definition will permit us to shed some light on a rather vexing problem of sociology, a problem that continually obstructs it in its empirical research. The question is, Who is Protestant? Who should be considered as a member of a Protestant church? This problem is solved relatively easily in regard to Catholicism: there are a certain number of canonically defined practices, and if these are not fulfilled, one ceases to be a Catholic. Le Bras has been able to establish his famous classification of Catholics on the basis of these practices, on their number, frequency, and repetition.[8]

These criteria are not *immediately* applicable to Protestantism for two reasons. First of all, Protestantism is anxious to avoid anything, no matter how insignificant, that might turn it into a religion of works-righteousness. Consequently, it resists defining and classifying practices. To be sure, for the Protestant as for the Catholic, there is no Christian without baptism. But not every baptized person is necessarily a member of the church, or at least he is a member only by the promise and not necessarily in fact.

Secondly, and we attach great important to this fact, practices (which the theology of the Reformation calls rather the means of grace) are never dissociated in Protestantism from the insertion of the member into the parish community. A Catholic can be in good standing with his church without being truly integrated into the parish community. He can carry out the practices outside the parish. He finds places of worship that are not parishes – a phenomenon almost unknown in Protestantism. He makes confession to any priest and receives absolution from it. The mobility brought about by modern civilization, coupled with the increase in the use of week-ends, have meant that at least in the cities the member spends less and less time in the parish to which he nominally belongs. This does not mean, however, that he does not go to mass or that he does not take communion: he can and does do so outside the parish. The Catholic engaged in parochial activities is certainly a good Catholic, but the converse is not true. One can be a true member without participating in the life of a parish. From the pastoral point of view, this fact is not entirely normal, but neither is it entirely abnormal. This is because the church, for the Catholic, is not primarily the local community: it is primarily the hierarchical ensemble of the institution.[9]

The Protestant discerns more clearly than the Catholic the reality of the church in the local community. For him, the church is not an institution and a hierarchy, but the place where the faithful gather to hear the Word, to receive the sacrament, and also to accept a certain number of responsibilities. To his view, it is in this assembly that the body of Christ takes form and that the church is edified. Certainly, not all the Protestant churches are congregationalist in the proper sense of the term.[10] Congregationalism, which is still strong among the Baptist churches, is clearly losing ground, and the Reformation did not acknowledge it. Yet nevertheless, Reformation ecclesiology contains a congregationalist dimension, even in the churches that have maintained or restored a very hierarchical episcopal organization. This dimension is tied to the very definition which Protestantism gives to the church. The result of this is that the Protestant must define himself by his integration into the parochial community and that the classification of Protestants must be made not directly in relation to the fulfilment of certain practices, but in relation to the degree of integration into the parochial life. This criterion is undoubtedly more delicate to handle than the somewhat mechanical criterion of practices, but it is indispensable for a sociology of Protestantism to want to respect the nature of its object. One of the tasks of sociologists who occupy themselves with Protestantism would be to elaborate the various indices of integration into the parochial community. *This elaboration goes beyond the framework of this present study.* Let us content ourselves with emphasizing that the very

Calvinistic idea of responsibility will undoubtedly play an important role in this elaboration. The ideal of an ecclesiology of the Protestant type would be to consider each member as exercising a particular ministry in the church. This would be the explication of the principle of the universal priesthood.[11]

The internal organization of Catholicism rests on the presence of priests ordained by a hierarchy, which is itself within the apostolic succession. Without the presence of this hierarchy, there is no real church. The internal organization of Protestantism rests on the building up of parishes. The parochial community plays the role in Protestantism that the hierarchy plays in Catholicism. For the Protestant, the church exists from the moment that there exists a community which assembles to hear the Word of God. Thus we see that the primary concern of the Reformation (more perceptible in the Calvinist than in the Lutheran Reformation) was to "raise up" churches, even when it was not prepared to place a pastor at the head of the church.

There is a need to analyse very closely the reasons for the spectacular growth of Protestantism in Latin America.[12] It would undoubtedly be seen that this growth arises from the Protestant concern to integrate the converts into a social group, whereas Catholicism, having a totally insufficient number of priests at its disposal, is not able to supervise the observance of practices – without which, appurtenance to the Roman church disappears.[13]

It has often been said that sociology is concerned only with institutions and practices, the most objective, most measurable, and at the same time the most superficial elements of social life. This maxim is restrictive enough when applied to religious sociology. It is very reassuring for those who are suspicious of religious sociology. It signifies that this discipline is not concerned with anything in the profound religious life and does not touch the reality of the church as mystery. It also delineates certain reserved sectors where sociology could not adventure without impiety, for instance, the domain of dogmas and creeds. Must a sociology of Protestantism be understood in this restrictive sense? We do not believe so, and would like to substantiate our viewpoint with two examples.

We have said that the sociology of Protestantism seems to us to be basically the study of communities which are differentiated and structured by the preaching of the Word and the administration of the sacraments. As E. G. Léonard writes, "All religious sociology rests on an ecclesiology."[14] To be sure, these communities are, indeed, visible empirical societies. Protestantism has never confused the church-mystery, known of God alone and constituted by all those, living and dead, who are united to Christ by the invisible tie of faith, with the visible and instituted church. The Reformation confessions of faith are very explicit on this point. But although they do not confuse these two realities, although Protestantism, unlike Catholicism, refuses to see the only true church of Christ in a particular institution, it is nevertheless the case that Protestantism refuses to separate these two aspects of the same reality constituted by the church visible and the church invisible. Calvin, who among all the Reformers insisted most on the necessary visibleness of the church, always affirmed that there were not two churches but only one.[15] Thus the mystery of the invisible church of God is expressed, through this very imperfect reality – with which it is not confused – which is the empirical community of believers. This community is not the church, but the church is expressed, manifested, and edified in it.

It results from this that a sociology which intends to respect its object (in this case the givens of ecclesiology) will also not separate the visible church, which it arrives at by its own means of investigation, from the invisible church. It cannot limit itself, to utilize a formula which we have previously proposed,[16] to the study of the *corpus christianum* and ignore the *Corpus Christi*. For the *corpus christianum*, although it has been affected by all sorts of social determinations, sees itself as participating in the *Corpus Christi*. Consequently, sociology cannot treat the church as if it were unaware that it lives in permanent tension with an invisible reality, that it is, in its profound intentionality, the visible and instituted expression of an invisible event.

Thus the diagnoses which sociology makes of the vitality of a parish, whatever be the hazards of error and of over-simplification that they entail, actually concern the profound life of the church in its empirical reality as well as in its mystery – and not only as a sort of sociological epiphenomenon. When J. Binet modestly proposes that sociological analysis "reaches only the external acts and is incapable of apprehending their motivations which alone give to the acts their true meaning",[17] it seems to us that his moderation is excessive. For example, take a graph that would show the curve of attendance at Sunday worship and the curve of attendance at the Holy Communion services of Good Friday and Easter Sunday. If, in certain parishes, the first curve is stabilized somewhere close to the zero level (around 8 or 10 per cent), whereas the second curve shows a marked upswing to around 60 or 70 per cent, we can say that in these parishes the Lord's Supper is the object of superstitious idolatry. We can say to the church that it must 'demythologize' the Lord's Supper, that the reasons which impel the faithful to communicate in such numbers once a year are not good and sound reasons. It is not possible to isolate the empirical church from the mystery of the church. Our sociological research, no matter how tainted it may be with relativism and error, concerns both the ecclesiastical institution in its historical contingency (the community of the faithful assembled by the Word and at the same time by other mundane factors) and the mysterious event of this assembling. Sociological research cannot be based on a dissociation between the visible church and the invisible church, for this would be to *truncate* and mutilate the experience lived by the community itself. It would be to submit the ecclesial reality to categories that are not in line with its effective intentionality.

This is why it is so difficult to execute the task which the Faith and Order Conference of Lund (1952) proposed to the member churches of the World Council of Churches, namely, to investigate the "non-theological factors" of division among the member churches.[18] We do not say that this task is impossible, for a sufficient historical and sociological knowledge effectively allows one to mark off elements of ecclesiastical life that are unrelated to the ecclesiology belonging to the church in question. But it is none the less true that some of these elements will have been valorized by the ecclesiology, that is, they will have become bearers of the church's intention to participate in the mystery of the Body of Christ. It is not possible to distinguish in any absolute way between the church in its essence and purity and the church in its concrete manifestation.

A second example concerns the view that doctrine and beliefs constitute a reserved sector with which sociology should not occupy itself. This is the position taken by many sociologists of Roman Catholicism, but against which H. Desroche has unceasingly protested. We think that to accept such a limitation would be to reintroduce, under another form, the dissociation between visible and invisible church, in this case, a dissociation between revelation as Act of God and revelation as it is received by a concrete community. Now, there are good theological reasons for rejecting such a dissociation. According to the Christian faith, that which is proper to God's revelation is effectively to reach those to whom it is destined and to reach them in their concrete, historical, and sociological situation. We do not understand the message of the New Testament as a timeless revelation; rather, it is a message received, understood, and taken up by a certain community which thought in terms of New Testament categories (grace, law, sacrifice, wrath, mercy, redemption) and of categories resulting from the contamination between Jewish thought and the Hellenistic world (*logos*). The exegete who explains these things to us is doing sociology. And throughout the doctrinal elaboration of Christian thought we come again and again across this indissoluble alliance between the exigences of revelation and the socio-cultural characteristics of groups and communities. This is indeed what was clearly seen in a courageous article by Father M. D. Chenu:

> From one end to the other of its elaboration, in its ecclesial supports and in its terminal structure, the pronouncement of a Council, be it doctrinal or disciplinary, arises out of a *communion* of thought, out of a social conscience. This is not the sum of efforts, of lights, of private passions, but the effect of a collective phenomenon, which, according to the sociology of learning, has its own laws and its own original movements ... When God reveals himself to man, he reveals himself not according to his own understanding but according to the mode of the human mind, beginning with the humble processes of grammar and language. Although this divine communication is made in a community called the church, it will still follow, in this humanization, the laws and processes of human learning, which each sociologist can observe in human societies.[19]

Father Chenu adds that any other interpretation, which would want in some way to isolate the core of revelation from the fashion in which it is communicated to us, which would want to distinguish between revelation-in-itself and revelation-for-us, would indicate an idealism related to the monophysite heresy.[20]

Father Chenu touches here on a very important problem: the sociologist who, out of respect for revelation, would go no farther than an investigation of religious practices and who would prohibit himself from going on to a sociology of doctrine and of faith, would in reality be committing a theological error, namely, that of dissociating that which revelation itself unites. He would succumb to the charms of docetism. Even the apparently innocuous distinction between the content and the form of revelation cannot be retained, for it is proper to the Christian revelation to be given to us under a certain form which is inseparable from the history of the Jewish people, of the Jerusalemite community, and of the communities formed by the Pauline preaching. Its *Sitz im Leben* does not constitute an incidental form: it is expressed through this *Sitz im Leben*.

Nevertheless, is there no limit to sociological investigation and comprehension? To be sure, these limits exist, and the sociologist cannot take the place of the dogmatician. But the difference between them does not bear on the extent of the sector that they study. It involves, rather, an attitude of mind: the sociologist refers himself solely to the intentionality of the collective consciousness of the Christian community; he takes account of the realities focused upon by this consciousness, of revelation, of all of revelation in so far as it is the intentional object of this consciousness; he studies the action which the object focused upon has on the group, its power in the formation and structuring of the group. But, differently from the dogmatician, he does not pronounce on the validity of this focusing, on the authenticity of this revelation; he is interested in the sociological power of this revelation. In other words, the sociologist's point of view is that of the phenomenologist: he puts the ultimate question, that of truth, into parentheses. He observes simply that a certain "religious object", having a certain structure, polarizes the intentionality of the collective consciousness. To put it still another way, the sociologist studies revelation as *given* to the collective consciousness and leaves to the dogmatician the concern of pronouncing on the manner in which this revelation is given to the consciousness, that is to say, on the very act of revelation.

Thus we have not gone beyond the limits which we have traced for the sociology of Protestantism: this latter is always anchored in the assembled community, in the local community. But in place of restricting itself, as contemporary sociology tends to do, to the pure morphology of this community, to its practices and institutions, the sociology of Protestantism attempts to reach the internal life of this community. It perceives then that this internal life remains impenetrable to the degree that we have not understood that this life is organized around a given which is objectively focused on by this community, and that, consequently, the sociologist must listen to what the exegete and the dogmatician teach him about this given. Thus the sociologist knows the Christian revelation as it is both focused upon and received by a community. If the sociology of Protestantism is a specific discipline, it is precisely because the Protestant community (under its parochial form as under its other forms) has its proper fashion of relating to revelation and of allowing itself to be structured by it.

NOTES

1. This chapter has already appeared in article form, under a slightly different title, in *ASR*, 14 (1962) and in *Kölner Zeitschrift für Soziologie und Socialpsychologie*, 6 (1962). It repeats certain observations presented in chapters one and two.

2. The same remark is true also of Roman Catholicism. Proof of this is seen in the many precautions taken by sociologists to justify the legitimacy of their enterprise (see Jean Labbens, *La sociologie religieuse*, ch. 1).

3. E. G. Léonard repeats this reaction in his study, "Les conditions de la sociologie protestante en France", *ASR*, 8 (1958).

4. See especially P. Bonnard's study, "Les manuscrits du désert de Juda et l' Evangile", *FV*, 57 (1958), No. 2. [Trans. note. On this point, see also Marcel Simon,

Jewish Sects at the Time of Jesus, translated by James H. Farley (Philadelphia: Fortress Press, 1967), ch. 6.]

5. Wach, *Sociologie*, p. 2.

6. See Rudolf Bultmann, *Primitive Christianity in its Contemporary Setting*, translated by R. H. Fuller (New York: Meridian Books, "Living Age Books", 1957 and London: Collins, 1960).

7. See the *Confession of Augsburg* (art. VII), the *Confession of La Rochelle* (art. XXVI), the *Belgic Confession* (art. XXVII), the *Scottish Confession* (art. XVI), etc.

8. See, in particular, his study, "Secteurs et aspects nouveaux de la sociologie religieuse", *CIS*, 1 (1946).

9. This "deparochialization" of the Catholic parishioner has been emphasized and analysed by Jean Chélini, *La ville et l'Eglise* (Paris: Editions du Cerf, 1958), pp. 168 ff. The causes that he indicates are certainly correct and arise from the traditional parish's poor adjustment to the human and sociological milieu. But it seems to us that these causes are put into play more easily by the Catholic idea of practice and by the ecclesiology taught by Catholicism.

10. Congregationalism is a system of ecclesiastical organization that rests on the principle of the autonomy of the local congregation and allows of only a federation of congregations.

11. Let us emphasize how much this is a matter of an ideal norm. But it has not lost all of its efficacy, since it is seen in the present efforts of the Protestant churches to delineate a great diversity of ministries, in accordance with the indications of I Corinthians 12.

12. According to *Settimana del Clero* (Rome), an average of a thousand Catholics daily pass over to Protestantism (April, 1962).

13. In opposing thus the two types of churches, we in no wise intend to prejudge the future. Even now, there are Catholic parishes of Protestant style and Protestant parishes of Catholic style (especially in the High Church type of Protestantism). The ecumenical confrontations are producing an osmosis. It is not impossible to attempt a sociology of ecumenism (cf. chapter ten).

14. Art. cit., 128.

15. See François Wendel, *Calvin; The origins and development of his thought*, translated by Philip Mairet (New York: Harper and Row, Inc. and London: William Collins, Sons and Company, 1963), pp. 294 ff.

16. See our study, "Dans quelle mesure la sociologie peut-elle saisir la réalité de l'Eglise?" *RHPR*, 31 (1951), No. 4.

17. "Sociologie religieuse dans le Sud Cameroun", *MNC*, 47–48 (1958).

18. *Official Report of the Third World Conference on Faith and Order* (Lund, 1952) edited by Oliver S. Tomkins (London: SCM Press).

19. M. D. Chenu, "Vie conciliaire de l'Eglise et sociologie de la foi", *Esprit*, new series, 12 (December, 1961). Note the wonderful audacity of the title of this study (Conciliar life of the Church and sociology of faith). The preparations for the Second Vatican Council and the efforts of certain Catholic theologians to discern what is reformable in the Church's doctrine and what is not reformable, called forth a great number of studies which tied in with those of Father Chenu. We would mention, in particular, Hans Küng's *The Council and Reunion*, translated by Cecily Hastings (London and New York: Sheed & Ward, 1961), and the study by Yves Congar, "Simples réflexions sur l'originalité de l'entreprise oecuménique", in the collective volume, *Découverte de l'oecuménisme* (Paris: Desclée de Brouwer, 1961).

20. Art. cit.

IV

The Christian Community –
Its Relationships with the World –
Secularization

Let us try to make more precise the exterior form of the Christian community, the form of its implantation in the world, and its relationships with this world. This study cannot be undertaken without reference to history, for there are essential differences between the small, isolated communities of the primitive church, the church incorporating and ordering the whole of the civilized world, and the modern church over against which the world stands its distance. These different modes of being present in the world obviously have repercussions on the very structure of the Christian community.

1. *The Primitive Christian Community*

The first Christian community was characterized by a double movement, one of withdrawal into itself (in relation to the synagogue and to pagan society) and one of a missionary thrust which enabled it to cross all ethnic barriers. The picture that the New Testament presents to us of the primitive church bears the evidence of this double and contradictory movement.

On the one hand, the apostle Paul fights openly and effectively against the infiltration of judaizers into the Christian community. Now, these judaizers had been able to form a bridge between the synagogue and the new movement, which at that time had not yet taken a well-structured form and which in the eyes of those outside was still poorly differentiated from Judaism (to the Roman observer, the new movement seemed to be a Jewish sect). The differentiation between the Christian community and the Jewish community came about slowly. In certain respects, the differentiation came about within the synagogue itself, which for several decades remained the place where the apostles and their group preached and prayed. (The same process is observed in the differentiation of the churches of the Reformation *vis-à-vis* the Roman Church.) Christianity is not tied to Judaism only doctrinally, as an extension of the history of salvation; there is also a sociological tie. After being denied the use of the synagogue, Christianity found its first supports among the peripheral circles of Judaism, namely, from among the proselytes and the "God-fearers" whom we now know constituted significant groupings throughout the Roman Empire. It was through these peripheral elements that Christianity spilled over into pagan society, and accentuated by this same movement its rupture with the synagogue. But the new communities were very prudent in relation to this pagan society. Their problem was one of retaining their originality in a world that was riven with all sorts of religious movements which were preoccupied, like Christianity, with the fate of individual souls, with salvation, with a direct contact of the subject with God. It was necessary for the Christian community to have a lucid understanding of its bounds, and Paul's first letter to the Corinthians is a good example of this effort to keep the Christian community from simply melting into the surrounding society. (This explains the importance taken, for example, by the question of eating food offered to idols, the abstention of Christians in regard to the tribunals of the state, etc.) In a period in which there was no particularly strong political interdependence (political institutions were largely external to individual life) nor economic interdependence (most men lived as craftsmen in a closed market), the Christian communities could organize themselves to a great extent in an autonomous way, although the totally communal life, with a community of goods, did not continue beyond the first attempt at Jerusalem. Paul's counsels concerning work show quite well that each individual had to feel solidarity with the others and was to take care of the poorer members of the community, but also had to watch over his own individual work to see that it did not fall to the charge of the community.

On the other hand, this distinctly separate community in no way constitutes a ghetto. It is conscious of a universal vocation and wants itself to be catholic, although not always without some reticence. The Jewish-Christian quarrel signifies that, sociologically, there was a desire to filter entrance into the church through the screen of Jewish institutions. But, in fact, this tendency did not prevail. Although the pillars of the church at Jerusalem confined themselves to action in the Jewish *milieu*, the primary current of expansion went beyond them, through Paul and his *milieu*. The missionary travels of Paul, and his companions, which followed the customary major travel routes of the Empire, mark quite well the considerable expansion of Christianity throughout the periphery of the Mediterranean,

that is to say, of the civilized world of that day. Nevertheless, and here we
see the first component at work, during the course of the first Christian
generation in the pagan *milieu* there was no massive and collective entrance
into the church (to the degree that the numbers given in the Acts account
of Pentecost are exact, they concern essentially Jews and proselytes). One
entered the church by a personal act of conversion, usually marked by
baptism; this was done in such a way that the community could guard its
purity and not be submerged by a wave of new arrivals. The massive entry
of pagans into the church did not come until the end of the second century
(and in this case it was often a matter of cultured elements). Thus the
Christian communities had a century of existence, which is to say that
their organization, their worship, their interconnections had time to
acquire a certain stability, and the communities were more capable of
welcoming the new arrivals. Communities at the same time concerned to
avoid all external contagion and yet missionary, communities convinced
of their catholicity yet decided to admit into their midst only men who
were personally linked by faith in Christ – such is the picture of the first
Christian communities.

This situation explains the structures of these communities. They were
characterized first of all by a relatively undeveloped internal organization.
This organization was based on the elders, the leaders of the parish, who
were charged with guarding the purity of the teaching and with the regulation of morals. But the elders did not constitute a hierarchy that was
clearly distinct from the whole: the principal letters of Paul are addressed
to the community as a whole. The community manifested its vitality in
an abundance of charismas, but these charismas were linked to persons
whose authority was recognized by the community; they were not fixed
in a function. There was no priesthood, no distinction between priests and
laity. The only function that was clearly set apart was that of apostle. But
the apostolate was tied to an event: the apostles were the former companions of the Lord, the witnesses to his resurrection. The case of Paul
was somewhat different, but it also was clearly tied to a singular event:
Paul's encounter with the living Lord on the road to Damascus. To be
sure, the very fact that there were *Twelve* apostles is related to the institutional complex of Israel. But the apostles themselves did not intend to
institutionalize their own function. There is no trace in the New Testament
either of a doctrine or of a practice of apostolic succession. As for the elders
– *episcopoi*, teachers, evangelists, even deacons – their functions were not
set out in any very strict way. They all had teaching and preaching in
common. One undoubtedly can find traces of a development in the New

Testament, and this development tends towards an increasingly elaborate institutionalization. Yet the first Christian generations none the less lived in a situation where dynamic communion and auto-discipline far overshadowed the organization. Authority was much more tied to the *de facto* existence of charisms than to the existence of a hierarchy.

In regard to the cohesion of the whole, it was primarily assured by personal contacts: the journeys of the apostles and of their envoys, the exchange of letters, encounters between men like Paul and the group of apostles at Jerusalem – encounters that were neither obligatory nor periodical (for example, what we improperly, and by analogy with later institutions, call the first Synod of Jerusalem). The only communal institution that appeared was that of the collection made for the poor in Jerusalem, an institution which took the form of the Jewish collection for the temple. The very fact of this uni-directional collection indicates that the Jerusalem church (or the Palestinian church) held a certain pre-eminence. Yet this pre-eminence was clearly related to a historical fact:

If the traditions and customs of the Palestinian church are authoritative for the whole church, it is, Paul says, because the Gospel started off there.[1]

At Jerusalem there were men who had been close to the Lord, who had accompanied him during the times of John the Baptist (Acts 1.21–22). The historical fact takes precedence over the institution. Fidelity to the origins is in no wise a juridical rule. There was indeed a tradition, and Paul, on every important occasion, invokes it. This is the case, notably, in regard to the Lord's Supper, but Paul is careful to note that although this tradition came by way of Jerusalem, it was not the see of Jerusalem that gave it its authority or its guarantee: "For I received from the Lord what I also delivered to you . . ." (I Cor. 11.23). The Gospel spread out from Jerusalem, because Jerusalem was the historical locus of the resurrection of the Lord. The principle of authority resides in the person of the resurrected and living Christ, who communicates his life to *persons* by means of the Holy Spirit.

In short, the historical, in its singular and unique aspects, plays a determining role in the constitution and life of the new communities. Menoud is designating this situation of the primitive church as a "Christocracy".[2] From our point of view, this means that personal relationships were more important by far than institutional and hierarchical relationships. In this case, microsociology is more important than the sociology of institutions. Many things attest to the existence in the primitive church of a spontaneity which has little in common with what we today call the church: the worship service itself, with its very free forms; the fact that the church took form in families; the fact that the religious community was not distinguished from the familial community. Obviously, what we have here is a temporary state, undoubtedly conditioned by the relatively modest number of members. Nevertheless, one is struck by the profound difference between the sociological non-organization of the first Christian communities and the strict, very carefully hierarchized organization and discipline of a sect like that of Qumran (whose membership was considerably less than that of the Christians).

It would be incorrect to assume that this absence of hierarchical and juridical structure was simply a sort of congregationalism, with each community withdrawn into itself and developing according to its own particular course. To be sure, such must have been the case from time to time: the existence of small groups linked to the baptism of John the Baptist is evidence of this. But this was not the general rule. The communities remained inter-related, acting upon each other by a sort of contagion. Paul writes to the Thessalonians that they had become a model for all the believers in Macedonia and in Achaia, and he adds:

For not only has the word of the Lord sounded forth from you in Macedonia and Achaia, but your faith in God has gone forth everywhere, so that we need not say anything (I Thess. 1.7–8).

The development of Christianity would later show that this sociological "model" was fragile indeed.

2. *The Western Church from the Twelfth to the Fourteenth Century*

We have chosen the church in the West between the twelfth and the fourteenth century as the antitype of the primitive community. Why this choice? For one thing, this period is considered to be the classical age of the church:

There is a striking contrast between the classical age and the first millennium. We will move from a time of dispersion, of empiricism, and of variety to a time of gathering, of logic, and of ecumenicism. Jurists and non-jurists will be impressed by the genesis, flowering, and triumph during this period of a harmonious system of rules which is nourished by legislation, classified by codification, and ordered by science.[3]

This period was one of great organization and institutionalization. The expansion of Christianity in the western world was practically completed, the frontiers established. When Innocent II was elected pope in 1130, Christianity occupied almost the whole of Europe: in the north it occupied

the islands of the North Sea and the south of Scandinavia; its eastern
frontier, although somewhat ill-defined, coincided more or less with the
outline of Poland and Hungary; in the south it skirted Sicily and cut
across Spain on a line running from the mouth of the Ebro to the head-
waters of the Tagus. Christianity collided in the north with the ancient
paganism of the Laplanders and of the Baltic peoples, in the east with the
solidly established schismatic Eastern Church, in Africa and in southern
Spain with Islam. The situation was only slightly modified in the next two
centuries. The frontiers advanced to the boreal seas and to the African
coasts, but this was an expansion of the body of Christendom rather than
a missionary conquest. In short, during this period we are in the presence
of a stabilized Christianity. No longer is it a stranger and exile on the earth;
it has found firm foundations and an almost undisputed security.

It was also a *standardized* Christianity:

For the third time, a principle of unity reigned in the West at the beginning
of the twelfth century; pagan Rome had established administrative unity;
Charlemagne, in his dream of an unequal dyarchy, attempted to impose the
unity of faith under the imperial sceptre (after his death, the church took the
first rank); the Gregorian reform proclaimed the unity of obedience of the
western world to the sovereign papacy.[4]

This unity which Rome brought about in the West was manifested in an
administrative consolidation of the church and in a centralization. This
work was completed by the end of the twelfth century. Primates and
metropolitans lost all authority and retained only an honorific pre-
eminence.

The progress of Roman centralization made the bishop the representative of
the Holy See rather than the king's man or one elected by the local clergy.
Properly speaking, election was taken out of the hands not only of the laity but
of all ecclesiastical dignitaries except canons.[5]

For all practical purposes, the princes no longer had anything to do with
the temporal investiture of bishops. At the end of the century the kings
had to content themselves with according or refusing their assent to the
person of the one elected. A direct and constant liaison was assured between the Holy See and the bishop. The authority of the latter increased
with the rapid progression of cases referred to ecclesiastical tribunals and
with the renaissance of Roman law. Parishes were progressively removed
from the authority of the descendants of the founders. The bishop began
to play a considerable role in the nomination of curés. Parishes were
redeemed from the laity and very often became the property of religious
establishments. The development of monastic orders increased the power

of Rome. An immense work of codification was accomplished, resulting in the formation of a veritable *corpus juris canonici*; this was constituted, essentially, by the *Decretum Gratiani*, which was universally accepted by 1150, and by the decretals of Gregory IX. Since the Gregorian reform, moreover, the papacy had won out over the councils:

The pope fixed the order of the day, he organized the meetings, he presided over the debates. Through his good offices the canons were drawn up, promulgated, and finally corrected before publication. They appeared and were distributed under his authority.[6]

This is not to say, of course, that all resistance to the pontifical authority had disappeared. It sometimes happened that the bishops and priests took their time in publishing papal decisions. Furthermore, relationships with the secular powers were not always good. Indeed, they were extremely strained under Frederick Barbarossa, Frederick II, and Louis the Bavarian. Sometimes the kings were in a state of open rebellion (Henry II and Philip the Fair). But excommunication is a weapon greatly feared in all echelons of the social hierarchy.

The political pre-eminence of the church was not established without hindrance, as the history of Germany shows. When the attempt was made there to reduce the coronation of the emperor to a simple rite, the papacy maintained that it alone was creator of the empire. During the period of the investiture quarrels, Gregory VII and his successors even laid claim to a certain control in the election of the emperor. In 1125 and 1138 this election was directed by the church, which attempted to turn the relationship between pope and emperor into a feudal tie. The spirited reactions of a Frederick Barbarossa (in particular, at the Diet of Besançon in 1157) did not impede the empire from being considered as a function of the church, since its purpose was the defence of Christendom. True, it is correct to say that the imperial *potestas* was also the power proper to the king of Germany, and did not come from the pope. But the pope, although he did not confer the *potestas*, did confer the *dignitas*. Although the emperor did not exercise a true authority over the other kings, at least as defender of the faith and of the papacy, he did acquire a moral pre-eminence, an *auctoritas*, over them. Formerly the pope and the emperor were the two eyes of the same mystical body (which was the measure of the state of non-secularization of the society) and one could be substituted for the other in the guidance of the mixed or inter-related society of clergy and laity. But the Gregorian reform brought a different conception into prominence: the organic church was a hierarchical society different from the empire. To be sure, the emperors reacted: they, for their part, claimed to build an empire truly independent of the church and with a universal mission. But this was in no way a secularization of the idea of the empire. The empire of the Stauffen maintained its own spiritual power (canonization and cult of Charlemagne). Moreover, on the death of Henry VI, Pope Innocent III felt that the time had come to restore his power as creator of the empire, and the great crisis of the empire that broke out from 1197 to 1215 demonstrated that the empire could be interpreted only in light of the mission which the pope confided to it. In the first half of the thirteenth century, pontifical omnipotence triumphed with Innocent IV and Frederick II: theocratic monism would supplant, at least for a time, the old Gelasian dualism.

The vicissitudes of this development which we have traced (following Robert Folz[7]), and which represents only a sampling of the relationships between the spiritual and the temporal, should make us wary of assuming that the classical age of the church was an absolutely stable period in which the supremacy of the church was affirmed without encountering any resistance. But even when resistance asserted itself and triumphed, it was careful to guard against introducing the seed of a true secularization. Furthermore, sociology could not restrict itself to this political superstructure: daily life is infinitely more revealing.

Men's existence unfolded uniformly in the framework which the church had outlined for them. From birth to death man was taken in charge by the church, and the sacraments marked all of the decisive steps of life. Parents were led to take their children to the sermon. The Decretals universalized parochial schools. The preaching exercised by the bishop or by the priest had a didactic and disciplinary role: commentaries on the Creed, on the Lord's Prayer, on the Ave Maria, even on synodal statutes. Sometimes the preaching was restricted to the reading of collections of homilies and various compendia. A severe discipline was exercised over the life, beliefs, practices, and morals of all. The day was regulated by several hundred canons concerning the nature and obligations of marriage, education, property, the repression of usury, professional relations, and relations between the social classes. This discipline was reinforced and made more precise by the fight against the Catharist heresy. A precise questionnaire was at the disposition of the bishop who wanted to utilize it. Numerous synods recommended that priests keep a register of paschal abstentions. Rumours and private conversations permitted the priest to keep an account of hidden sins. The priest, to use Le Bras' phrase, exercised "a policing of the faith".[8] There were numerous means of coercion: discrete reprimand, solemn warning, denunciation to the curia. When the

sinner persisted, justice was quick. It punished heresy, schism, superstition, all shortcomings of ethics and practice. Punishments ranged from
amends to major excommunication, which, in that relatively integral
society, could amount to a death sentence. To be sure, such a picture is
not greatly different from what still exists in the church even today or, with
certain qualifications, in the Geneva of Calvin. But the originality of this
situation resided in the universality of the system. It was applied in a world
without imperfection, a world in which heresy was quickly repressed and
where unbelief was impossible.

Moreover, the church was present in all the forms of human activity.
It was truly the *Ecclesia regens*, and its authority was exercised in particular
over the world of thought. The church controlled the whole of university
teaching, especially by means of the *studium generale* or *universale* or
commune, which the religious orders created in important cities, and by
means of the universities. These universities were spontaneous creations
at the beginning of the twelfth century: students grouped around a celebrated teacher, forming a school and giving birth to a tradition. The number of students in certain cities, notably at Paris, became such that it was
necessary to organize the university. The kings of France played only a
secondary role in this organization. The true founder of the University of
Paris was Innocent III. When the University spontaneously became a
centre of free research, Innocent III and Gregory IX turned it into a
guarantor of religious orthodoxy. As Etienne Gilson writes:

From the point of view of Innocent III or of Gregory IX, the University of
Paris could be only the most powerful means of action that the church had for
the spreading of religious truth throughout the entire world, or an inexhaustible
source of errors capable of poisoning the whole of Christendom. Innocent III
was the first to have resolutely desired to make the University a mistress of truth
for the entire church. He transformed this centre of study into an organism
whose structure, function, and defined place in Christendom were explainable
from this point of view alone . . .

The *studium parisiense* was a spiritual and moral force whose most profound
significance was neither Parisian nor French, but Christian and ecclesiastical.
It was an element of the universal church in exactly the same way and with
absolutely the same meaning as the priesthood or the empire.[9]

In fact, by prohibiting the teaching of Roman law in favour of canon
law alone, by prohibiting the teaching of Aristotelian physics and meta-
physics, by introducing Dominicans and Franciscans into teaching, the
papacy provided itself with a first-rate instrument for directing the intellectual development of Europe. This instrument was then supplemented
by other universities.

But the church's presence was not limited solely to the worlds of law, juridical organization, and thought. The church was present in all creative centres. It contributed in large part to the resurgence of business. As Le Bras points out, the church

had patronized the fairs, near its sanctuaries; it gave rise to the Crusades, founded or supervised the development of cities, transformed the rural countryside around its monasteries. Its immense fortune gave it reason to hope for a dominant role in the business world. The financial operation of the papacy entailed an international economy.[10]

Certainly, there were shadows in this picture: the great monastic domains depreciated, and monetary manipulations diminished the revenues of the church. Moreover, the cities that the papacy had sustained, and whose administrative autonomy it had defended, deprived the bishops of their rights. States began to revive, and were jealous of their sovereignty. The church exercised its influence everywhere, but everywhere it was confronted by powers that claimed their share of autonomy, although they did not want to cast off the ecclesiastical yoke completely and respected the church's spiritual authority. The conflict between the priesthood and the empire continued to have repercussions for many years.

Yet the church could preach a third crusade, which it organized for the most part. And the financial measures taken by the kings and princes in regard to the crusade were backed by the church in the form of spiritual sanctions (indulgences for those who left, for those who financed it; the promise of eternal life for those who died in the crusade). These facts attest that the church's empire extended over all souls, that it was master not only of civilization, of the great currents of thought, of the forms of individual and family life, but of the great politico-social movements as well.[11]

The church was a power, the first among all the powers, and the secular authorities had to come to terms with it. Religion in no wise was a private affair; it was extremely institutionalized. Its institutions permitted it to cover the whole field of human activity. It constituted both a sociological state of fact and a voluntary creation. The church appeared to everyone as an institution of salvation, the only institution of salvation; thus everyone was ready to defend it. The church had always remained a teaching church like the primitive church, but it had ceased to be missionary. It guaranteed salvation more than it preached good news. It assured a harmonious, well-regulated, and juridically formulated communication between the earthly community and the supernatural world. It resurrected the synthesis of pagan antiquity between the city and the world of the gods. By its presence, it gave the city an ontological foundation. It founded, or at least guaranteed, a civilization which bore the mark of the sacred.

3. The Situation of the Contemporary Church. Secularization

In order to understand how the balance which we have described was upset, it is necessary to deal with the process of secularization, by which the relations between the world and the church were profoundly modified.

Secularization is a historical process, characteristic of the western world. In the West, religion has been increasingly taken out of the public sector of life and placed in the private sector. At the same time, the development of the global society has tended to reduce the private sector of our existence.[12] At the extreme, religion no longer is considered as anything but a private affair, and the exercise of worship tends to be enclosed in very narrow limits, with the state regulating more or less liberally the public manifestations of the churches. These restrictions can constrain the churches to a clandestine existence, to a return to the catacombs.

The process of secularization began very early in the western world. It began as a reaction of the political power that wanted to disengage itself from the hold of the church, which itself had become a power. The first outlines of secularization began to be drawn during the height of the Middle Ages (and not only beginning with the French Revolution). At first it took a very unexpected form. The political power attempted to usurp that which it felt to be the source of the church's power, namely, the church's claim to possess and to dispense a supernatural force. Consequently, the secular power was led to try to utilize religious ideas and forces. There were various ways to accomplish this. A brutal method, but one that did not have long-term consequences, involved domesticating the religious power (the papacy). A second course, one involving a long conflict between the priesthood and the empire, resulted in the sharing of power. Finally, a method that was far more consequential entailed modelling the state on the church.

This third attempt took its most original form in England under the Tudors. It resulted in the famous doctrine of the King's *Two Bodies*: the king, just like any other mortal, possesses a natural body, a body subject to suffering and death; but he also possesses a political body, a veritable "corporation", of which the king is the head and his subjects the members. This body does not die at all, for on the death of the natural body of the king, the political body is immediately transferred to his successor.[13] In the *Treatise of the Anonymous Norman* (composed ca. AD 1100), the king is described as *personna gemina*, a double person: one is natural, the other is a new creature who is born from the coronation, the sacramental grace of which confers on him a body inhabited by the spirit of God. By this sacrament, the king becomes the figure and image of Christ. The church was well aware that this constituted a capturing, as it were, of religious forces, to the benefit of a non-religious power. Consequently, the church later removed coronation from the list of sacraments, although it left the ceremony a religious significance (somewhat incompletely defined, however).

The essential element in this doctrine rests in the transfer of the *corpus mysticum* from the church to the state. The state was even sometimes qualified as *corpus reipublicae mysticum* (Vincent de Beauvais). The dogma of Chalcedon on the two natures of Christ was at the same time applied to the person of the king. This doctrine became general, and in France it was said that the king was the spouse of this mystical body, as the church is the spouse of Christ. Thus the whole of christology and ecclesiology were taken over by the secular power; they were secularized, but without their ties with the religious world being cut. The concept of the fatherland, with all its affective and religious potential (the fatherland is *holy*), would later be the direct inheritor of this *corpus reipublicae mysticum*.

The idea arose that the king possessed a sort of immortality. The king does not die; he survives in the dynastic continuity. With the triumph of rationalism in the social life, this idea foundered and became increasingly difficult to justify. Or rather, its justification was sought in a completely different domain: it was turned into the symbol and guarantee of the continuity of the nation (as we see in modern constitutional monarchies). This perenniality of the king throughout time is also expressed, especially in England, in the symbol of the *crown*, a concept which designates the inalienable rights and domains of the kingdom, of which the king is the temporary holder. The crown is thus the *signum gloriae* of which the rite of coronation speaks.

Thus the king has two bodies blended in one sole person, and this person is the possessor of the *regia dignitas*, which unites in it genus and species, the political body and the royal individual. The king, having two bodies, is reborn from his own ashes, like that mysterious bird, the Phoenix.[14]

These notions are not simply the individual speculations of philosophers and legists, although such people naturally had an important role in the technical elaboration of these ideas. What is involved is truly a collective thing, which is expressed in the famous popular cry: "The king is dead, long live the king." Art has also contributed to the expression of these ideas: the funerary art of the Middle Ages and of the Renaissance represents two recumbent effigies superimposed on the royal tombs – the one effigy is cadaverous, the other is adorned with the symbols of office.

All this is indeed a matter of a secularization, because it causes originally religious concepts to pass over into the realm of the profane, and because it progressively empties them of their religious content while at the same time pretending to preserve their religious dynamism. In the end, we see patriotic worship substituted for religious worship. The French Revolution was not content to secularize the goods of the church. It also tried, with very limited and fleeting success, to secularize the whole Christian worship and to nationalize the clergy. After this attempt failed, it tried to create *ex nihilo* a worship of the nation and of reason.[15] By demanding to be crowned by the pope, Napoleon I indicated that he had not abandoned the idea of turning religious forces to his own benefit.[16]

At a later time, when the church forcefully disengaged itself from this type of compromise and wanted to claim its patrimony, the state would turn towards other religious forces. National Socialism hesitated between two formulas: on the one hand, the Nazi state attempted the difficult resurrection of ancient Nordic paganism; on the other hand, it tried to create a new Aryan church by blending all the confessions in a syncretistic synthesis. Anti-semitism was to be the cement of the new organization, and the "German Christians" constituted its lineaments.

In regard to the Soviet state, this development is less clear. It has frequently been maintained that Marxism, in many respects, is a secularized Christianity. Although this assertion cannot be justified on the level of the technical elaboration of the system, and in any event cannot be imputed to the original intention of Marx, it is none the less true that Marxism presents certain objective structures which have an incontestably Judeo-Christian resonance. The proletariat, with its universal mission, plays the role of the Messianic people. It is the one who will lead history to its fulfilment; yet at the same time, this fulfilment is a sort of eschatological necessity inscribed from the beginning of history itself. Truth, tactics, and strategy are elaborated by a party, which claims the ability to read history and to interpret the signs of the times. It is provided with a sort of infallibility, like the Catholic Church. To be sure, Marxism does not claim any kind of innate genius and does not pretend to develop doctrine outside of the proletarian masses. But neither does the Catholic church think that its hierarchy can define dogma without contact with the people of the faithful. Alienation is not unrelated to the fall, and as such, it requires a kind of redemption. Thus we feel that Raymond Aron is not wrong in speaking of communism as a "secular religion".

The current of secularization that began to take shape from the time of the Middle Ages, and consists in a taking over of religious forces and concepts to the profit of social and political powers, is far from being totally arrested. But it has encountered certain limits in the scientific and rationalist movement, as well as in the dechristianization of the western world.

However, secularization has another aspect, that which we have described in our initial definition. This aspect, we believe, represents the very intention of secularization. The profane world, the world of daily life, the world of production, of politics, and of cultural creation avoids the influence of the church. It rejects the church's presence and encloses it in a sphere that is clearly differentiated from the global society. This socio-logical development was favoured by Christianity at first, perhaps not consciously but because of the essence of Christianity. Since Christianity, unlike other religions, does not rest on the distinction or the dichotomy between the sacred and the profane, it considers that God alone is holy and that all the rest is profane. This is not meant in the sense that the rest does not come from God or does not belong to him. It means simply that the rest does not partake of the character of the holy: neither the world of things, nor civilization, nor art, nor politics are holy. It is typical that Christianity, from the very beginning, refused to impute any holy character to the state (and consequently rejected emperor worship), while at the same time it considered the magistrates to be God's agents. As God's agents, they were due a legitimate submission, not solely from fear but from motives of conscience.[17] It is no less typical that secularization essen-tially developed in the countries of the Christianized West, and that it encountered strong opposition in Moslem countries, in the Near East, and in the Far East.

Secularization, in this new meaning of the word, manifested its first stirrings in the twelfth and thirteenth centuries in the realm of science and within the university. It was expressed as a rebellion of the arts and of philosophy against a theology that magisterially claimed to know every-thing. Although Aristotle was of primary importance in the overall con-stitution of medieval theology as a universal system of knowledge, it should not be forgotten that Aristotelian physics and megaphysics served also to give rise to the idea of an autonomous science which escaped theological and ecclesiastical control. Recourse to experimentation with Bacon, then the application of mathematics to physical research (both of which could claim a perfect religious neutrality), greatly assisted science in freeing itself from all clerical control and in affirming a self-evidence which led to an independence regarding all authority. To be sure, at the beginning of the seventeenth century, the church could still condemn Galileo and obtain his retraction; although Descartes had been quite prudent, the church could constrain him to destroy his *Traité du Monde*. These were only rearguard skirmishes; in actual fact, the physical sciences were entirely secularized. Religion no longer exercised any control over them. Indeed, it was the physical sciences that claimed to call into question the assertions of the church.

Two centuries later the same phenomenon would take place with regard to the biological sciences: the crisis of evolutionism and of transformism would show that although the church had abandoned the physico-mathematical sciences to their destiny as autonomous sciences, it was not yet ready to do the same for sciences that were so closely concerned with man. However, evolutionism came to be accepted in scientific thought, and even accepted by the church or at least by Catholic scholars and philosophers (Teilhard de Chardin).

The same crisis and the same solution manifested themselves in regard to the humane sciences, especially the historical sciences, when they sought to apply their methods to the study of the sacred Books. To be sure, secularized historical science evidenced a certain aggressiveness that was expressed in certain excesses (hypercriticism, the Modernist crisis). But in the long run, once these methods were given their proper neutrality and scientific objectivity, recourse to them was made by theologians of various confessions (Protestants first, Catholics notably later). It is beyond any doubt that a science continues to exist which poses serious theological problems, and which poses them all the better because it is more neutral, more secularized. Indeed, the neutrality of science has advanced to such a point that the Christian churches, on occasion, have been led to defend the freedom of scientific research, particularly at times when totalitarian political systems have appeared.[18]

The secularization of science has been accompanied by the secularization of political life. To be sure, political life initially took the form that we have indicated, namely the usurpation of a sacred aura, of a religious prestige, on the part of the political power. But a movement towards the secularization of the political life was made possible in the West when the unity of faith was broken at the time of the Reformation. It certainly did not come about immediately after the Reformation: for a long time Catholic states and Protestant states continued to exist. Up to the eve of the Revolution, the French monarchy continued to make the unity of faith the guaranty of national unity. This idea has retained its force in a number of countries even at the present time; for example, Spain, or Italy, which admitted full religious liberty only with the constitution of 1946 (and religious liberty is still sometimes only theoretical in Italy). But the great movements of population, and the mixing of nations and of ideas, have permitted unity of faith and religious practice to subsist only in rare regions. The advance of unbelief and of practical dechristianization have broken the unity in those places where religious pluralism had not become prevalent. The result has been that states have been obliged to define a law, a legislation, and a policy of a general type that will be valid for all religious confessions. Political life becomes secularized, political parties are most frequently without any confessional connections, or are led to relax these confessional ties and to maintain a certain freedom of action vis-à-vis ecclesiastical authorities. Even though certain political themes (for example, the school) still give rise to religious questions, it should be recognized that the majority of political problems have been deconfessionalized.[19] They are located on a technical level where religious motivations no doubt can still play a role in the options taken, but where the churches as such cannot easily take a position. We do not say that the religious life and the political life are without any communication: the maps established by Boulard showing the relationship between religious practice and the distribution of votes in elections, attest quite well to the solidity, depth, and antiquity of this tie. For one thing, political problems themselves are posed in neutral terms, and often in technical terms. They rarely are resolved under the impetus of individual confessional groups. To be sure, it is justified to include the churches among the "pressure groups" that act on the political life of a modern country. And the less clerical churches do not neglect to make their voices heard, especially on political problems that are integrally related to ethical problems (social justice, the peace movements, atomic disarmament, decolonization, etc.). But the churches are only one group among others. They exercise no monopoly on the political life.

But what seems even more important is the secularization of daily life. The grip that the ecclesiastical power once held over all of human existence has now loosened to the point that a man can live a normal life from birth to death without coming under ecclesiastical pressure or even influence, or in any case, without the essential times of his life being controlled and marked by the church. To the degree that this man comes to a certain level of culture, he will indeed encounter Christianity as an essential component of civilization, at least in the West. But he is free to maintain a certain distance in regard to this Christianity.

In any event, he can quite legitimately be born, received and integrated into a family, a social group, receive an education, marry, exercise a profession, voice political opinions, enter public service, receive various honours, and finally die without ever having taken notice of the existence of one or of several churches. The only thing that will have happened is that his contacts with certain social circles may have been made difficult because of his estrangement from any religious confession. It can be objected that this type of existence does not unfold in every country of the world. In the case of Europe, one can cite the example of Spain, where civil life, economic prosperity, and access to public office are available only to Catholics. But it is also a fact that Spain is viewed with a certain dread by the rest of the western world.

Secularization was historically tied to the movement of tolerance first of all, and to dechristianization later. Does it follow that this was a matter of one and the same process? We would not contest that they came together at several points. But it is very clear to us that secularization does not necessarily accompany the decline of the churches or their loss of vitality. To be sure, by pushing religion towards the private sphere of life, in making religion simply a private affair (along with philosophical opinions, artistic tastes, etc.), secularization implied a pejorative judgment, or at least a deprecating opinion concerning the role of the churches.[20] When a practice or an institution takes on a free and non-obligatory nature, it ceases to be an inherent part of the common society, since the latter is characterized precisely by the fact that its practices and its institutions are obligatory.

But since Constantine made Christianity official, it has progressively become a social component. The church was blended into a half-civil, half-religious society, *Christendom*. It had covered a whole civilization with its authority, inspired a politic, and had become an essentially western reality. The Christian churches have been led to appreciate more positively the process of secularization of which they were initially victims, and this appreciation is due to a tripartite process: first of all, Christianity resumed its world-wide expansion through mission; then this expansion ceased to be disguised and protected by western nations and civilization; finally, the young churches born of mission efforts now seek to separate the Gospel from western civilization. Thus the churches are called to return to a situation that is closer to the primitive church than to the church of the Middle Ages. The *corpus Christi* ceases to be confused with the *corpus christianum*, and the church has become a differentiated society in relation to the total social body. Thus it is possible for the church to rediscover its specific nature.

How should one describe the situation of the church in a secularized society? Here the description becomes very difficult, for it varies according to the continents: the church can be left behind, on the margin of the global society, an official or at least a respected power, it can be tolerated, ignored (the situation of minority churches), persecuted, reduced to a clandestine existence.

Let us restrict ourselves to a description of the western situation, that is, to a description of the situation in that region of the world where secularization was born and developed.

Certainly, in the West, the social presence of the church is perfectly visible. Yves Congar describes it in the following way:

In our countries of ancient Christendom, the church not only occupies a considerable place but has a certain conspicuousness. One cannot help but encounter it in its monuments, in its clergy, in the signs or traces of its influence. It is present everywhere and can indulge itself in the feeling of being a very great thing. If we go from our own country to lands that are even more Catholic, this feeling of prominence grows. Whoever has made the journey to Rome or has stayed there knows how the church and the papacy impose their presence in that region.[21]

Well, this description, with a few qualifications, would be equally valid for the Anglican church, for the Lutheran church in Scandinavia, for the Evangelical church in Germany. In our secularized West, the church has retained a grandeur that must be taken into consideration, that inspires a certain respect, that forms a part of social decorum. In many countries membership in the church is the mark of a certain social level. But precisely this fact indicates sufficiently that the church no longer covers the whole of the social body. In particular, it no longer includes the working class, which arose abruptly in the nineteenth century and since then has not ceased to grow in importance. The working class has become one of the most dynamic classes, and has succeeded in wrenching numerous concessions from bourgeois society. Indeed, it constitutes the foundations of a new civilization. This class, with which or against which governments govern, is not in the church. One could not speak of dechristianization in regard to the working class, for as working class it has never been in the church. It is a missionary field for the church no less than paganism is. One of the experiences of the worker-priests who have worked in the northern mining region of France can be bluntly stated as follows: for persons belonging to the upper echelons of management, to the world of engineers, it is normal to be practising Christians; for those belonging to the world of employees, it is possible but not obligatory to practise; for those belonging to the category of miners, it is abnormal and exceptional to practise. On the Protestant side, a similar analogy can be mentioned regarding evangelization among the proletariat: the worker who is won over to the Gospel separates himself from his social class, and becomes "embourgeoised", or at least he begins a path of social ascension. Thus our first observation would be that the church in the secularized West is affected by social cleavage. Only in exceptions does it remain a *Volkskirche*, and is no longer capable of reaching the whole of the social body. Of course, this diagnosis is not a prognosis: it is possible for the church to overcome this social cleavage, and obviously it is tending to do so. This is evidenced by the ongoing research, in both Protestantism and Catholicism, concerning new forms of evangelization. We also see an effort being made to transform parochial structures in order to make them more receptive to various social categories (an example in Catholicism would be the specialized movements).

A second observation is that the church no longer is spontaneously present in the creative centres of culture. Culture is elaborated independently of the church. The great works of literature and art are born outside it. This is all the more obvious because of the fact that up to the end of the seventeenth century the opposite was true: it was under the inspiration of the church, and often for it, that the great works of culture, architecture, music, art, and literature were created. Science is not alone in having affirmed its autonomy. One cannot even say that culture is elaborated in reaction against the church. The result of this is that the churches are faced with the necessity of making what to them is a completely new effort, namely, that of understanding a culture that is foreign to them by its origin, that of retrieving this culture, that of elucidating its meaning and, if possible, of rooting it once again in a Christian soil. The church is called upon to take the *initiative* of a dialogue with the culture, whereas formerly it inspired and controlled culture. The church is aware of being questioned by a culture that formerly posed no questions. Witness, for example, the immense contemporary literary output that seeks to understand and critically evaluate communism or existentialism, and to give them meaning for the Christian. In a secularized situation, the churches perceive that the culture is not Christian and yet has a meaning for the Christian that the churches must draw out. Instead of being the *ecclesia regens*, the church becomes the church of dialogue (on condition, of course, that it does not accept with dejected resignation the situation in which it finds itself and does not enclose itself in a ghetto).

That which we have said of culture is also true for that aspect of culture which we call politics. Politics was emancipated earlier than the culture from the tutelage of the church, but this emancipation had a more progressive character. In the long conflict between the priesthood and the empire, the latter quickly won the battle. Yet it did not seek complete victory; it did not want to crush the priesthood, and was content to arrange its relationships with the priesthood in a profitable fashion. On the other hand, the priesthood never held scorn for the empire. The empire brought a reign of order in which the priesthood found its place. And this order assured the church its position of power. Thus we have a new fact in this development of politics in a democratic and secular direction, in the creation of a political ethic that claims to define the common good without utilizing any ecclesial criterion. And here the conflict between politics and the church has taken on tragic dimensions in the secularized world.

Pierre Burgelin characterizes this new situation in the following way:

The new fact, consequently, is that henceforth the Christian church is called into question as the foundation of the social order. In this sense, the Constantinian era is closed. And on the other hand, religion is no longer admissible except in relation to the politics that is constructing a new world. Politics has monopolized the profound feelings, the most impassioned ideals sought by men. It proposes a salvation here below. It takes the place of religion.

Here is where the problem becomes complicated. For the church has often reacted in the face of a secularization that threatens to strip it not only of its privileges from the Constantinian era but even of a large part of its influence. It once made use of education, of prestige, of established tradition, even of the support of the secular arm. Now, the elements of power are crumbling bit by bit. But in its reaction, the church often has been led to take a pure and simple position of opposition, and to ally itself with conservative and reactionary ideologies. Is it necessary to recall the celebrated condemnations of Pius IX in the encyclical *Quanta cura* and in his *Syllabus*? Is it necessary to recall the opposition of Christians to social laws, to the limitation of work by children for example? Or the condemnation of liberalism? and of tolerance?

There is an ecclesiastical paternalism that denies the faithful their majority and treats them like ignorant children. There is a prudence that looks at all change in traditional mores as bad. Thus Christianity often will appear as a political element, which attempts to oppose demands even when the moral conscience approves of them. It will appear, in Marx's words, as the "opium of the people". In the outlook of the modern world, the church necessarily will become the enemy to strike against. This is what happened in France, where the Catholic church had particularly compromised itself with monarchist parties and with the Roman politics of Napoleon III in the second half of the nineteenth century. Everywhere, the state found it more and more difficult to put up with ecclesiastical interference in its affairs, even when it was a matter of moral questions, as would be shown by the difficulties raised by divorce or birth control.[22]

One could easily continue along these lines by recalling the present conflict between the churches and the political regimes behind the Iron Curtain. This conflict is a good measure of the degree of secularization, and of the difficulties that churches find in the secularized world of preserving a political influence even in those matters that only touch moral questions (concerning respect for individual life, human honour, to say nothing, of course, of the right of property).

What are *the responses of the churches* in face of this situation? Naturally, they will vary according to the degree of secularization of the surrounding society, and also according to the particular confessional ethic involved. Broadly speaking, it is possible at present to discern different types of reactions.

1. The first reaction, to which Burgelin's comments allude, is the pure and simple reaction, that is, a withdrawal into a pre-formed set of traditions and privileges. In such a reaction, one finds a will to refuse to recognize all social development and to deny the fact of secularization. This attitude is particularly noticeable in the Catholicism of certain countries, but it is not entirely foreign to Protestantism. "Integrism" is the term currently used to refer to this attitude, a term that gradually has shifted from a doctrinal meaning (in opposition to the excesses of Modernism) to a political and social meaning. In such a reaction, the church lays claim to control of education, of morals, of culture, and of politics. But because the church is in a defensive position, this attitude is no longer creative and, indeed, ends in condemnations that stifle all creativity. Yet today there are few regions where political and social conditions permit ecclesiastical authorities to use the means of this control (Spain, and, to a degree, Italy). One of the major points on which this delaying action is fought is that of the maintaining in civil law of the principles of canonical legislation concerning marriage and divorce. Thus, for example, the Roman Catholic Church agreed to sign a concordat with Mussolini's fascist regime (which, moreover, was hostile to the church) on the express condition that divorce would not be recognized in civil legislation. But, in fact, this integrist reaction rarely obtains its objectives, and it is easy to understand why it does not: the sociological bases that would permit its triumph to be assured – namely, the existence of a Christendom – no longer exist. The situation is such, indeed, that the combat takes on another visage in the

organization of a kind of Christian ghetto. The church attempts to restrain those who submit to its authority from the influence of the modern world. It organizes narrowly confessional schools, and extends this procedure in youth movements and organizations that are carefully overseen by ecclesiastical authorities.

There are other aspects to this picture: the formation of political parties, of narrowly confessional labour unions, even of corporations (which tend to ignore the fact of the division of social classes) and of a press that daily filters down news for the benefit of the faithful and teaches them its precise meaning. The outcome is that the church feels able, by these means, to maintain its own vision of the world in a world that no longer corresponds to it in any way. In fact, this defensive system is manifestly fragile: it can continue to exist only in a well-cloistered rural organization. It simply becomes illusory under the impact of the mobility of populations and of modern means of communication. Even the so-called Christian school does not succeed in maintaining a total segregation of young Christians: it is obliged to teach a science that is just as secularized as in other schools. This is why the faithful themselves so often call this tactic into question today.

This tactic is not completely harmless for the church's ministry itself, for the church exhausts its strength in erecting protective barriers and meanwhile is obliged to abandon its missionary tasks. Thus, for example, in France many parishes have been deprived of priests in order to recruit a greater number of teachers for Catholic schools. On the other hand, the priest who lives within this ghetto is in danger of holding illusions regarding the vitality of the church: between him and the world of the dechristianized faithful is a "protective muff of the Pure".[23]

This type of reaction is less clear-cut in Protestantism, because Protestantism brings a less negative judgment on the fact of secularization. It has a tendency to see secularization as the end of an equivocation, that of Christian civilization, of Christendom. Its idea that God alone is holy and its rather strongly eschatological orientation make it incline to the view that Christian civilization, in a strict sense, does not exist, that every civilization, even when it has been under the historical influence of Christianity, remains profane and that it is always mistakenly that a civilization wants to pass itself off as Christian. Indeed, Protestantism has the tendency to *make profane* every civilization that would claim to be Christian. This is why a *tradition*, even when impregnated by Christianity, has no absolute value for Protestantism. It does not think that it is possible to Christianize the social order (although this was the slogan of the first generation of the

Social Gospel movement[24]). Every human accomplishment remains tainted by imperfection, and to proclaim it Christian would be to anticipate the judgment that God alone can bring. It is necessary for us to take our part in a world broken from within, in which the absolute truths of faith encounter truths of science, which are no less absolute in their order but at the same time unco-ordinatable to the truths of faith. For Protestantism, the role of the Christian is not to withdraw from the world, but to live dangerously in a profane world.[25] These theoretical considerations explain the attitude that Protestantism has had in the contemporary world: with the exception of the Netherlands and of some cantons in Switzerland, Protestantism has not sought to organize Protestant parties, let alone Protestant labour unions. It is not opposed to the secularization of the state, in which it has seen a guarantee of religious freedom. It is less tied than Catholicism to the confessionality of the school. To be sure, Protestantism has had its integrist reactions, notably under the form of Pietism. Such reactions, however, have had a less systematic character than in Catholicism.

2. Opposed to the conservative and integrist attitude is what could be called the *progressist* reaction. This consists in introducing the thought, methods, and ways of feeling of the secularized world as widely as possible into the church. The assumption is that the Christian faith is dynamic enough to be able to support a necessary confrontation with a secularized culture and civilization, and to draw out the positive meaning from it. The progressist reaction is more recent than the integrist reaction, and its doctrinal background is somewhat confused. As a general rule, the Christian churches have accepted it only with extreme reserve. The Catholic church has condemned the most flagrant manifestations of progressism, which ordinarily attempts to bring Christian thought to accept the Marxist analysis of the economic and social world[26] or to accommodate the idea of a civilization of work to Christian terrain. In many respects, the efforts of the worker-priests had the same meaning. It should be emphasized that it is not a question of abandoning the Christian faith. Rather, it is a matter of bringing about the coexistence, on the one hand, of an interpretation of society and of its development that has been inspired with a typically secularized ideology, namely, Marxism, and, on the other hand, a Christian faith purified of the adventitious elements with which it has been burdened by several centuries of so-called Christian (or in any event, bourgeois) civilization. The idea of rediscovering contact with the world inspires all these Christian adventures. This contact is to be accomplished by a new engagement of Christians in the great social and political battles that

characterize our times.[27] As Burgelin emphasizes,[28] the danger inherent
in these attempts is the intrusion of political ideologies into the church
and the appearance of schism by this means. Given the socio-professional
composition of the churches, especially in the West, and their bourgeois or
rural character, such efforts necessarily run into an incomprehension that
does indeed risk calling the unity of the church into question. The Protestant churches share this uneasiness, even though, because of their own
spirit, they do not react in the same fashion as the Roman Church and have
never officially condemned progressism. It seems, however, that whenever
a fundamental change is produced in social and political structures, as is
the case for the regions behind the Iron Curtain, the Protestant churches
show a greater flexibility than the Catholic church and somehow manage
to maintain the fundamental exigencies of the faith while at the same time
opening themselves to a vision of society, of social relationships, and of the
relationships of man to his work that were not familiar to them. But the
experience is too short and the information that we possess too fragmentary
to be able to evaluate this new situation.[29]

3. Naturally, a whole gamut of intermediary reactions lie between these
two extremes. The most typical reactions on both Protestant and Catholic
sides are the birth of a Christian social movement, the formation of study
and action groups that try to find original formulas for permitting the
alliance of an authentic Christian witness and a presence in the secularized
world. Such reactions have contributed in great measure in several
western countries to the weakening of the traditional link between
Christianity and conservatism. In this respect, the initiatives taken by
the World Council of Churches witness to the great seriousness with
which some are attempting to build a social ethic and to enable Christians
to take an effective role in the great social transformations of our age.

The multiplicity of reactions that the growing secularization of the
world awakens in the churches is probably a good sociological indication
of the vitality of the different Christian confessions. The churches, coming
from differentiated societies in relation to the global society, have not
accepted their rejection to the periphery of social life. They tend to affirm
their presence under new forms. A new Christian social ethic will one day
come out of the many experiences that are happening.

When the church finds itself confronting a world without religious structure, a world enclosed in its own autonomy, precisely then will it discover the
negative or absurd nature of the separation between sacred and profane.
Understanding that a non-Christian world cannot have ecclesial structures
imposed from without, the church will cease to seek or will seek less to

impose its laws on the world. It will understand that an ethic is rooted in the world through the ministry of its laymen. It is symptomatic of a situation of secularization that the role of laymen takes on greater importance. This is not only because the priests are no longer sufficient for the task, as G. Le Bras has rightly emphasized,[30] but because laymen can be living bearers in the city and in society of a Christian ethic that law can no longer impose. This call to laymen which characterizes the whole effort of the ecumenical movement is heard no less vigorously on the Catholic side, although there is more reticence present in regard to the tasks that are confided to the laymen and the freedom they enjoy in carrying the tasks out. The church finds itself obliged to think out a Christian ethic for a non-Christian world. To do this, it is necessary for the church to re-evaluate its old ethic, which was valid only for a non-secularized world and was primarily an individual ethic, since man necessarily found himself in a network of canonical dispositions that controlled social functioning. There is nothing astonishing about the fact that the new ethical forms that are being sketched out are essentially social ethics.[31] Whether it be a question of pontifical encyclicals or of declarations of the World Council of Churches (and of its Department of Church and Society), the accent is placed on problems of social ethics. To be sure, individual values retain their place, but they are designed to authenticate the witness, the service, and the action that Christians will have to give and accomplish on the social level.

The critical time for a religion, [Le Bras observes] is when it submits to the action of civil society rather than inspires it. But in this reversal, the religious society does not lose all its strength. It applies itself to reconquest and to persuasion.[32]

We would quickly add that the reconquest is primarily a persuasion by witness and service.

This period, which today would seem to be well under way, is often preceded by a period (which continues into the present) in which the churches, knowing themselves to be differentiated in relation to the global society and opposed to it, attempt to have all the organs and institutions that the global society has at its disposal. They constitute societies parallel to the global society. This is the source, as we have already noted, of a vast network of Christian schools, Christian hospitals, Christian cultural and athletic associations, a Christian daily press, Christian political parties and labour unions, etc. In short, the churches try to be sufficient unto themselves. But besides the churches becoming quickly winded in this competition, one can wonder if they are not making a mistake in terms of their own mission in the world. In so far as they content themselves with responding to the unsatisfied needs of society by creating model institutions that sooner or later will be reproduced by society (as was the case with hospitals, the creation of social welfare functions, and in part, the schools), they are truly the salt of the earth and participate in the renewal of the world. Beginning with the moment that they enter into some type of competition that encloses them in the ghetto which secularization has prepared for them, the enterprise becomes much more questionable from the point of view of the finality proper to the church. It seems indeed that in our age, at least on the Protestant side, the problem is felt in the terms that we have discussed.

We cannot close this chapter without calling attention to a rather paradoxical phenomenon that is manifested in the very midst of secularization. Will Herberg, in his book *Protestant-Catholic-Jew*,[33] has shown that the three great religious bodies play and have played for several decades an unexpected role in the secularized global society. Not only do they constitute one of the most powerful forces of social integration in the United States, but almost everyone aspires to become a member of a religious community (which explains the formidable rise in church membership). By becoming part of a religious community, the individual finds a means, if not the means, of social identification and access to personality. It is true that American society constitutes a peculiar social world: the melting-pot of Americanness quickly relieves the successive waves of immigrants of their ethnic, linguistic, and cultural particularities. Individuals thus find themselves deprived of that which gave them personal identity and individual worth. The social advance that many of them experience in the second or third generations is not sufficient to fill the void. On the contrary, it demands in an imperative way the recovery of personality. Religion, which integrates them into differentiated social groups, often corresponding to their social rank, comes at the appropriate time to help them. Consequently, the churches, far from being marginal societies, such as are found so often in secularized orders, seem to participate directly in the great process of integration into the global society. Nevertheless, it is necessary to keep in mind, as Herberg emphasizes, that this religion that plays such a positive and unconstrained role in American society is, in reality, a sort of religion common to the various denominations; it is a religion whose essential dogmas are the existence of a Providence, the worth and freedom of man, democracy, etc. To be sure, the specifically Christian doctrines have been grafted onto this common base and nourish the piety of individuals and parishes. But one can wonder if it is not what Henri Desroches has called "the religion of Americanness" that comes into play when it is a question of integrating Americans into their society, of integrating them in a more happy fashion. Undoubtedly, Christianity, by reason of its communal essence, possesses on its own "the paramount force of social integration".[34] But this does not necessarily work in favour of a peaceable and problemless integration into a secularized society, a society of comfort and opulence. It is not certain that it is Christianity as such that plays the role of social catalyst in the United States. It is indeed possible that it is a secularized deism grafted onto Christianity, at least among large segments of the faithful, and thus something that involves an illusion.

NOTES

1. Ph. H. Menoud, *L'Eglise et les ministères selon le Nouveau Testament* (Neuchâtel and Paris: Delachaux et Niestlé, 1949), p. 15. See also A. Benoit, "La paroisse dans le christianisme primitif", *FV*, 50th Year, May–June, 1952.

2. Menoud, op. cit., p. 56 et seq.

3. G. Le Bras, *Institutions ecclésiastiques de la chrétienté médiévale*, vol. 1 (*Histoire de l'Eglise*, vol. 12) (Paris: Bloud et Gay, 1959), p. 19.

4. Le Bras, ibid., p. 21.

5. Raymonde Foreville, in *Histoire de l'Eglise*, vol. 9 (Paris: Bloud et Gay, 1944), p. 228.

6. Le Bras, op. cit., pp. 57–58.

7. Robert Folz, "Réalité de l'Empire au XIIᵉ siècle", in *Etudes politiques* (Strasbourg: Cahiers de l'Association interuniversitaire de l'Est, 1960).

8. Le Bras, op. cit., p. 141.

9. E. Gilson, *La philosophie au Moyen Age*, vol. 1 (Paris: Payot, 1922), p. 132.

10. Le Bras, op. cit., p. 29.

11. Pacaut, in his book *Alexandre III* (Paris: Vrin, 1956) shows that although Alexander III took up the defence of the spiritual power of the papacy by slapping spiritual penalties on the sovereigns who had attacked the liberty of the church (Frederick I and Henry II), the very idea of the spiritual and of the sacred continued to spread following the "secularization of the church and the clericalization of the secular world" (p. 197). This idea tended to include everything that was useful to the church. The idea of *auctoritas*, taken from Roman law, was added to the enlarged spiritual power to give the means of intervening very effectively in the temporal world. This provided the basis for the progress of ecclesiastical centralization in all domains. Thereafter the Emperor would take only second place in the temporal order. *Auctoritas* was set in opposition to simple temporal administration or management.

12. Secularization and dechristianization should not be confused. Although, as we shall see, dechristianization gave support to the movement of secularization, the state of non-secularization did not hinder dechristianization from taking place. Historical inquiry reveals that in an age in which no social structure was secularized, the dechristianization of the age was none the less profound (cf. Jacques Toussaert, *Le sentiment religieux en Flandre à la fin du Moyen Age* [Paris: Plon, 1963]). The literature on secularization is considerable. Let us refer only to two works of synthesis: F. Delekat, *Ueber*

den Begriff der Säkularisation (Heidelberg: Quelle and Meyer, 1958); R. Mehl, "La sécularisation de la cité", in the collective volume *Le problème de la civilisation chrétienne* (Paris: PUF, 1951).

13. Shakespeare, in *Richard II*, described the tragedy of the King's two bodies.

14. We have borrowed this whole analysis from the monumental work of Ernst H. Kantorowicz, *The King's Two Bodies* (Princeton: Princeton University Press, 1957), especially pp. 317–450.

15. See, for instance, the study by R. Voeltzel, "L'Etre suprême pendant la Révolution française", *RHPR*, 38th Year, 1958, no. 3.

16. The Catholic forces were of primary concern, of course, but others were not forgotten: a delegation of robed ministers attended his coronation.

17. See O. Cullmann, *The State in the New Testament* (New York: Charles Scribner's Sons, 1956 and London: SCM Press, rev. ed., 1963).

18. This was particularly the case with the ecumenical movement. At the time of the Oxford Conference (1937), Nazism aspired to impose its ideology on scientific research.

19. Qualification is necessary here: what has held back the formation of European unity and has sometimes given rise to distrustful reactions from the Protestant side is that people have thought that European unity is an attempt to recreate a European Christendom in order to give Catholic authorities a European leadership. See our study, "L'Europe protestante", in *Problèmes de civilisation européenne* (Strasbourg, 1956). See also: *Forces religieuses et attitudes politiques dans la France contemporaine*, edited by René Rémond (Paris: Armand Colin, 1965).

20. In France the parliamentary debates on secularism have given precise expression to this judgment. See L. V. Méjan, *La séparation des Eglises et de l'Etat* (Paris: PUF, 1959).

21. Yves M. J. Congar, *Vaste monde, ma paroisse* (Paris: Témoignage chrétien, 1959), p. 17.

22. Pierre Burgelin, "La fin de l'ère constantinienne", *FV*, 58th Year, 1959/1, pp. 14–15.

23. Father Daniel even thinks that the present structure of parishes constitutes such a buffer zone (cf. *Informations catholiques internationales*, April 15, 1960).

24. See our study in *Encyclopédie française*, vol. IX (Paris: 1960), entitled "La vertu de la promesse".

25. See our study, "Source et signification de l'idée de laïcité dans la pensée protestante", in *Cahiers d'histoire*, vol. IV/1, 1959.

26. See two typical works (both condemned by Rome): *Les événements et la foi* by Father M. I. Montuclard and the team of Jeunesse de l'Eglise (Paris: Editions du Seuil, 1951); and H. C. Desroches, *Signification du marxisme* (Paris: Les Editions Ouvrières, 1950).

27. On the reactions of the Catholic hierarchy in regard to Progressism, see the article by Father P. Bigo, "Le progressisme; Aspects doctrinaux", *Revue de l'Action populaire*, May 1, 1955. This article contains, in particular, a list of the warnings and mandamuses of the hierarchy. The article underscores, although somewhat acrimoniously, the dangers that Progressism posed for Catholic doctrine, especially in the status of the priesthood.

28. Burgelin, art. cit., p. 17.

29. Cf. R. Mehl, "L'Europe protestante", op. cit.

30. G. Le Bras, "Mesure de la vitalité sociale du catholicisme française", *CIS*, 1950, vol. 8, p. 8.

31. In an article entitled "Aux origines de la démocratie chrétienne" (*ASR*, no. 6, July–December, 1959), Montuclard rightly emphasizes the opposition, at the end of the nineteenth century, between the attitude of movements related to employers and to

mixed unions, on the one hand, and those of worker groups influenced by social Christianity. Whereas the former attempted to prolong the myth of a Christian society in which there are only problems of individual ethics, the others brought to the foreground the problems of structures, institutions, and social justice. They inverted the order of the terms in regard to the relations of love and justice. For them, love has no meaning except when justice is realized (p. 79).

32. G. Le Bras, "Sociologie religieuse et sciences des religions", *ASR*, no. 1, January–June, 1956, p. 10.

33. Herberg, *Protestant-Catholic-Jew* (Garden City, N.Y.: Doubleday Anchor Books, 1960).

34. J. Wach, *Sociologie*, p. 382.

V

The Religious Object: Doctrine, Myth and History

1. *Christianity, a Doctrinal Religion*

After having situated the Christian community within the context of the global society, it is necessary to penetrate into the interior of that community, to see how it lives and where it itself locates its own ground. That which is proper to every society is to be gathered or to be able to gather itself around a reality from which it receives its vitality, which commands at one and the same time its institutions, practices, and beliefs. But it is entirely possible that the community will be ignorant of the exact nature of this ground or that it will have only a confused idea of it and will take a purely affective approach to it. The reality which gives the nation its moral consistency and its unity is the fatherland, but what citizen is capable of defining the fatherland, even though he feels its constraining reality? Religious groups are distinguished from other social groups in the sense that the religious object is always immanent in the practices, beliefs, festivals, and institutions. It makes its presence felt in a particularly clear way and inspires sentiments *sui generis* of respect, fear, of sacred awe, of jubilation. This fact does not mean that the intellectual representation of the sacred object will be especially lucid. Indeed, confusion is more the rule, as is attested by the numerous syncretisms and by the very evolution of the personality or of the function of the gods.[1] At least the collective consciousness comprehends a mode of presence or of appearance of divinity.

The particularity of Christianity rests in the role played in it by theology (taken, of course, on diverse levels), teaching, the instruction of catechumens (although this term has changed in meaning in the course of its history), the concern for doctrine and for orthodoxy, in short the concern to explicate the specific nature of the God which it worships (this same concern already appeared with clarity in Judaism). How is this sociological particularity to be explained? It is impossible to explain it by the cultural level of the faithful, since from the birth of Christianity and up to the end of the second century Christianity counted few members from the intelligentsia or from the upper classes of society. Yet we should recognize that the massive entry of pagan intellectuals and of philosophers into the church following Justin Martyr accentuated the importance of the doctrinal element, and at the same time hastened a development that Paul had already begun to make precise in his first letters. But the profound cause must be sought in the manner in which God appeared to the Christian consciousness, made himself known to it, and revealed himself. Certainly the Christian revelation is not, in the proper sense, a doctrinal revelation as it is in the Koran. It does not consist of a series of doctrinal propositions, but rather is the revelation of God himself. That which is proper to revelation in Christianity is that its content is not distinct from the subject who reveals himself: it is always the affirmation of a merciful presence of God with men. It is always the revelation of a God who walks among his people. This revelation alone is made in and by the Word. The God of Christianity, like that of Judaism, is a God who speaks. Theophany is brought about essentially in a word. If the incarnation of Christ is not a theophany in the sense of pagan religions, it is because it is the incarnation of the Logos. In fact, Christ does not restrict himself to teaching about God: he is himself the Logos made flesh, the living Word. Christianity is essentially a religion of the Word, a Word which the faithful can receive, understand, assimilate. Even when God acts (creation, resurrection, judgment), he acts always through the word. This word is addressed to man, not as an ambiguous word, which only the initiated can understand or which would have several possible meanings, but as an intelligible word. To be sure, this word is mysterious, in the sense that the human mind is not naturally capable of it; but the Holy Spirit comes to clarify it for man, provoking a renewal of his understanding, in such a way that he can be persuaded by this word, since his will and his understanding are associated in the comprehension of God's work.

This explains why Christianity has become a religion of the book, of the writing, of preaching, and why the education of Christians is accomplished not by a ritual or mystical initiation but by instruction. It also explains why the revealed Word, attested by an intelligible word, has called forth an immense work of exegesis, interpretation, and systematization, to the point that in certain ages it has been this work and the propositions resulting from it that have appeared to be decisive. The ever-present risk is that Christianity will be turned into a religion of intellectuals and, since this doctrinal elaboration has been accomplished in the conceptual world which Greece bequeathed to the West, that Christianity will become the religion of the West. In many respects, of course, it has become this, in spite of the fact that missionary work has transported it to Asia and Africa.

It is on the side of Catholicism that this risk is most fully developed, in the sense that the continuous elaboration of dogmas, which supposedly lead into one another following a logical order, impose an adherence to the doctrinal contents that are considered to be the equivalent of faith in the very person of God. The risk is that when this doctrinal system no longer finds supports in the reigning culture, when the civilization in which this system has been progressively formed begins to break up, faith itself can crumble. The faithful are no longer able to put up with the dichotomy between their faith and their culture. The latter has been constructed with concepts that are totally foreign to those which theology utilizes, and thus religious decision is presented as a choice between two contradictory systems of thought. Whereas Catholicism has emphasized the *quid* of Revelation, Protestantism generally, except in times of rational-ist orthodoxy, has put the emphasis more on the act of Revelation, on the fact that God communicates himself in Revelation.[2] Thus it insists more on the personal character of Revelation. Yet since it is obliged to express the latter in an accessible language, it encounters in a less dramatic fashion the same difficulties encountered by Catholicism. This is the source of the many present-day attempts to create a new theological language, attempts that are expressed as well in technical research on demythologizing as in practical research on the contemporary relevance of preaching.

Of course, by rights Christianity should be able to escape these diffi-culties of language and of expression, since it does not present itself as a religion among religions and simply seeks to express the intervention of God under the form of historical events. It should be able to express itself in all categories and in all cultures. But Christianity has a history, and this history is essentially western. Christianity has been led to express the content of Revelation in a mould that was created in advance and for other purposes. The very idea of truth that Greek thought proposed to it was different from the idea of truth that it owed to its Jewish origins. Whereas the Greek idea of truth is the idea of a true proposition (because it is non-contradictory or verifiable), the Judeo-Christian idea of truth concerns authenticity, the absence of fraud and duplicity in personal relationships. The first form of the idea of truth is that which science has inherited, and there is a certain filiation between Greek science and modern science. The second form was destined to found an ethic of personal relationships, not an ethic of right and wrong considered as objective realities. Thus Christianity has had to bend itself to an idea of truth that was not made for it: Christ's assertion that he is himself the truth was perfectly unintelligible and properly scandalous to the Greek mind. In the same way, Christianity has had to express itself in ontological categories of nature, substance, and accident. These categories were conceived to express a hierarchical cosmos, in which God is the first principle, the unmoved mover. They were not meant to express the living God who goes before his people, who intervenes in history, and who finally becomes incarnate in this history: the idea of the Word made flesh (and not metamorphosed into flesh) is in complete contradiction with the idea of substance which excludes all becoming. Such are the difficulties that Christianity has encountered from the fact of the resistance of a language which was imposed on it. This was undoubtedly the source of all the christological misadventures, for example, the docetic and monophysite heresies. These must not be considered only in the absolute, as false doctrines (from the theologian's point of view), but also as solutions of a sociological problem, as the insertion into an ill-suited culture not of a doctrine but of a message which is held prisoner there. This is also the source of the great enterprise of Chalcedon: the expression of the christological doctrine obtained by joining the term of nature (Greek) with the term of person. Finally, this is the source of the quarrels concerning the real presence of Christ in the Lord's Supper, quarrels which have not been resolved even today because they also have a sociological background: with our conceptual apparatus, is it possible adequately to express the modality of this presence and to give an account of it? Catholicism has believed this possible, but already by introducing the idea of transubstantiation it came into collision with the idea of substance. Catholicism claimed to introduce a flexibility into the idea of substance, which it does not have, and was thus able to keep the term and the type of thought which it represents. For a long time, the idea of transubstantiation was on the level of scientific culture, and up to the seventeenth century was able to be presented as an intelligible doctrine. When science succeeded in repudiating all idea of substance, Catholicism was faced with the necessity of referring to a pure miracle (but at the same time a physical miracle), of presenting a sort of sacramental chemistry guaranteed by a ritualism.

Protestantism, born at the dawn of modern times, and more aware of the specific nature of Christianity, manifested a greater prudence in the formulation of the Eucharistic mystery. It sought to avoid tying itself to well-defined categories, and attempted to invent other categories for the mystery. But in this search, it lost its unity (consubstantiation, spiritual presence, commemoration). Now, with a great deal of difficulty, it is seeking a faithful and intelligible expression of the mystery recognized by faith. One could not claim that Protestantism has been successful in its search. It is at the stage where it is ready to abandon the classic formulations, to make a sober effort, to indicate, to circumscribe, to describe, without formulating the mystery with the precision of former generations yet without seeking to remake its unity around simple formulas.[3] It knows in what direction it must orient itself, or at least it is moving in that direction without having yet arrived.

All these difficulties undoubtedly have a theological character; that is to say, they express different basic theological tendencies. Yet it would be dangerous not to see their cultural background, that is, their sociological background.

This problem that western Christianity has encountered on particular points appears on a much vaster scale when one considers Asia and Africa. Here we are not speaking of Asian and African Christianity as a product of importation, reserved, in short, for the élites who are already strongly westernized. We are speaking of that Christianity which has become autonomous, rooted in the vast layers of population which have had no contact with the western culture of the past centuries. The problem that one calls the indigenization of Christianity will appear in all its fullness. It is easy to understand why the churches have exercised such great caution in this area: they are well aware of the dangers of syncretism that seem tied to any effort of indigenization of Christianity, and they also know that the indigenization process up till now has reached only the cultic forms, whereas the doctrine continues to be taught under its classic, i.e., western, forms. Nevertheless, there seems to be a growing indifference among the younger churches in regard to the confessional divisions of the West and a very strong pressure towards unity, which is good evidence of their desire not to take on the whole theological development that has been produced in the West. The Protestant churches of China, which have grown very far apart from the West since the triumph of the Communist revolution, proclaim their desire for a triple independence: administrative, financial, and theological. The experience could be interesting and important theoretically, but it has become involved in a political context which falsifies its meaning.

In sum, the fact that theological problems, that is to say, problems of truth, are implied in the doctrinal controversies and development of Christianity should not make us lose sight of the other fact, namely, that

Christianity does not have at its disposal a language of its own. It has had to express itself in the language of a cultural and philosophical tradition, with which it has formed a profound solidarity throughout the course of history. Now that this tradition has been called into question, Christianity has two possibilities open to it: either it can maintain archaic forms of expression at the risk of losing its substance in this new expression (this is what, for example, is to be feared in an attempt like that of existential theology). In any event, these facts authorize a sociology of dogmas themselves, to the degree that every dogmatic formulation is tied to a type of culture and to the degree that this culture reflects a social state.

The problem is more acute in Christianity because doctrine plays a major role there and because the forms of worship and piety, the rites and the ceremonies, are commanded by the doctrine, whereas in other religions the doctrine represents nothing more than a *possible implication* of the rite, that is to say, the rite progressively engenders the doctrine instead of being fashioned by it. The subordination of forms of worship, piety, church government, and community organization to doctrine is undoubtedly most clear in Protestantism. It is also in Protestantism that we find the concern for a doctrinal purity which makes the problem of language even more acute. Ritual is relatively undeveloped in Protestantism, and this is due to a conscious decision: the purpose was precisely to keep ritualism from covering over and hiding the doctrinal assertions. In the Catholic church the development of mariological doctrine is certainly inscribed in the very logic of theology and has been carried on throughout history, beginning with the assertion of Mary *theotokos*, mother of God. But it is also required by the very exigencies of a piety that has developed outside all doctrinal control and very quickly manifested a considerable pressure in the life of the church: the Assumption of the Virgin had been the object of popular piety three or four centuries before becoming a dogmatic formulation.

2. *Doctrine, History and Myth*

The specific nature of doctrine in Christianity is made more precise in the ties that it maintains with history. The doctrinal revelation is tied to an event, to a personal intervention of God in history, and this event or act alone gives doctrine its plenary significance. Thus the doctrine could never be constituted without reference to this history. It will itself be historical doctrine, significant history, holy history. This is what had already appeared in Judaism[4] and it continued in Christianity. The truth of

Christianity is thus not a non-temporal truth, but the truth of a historical event or events. This is why it is necessary for the community to preserve the memory of these events, to remain in contact with this past, and to conserve the link between this past and the rest of history. In so far as it is a question of a community close to the event (the primitive church), no real problems will arise, except perhaps those of warding off false witnesses, or of making a choice from among the witnesses: this is the work that was carried on during the course of the first two centuries with the fixing of the canon. But as the events become more and more distant, and as the ensemble of society becomes secularized and no longer is concerned with preserving these living memories, the community must make an effort not only for the continuous holy history to be an integral part of the religious culture but also to be careful that the join be made between this holy history and the other historical references of the culture.

Holy history, in effect, has a double character of being a history, but a history whose meaning and sometimes whose events escape the historical witness properly speaking, and which can be established only by historical criticism. This is the source of the tendency which is manifest in western civilization of throwing back Christian holy history into the realm of *myth*; not necessarily to the realm of legend, but to the realm of that complex of historical elements and interpretations added by the community, which seeks to render account to itself of a lived experience and can do so only by tending towards a historicization of mythic figures or events. The Christian community in modern times is faced with a twofold necessity: on the one hand, it must throw out the ballast (in regard to the wise men who came from the East, to take an inoffensive example) and must recognize that the boundary between the historical and the mythical is a rather uncertain boundary, above all since the Christian church is based on the old covenant and consequently interprets, of necessity, the historical events and the historical figure of Christ on the basis of mythic archetypes (the Suffering Servant, the new man coming on the clouds of heaven, Elijah risen from the dead); on the other hand, it must not permit the biblical history to be driven back to the realm of myth, that is to say, to that time outside time, to that time anterior to time and posterior to all times, *in illo tempore*. It must not neglect to underscore the historical coordinates of the events on which it is based (whence the mention of Pontius Pilate in the Apostles' Creed).

To be sure, in so far as holy history is rooted in events of foundation (creation), events which perhaps are plausible but which by definition escape all verification, and is completed in eschatological events whose character excludes historicity, to that degree the Christian community must not repudiate every alliance of its essentially historical thought with myth. Christian thought approaches history both forward and backward. But it would be the end of the specific character of Christianity if it were to abandon the historical nature of its foundation, the relationship between the events of Palestine and the general history of the world. One of the major difficulties in the missionary diffusion of Christianity among pagan peoples is precisely to make them understand that Jerusalem is located well and truly in real space, that one can reach it by ordinary means of communication, and that Jesus Christ belonged to the same history that we live today:

The entire being finds himself engaged in the distance covered by this space which is finally open to him. After the word of the gospel has been brought into the midst of the society and has determined a new form of life, the individual finds himself dominated, for the first time, by a space and a time which separates him from the Jerusalem of Christ – a measurable space and time, where rationality and dialectic become possible. He situates himself in the place of the event which is his own time and that, at least, of the historical Christ. In that way he knows a history which is that of Jesus Christ and, in relation to it, he follows his own history. He truly lives his own time, he has of himself a means of control . . . a self-possession, a knowledge that no longer has anything in common with the identification that he had formerly, when he adhered to the world so intimately that space was hardly perceptible to him. He no longer is a person in his society. He is a personage in the world, with his own history.[5]

This passage from Leenhardt's *Do Kamo* shows clearly how the Melanesian, leaving the world of myth where totemic identifications are produced and where, consequently, the person does not have its own originality, discovers a historical time and a space where persons encounter each other and where they are situated in relation to each other by their differences. Now this dimension is essential to Christianity, where a personal encounter between the faithful and Christ is involved, where faith is located in this encounter with the Christ who is the eternal Christ only to the degree that he is also the Jesus Christ of past history.

It is because the Christian community is aware of the specific nature of its object and of the link between this object and concrete history that it unceasingly pursues what could be called a work of commemoration. It does this on the level of preaching, catechetical instruction, and theological research. This is also why the appearance of methods of historical criticism and their application to the biblical texts have brought about a crisis within the Christian community, namely, the crisis of modernism or liberalism. This crisis was long in being resolved, for it involved no less than a re-evaluation of the relationship of doctrine and Christian teaching to history, such as science had reconstructed it. The fact is that Christianity cannot be formulated in timeless aphorisms; its doctrine is always related to historical events, even if historical science cannot draw out the profound meaning of these events as faith alone can. This fact makes Christianity a case apart in the world of religions. Christian theology can never pass over the problem of the relationship between the Jesus of history and the Christ of faith, however much the terms in which the problem is posed vary.

The position of Christianity is no less original in regard to the question of myth. Christianity cannot confine itself to myth, for then the God whom it invokes would not really be involved in the history of men. Nor can Christianity reject myth entirely, for Christianity is a total vision of history. From this fact, it is obliged to take into consideration both a beginning of history – a creation for which it has no historical witness – and an end of history. It can express its doctrine of the beginning and end of history only through myths: thus it bases itself on a history that reaches out in two directions via myths, the myths of creation and of the final fulfilment.

By qualifying them as myths, we do not mean to make any judgment on the revealed truth which they bear, but we are simply saying that objectively this truth is presented to the community under a mythical garb. Certainly the tendency of Christendom throughout the ages has been to camouflage their mythical nature (at least concerning the creation) and to turn them into historical narratives on the same level as the texts dealing with King David or Jesus. Even more, they have served as reference points for a pseudo-historical chronology. But to the degree that the development of culture, including biblical culture, makes the mythical nature increasingly clear to the community, the teaching of the church is obliged to modify itself and to admit that revelation also reaches man by means of myth. However, not just any myth will suffice, for the myth has to be correlated to and even taken in charge by a history. The myth of creation as well as that of the Parousia are not independent elements: they are brought into relationship with the central history in which Christian faith reads historical revelation. Instead of being determinants and absolutes as in other religions, where they for ever order all cultic and ritual activity, these myths are conceived of in relation to the history of Christ. The narratives of creation and of the Fall take their significance in relation to the redemptive work of the historical Christ. The same is true of the Parousia: it has meaning only as the radiant manifestation of the lordship of Christ that history has revealed only in an ambiguous and hidden fashion.

The history of religions has shown clearly that the biblical myths contain many elements that belong to them as well as to other myths (Babylonian and Sumerian, for example). But since the history of religion ordinarily restricts itself to being purely analytical and to drawing out relationships and parallels, it does not sufficiently emphasize that the biblical framework gives these mythical elements a certain internal adjustment precisely in order to render them capable of being put into relationship with a true history. Oscar Cullmann states that the chief fact is

the recognition that the New Testament faith extends the historical incarnation even beyond the time of the actual preparation into the primal history, and in the other direction extends it past the time of the development in the church into the history "of the last things", because even for these parts the historical event in Jesus is the orienting mid-point. The Primitive Christian understanding of the history of salvation is correctly understood only when we see that in it history and myth are thoroughly and essentially bound together, and that they are both to be brought together, on the one side by the common denominator of prophecy and on the other by the common denominator of development in time.[6]

Obviously, the conception of the relations between history and myth that Cullmann analyses is that of the first Christians; but this conception engages the whole Christian church in so far as Christianity adheres to a permanent effort to place itself on the level of the Primitive church, and to think through and extend in time the Primitive Christian view of history.

In any case, the doctrinal particularity of Christianity consists in making history prevail over myth, of seeking in history the meaning of myth instead of *vice versa*, and, consequently, of restoring time instead of annulling it as in religions of archetypal myths and myths of the eternal return. The restoration of time consists in the conception that God is not only the One who is at the beginning of time, who accomplishes the archetypal and auroral act, *in illo tempore* as the Roman myths say, in the great time which precedes history. He is the One who unceasingly intervenes in history to accomplish an original work there, to call men not to a repetition of the primordial act but to a fulfilment, to an entry into newness of life. He is the One who is present in the history of men and with them through the historical ministry of his Son as well as through the permanent action of the Holy Spirit. Historical time has a value in the sense that "historical facts thus become 'situations' of man in respect to God".[7] Mircea Eliade even thinks that there is a sort of convergence between Christianity and modern man, because the latter is involved in history and progress and, consequently, would be stifled in the world of cyclical time, of repetition, of archetypal acts which would send us back to a mythical origin without offering us any opening on the future.

> We may say . . . that Christianity is the "religion" of modern man and historical man, of the man who simultaneously discovered personal freedom and concontinuous time (in place of cyclical time).[8]

Sociologically, one can only point to the concurrence between Christianity's vision of history and the experiences (not all of which are religious by any means) of modern western man. There is undoubtedly a link between Christian doctrine and these experiences, but it is difficult to be precise in this respect. In any case, the collective experience of the Christian church regarding the nature of time and of history has largely overflowed the limits of the church, since it has tainted the global experience of western man.

3. *The Problem of Tradition*

How is the transmission of doctrine guaranteed in Christianity? How is the doctrinal continuity of the church maintained? It is evident that the problem is posed in Christianity in different terms from those in other religions, and in the philosophical schools. Many religions have guaranteed this continuity by means of an initiation. We still find many examples of this at the present time, although the initiation is no longer essentially ritual but intellectual; nevertheless, it still requires the presence of a master who alone is capable of guaranteeing this initiation, of transmitting this deposit (Islam, certain currents of Judaism). As far as the philosophical schools are concerned (and this remark could be extended to the theological schools), it is evident that continuity is accomplished through a direct contact, individual or organized, with certain master-works. But this continuity, at least in the framework of western civilization, is not rigid: the master-work is viewed as a point of departure, meant to nourish a personal reflection. Orthodoxy plays only a very unobtrusive role. In fact, it is more a matter of continuity by renewal: hence the epithets that point to both continuity and renewal; neo-Platonism, neo-Kantianism, the Hegelian left. In philosophical as well as theological reflection, it is a matter of taking up the primary reflection in order to integrate it into a broader perspective or one reputed to be such. And this phenomenon naturally can be found within Christianity. But it constitutes only one aspect of the transmission of doctrine. This transmission goes beyond the limits of the particular schools. It is of interest to the whole Christian people. It belongs to churches as social bodies. It aims both to conserve and to actualize. Primary emphasis is placed on conservation (whence the expression *depositum fidei*), and to understand it one must refer to the Christian idea of revelation and to the role of scripture which this idea of revelation implies. But at the same time, the church must show that it not only is conservative, that the deposit is not an inert reality, that it retains an actual power. This is the second aspect of the transmission.

Preaching, for most churches, is that instrument by which continuity and renewal are assured and are assured at the same time.[9] *Preaching*, from a sociological point of view, has a double function: to affirm the unique and decisive nature of the same Revelation; and to show how this unique Revelation concerns all the aspects and the most current concerns of our existence, despite the movement of history. The balance between these two functions is often difficult to discover. Examined from a sociological point of view, a history of Christian preaching would show how these two functions have been carried out in variable fashion, with the church sometimes being more attentive to the unshakable foundation, sometimes being more concerned with adapting it more or less well to the development of minds in the cultural and sociological context. It is precisely to guarantee this necessary and difficult balance that the Christian churches give preaching a norm through the means of the confession of faith. The role of the *confession of faith* in the transmission of doctrine is that of recalling, in clear formulas, the basic aspects of Revelation, of putting them in an order of importance, and thus of making precise the contours of an *orthodoxy*. The latter carves out the domains and sectors in which the church will have a certain latitude of adaptation to changing circumstances. Whereas the principal symbolic texts of the Catholic church have tied orthodoxy to a Thomist view of the universe, the confessions of the Reformation emphasized that unanimity in the preaching of the gospel and in the administration of the sacraments would suffice to guarantee the integrity of the church. As a consequence of this, the Reformation confessions held that the form of worship, ecclesiastical organization, and even the forms of piety and action could have a certain diversity and flexibility.

But preaching and confession of faith, as characteristics of each Christian church, are ordained by a reality which goes beyond them, which commands them, yet which is more difficult to grasp and define: Tradition. Certainly, every social group has a tradition to which it refers and which moulds its behaviour and sensibility, while at the same time taking on new elements throughout the course of history (to the point that tradition sometimes is altered despite its claim to remain the same). But tradition has much more importance for the Christian communities, from the very fact that they refer to an original and fundamental event, to a precise act of foundation. Tradition is the constant reference throughout history to this original event. It is also the fact of transmitting this primary content from one generation to another (by means of preaching, teaching, and confession of faith). It is both content and act. As content, tradition dominates and directs the community, as act, the subject of tradition is the community itself, which in one way or another has a hold over tradition. The act of transmitting tradition gives birth to traditions which will attempt to become grafted onto the Tradition, but which can also obliterate the Tradition. The Christian churches have lived and will live in a constant dialectic between Tradition and traditions, even when they claim to reject all traditions that had been grafted onto it and had altered it; this is what is expressed, sometimes rather naïvely, in Protestantism's desire to reproduce the primitive Christian community. And certainly the operation is effective: all kinds of doctrines and practices have been abandoned. But at the same time, Protestantism creates new traditions, be it a certain way of reading and of explaining scripture, or of grounding an ethic in the biblical Revelation, or a certain style of piety and of worship, a certain predominance given to the preached Word, to the intellectual elements of Revelation. To be sure, it would be false to bring about an absolute separation between Tradition and traditions. The latter are always rooted in some fashion in Tradition. But the link can be more or less strong, more or less lax, more or less apparent or more or less subtle. At one time or another, every church attempts an effort to relocate the sources of the traditions in Tradition, and to prune the wild branches of the latter. Thus the idea of reformation is inherent in the very life of the Christian churches (or the idea of a return to the sources). But these operations themselves are dominated by traditions. It is certain that, on the whole, the Protestant tradition is more of a tradition of refinement, whereas the Catholic tradition is more of a tradition of integration.[10] Protestantism, at least in intention, has nearly always been an *Ecclesia reformata semper reformanda*; Catholicism, at first in practice, and then beginning in the nineteenth century, on the theoretical level, has slowly built up the idea of an organic development of Tradition, the idea of a movement from the implicit to the explicit. This permits the least possible pruning of the traditions; indeed, the very idea of the growth of all living organisms provides the justification for all of the proliferations of Tradition. This is why Protestantism has a greater rigidity and Catholicism a greater capacity in regard to adapting to changing situations. This is also the source of the danger that Protestant communities have of isolating themselves from the surrounding society, and the source of the risk that Catholic communities face of being sub-merged in the surrounding society. This risk should not be overemphasized, for it has not always operated. In the eighteenth and nineteenth centuries, Protestantism as a whole was more receptive than Catholicism to the new ideas, to the philosophy of the Enlightenment, to the thought of Rousseau, to Kantianism, Hegelianism, and finally, to biblical criticism. But it should be pointed out that the reason why Catholicism has not been quite so receptive to these philosophical currents and has only recently begun to be open to biblical criticism is that it had already received a more massive philosophical tradition, namely, Aristotelianism and Thomism. This tradi-tion, along with several others, was sufficiently viable and productive to discourage Catholic thought from directing itself elsewhere. We should also mention that biblical criticism, perhaps excessively, has played a refining role in Protestantism in regard to traditions. In intention, at least, it has sought to lead Protestantism back to its sources, and has enabled Protestantism to rediscover aspects of its sources that non-biblical tradi-tions had set aside (for example, the rediscovery of the eschatological dimensions of the New Testament with Albert Schweitzer).

There are numerous sociological reasons that explain the enlarging of Tradition and the more or less successful grafting of traditions onto Tradition.

First of all, no community can be the bearer of a tradition without seek-ing to penetrate the meaning of it, without seeking to make it explicit. Such an operation is even more necessary in Christianity, since the re-vealed given is not constituted by a body of doctrinal propositions having the fixed and univocal character of a juridical code; rather, it is constituted by a mystery that contains a considerable number of meanings to elucidate and evaluate. Thus the theological schools, and the particular communities that support them, are creators of traditions. To be sure, this work does not take place in an academic fashion; it is always a response to the chal-lenge of the present time, a response to the difficulties that the community undergoes. It is the historical situation of the community that largely dictates the work of explication and elaboration that eventually enlarges the Tradition. This explains why very often it is the history of the com-munity itself that is inserted into the Tradition. The people of Israel always strove not only to understand its own history in the light of the basic events that constituted its tradition (the Exodus from Egypt, covenants, the revelation on Sinai), but also to unite this history with these events in order to give both value at the same time. Such is the process of the constitution of holy history. And the Roman Catholic Church integrates its own history into that of salvation, all the while proclaiming the sufficiency of the biblical canon. The idea of doctrinal development, which has become a classic idea in Roman Catholicism, represents an *a posteriori* justification of this operation: it is not invalid to enrich the Tradition by the contributions of historical traditions which are born of the very life of the church, for these traditions only make explicit the unperceived meanings of the Tradition. In the same way, there is a neutralization of that in the Tradition which is too exclusive, that which it lacked of universalism in extension. The process is obviously tied to the extension of the religion considered: as Catholicism became increasingly diffused throughout the world, it felt it necessary not only to recapitulate its own history and to integrate it into the Tradition, but even to include foreign forms of thought and piety in this Tradition.[11]

A second motif in the enlarging of the Tradition would seem, at least in intention, to be antithetical to the first, but which, in fact, leads to the same results. This second motif is that of apologetic and the fight against heresy. Certainly, this fight can take on the aspect of a return to the sources, as was seen in regard to the birth of Protestantism; consequently, it will take shape as a purging of adventitious traditions, as a tightening up of the Tradition, as a movement towards wholeness. This does obviate the necessity of being situated among adverse doctrines, especially regarding the heresies that must be refuted; and to do this, the Tradition must be made more explicit, it must be deployed in all its meanings, indeed, meanings that are not yet perceived must be brought out in order to respond to this new situation. It is rare when one does not thus integrate something of the adversary's perspective. But even when one has successfully avoided this danger, one cannot avoid disjointing the Tradition, explicating it in new doctrinal formulas, having recourse to modes of thought that are foreign to it. It was thus that in Christianity, the apostolic Tradition, Revelation grasped as a whole and centred upon the person and work of Christ, *the dogma* of Christ with all the exigencies it involved regarding the faithful, were split into multifarious doctrines, into propositions that were rationally linked to one another (in order better to refute the adversary); this operation, of necessity, had recourse to categories that were completely foreign to the Tradition itself. The sociological necessity of fighting against heresies while at the same time taking account of the socio-cultural context in which Christianity developed had the result of introducing the concepts of nature, substance, attributes, and the communication of attributes (at the time of the Eucharistic controversy) into an essentially historical Tradition. Joseph de Maistre observed, not without justice, that

if Christianity had never been attacked, it would never have written in order to fix dogma; but also, dogma would never have been fixed in writing except for the fact that it existed anteriorly in its natural state, which is that of the word.[12]

By "word" in this case, we mean the Tradition, that is, both the original deposit and the fundamental event (in this instance, the Word made flesh), which are not reducible to a set of doctrines; by "dogma" we mean the body of speculations and elucidations that theology and the magisterium have continued to develop in order to confront a certain socio-cultural world. In their desire to return to this original deposit, the Reformers certainly uprooted a great many traditions; furthermore, they could not avoid creating new traditions, if only a certain exegetical, sometimes literal, one.

A third factor in the enlarging of the Tradition also is related to the necessity of making it relevant to current situations. The preaching of the church creates traditions from the sole fact that it exercises a choice in regard to the deposit. It orients the deposit in a certain direction. It creates the language of piety, and favours certain biblical images at the expense of others. It gives birth to a certain style of biblical reading, and raises and maintains certain exegetical traditions. It accents the doctrinal aspect or the ethical aspect. It demythologizes in a certain fashion directed by the age and by cultural imperatives. It harmonizes or refuses to harmonize the revealed given with the image of the world that is proposed by the science of the age. It is concerned to clarify political problems, or, on the contrary, it encloses itself in a pietistic attitude. It attempts to build up the community, or it interests itself only in the individual.

In any event, these traditions which enlarge the Tradition represent an influence of the ecclesial community over the original deposit. This influence, even when it is not avowed as such, is a response to a fundamental intention, namely, the concern to avoid a fatal rupture between the original Tradition and the unfolding history. It may be said that, in a general fashion, Tradition roots the community in history and permits it to assume history, that is, to give history a meaning. But it should also be said that the traditions develop and proliferate above all when the community, rightly or wrongly, no longer feels capable of assuming the history that it lives through the means of the one Tradition. The traditions attempt to render to the Tradition the authority which it has lost, and intervene at the moment where the tradition is put in doubt (generally when a considerable lapse of time has passed since the founding event). By engrafting traditions onto the Tradition, the community attempts to breathe a new authority into it. It was when the authority of Christ the Lord, elevated to the right hand of God, was no longer felt with sufficiently grasping force that the Mariological traditions developed in Christendom. These traditions aimed to interpolate between Christ and men the reputedly closer mediation of Mary (and it is reputed to be closer because it is rooted in some completely different religious traditions that have not ceased to inhabit the sub-conscious of Christendom). As the theologians of Mariology say, the mediation of Mary does not impair that of Christ; on the contrary, it reinforces it. The theological error here is accompanied by a quite correct idea concerning the sociological process.[13]

It was inevitable that in the course of thus abrogating to itself the right of rendering to Tradition its authority, the community itself would benefit from an increase of authority. A comparative phenomenology of Protestantism and Catholicism would easily show that the ecclesiastical power in the Protestant churches has always remained relatively weak and diffuse (lack of monarchical government; power devolving upon assemblies and councils, or at least controlled by them), whereas power in Catholicism has continuously been reinforced and concentrated; it would also show that this is precisely because Protestantism, being bound to the scriptural principle, is constrained to limit the influence of the community on the Tradition and to proclaim that the traditions which it creates are relative (for example, by asserting that the confessions of faith are not *norma normans* but *norma normata*), whereas Catholicism has viewed the enlarging of the Tradition as the very mark of a living religion. Social power in the religious community grows in exact proportion to the emphasis that is placed on the importance of the act of transmitting, making explicit, and enriching tradition, rather than on the content of the Tradition itself. The constitution of a monarchical pontifical power in the Catholic church has been made necessary by the development of traditions; otherwise, the proliferation of traditions would proceed in an unregulated fashion. There is a certain (but not univocal) relationship between tradition and the magisterium: the traditions have developed the role of the magisterium, and the magisterium exercises a control over the traditions. Catholic theology speaks readily today of a living tradition, that is to say, of a tradition sustained, directed, and administered by the magisterium which is at the same time the reflection of the tradition. The idea of the apostolic succession is important to consider in this regard: it is an integral part of the Roman, Orthodox, and Anglican traditions, but at the same time it is above and beyond traditions. It constitutes a lateral chain in the traditions, and thus those who benefit from the apostolic tradition have power over the traditions, to define them, make them explicit, and check them.[14]

Of course, these remarks do not mean, as one might naïvely imagine, that the Protestant churches do not have traditions and that they have only the vertical line with the immutable Tradition. We have seen that every community is the creator of traditions. It has been due to the necessity of making the Tradition relevant and contemporary that the Protestant churches, through their preaching and teaching, also have been creators of traditions. It is even necessary that these traditions have a certain force, which is witnessed to by these churches in their relative resistance to unification attempts and in their attachment to the national framework which has been theirs since the Reformation. One can even say, without being paradoxical, that the Protestant churches are quite strongly traditionalist, because their sociological cohesion exacts this price: the absence of a monarchical magisterium that asserts its power over the traditions themselves must be compensated for by these traditions having power in and of themselves. Generally speaking, democratic communities have need of strong traditions in order to survive. They do not take well to precipitous developments. When economic, social, or ideological necessities impose a radical change on them, it is usually the democratic style and the democratic traditions of the community which bear the expense of the operation. A dictatorial power is installed which denounces the worthlessness or harmfulness of the old traditions and asserts itself as a power over these traditions; it has a new style, that is to say, it constitutes the point of departure for new traditions. To the degree that these new traditions are established, and find sympathetic reception from the community or clandestinely come into conjunction with old traditions, the dictatorial regime becomes normalized and adopts certain democratic aspects. The hardening of its traditions weakens its dictatorial virulence.

Perhaps we are witnessing such a process in the Roman Catholic church, although it is a process that unfolds much more slowly than in political societies. Monarchical authority which was strengthened over a long period of time reached its apogee between 1870 and 1950. During this period, the magisterium was affirmed as the master over traditions, in opposition to those traditional institutions which are the episcopacy and the councils. Unless contrary factors intervene, we shall undoubtedly see a certain relaxation of pontifical authority in favour of the bishops and councils. This will undoubtedly be one of the sociological significances of the Second Vatican Council.

In a general fashion, one can say that the traditions are indeed basic to the authority of the leaders; that the strongest power is that which supports itself on the traditions while at the same time channelling them to its profit; but that the traditions, when they are strong, have the effect of effacing or weakening that which is too violent, too authoritarian, or too revolutionary in the power. There is also a kind of dialectic between the power and the traditions. The power has a tendency to fight against the traditions, but to the degree that the latter remain living, the power must necessarily come to terms with them.

In this dialectic to which we have referred the power can never break away from the traditions without weakening its own bases and its own chance for survival; nor can it lord it over the traditions without at least partially submitting to them, if only in order to bring new traditions into existence which could then be grounded on the authority of the old ones.

Reason, on the other hand, directs a much more radical attack first against the traditions, then against Tradition itself. The western world, and with it Christianity, has been undergoing this crisis for several centuries. The outcome has never appeared with any clarity. To be sure, the reason that directs this critique is not an absolute and timeless thing. It is itself situated in the world of traditions: it is Aristotelian or Platonic, it is the reason of the Enlightenment or the reason of Positivism. But it presents itself as absolute and sovereign reason which, in the name of this sovereignty, sets about criticizing the Christian tradition or traditions, throwing doubt on the authenticity of these traditions, then attacking them on the basis of their claim to truth, while, at the same time, occupying itself with detaching the city from the church. In a general fashion, reason (even if it does not have the right to claim absoluteness) substitutes an attempt to take a *direct hold* on history for the attempt to become inserted in history and to assume history by means of Tradition (which is itself inserted in history and dominates it). Instead of referring to a fundamental and normative event for our faith in God, reason would like to establish "reasons" for knowing the existence of God and for considering God to be providential. It would establish these "reasons" by means which owe nothing to history, by means which are related solely to our present and timeless capacity to judge the true from the false. Evidence of this intention is found in the proofs for the existence of God and the various forms of natural theology, for which Christianity, for better or for worse, has tried to make a place.

But in fact, no community has ever succeeded in gaining this direct hold over history without the mediation of Tradition and of the traditions which derive from it. The reason which was expected to give birth to a "New Christianity" (it is not by chance that we borrow this term of Saint Simon) never succeeded in animating a religious faith, and so-called natural theology has compromised Christian theology much more than it has bolstered it up. Moreover, it is as tradition that natural theology has survived within Christian teaching, and the reason invoked by this natural theology is considered by other forms of rationality as tainted with irrationality.

Attached as it is to the idea of an essential historicity of man, Christianity can neither escape Tradition (where it discovers the meaning of this historicity, and the misfortune and the hope that are linked to it), nor eliminate once and for all the traditions that give rise to the very fruitfulness of the Tradition. Under its Catholic form, Christianity has tended to establish the strongest possible ties (often reputedly rational) between the Tradition and the traditions. The tie is a little less strong in Orthodoxy, which holds to a view that there is a cut-off point in history between the period of the authentic Tradition (corresponding to the first seven councils) and the period of aberrant and doubtful traditions. This cut-off point is made, moreover, in conjunction with the history of schisms, which implies that a Christianity regrouped and reconstituted in its unity would have more chance of maintaining itself in the times of the authentic Tradition. Protestantism, in theory, engages in a process of choosing from among the traditions in the name of the Tradition: this is both the sociological and the theological meaning which it gives to the primacy of Scripture and of the Apostolic age. Its doctrinal attention bears more on the events than on the signs that these events have left in subsequent history. But it could not prevent the living Tradition, because it is living, from giving rise to traditions. The vigilance that Protestantism takes in regard to traditions is, in theory, not a negation of traditions.

The ecumenical problem of our age is precisely that of the relation between the Tradition and the traditions, of the boundaries between these two phenomena, of the nature of the tie that unites them. Catholic tradition is more ready to make readjustments and refocusings as they are required, whereas Protestant tradition calls for a more radical and more surgical operation. Protestantism maintains that not only do the traditions obscure the meaning of the Tradition, but disjoint and pervert it as well. For example, it sees the development of Mariology as an attack on Christology, whereas Catholicism maintains that Christology is undergirded and affirmed by Mariology – the latter being a sort of presupposition and extension of the former.

Although the relation between the Tradition and traditions is a problem among the Christian churches, they at least have in common an affirmation of the Tradition, of the founding event, of the event of Christ incarnate, dead, and resurrected. And this Tradition has such a power in the various churches that, despite all the ruptures, the term "Christianity" still has a full meaning. It is not the task of a socio-phenomenology of Christianity to say whether or not this Tradition has an inalienable authority, or whether it is capable of resisting not only the various forms of historical criticism, but also the fundamental change of the human *Weltbild* in the age of science and technology. Nor has such a socio-phenomenology any criterion by which it could recognize an exceptional value in the events that took place in Palestine under Pontius Pilate and during the Apostolic age, a value that would give these events a hold over all times and over all civilizations. It can only state, without making any value judgment, that the church and theology have never in the past been totally without resources for confronting the change in morals and attitudes. It can also state that, in fact, this Tradition, this living Word, this Apostolic *paradosis* has never ceased, in the diversity of times and places, to give birth to faith and piety, to create and reform communities, to inspire movements of charity, and to give rise to hope, and, consequently, to assume history.

4. *The Formation of Doctrine and Sociological Development*

Although it is evident that the formation and growth of religious and ecclesiastical traditions are closely related to the development of community structures (and even to the development of the structures of the global society), the relationship between doctrine and sociological development often is disputed. There undoubtedly is good reason for this: the prestige that doctrine and the biblical revelation have enjoyed has contributed to their isolation, which is meant to protect them from the influences that other currents in society would have exercised over them. Yet it has never been possible for this sheltering to be complete. If it were, Christian doctrine would risk becoming an erratic block in the midst of the culture; there would no longer be any dialogue between the two. Indeed, such dialogue would be impossible, since Christian doctrine and the culture would speak a language without any terms in common. Even if the central core of biblical revelation is considered to be intangible (especially in Protestantism), it is none the less true that the doctrinal formulations which appear in the creeds and confessions of faith bear the imprint of a culture and world-view, and of the social groups that carry this culture and world-view. Thus religious sociology looks out over a vast, hardly explored field of investigation, one which includes all the socio-logical conditioning of doctrinal formulas. G. Le Bras poses the problem in the following terms:

In what society do these dogmas take shape? Even for the most orthodox and most convinced of believers, there is a problem of origin and of expression: under what influences, and to respond to what collective needs, did such and such definition intervene? And what meaning could the terms of this definition have had in the milieu of those who formed the definition (since language itself is also a social datum)?[15]

M. D. Chenu, in analysing the work of the Council of Trent, writes:

In fact, the *Mediterranean* character of the participants, the majority role played by the religious, the formulation of a *doctrina* by men experienced in university proceedings, the deliberative power of the theologians in support of the prelates, the inclination for the security of verbal definitions, the crystalliza-tion of an orthodox state of mind, the total inattention to socio-economical con-junctions which were even then transforming the earthly condition of men and the Christian comportment of the faithful: all these sociological elements, of profane origin, were woven into the conceptual-doctrinal fabric of the most theological definitions, as well as into the most religious inspirations. . . . The major business of sociology is the analysis of connections which, in various ways, condition events and decisions not only from outside but in their internal dynamics as well.[16]

It is evident that the religious consciousness encounters a certain diffi-culty in authorizing such investigations. It is a victim not only of its own respect for the religious object, but of too narrow and too scientistic a conception of sociological determinisms. It is disturbed by such things, as if they were an impiety. Consequently, we see this type of research given priority in areas that seem to touch less directly on the content of lived faith. Let us point out, for example, that sociological studies concern-ing the beliefs of the Old Testament are much more in evidence than similar studies concerning New Testament faith.[17] In the same way, in regard to Protestantism, such studies have more often been directed towards the movements parallel to the Reformation (illuminati, Anabap-tists) than towards the Reformation itself.[18] We are convinced that the method could be extended more widely.

For example, it has often been observed that the Reformation creeds, especially those of Calvinist inspiration, put strong emphasis on double predestination and almost pass over the missionary vocation; however, during the age in which they are engaged in missionary action, the teaching of the Reformation churches tends to tone down the doctrine of double predestination, or to re-evaluate it in a sense quite different from that of Calvin (e.g., P. Maury, K. Barth). One can draw a properly theological conclusion from this fact, namely, that there is a doctrinal incompatibility between a certain conception of predestination and the missionary vocation of the church. But one can also wonder (1) if the maintaining of a self-contained Christendom at the time of the Reformation did not necessarily veil this missionary vocation; and (2) if the accentuation of the doctrine of predestination did not serve as a facile explanation for the survival of a paganism on the periphery of Christendom. If these hypotheses were to be shown to be correct, this would obviously not mean that the end of Christendom deprived the doctrine of predestination of all theological significance.

Certain recent theological and historical works show quite clearly that the doctrine of the Calvinist Reformation in the area of economic and social ethics is quite strongly influenced by the great economic, technical, and social upheavals of the age. Calvin was at Geneva after the resurgence of business which was brought about by the massive influx of refugees. Thus he had a particularly fortunate sociological observation post (which Luther did not have). This helps to explain why Calvin was so attentive to the social dimension of man, and to the decisive importance that economic exchange had for the entire society. It explains why he formulated an ethic of work, an ethic of money and of wages. It explains why he declared the lending of production at interest to be legitimate, and why he did not apply to this form of lending the interdictions which the Old Testament formulated against usury. This attention to the socio-economic conjunction did not hinder Calvin seeking and finding a biblical foundation for his ethical position. But he would not have sought in that direction, nor would he have manifested such an exegetical sureness there, had he not been led by the urgencies and needs of the merchant and semi-industrial society in which he lived.[19]

Today it has become a common, and well-founded, assertion that the western church is characterized by a certain juridical outlook, in which is expressed the desire

to give their maximum consistency and perfection to the human realities which the grace of God has impregnated and charged with a divine virtue, whereas in the eastern church there is concern less with these human realities in themselves than with the divine virtue to which they have been ordered.[20]

Dumont goes on to say that this explains

the growing importance attributed in the West to the juridical aspect of things (in the order of ecclesiastical institutions and even in ethics), or the rational element in understanding and the theological formulation of revelation. In the East, on the contrary, although the juridical aspect of institutions has never been neglected (nor has the assistance of rational thought in theology), it is primarily the *sacramentality* of things that occupies attention; further, there is an awareness of the limits which the sacramental nature of things imposes on law as well as on theological reflection . . . The place attributed to the juridical element in the structure of the Catholic Church has progressively resulted in priority being given to the juridical over the sacramental.

This is certainly a correct phenomenological statement. But can we view these divergent developments in the western and eastern churches only as the consequences of doctrinal choices? Assuredly not. We are here in the presence of completely different spiritual and human climates. One could not account for this progressive opposition between the juridical and the sacramental, between the rational and the symbolic, without appealing to the data of social psychology and sociology. Everyone now recognizes that the schism of 1054, even if it used the pretext of and supported itself on doctrinal conflicts, was rooted in differences profoundly anchored in the two civilizations.

The sociological analysis of doctrinal formulations, and even more of doctrinal conflicts, promises to have a fruitful future. However, it will retain its validity only to the degree that the inverse research is not systematically eliminated, that is, the study of the influence of doctrinal content on the organization of the community, on social comportment, and even on the general structures of society.

NOTES

1. Marcel Simon, in *Hercule et le christianisme* (Paris: Les Belles Lettres, 1956) has shown how the religious consciousness of decadent paganism conferred on Hercules the titles and dignities of Christ and how a sort of Christian Hercules was created.

2. Cf. André Malet, "L'avenir de l'interprétation biblique", in *FV*, 59th Year, 1960

3. For example, see the Theses of Arnoldshain, formulated by a theological commission named by the Evangelical Church in Germany and published in 1958 by that church under the title *Abendmahlsgespräch der Evangelischen Kirche in Deutschland 1947–1957*.

4. Cf. Edmond Jacob, "La tradition historique en Israël", *ETR* (Montpellier), 1946.

5. M. Leenhardt, *Do Kamo ; La Personne et le Mythe dans le monde mélanésien* (Paris: Gallimard, 1947), pp. 232–233.

6. O. Cullmann, *Christ and Time*, trans. by F. V. Filson (Philadelphia: The Westminster Press and London: SCM Press, 1951), pp. 105–106.

7. M. Eliade, *The Myth of the Eternal Return*, p. 104.

8. ibid., p. 161.

9. Contemporary exegetical works, especially those of the *Formgeschichtliche Schule*, have shown that during the time of the primitive church, preaching as a vehicle of the tradition was not the simple transmission of a historical fact. Rather, it was an effort to give contemporaneity to the deposit. Tradition is the presentation of the Christian demand coupled with the announcement of the Good News. Preaching has a kerygmatic character. This is what Bonnard shows especially well: ". . . No matter how far back in time one goes with literary analysis, the gospel traditions preserved in the New Testament possess a kerygmatic style and content. At the origin of the process of transmission (at least as we are able to perceive it), there are no documentaries or biographies, more or less objective, concerning Jesus of Nazareth and the first days of the church. On the contrary, one is *immediately* in the presence of two significant literary facts. On the one hand, in the Synoptic Gospels there are the *logia* of Jesus. These logia are clothed in narratives, no matter how variable and even contradictory they sometimes are, that are one in giving these logia an authority based on an already developed Christology. Furthermore, the Epistles and the Acts of the Apostles contain hymnological or catechetical formulas which are really summary proclamations of faith in Christ: Jesus crucified and raised for the salvation of men. No matter how different they are one from another, the logia of the Synoptics, the most ancient passages of the Book of Acts, the catechetical or hymnological texts running through the Epistles, and even the Johannine discourses can all be held to be ecclesiastical redactions responding to the needs of the primitive catechesis and worship."

This brings us to the second characteristic of the gospel tradition: "This kerygmatic nature of the gospel tradition makes it coherent with its base, and also gives the tradition its amazing freedom. In other words, the tradition is not charged with *transmitting* a teaching of faith; rather, it is more qualified to preach, that is, to explain and to apply the common treasure of the church to the concrete needs of the very diverse communities that it was to nourish and that nourished it" (P. Bonnard, "La Tradition dans le Nouveau Testament", *RHPR*, 40th Year, 1960, no. 1, pp. 21–22).

10. Cf. F. J. Leenhardt, *La Parole et le Buisson de Feu* (Neuchâtel: Delachaux et Niestlé, 1962).

11. This has been noted by Lestringant: ". . . how can Catholicism respond to this vocation of religious universalism if not by welcoming, century after century, the supports of tradition in order to preserve them? Whether it be a matter of Jewish legalism, of Neoplatonic mysticism, of the juridical mind of Rome, of the thought of Aristotle, of Bergsonian philosophy, or more simply the piety that is attached to each new saint, its order of the day can never be anything but to place in juxtaposition that which history successively offers it. In order for nothing to be lost, it must integrate everything. Each day it must offer its faithful the spectacle of a vast recuperation. The credit given to the transmission of religious forms is not, therefore, one element among many of the life of Catholicism. Tradition is the means of its universalism and the genesis of its faith" ("Tradition catholique et Tradition protestante", *FV*, 44th Year, 1946, no. 7, p. 747).

12. *Des Constitutions politiques et autres institutions humaines*, ed. by R. Triomphe (Paris: Les Belles Lettres, 1959), p. 35. In the same spirit, de Maistre wrote: "The church is not at all argumentative by nature. It believes without disputing . . . But if someone contests some doctrine, it leaves its natural state. Being foreign to any contentious idea, it seeks the basis of the contested doctrine. It interrogates the tradition. It creates words everywhere, of which its good faith has no need but which have

become necessary in order to characterize the doctrine and to put an eternal barrier between us and the innovators" (*Du Pape*, 1/1). It is significant that this text is cited in the conclusion of the article "Tradition" (by A. Michel) in the *Dictionnaire de théologie catholique*.

13. Of course, we do not argue that there has been a theological evolution of mariology beginning with the doctrine of Chalcedon and that this evolution has been relatively autonomous. But we should not forget the proliferation of mariological beliefs on the level of popular piety that have been progressively integrated by the theologians.

14. Cf. M. J. Le Guillou, "Plénitude de catholicité et oecuménisme", *Istina*, 1959, no. 3, p. 273.

15. G. Le Bras, "Réflexions sur les différences entre sociologie scientifique et sociologie pastorale", *ASR*, no. 8, July–December, 1959.

16. M. D. Chenu, "Vie conciliare de l'Eglise et sociologie de la foi", *Esprit*, new series, December 1961, no. 12.

17. For a perceptive and lucid example of the sociological analysis of the faith of ancient Israel, see the study by H. H. Féret, "La mort dans la tradition biblique", in *Le Mystère de la mort et sa célébration* (Paris: Editions du Cerf, 1951).

18. However, we should mention the fine studies of Norman Birnbaum on the Reformation at Zurich ("The Zwinglian Reformation in Zurich", *ASR*, no. 8, December 1959).

19. For more precise details, see the works of André Biéler, *La pensée économique et sociale de Calvin* (Geneva: Georg, 1959), and *The Social Humanism of Calvin*, trans. by Paul Fuhrmann (Richmond, Va.: John Knox Press, 1964).

20. C. J. Dumont, "Catholiques et orthodoxes à la veille du Concile", *Istina*, 1961–1962, no. 2, April 1962.

VI

Religious Practice

1. *Practice and Beliefs*

It is not altogether obvious that the study of religious practice should follow that of doctrine and beliefs. If there is anything that sociology and the history of religions have clearly demonstrated, it is the subordination of myth to ritual. Ritual, the ensemble of practices, comes first, and myth elucidates, amplifies, and sometimes rationalizes the meaning of ritual. The gestural origin of myth has been advanced: the mythic account is only the development of a significant gesture.[1] We do not claim that this theory is inadequate in a sociology of Christianity. It is remarkable that the New Testament account of the institution of the Lord's Supper gives secondary place to doctrine; the Lord completes a certain number of gestures (the breaking of bread and the blessing of the cup), and then gives an order instituting a practice: "Do this in remembrance of me" (Luke 22.20). To be sure, the gesture is accompanied by a word which reveals its meaning: "This is my body . . . This cup . . . is the new covenant . . ." (Luke 22.19, 20). But these words constitute only the seed of one or another of several possible doctrines. They designate the mystery contained in or tied to the ritual; they do not constitute an explanation. Moreover, all doctrines of the Lord's Supper are constituted on the basis of the gesture and order of the Lord. The ritual does not arise as a means of illustrating a doctrine of the presence of Christ. Quite the contrary, it is the doctrine which would later be induced by the community on the basis of the celebration itself. Consequently, we do not deny that in regard to Christianity, one can verify the thesis of the priority of practice over doctrine and beliefs.

Yet Christianity as a whole did not appear in a sort of doctrinal void. It appeared in the midst of a people who practised a scriptural religion. And the two poles of this religion were the Revelation of God in a Word and in a Law, and the expectation of a messianic and eschatological fulfilment. Christ appeared as the living Word, the incarnate Law, the fulfilment of eschatology. In short, the background of the Christian revelation is a coherent doctrinal ensemble; the event comes to confirm the doctrine, to makes its truth apparent. Thus Christian preaching will always support itself on the Law and the Prophets, on the historical doctrine which alone renders the mystery of the event intelligible. Thus it is not by chance that Christianity developed under a doctrinal form and that teaching and preaching played an essential role in its diffusion and maintenance. The encounter of Christianity with pagan philosophy, with the entrance of pagan intellectuals into the Church, would accentuate this character. Moreover, Christianity had to defend itself against the temptation for magic, ritual, and practice to have value in and of themselves (it defended itself with variable success); consequently, it was important for it to keep ritual from becoming isolated, from cutting itself off from the doctrinal Word which clarifies it and refers it back to the only efficacious Word. This explains the importance of the magisterium of doctors in the entire Christian church and the fact that priests and pastors, especially since the sixteenth century, have been given a teaching function. The essential practice in Christianity is *worship*. But worship is penetrated in its liturgy and its preaching with doctrinal elements; each gesture in worship receives a doctrinal explanation and justification. This is why it does not seem invalid to place the sociological study of practice after that of doctrine.[2]

2. *The Domain of Practice*

In any case, these considerations should not make us minimize the importance of practice in Christianity, for its domain is considerable. On the one hand, it includes the public practice of the assembled community; on the other hand, it covers the private practice of individuals and families, which is subordinated to and controlled by the former. Family worship and personal prayer are guided by the instruments which the ecclesiastical authorities put into the hands of the faithful (for instance, prayer and hymn books, missals, rosaries, tables of biblical readings, etc.).

The field of practice can be extended even more (and this is a characteristic of Christianity and of Judaism). In effect, the God to whom worship is rendered and to whom prayers are addressed is a holy and demanding God. The worship service is the occasion on which he reveals to us this demanding will; the reasonable worship pleasing to God is that of the

offering of a living sacrifice, of the sacrifice of the entire person who
stands before God to do his will. Christianity has contributed the idea of
service to the world of worship (cf. the expressions "service divin",
"office", "worship", "Gottesdienst"). Worship, thus, must be extended
in service, service conforming to the summary of the Law, that is to say,
service of love in regard to God and in regard to men. All that one calls
"the Christian life", with all its ethical components, is thus integrated
with practice in Christianity. Christianity, following the example of
Judaism, has never ceased to denounce the formalism and vanity of a
purely ecclesiastical action, one that would have no extension into daily life.
This concern has even created a conflict during certain periods between
ecclesiastical and ceremonial practice and ethical practice. Already in
Judaism, the prophet Amos set in opposition the hate and disgust of the
Eternal for feasts, assemblies, burnt offerings, and the noise of songs, and
his love of justice and righteousness (Amos 5.21–25). And the same theme
reappears in the invectives of the Reformers in regard to the "Papist
ceremonies" and the practices of monachal asceticism (in a general way,
Luther denounced in monachism a weakness regarding the need of God's
love).[3] And it should not be forgotten that, in Catholicism, the contemporary movement of purification, of liturgical simplification, of the decline
of the religion of the rosary, have been preceded by the whole movement
of social catholicism, of Catholic Action, in short, of movements that tend to
give practice its social dimensions. One can say that this extension of
practice to the totality of the believer's existence corresponds in Christianity to the fundamental refusal (although often forgotten) of making a distinction and an opposition between the sacred and the profane.

A sociology of Christianity could never forget the fact that practice
goes far beyond the bounds of rite and ceremony. But it is true, however,
that it scarcely has the means of observing this practice when it takes the
form of individual piety, of spiritual devotion, or of charitable and secret
action. Practice in the ecclesiastical sense remains the most objective
aspect of practice, the aspect on which science has seized. It is, in the
words of Le Bras, "the accountable element of Christianity".[4]

Once again, a distinction should be made here between Catholicism and
Protestantism. In Catholicism, canon law has become considerably more
broad and juridically more precise, fixing the cultic, sacramental, and
moral precepts to which a good Christian should submit and requiring the
curé to maintain a *Liber status animarum* in which are recorded the acts of
religious practice of each of his parishioners. Protestantism, on the other
hand, admits of only elements of canon law. But even these elements

concern scarcely more than the practice of the ecclesiastical institution and, when they concern the faithful, have more of a negative character; forbidding of non-baptized persons to participate in the Lord's Supper, very rare cases of excommunication, forbidding of marriages during certain periods, etc. This absence of organized canon law betrays the fear of Protestantism that acts of practice take on a value for themselves and take on a meritorious value, thus becoming accountable elements not only in the sociological sense but in the religious sense as well. Consequently, the sociology of Protestantism cannot be fashioned on the same bases as the sociology of Catholicism. For Catholicism, practice corresponds to an ensemble of well-defined acts whose non-fulfilment puts the salvation of the faithful in question; for Protestantism, practice consists both in acts and in attitudes which are the often unforeseeable and non-codifiable responses of faith to God's grace. They are not conditions of salvation, but consequences of salvation. This is why Protestantism is loath to make them something to be reckoned. The only thing which Protestantism considers legitimate is the recording of the acts of communal practice: the numbers of those present at worship, variations in the number present on ordinary Sundays as against the number present on feast Sundays, the number of participants in the Lord's Supper, the size of offerings, the volume of offerings for mission, etc. But it is obvious that these data, although Protestantism attaches a less absolute value to them than Catholicism does, still provide a means of determining the religious vitality of the community and make it possible to sketch a religious profile of the community.

Again, it is necessary here to know how to interpret the statistics and not to claim that they say more than they do. It is a sociologist of Catholicism, a Catholic himself, Gabriel Le Bras, who puts us on guard against too absolute a confidence in the statistics of religious practice.

Practice is far from revealing the whole religious vitality of a nation, parish, or individual. Above all, Christianity is a life of the soul; the feeling which it awakens towards God and the neighbour, the acts which it calls forth constitute its originality. Now, religious practice makes us presume the love of God and lets us ignore the practice of virtue. It does not at all assure fidelity to custom, since the church-goer from the provinces becomes a simple conformist once transplanted to Paris. Individual practice is all the less rooted in the individual as it is more generalized in his group. Thus it is necessary to look further afield.[5]

The very immensity of the field of practice makes it difficult to discern the truly decisive areas there.

Can one envisage a classification of religious practices? Here again we will see that this classification differs according to the Christian denominations. Le Bras proposes the following principles:

The classification of the acts of sacramental and cultic life is easily made on the basis of their frequency. There are *solemn* acts which introduce to a group or to a state: baptism, first communion, marriage, burial. There are *periodical* acts whose regularity attests to orthodoxy, maintains submission, vitalizes prayer: each week the Sunday mass, each year the confession and Easter communion . . . Finally, there are *exceptional* or *repeated* acts, which express and heighten devotion: on the one hand, pilgrimages, retreats, consecrations; on the other hand, attendance at daily mass, at minor offices and processions, frequent communion . . . In fact, from the first surveys, it became increasingly certain that the great majority of Christians can be grouped into three categories: they are conformists, seasonals, observants, or devout according to the way in which they regard the solemn, periodical, or exceptional acts.[6]

Is such a schema entirely valid for Protestantism? We doubt it for several reasons. For one thing, the gamut of acts of religious practice is infinitely less diversified and less codified in Protestantism. Secondly, Protestantism does not accept the Catholic distinction between the necessary and the supererogatory, between a minimal practice and a meritorious practice. Finally, Protestantism does not attach a particular value to the repetition of certain acts. To be sure, the constant effort of the Reformers from the very first was to integrate communion into the Sunday service. To the degree that the Lord's Supper was no longer viewed as a pure symbol or a pure memorial, it effectively became more frequent. Yet it never became a weekly observance, except in certain limited groups. For one thing, this tendency encountered many more or less justified obstacles, and secondly, it never occurred to ecclesiastical authorities to make weekly participation in the Lord's Supper the indispensable sign of true piety.

In other words, although Protestantism does not come under the same general categories of religious practice that Catholicism does, it is not because Protestantism does not have the same groups of church-goers such as Le Bras has delineated. It is that practice does not have the same meaning for Protestantism that it has for Catholicism. The latter views practices as the necessary consequences of belonging to an institution which decrees the rules of salvation. For Protestantism, practice is more directly related to the spontaneity of faith. It is less the consequence of belonging to an ecclesiastical institution than the consequences of belonging, known in faith, to the Body of Christ. It is more related to the awareness of the grace which is given to us through participation in worship, in communion, and in all the activities of the church. Submission to the salutary prescriptions of the church versus the spontaneity of faith: these two types of attitudes should not be set over against each other in an absolute way, as though the first were exclusively Catholic and the second exclusively Protestant. Both are encountered in the two confessions. But Catholic practice is coloured more strongly by the one, and Protestant practice more strongly by the other.

This thesis, moreover, can be demonstrated. Let us take the example of the region of Alsace. We choose this region by design, because, to a certain degree, Alsace is still a region of Christendom, the two confessions are strongly established there, the number of non-attached is not very high, and, finally, the religious practice in the two confessions is supported on firm family traditions. The statistics of the practice of religion give us figures much higher for Catholicism than for Protestantism: Catholic practice averages around 35 per cent; Protestant practice only around 12 per cent (in both cases, we will consider only participation in services and worship). A simple comparison of figures for Sunday practice should make us conclude that there is much stronger vitality on the Catholic side than on the Protestant side. Without going into the root of the problem, we would say that the comparison of the figures in question is not sufficient, because practice does not have the same meaning for Catholics and Protestants and, consequently, does not inspire the same sentiments. For the Catholic practice increases his chances of salvation; for the Protestant, there are no means of obtaining salvation. Participation in worship is a grace given to him: from the doctrinal and moral point of view, abstention from worship is indeed an infidelity and a culpable thing, but presence at worship does not mean that this salvation is assured. Thus it is undoubtedly easier for the Protestant to neglect duties which have a strict value for the Catholic. Although deficiency in practice is truly an alarming sign for Protestantism, it is even more alarming for Catholicism.

These differences in practice thus bring us to different ideas concerning the very nature of worship. Undoubtedly worship could be initially defined in a fashion valid for all forms of Christianity. As the *Dictionary of Catholic Theology*[7] points out, among Christian theologians there is a certain consensus which enables worship to be generally defined as "a mark of submission in recognition of the superiority and excellence of someone". Christian worship is primarily the act by which the assembled community expresses its obedience and its recognition for the excellence of the work of salvation that God brings about. Far from being the expectation of a theophany, of a new and miraculous event, worship is the collective expression of an already-existing faith:

The man who yields himself to worship [writes R. Will] is already faithful and he is faithful because God has awakened his faith.[8]

However, the aspect of expectation and seeking cannot be excluded from the phenomenology of Christian worship: the faithful expects a new grace from worship, a new witness of the benevolence of God, a strengthening of his faith. "Because eternal reality is found," writes R. Will, "it asks that we seek it with new ardour." God makes himself known to the faithful in worship: although there is no new revelation, there is a witness to revelation; although there is no new objective revelation of God, at least the faithful can have the individual discovery – for him – of the reality of revelation. The Word of God proclaimed in worship thus becomes an event. It is as though the congregation heard it for the first time. It has a new presence and perhaps a new meaning in relation to the situation in which the community and the faithful now find themselves. Such is the relationship of Christian worship to *mystery*: the proclaimed Word of God unveils its own mystery. This is the source of the various emotional phenomena brought about by worship, of which the highest undoubtedly is ecstasy but which can also take the form of all sorts of unsettled phenomena. Christian worship oscillates between these two poles: the action of submission in recognition (which implies sacrifice on the part of the faithful, offering of faith and of the body) and mystery. Christianity is characterized by this permanent tension of worship between sacrifice and mystery, the one imitating the other, the one orienting the other. Sacrifice, being *act* of humiliation and obedience, keeps the community from being completely absorbed by mystical contemplation, from being plunged into the expectation of a new revelation. Faith is manifested under the form of obedience, and contemplation is more oriented towards what God has already done, towards the sacrifice that God has already accomplished and which motivates our sacrifice of gratefulness. Although the mystery is thus limited by the present aspect of worship, it does turn the community from all activism. In worship, such activism necessarily would take the form of a ritualism, which would risk degenerating into magic. The idea that God is the subject of worship, that he makes his presence real in an eminent or particular way in worship, that it is the living Word which makes us penetrate his own mystery, orients worship towards contemplation, towards knowledge, towards recognition (in the noetic as well as the ethical sense of the word) of the action which God has done for men. In Christianity, as well as in all religions, worship is action, even when it is mystery: in the language of the New Testament, sacrament and mystery are one and the same thing. But it is action in a very special sense. As R. Will expresses it:

In the *sacramentalia* and in the sacrament, the sacred action is a service, *ministerium* or *officium*. For, in worship, the *agens* properly speaking is neither man nor the human communion. It is the holy power, whether it be a question simply of the holy community or of a holy will. "To do", "to act", in the cultic sense, is always sacramental ... A person does other and more than he accomplishes, he handles things which he does not dominate, he is *in* a holy action, not above it ... In this sense, cultic action is a *representative* action, not in the sense which Schleiermacher attributed to this word (symbolic representation of the faith possessed), but in the much more profoundly established sense of the representation of the original and holy action. *It is done* or *God does*: in both cases, man can only repeat, renew, "follow", "represent". Cultic action is always function and representation ... The priest acts and speaks "in the name of Jesus". In reality the one who has the word and who is the unique *actor* is God.[9]

The act of God acting in history is the axis of this cultic representation. It is not unrelated to theatrical representation (the religious origin and significance of the theatre is well known), where it also is a matter of attesting to the permanence of the sense of drama, of reproducing an ancient gesture which conserves its value, without for that reason the actors being really the authors. In short, in Christian worship it is a matter of *gesta Dei*, which are the living Word.

In Christianity [writes van der Leeuw] the ἱερὸς λόγος occupies the very centre of worship, in the cycle of its constantly recurring celebrations which, theoretically, repeat the typological history of Christ. Repetition transfers to the life of the church the potentiality of that history.[10]

The tie between worship and the unfolding of the church year, the insertion of worship in a liturgy developing in different stages, indeed show that worship is tied to the action which unfolded at the time of Christ. Worship repeats a history precisely in order for the faithful to be integrated into it, in order for him to take part in it, in order for the ὑπὲρ ἡμῶν, which is the vector of all the acts done by Christ, to be received as true by the faithful: To be sure, on the occasion of this action into which he is inserted, the faithful must also be instructed. Christian worship is characterized by a didactic aspect, which is emphasized by the sermon, but it is not a matter of a διδαχή pure and simple. The church is not the school. Rather, it is exercise, *Einübung im Christentum*. And the truth of the sermon rests less with its didactic qualities, with the tightness of its logic, than with its constant reference to the action represented in the whole worship. Here the διδαχή is a kerygmatic proclamation, a "living preaching" (Calvin), a *viva vox Evangelii* (Luther), that is to say, the instructive word is itself action which reaches a living being, transforms him, wrests him from his own history in order to make him participant in another history, in order to insert him ἐν Χριστῷ. It sometimes happens that in certain over-intellectual periods (theological liberalism was a form of intellectualism), the character of the lesson or of the "lecture" dominates and the very nature of worship is lost sight of. This is a danger especially for Protestantism, but the worship lecture results in rapidly becoming void of substance. Worship is not instruction on a religious subject. The biblical text is not the theme of a dissertation, but the guarantee that the word of preaching is not only the autonomous unfolding of a system of thought (even if it be a theological system) but the proclamation of the masterwork of God which is accomplished for the faithful.

Such is the general arrangement of Christian worship, where the sacrifice of gratefulness and of obedience and unveiled mystery is ordered according to a sovereign act, the act of that God to whom, precisely, the faithful pray that he act: "Be pleased, O God, to deliver me! O Lord, make haste to help me!" (Ps. 70.1).

But the various Christian confessions have introduced variations on the very basis of this arrangement. It is possible to construct a typology of Christian forms of worship and to see how various confessional orientations of worship derive from the basic schema.

Protestant worship has placed much emphasis on the overshadowing of all human participants. This concern is manifested by the refusal to confer a special quality on the officiant, to turn the officiating clergyman into a priest who possesses a special power which renders him a participant in the divine act in a way different from the other faithful. This is the source of Protestant prudence regarding the utilization of formulas of absolution and blessing. The officiating clergyman is restricted to inviting the faithful to receive a pardon and a blessing of which God alone is the agent. This is also the source of the relative poverty of the officiating clergyman's gestures (the return of the sign of the cross is encountering quite strong resistance, because of the pious fear that with the sign of the cross the clergyman is raising himself to the rank of a priest who performs a sacred sign on the faithful). This is also the source of the insistence of Protestant piety on the communal aspect of the Lord's Supper (the body of Christ takes form there), and on its *commemorative* and *kerygmatic* aspect. It is commemorative not in the symbolic sense (attributed rightly or wrongly to Zwingli), but in the sense of repristination or anamnesis of the event of the Lord's death: it is affirmed that the event has not at all been effaced. It is kerygmatic in the sense that the celebration truly constitutes the community's proclamation of the Lord's death and his return. Finally, this Protestant concern to overshadow all human participants is the source of the divisions and uncertainties of Protestantism concerning the real presence of the Lord at the time of the celebration of the Lord's Supper. The difficulty does not concern belief in the real presence, but how to formulate it dogmatically. The very diversity of formulas used and their difficult nature to understand (for example, consubstantiation) clearly and even vigorously shows that Protestant piety has refused to follow Catholic piety. The latter, by accentuating the present aspect of the Eucharistic sacrifice and tying it to the fulfilment of certain rituals (consecration of the species, reservation of the species) inevitably tends to give the priest an essential role in worship. The celebrant is turned into an agent and an author: without him, without the rituals which he performs and the words which he pronounces, the ceremony is not valid, in the same way that a baptism is not valid if the Trinitarian formula has not been pronounced at the very moment that the water flows over the candidate for baptism. All these Protestant hesitations prove that piety fears a drift towards a sacrifice which would not only be commemorated, represented, made present in a commemoration, but which would somehow be accomplished again, so that worship, as in a pagan mystery, would become a present accomplishment and not the proclamation of something accomplished once and for all by the divine subject.

Of course, Protestant piety has not always been able to maintain itself at the level of its own scruples; the drift was too easy. The idea that only an ordained minister can validly administer (this word has lost its etymological meaning) the sacrament is widespread. Lutheran consubstantiation has experienced certain drifts towards transubstantiation, not on the doctrinal level, but from the sole fact of the practice of reserving the species.[11] But the doctrines, for all their ambiguity and uncertainty, reveal a tendency in Protestant piety by which worship is coloured by a nuance not present in other forms of Christianity. The Protestant does not attend the Lord's Supper with the idea that, whether he wants it or not, there is objectively an operation produced to which he is ritually associated. The eyes of faith perceive what is promised to it; the presence of Christ is produced neither by certain gestures nor by certain words. It is given and communicated only in the act of faith. Certainly this is a difficult position to hold, as is attested by the drifting of Protestant thought towards either an attitude of sacramental realism or a pure symbolism. But this position also gives Protestant piety its particular character. It does not see the elements of the Lord's Supper as something sacred which must be handled with particular precautions. Yet it does enclose the Supper in a special respect. It gives the Lord's Supper more solemnity than an ordinary worship service (the Eucharist generally, but not exclusively, is celebrated on feast days), although it knows that the presence which is given in the sacrament is not in itself different from the presence given in the Word.

The nature of piety governs practice. Consequently, Protestant practice will have an aspect less ritualistic, less tainted with magic and superstition than in other forms of Christianity. It is more tied to the spontaneity of the religious life than in Catholicism. According to Gabriel Le Bras (analysed by H. Desroche), practice in Catholicism appears as a middle area, an intermediate zone between

the zones of more or less creative spontaneity (for example, the zone of individual prayer or of mystical contemplation) . . . and the formal regions of ecclesiological organization and conscience.[12]

Participation in the Lord's Supper, in worship in general, is certainly a duty formulated by the disciplines of the Protestant churches. But this is not a canonical prescription, in the sense that its observation does not determine salvation and rejection. The very term "means of grace" which the Reformers took from Catholic thought is coloured, thus, with a new meaning in Protestantism. The sociologist should be aware of this; the observation of cultic practice does not provide as perfect a means as in Catholicism for analysing the religious vitality of a Protestant group.

Catholic worship receives its particular coloration from the *mass*, that is to say, from the Eucharistic sacrifice. The words of institution which are related fundamentally to the elements bring about what they proclaim because they are pronounced by Christ himself or, more exactly, by the priest to whom Christ delegates his power. Christ giving his body and blood becomes present by the fact that these words are said. What happens in transubstantiation is certainly not a repetition of the sacrifice accomplished once and for all on the cross, but a kind of real reactivation of the act accomplished by Christ on the cross. The Catholic church has not pronounced on the relation between the historical sacrifice accomplished on the cross and the sacramental sacrifice, and considers it an open question.[13] In the proper sense, it is not the priest who brings about the effect, but the words pronounced by the priest who is ordained in the apostolic succession. The operation of man is not so much in the miracle of transubstantiation as in the fact that this presence of the crucified Christ, given by himself, is offered to God in sacrifice by the community (priests and faithful). Thus the community becomes a participant in the sacrifice of Christ; it indeed exercises a sort of priesthood. In Protestantism, on the other hand, it is the sacrifice of thanksgiving (with all its implications for personal sacrifices) which links the community to the sacrifice and offering which Christ alone accomplishes.

Consequently, Catholic piety (which undoubtedly is closer to that of Israel during the Temple period) has more of a sense of sacred action and of present action than has Protestant piety. Catholic piety is less tied than Protestant piety to history, to the unique, unrepeatable element of holy history. In short, it is essentially a sacramental piety. Of the two sides of Christian worship, Word and sacrament, it gives primacy to sacrament. It moves from sacrament to Word (whereas Protestant piety goes from Word to sacrament) and does not easily tolerate a worship service which is not the unfolding of a sacramental act. Catholic piety is nourished by the celebration of a mystery, with which the faithful want to become contemporaneous.[14] It is at the very moment of the celebration that, with Christ, they offer to God the actual sacrifice of Christ himself. For Catholics, the *church* is less the body of Christ, in submission to the head, than it is Christ himself. The Catholic idea of *Integer Christus* is Jesus and his church. At the moment of the Eucharistic sacrifice the faithful is inserted into Christ; this is not essentially insertion by faith, but sacramental, effected insertion.

Thus the term "practice" takes on its full meaning: it is truly a praxis, an efficacious act which, at the extreme, can give value by itself. It is a mode of sacralization. This is why this practice can be defined with a juridical precision and codified. No matter what, there is a minimum of practice required (for example, an annual communion). The Catholic is conscious of doing something, whereas the Protestant is conscious, rather, of receiving gratuitously without doing anything. Consequently, Catholic practice is infinitely better observable and countable for the sociologist than Protestant practice is. The latter puts a kind of limit to certain forms of sociological inquiry. The source of this limit is found in *sola fide*.

Orthodox worship is similar in many regards to Catholic worship. However, there are a certain number of nuances which make Orthodox worship distinctive. For one thing, Orthodoxy has a more continuous interpenetration of theology and the mystical life:

Far from being in opposition, theology and the mystical support each other and are mutually complementary. One is impossible without the other. The mystical experience gives a personal value to the content of the common faith; theology is an expression, for the use of all, of that which can be experienced by each person.[15]

This alliance between the mystical and theology means that worship (through the celebration of the liturgy and the various sacraments) is a process in which the growth of the person is realized effectively up to his perfect stature (a growth which Protestantism sees primarily under an ethical form). An Orthodox theologian qualifies this liturgy as follows: it is

an ever-alive, dramatic liturgy which has served as the only refuge for all theology and all church life during the centuries of decadence and which has shown itself able to preserve what is essential in the Christian message. Whatever be the age or the conditions in which it lives, the Orthodox Christian, in entering the temple, will be conscious of finding there heaven descended on earth, the Kingdom of God already present. He will know that Christ is present there in the sacramental communion in his Body and Blood, in the Gospel read by the priest, in the prayer of the church.[16]

Thus worship in Orthodoxy is a sort of parousia. Here, also, the historical element is abolished, or at least veiled, but it is a matter less of the history separating us from the events of the gospel than of the history separating us from the coming of the kingdom. Consequently, Orthodox piety, influenced by the powerful movement of "Hesychasm" (quietude or contemplation) born in the fourth century, considers that it is fulfilled only in deification. As Maximus the Confessor wrote:

Man becomes God by deification. He fully enjoys the relinquishment of all that which is his by nature . . . because the grace of the Spirit triumphs in him and because God alone, manifestly, acts in him. Thus God and those who are worthy of God are nothing but one and the same activity in all things.[17]

Although the above passage concerns the summits of Orthodox piety, one can say that liturgy and prayer have a deifying value for Orthodoxy. Thus practice has a more mystical import, and is less comprehensible through juridical categories. Although we know of sociological studies of Orthodoxy (and the eastern church undoubtedly would feel repugnance for them), it is presumable that practice in Orthodoxy is less of a countable element than it is in Catholicism, where the juridical mind of the Latin world has played a considerable role.

In order to understand the practice in a church, it is necessary to go back to the cultic archetypes which belong to it. It is these archetypes which determine the style of practice and which make it possible to develop variable methods for studying practice.

It is still necessary to emphasize a very profound difference between

Protestant practice and Catholic practice. Catholic practice is constituted of defined canonical acts, with well-determined contours and having a certain degree of value by themselves. Thus it will be essential that these acts be accomplished. On the other hand, the church is one single body, the framework of which is constituted by the hierarchy (and the church is not really the church except in this hierarchical catholicity). Consequently, the local parish will have only a secondary importance: there is no trace of congregationalism in Catholicism. The reality and the authority of the local community were not defined at the time of the Vatican Council of 1870.[18] And since the fight against the Church of England and Gallicanism, the Catholic church has consistently tried to reduce all particularities and tendencies towards autonomy of the national churches. These two inter-related causes explain why the Catholic member is theoretically less integrated into a parish than the Protestant member. For the Protestant, the church is present in its fullness wherever the Word is preached and wherever the sacraments are administered, that is to say, it is fully a reality in the local parish. This is the source of the congregationalist tendencies inherent in Protestantism. This is the source of its relative insensitivity to the problem of church unity, a problem which it has taken more than three centuries to discover.

On the contrary, the Protestant is theoretically more attached to his parish than the Catholic is, and ties his practice to his participation in the life of his parish.[19] All of this is true, of course, only in principle. In actual fact, for emotional reasons the Catholic manifests just as much attachment and generosity in regard to his parish, to the church building, to his pastor, as the Protestant does. But a profound modification is manifested in the practice of the Catholic whenever the social conditions of his life change or when his habitat loses its importance, or when the parish no longer coincides with the city. According to surveys made by Fichter, to which we have already made allusion, the religious practice of citizens of large cities and their participation in parish life at the present time constitute independent variables: although the member who is active in his parish and in religious work is a regular church-goer, the contrary is not true. It is not at all necessary for a parishioner to be integrated into the social institution of the parish in order to remain faithful to his religious duties. The member practises in any sanctuary whatever, and many authentic Catholics even practise in small sanctuaries (convent chapels, for instance) which are not even parishes. The phenomenon is not limited to America. The development of leisure-time activities, of winter sports, of week-end practices, which are increasingly important in urban, middle-class circles, mean that many members are regularly absent from their parish on Sunday. Yet they remain regular in their church attendance. The colossal size of parishes in the large cities make them ill-suited to being communities, and the relations between priests and faithful are extremely lax. Practically speaking, the priest approaches the families only on the occasion of surplice fees. Such events, again, are essentially of the nature of a rite and can be celebrated without any personal relation being established between the priest and the faithful. Even in smaller communities (the hospital, for example), it is quite easy to see that there is a clear distinction between the ritual and sacramental act of the priest, which is one thing, and his occasional personal relations with the sick person, which are another thing. The very rules of auricular confession amaze the Protestant, for he sees in them a phenomenon which is unthinkable for him, namely, a pastoral counsellor *in incognito*, a pastor without personal relationship. Consequently, the person of the priest plays a much less important role for the faithful than in Protestantism. The essential thing is that the priest be regularly ordained, in order that his presence render the practice valid and efficacious. This is strikingly expressed in Graham Greene's novel, *The Power and the Glory*. The absence of the priest at least renders practice uncertain, whatever be the religious fervour expressed (as is shown in Quéfelec's novel, *Le recteur de L'île de Sein*). Bernanos has not ceased to be an admirable Christian, a quite regular church-goer, respectful and submissive to the hierarchy of his church, while at the same time subjecting to abuse some of the highest dignitaries of his church (cf. *Les grands cimetières sous la lune*). Here we are in the presence of some type of law of Catholic practice: it consists of canonically defined acts which certainly presuppose fervour, piety, and faith, but to which these elements are not sufficient to confer validity. To be sure, the Catholic church has unceasingly fought against the danger of ritualism, but it could not completely avoid it.

Protestant practice, on the contrary, is inseparable from integration into the life of the community. The Protestant faithful is not one who adds devotions to ordinary practices, but one who participates in the life, witness, and charitable action of the community. Consequently, one is more easily outside the church in Protestantism than in Catholicism, and Protestant statistics have a more severe and more abrupt nature than those of Catholicism. Of course, Protestant churches in urban areas have the same problem that Catholicism has: parishes too voluminous to be communities, absence of structures which favour the birth of a community, worship services which turn into audiences. The sometimes too-didactic nature of Protestant worship accentuates this auditorium aspect. But the circumspection of private communion, and sometimes (for example, at the time of the Reformation) the refusal to give the Lord's Supper in private, the present tendency to integrate baptism into the worship of the community, have brought out a profound tendency in Protestantism, namely, the tendency to build up living parishes in which practice is the occasion of giving form to the community. The role traditionally given to the preaching of the word is precisely that of forming this community. The very divisions of Protestantism witness to this concern to consider as belonging to the church only those who visibly can be attached to the community. This, finally, is the source of the Protestant tendency to consider the unity which results solely from the presence of a hierarchy and of a unity of discipline as an artificial unity.

One of the characteristics of the churches of the Reformation is that of having developed a ministry of counselling having a clearly personal aspect; the relationship of pastor to faithful is decisive here. The pastor is not only the man who officiates in a sanctuary. He is also one who visits his members and seeks to call them to a personal involvement, which is the very mark of true practice in the eyes of Protestantism. Naturally, the result of this is a sort of excessive personalism: the life of the parishes often is very dependent on the personality of the pastor.

Despite all these permanent resemblances which exist among Christian churches, Catholic practice and Protestant practice are difficult things to compare because they lack a common denominator. The opposition which is evident between Catholicism and Protestantism on the doctrinal level (for example, regarding the question of good works) is rooted in a difference that is perhaps more basic, in the very conception of practice.

3. The Social Factors of Practice

Although the forms of practice are grounded in a doctrine of worship and consequently in a theology, being traditional, they also participate in all the manifestations of tradition: the doctrine preserved by the clergy is less exposed than practice to all the influences of the social milieu; doctrine is more open to the critical and purifying effort of theologians than practice, over which doctrinal teaching has little hold. It even happens that a practice, in becoming more general, shapes a doctrinal development, such as is the case in Catholicism in regard to the formation of Mariological dogma. Although Protestantism does not present such a clear example of a dogma progressively produced by practice, the fact should not be overlooked that a certain coloration of doctrinal truths can come from practice.

As an example, the funerary character given to the Lord's Supper in certain Protestant churches (especially on Good Friday) has succeeded in reflecting on the very nature of the sacrament and has substituted a theology of the blood (attested by our hymns) for a theology of the cross.

What social factors are capable of making variations in practice, of augmenting it or rarefying it? Several recent surveys have dealt with this question.

The most spectacular fact is the variation of practice according to membership in the various social classes. Thus it seems that what men expect from the church is determined by their appurtenance to the various social classes: the member of the well-to-do class, assured of his well-being here below, wants the church to assure his salvation in the beyond; the proletarian who still has his temporal "salvation" to accomplish wants the church to take positions concerning the realities of this world; the lower middle-class persons, who are progressing upward and who need to be sustained in their hopes, are rather satisfied with the present form of the church, for it represents their means of being integrated into the bourgeoisie.[20] With only a few qualifications regarding the interpretation of the idea of salvation, it would be possible to apply this diagnosis to the Protestant social classes. This social variation of religious practice is spectacular because today it is general. In the sixteenth century, practice was homogeneous in all classes of society (although it undoubtedly already took on a particular coloration according to the social class). For example, we know that religious interest was the same in all classes and that the Reformation almost equally affected the nobility, the bourgeoisie, the peasants, and the artisans.[21] In the eighteenth century, the bourgeoisie was libertarian, Voltairian, and incredulous, more so than the common people (with the exception of certain regions of France, where dechristianization had commenced well before the Revolution). In the twentieth century, it is in the working-class that practice is the most feeble. On the basis of a survey made at Saint Etienne (France) on Sunday, March 8, 1953, it was ascertained that 28·5 per cent of the city's population were present at mass (a relatively slight proportion). The social distribution of the communicants was as follows:[22]

Engineers: 60%
Liberal professions: 40%
Craftsmen: 20%
Workers: 10%
Miners: 5%

Analogous observations have been made in the mining regions of northern France.

An extremely detailed monograph has been made by Jacques Petit[23] in regard to the Parisian Catholic parish of St Laurent, which includes most of the Tenth Ward (an extremely mixed ward). The actual population of the ward is broken down as men, 23·5 per cent; liberal professions, 5·6 per cent; managers, 2·1 per cent; other, 7·4 per cent. The distribution by profession of practising parishioners is as follows:

Workers: 5%
Clerks: 38%
Civil servants: 15%
Merchants, craftsmen: 21%
Liberal professions: 10%
Managers: 3%
Other: 7%

Put in relation to the population of the parish territory, these figures enable us to determine the rate of the socio-professional groups' attendance at Sunday services. In decreasing order, we find:

Without profession: 12%
Liberal professions: 9·5%
Civil servants: 7·9%
Clerks: 6·3%
Managers: 5·2%
Merchants and craftsmen: 5·1%
Workers: 1·7%

Thus, although the workers still represent 5 per cent of the population of the parish, they represent only 1·7 per cent of the worker population of the ward. In other words, they are practically absent. The numerous surveys that have been made in France in the course of the last twenty years[24] have generally confirmed the impression of individual monographs: although the bourgeois classes are widely enough represented in the Catholic church, the proletariat is almost totally absent from it. The proletariat lives outside the church and practises only exceptionally. (One should take into account regional diversities: the presence of practising workers is a known fact in Alsace, Moselle, and Brittany.) These surveys have reinforced an impression that many observers had already had. Godin and Daniel, writing in 1943, stated:

In the present state of things, the conversion of a proletarian living in a proletarian milieu offers difficulties comparable to the conversion of a pagan in far-off mission countries. The worker, also, must abandon not the evil that was in his life, but *his whole life*: his friends, his relations, his customs, his Sunday holidays; he must change his mode of living, he must leave his milieu.[25]

In 1952, it was ascertained that religious attendance at Paris was 6 per cent of the population of the lower-class sections and 20 per cent in the wealthier sections.[26] Thus there is indeed a very clear relationship between social category and religious practice. Certain social classes have almost totally lost contact with the church, despite the persistence of recourse to baptism.[27] This cleavage of religious practice according to social classes is manifested morphologically in the variations in practice according to the sections of the cities: at Grenoble, where the overall percentage was 14 per cent, it rose to 21 per cent in the parish of Saint Louis (bourgeois), to 16 per cent in the parish of Saint André (lower class), and fell to 7·5 per cent in the parish of Saint Laurent (majority of poor Italians). At Marseilles, the deaneries of bourgeois majority show a practice of 20–30 per cent, whereas the industrialized suburbs of the north show only 7 per cent. At Brussels, the Leopold section (bourgeois) shows 35–60 per cent, while the lower-class sections of La Senne and Forest show 15 per cent.[28]

Although we do not have comparable statistics for Protestantism,[29] the percentages of practising workers seem to be quite low. In any case, Protestantism has encountered the same difficulties in its evangelization work which were noted by Godin and Daniel: the conversion of a worker is a difficult thing because he does not succeed in becoming integrated in the parishes of bourgeois majority. This explains the creation of brotherhoods in worker regions (the north of France, Paris suburbs, Nantes, St Nazaire), that is to say, in fact, the creation of purely worker parishes, since the workers could not become acclimatized in parishes of bourgeois structure.

The generality of the phenomenon in Protestant circles is incontestable. The Anglican bishop E. R. Wickham, at the time a minister in the working-class sections of Sheffield, made numerous surveys and then formulated the following opinion: at the adult age, the worker is outside the church and he is convinced that what takes place in the church is unrelated to his worker existence. In Wickham's words,

From the emergence of the industrial towns in the eighteenth century, the working class, the labouring poor, the common people, as a class, substantially, as adults, have been outside the churches. The industrial working class culture pattern has evolved lacking a tradition of the practice of religion.[30]

The studies made by F. G. Dreyfus[31] on Alsatian Protestantism show that although the percentage of practice has a tendency to decline in a very accentuated way, this phenomenon is accompanied by a demographic and socio-professional modification of the Protestant population of Alsace (in Upper Rhine, 21,900 of 46,000 Protestants now live in cities; in Lower Rhine, 96,000 of 196,000 Protestants are city-dwellers). In the country and in small towns, religious practice oscillates between 20 and 30 per cent; it falls to between 8 and 10 per cent in the large cities (for those who regularly practise). In the Strasbourg area, the percentage of the faithful in worker circles oscillates between 7 and 12 per cent, that of management between 50 and 80 per cent. The sociological study of the Reformed parish of Grenoble undertaken by Pierre Bolle, which established precisely the socio-professional composition of that city, shows that the well-to-do and bourgeois classes represent only one-third of the city's total population, but two-thirds of the responsible (voting) members of the parish, i.e., of those who show an active attachment to their parish.[32] In his monograph on the Reformed Church of Alsace-Lorraine, Francis Andrieux established that in the parishes where the percentage of the agricultural population exceeds 10 per cent, the average participation in worship is 30 per cent, whereas in the parishes where the percentage of the worker population exceeds 25 per cent, this participation drops to 10·5 per cent.[33]

However, it is not sufficient to state the fact; it must also be interpreted. Why does membership in the proletarian social classes result in abstention in regard to religious practice and the loss of contact with the churches?[34]

We cannot propose an exhaustive explanation. It is necessary to content ourselves with suggesting some points of reference.

In Europe, at least, the Christian churches (especially the Catholic churches) are the witnesses of "Christendom", that is to say, of a form of society that has disappeared and whose disappearance became complete at the very moment that the working-class was constituted (at the end of the eighteenth century). The Christian churches became aware only slowly of the disappearance of Christendom, and persevered for a long time in the attitudes and methods which had belonged to Christendom. The upsurge of the working-class took place so rapidly during the nineteenth century that the phenomenon escaped attention. It was not that no one paid any attention to the fact of worker concentration, but that no one saw that the working-class was acting as a completely new class, having a very acute class consciousness. The social structures had not provided for a welcome for this class. The European society in which this working-class grew up was a liberal and individualistic bourgeois society. As a bourgeois society, it felt that social responsibility belonged to the property-owner. This is why it tried to fight against universal suffrage and sanctioned a régime – in society and even in the church – where the franchise was given to copyholders and freeholders (cf. the Concordat of Napoleon and the Organic Articles). As the Protestant Guizot said, "Enrich yourselves and you will become electors."

As a liberal society, it was hostile to all state interference in the social and economic domain. Consequently, it was hostile to legislative provisions which would have led to a reception of the working-class in the nations.

As an individualist society, it did not believe in the existence of social classes. It viewed class consciousness as a rebellion, and naturally was hostile to the workers' right of association. It considered the workers only as minor beings, incapable of economizing and of managing their affairs. Thus strikes were revolts to be crushed. Certainly, "pauperism" was manifest. But bourgeois society viewed it either as a witness to the necessary inequalities of all society, to which one must be resigned, or as a witness to the infantilism of the workers, who must be held in tutelage and directed paternally. The social patronage in France was initially a form of paternalism. The Protestant industrialists of Mulhouse attempted a significant effort to ameliorate the precariousness of worker housing and built cities which long served as a model. The workers' response was one of the most difficult strikes of the century, which led, of course, to the denunciation of the workers' ingratitude.

The initial efforts of the Catholic church to become interested in the plight of the workers were significant enough. The first attempts were veritable corporations or mixed unions in which the effort was made to gather workers and management together (Lille, Roubaix, Tourcoing). Worker associations also appeared at the end of the century, but one cannot say precisely that all of their members were characteristically workers. In any case, priests and intellectuals often played an important role in these groups.[35] Generally speaking, due to the influence exercised by intellectual and ecclesiastical groups (The Worker and Democratic Christian Movement, for example), the ideology often remained foreign to the concrete demands of the proletariat. Moreover, the number of workers touched by the movement was relatively slight. At the time of the Congress of Reims in 1896, the report estimated that there were 20,000 worker groups. It is enough to say that as a whole the working-class remained foreign to the church, even to its social efforts (which does not at all mean that all seasonal practice had disappeared or that the workers were no longer baptized nor had their children baptized). Also, many bosses required at least external practice of their workers, and maintained it by threat of dismissal. But there is a great difference between official membership in the church, and real insertion into that church. The official ties between proletariat and church disappeared when external constraints ceased, when the workers possessed vast and solid international worker organizations (Confédération generale du travail after 1906) which were tainted with marxism and socialism.

Marx's formula: "the proletarian camp in the nation" is sociologically exact. It is a foreign camp which the nation initially did not know how to integrate. The churches which were part of this society closed to the proletariat, had no point of contact with it. It cannot be said that they cut themselves off from the proletariat, or that the proletariat had withdrawn from them. As a collective group, the proletariat had never been integrated into the church because the proletariat was outside the very bounds of the nations. Such is the heritage of the nineteenth century. To be sure, this situation is not definitive. To the degree that the proletariat wins not only its political rights, but its social rights and a legislation which will take account of the nature of its work (unionism, social security); to the degree that the isolation of the proletariat in relation to the total population diminishes, the proletariat will cease to be a camp within the nation. It will become less impervious to the influence of the church. In France, the development of Catholic Action and of specialized movements (Jeunesse ouvrière chrétienne – Christian Worker Youth), and especially the union Confédération française des travailleurs chrétiens (French Confederation of Christian Workers) attest to a rather close contact between the church and the working-class. However, this contact is still made by intermediaries and many workers enrolled in the CFTC still maintain a certain distance from the church. We should point out also that in 1964, after a long period of hesitation, the CFTC secularized itself by suppressing the "Christian" in its title.

But this reconquest, which would take several generations, is possible only in worker circles where there is not a solidly established ideology such as communism, that is, an ideology which has been able to persuade the workers that religion, Christianity, the church are aspects of the alienation that the working-class encounters on all levels. Christianity presented as the ideology of the triumphant bourgeoisie thus becomes the enemy, and the emancipation of the working-class will follow infallibly to the degree that the bourgeois ideology declines. If an open and violent conflict is rare, it is because Christianity, like any ideology, is only a superstructure. Any superstructure crumbles of its own weight when its supporting economic and political infra-structure no longer exists. The stability of communist establishments in west Europe, especially in the Catholic countries of

Europe, indicates that the social action of the Christian churches has not been able to encroach upon communist ideology.

Communism, indeed, is an ideology which has been thought out on the level of the worker experience, an ideology in which the working-class has recognized its own visage. Communism has given the working-class the assurance that by thinking through the consequences of its own alienation, the proletariat will succeed in overcoming this alienation. Christianity too often and for too long has been presented as a sort of justification of social inequalities, as an ethic of obedience to established authorities, as the reflection of the primacy of a social class. Moreover, it has posited another world in which compensation will be received for misery here below. Thus it offered an opening for Marxist criticism, which denounced it as the opium of the people, that is, as an ideology which drugged the energies of the lower classes and hindered the working-class from achieving its destiny. It must be recognized that the Christian churches have often manifested a singular timidity in their social doctrine, and that the so-called Social Gospel movements have remained more or less marginal. Indeed, those movements themselves have not possessed a sufficiently developed doctrine, one sufficiently concerned with thinking through the worker condition and envisaging basic changes in social structures in order to provide an obstacle to communist propaganda.

In fact, at the present time, a stable front has been established in the West between Christians and communists, and it does not seem probable that there will be a thaw in the situation.

However, this analysis requires some qualifications. It is a fact that communism has more profoundly succeeded in Catholic countries of the West than in Protestant countries. Although the absence of a strong communist influence in the United States and in West Germany is explained by particular economic and political circumstances, this absence is even more striking in England and in the Scandinavian countries. But the absence of communism does not mean *ipso facto* that there is unhindered contact between the church and the working-class. The low rate of church attendance in the Scandinavian countries and the profound religious crisis affecting England testifies that the working-class is also detached from the church in these industrialized and urban countries.

Furthermore, urbanization itself seems to be a cause of low rate of religious observance.[36] The rate of religious observance in Catholicism is quite low in the large cities: 14 per cent at Grenoble, 15 per cent at Marseilles, 20 per cent at Lyons, 24 per cent at Brussels, 12 per cent at Barcelona, and 15 per cent at Rio de Janeiro. Obviously, it cannot be maintained that this rate is always and absolutely lower than in the rural areas, for there also are rural areas where observance is low. Moreover, there are considerable variations in the rate of practice among the various quarters of cities: the rate varies from 10 per cent to 25 per cent at Barcelona, from 5 per cent to 45 per cent at Lyons. The city itself does not kill off practice; the action of certain quarters should be blamed. All the same, considered as a whole, the phenomenon of urbanization is accompanied by a decline in religious practice. Boulard has compared the degree of urbanization of French *arrondissements* with the map of the fecundity of priestly vocations.[37] It appears that the very urban *arrondissements* (Marseilles, Lyons, Bordeaux, Nice, St Etienne, Versailles, Pontoise, Toulouse, Nancy, and Seine) generally belong to the category where the rate of sacerdotal vocations does not exceed fifteen priests for 10,000 inhabitants. But this ratio increases to thirty-five per 10,000 in the less urbanized *départements* (Aveyron, Lozère, Haute Loire, Cantal, the two Savoys, Vendée, Pyrenees, and Hautes Alpes). Here again, notable exceptions (pointed out by J. Labbens) are Moselle, Haut Rhin, Nord, the Territory of Belfort, the region of Rennes, which, although highly urbanized, furnish a notable contingent of priests. But the phenomenon of total, avowed, and recognized unbelief has indeed appeared in the cities. In the 1904 census at Buenos Aires, where the Catholic majority comprises 86·6 per cent of the population and where the Catholic church is officially supported by the State, there were 823,936 declared Catholics and 13,335 persons who stated that they belonged to no religious group. A study made in the Netherlands after the 1920 census showed that the "godless" were distributed in the following fashion:

2·1% of the population of townships of less than 5,000 inhabitants,

3·57% for the small towns of 5,000 to 20,000 inhabitants,

5·14% for towns of less than 50,000 inhabitants,

9·92% for cities of between 50,000 and 100,000 inhabitants.

Statistics of the same type are furnished by the *German Catholic Church Yearbook*: religious practice is

52·4% in rural areas and in cities of less than 100,000 inhabitants,

39% in cities of 100,000 to 200,000 inhabitants,

31·6% in cities of more than 200,000 inhabitants.

It should be pointed out, however, that the percentages are higher in certain cities of the Ruhr:

39·8% at Essen,

34·9% at Dortmund,

39·1% at Bochum.

In the northern port cities, practice falls to:
  26% at Bremerhaven,
  26·3% at Hamburg,
  26·1% at Lubeck.[38]

Atheistic propaganda is tied to culture, above all in Catholic countries, as has been obvious in the West since the beginning of the eighteenth century. It is in the city that the cultural movement and the movement of ideas are the most intense. The influence of the city upon the surrounding countryside is beyond doubt. The large cities are the centres of religious transformation. As E. Pin observes,[39] the large cities are the departure points for influences, and the small cities are relay stations.

We cannot entirely corroborate these statistics from similar information from the Protestant side. The few surveys made do indeed indicate a decline of practice in the cities. On the other hand, the work of J. P. Boilloux[40] shows that pastoral recruitment in Alsace and Moselle from 1918 to 1957 is clearly higher in the cities. He even established that the less urbanized a region is, the weaker its pastoral recruitment is, despite the fact that the regions of urban majority have only a diaspora of Protestants. The majority of urban zones have an average ratio of ·9 per cent per 1,000, whereas the majority of rural zones have a ratio of less than ·9 per cent per 1,000.

Of course, Boilloux's study involved a relatively small number (354 students), and does not permit general conclusions: the accidental causes, the greater facilities offered to urban children for secondary education, and the socio-professional characteristics of urban Protestants could indeed have neutralized the general effect of the cities. As always, the results of this survey, like the numerous exceptions recorded on the Catholic side, should lead to qualified judgments. There is no absolute determinism, and each city must be considered not as a homogeneous unity but as an ensemble of quarters which have varying influence on religious practice.

And yet, urban civilization does tend to disengage a new type of man, over whom the traditional organization of parishes undoubtedly has less of a hold. The parish is modelled on the commune or village, and presupposes a stable population. The place of work is in the vicinity of the church, on the territory of the parish. The church is there to invite man to turn his thoughts to God when his work is done. But the modern citizen, as J. Labbens points out, is a migrant. He is a migrant in several ways. He comes from the country, he has broken with local traditions, he has not been welcomed and taken in charge by a church at the moment when he arrived in the city, he has not been hurried off to church by his fellow-workers. The phenomenon of emigration from the country to the cities has often been a phenomenon of negative selection. The emigrant has been rejected by the country, where he was useless. He has few outlets, and is given over to rapid proletarianization (even to vagrantization). The citizen is a migrant, and remains such, in the second place, because he is in a process of continual change of place. There no longer is the tie between the home and the place of work. The city worker spends only rare moments in his home (but the church claims to reach the home, and the man in the home); it is the milieu of work and not the family which creates in him the strongest feeling of community. Thirdly, he is a migrant because he perpetually remains a stranger; the city is a juxtaposition of quarters or neighbourhoods all foreign to one other. There is no tacit consensus on the values accepted by everyone. Finally, the citizen is a migrant because he is in perpetual social mobility: frequent changes of employment, social advancement (very frequent, when it is only a question of coming up from the lowest ranks) and the permanent possibility of failure (cf. the numerous bankruptcies on the level of small business).

There is a profound difference between rural life and urban life. The abrupt passage from one to the other, so characteristic of our civilization, produces all sorts of traumas:

From the classic small villages of Christendom, where sociological pressures and a certain ground-work of faith maintain either real or external traditions and fidelity, the modern person moves to the urban quarter – without yet being of full age; from the secular village order, he moves to the anarchic disorder of populous blocks; from the continuous surveillance of priest and neighbours, he moves to the freedom of a completely different world, where he still feels himself observed and where he accepts the patterns of behaviour; from one conformity, he moves to another conformity . . .[41]

But from one conformity to the other, the rupture is profound. And it is all the more traumatic, because it is less well-prepared for:

For many Bretons (even children of Mary), the Montparnasse Station marks the threshold of unbelief, and for most Bretons, it marks the threshold of an indifference which is expressed by the forgetting of mass and Easter communion. In other words, the roots of practice are sunk in tradition and not in the conscience, the gregarious customs mask the absence of any personal religion. The city delivers the individual from the social bond of origins and releases him from all homage to a God who was the God of his community.[42]

This brings us to a basic point: what the comparative statistics of practice in the city and in the country are not able to say is that the passage from country to city is often only an incidental cause. It demolishes the superstructures which were poorly rooted in the personality. It lays bare the superficial Christianization of the West. Thus it would be false to put city over against country in any absolute way.

In order for practice to be maintained with absolute stability and not to be lost in the city, it would obviously be necessary for the church to accompany men in their migrations.

Other social factors can influence practice. In many respects, the distinction of sexes is a social distinction, for the sex is seen and interpreted through collective representations. The education of children is entrusted to women; because "religion" has a manifest effect on children, and because it involves and motivates feelings and emotions, it is considered as a woman's affair. The action of the clergy, generally speaking, is more powerful over women than over men. Feminine practice is almost universally higher than masculine practice. The difference of age also plays a part, although in a less regular way: in general, it is the middle age which is absent from church (that is, the age which corresponds to the particularly active period of life). The level of culture is a decisive factor in religious practice, although its action is difficult to determine. It is usually combined with socio-professional factors. Sometimes it turns a person away from practice. It was the progress of the Enlightenment of the eighteenth century which turned the cultivated bourgeoisie from the church; it is culture which tends to lead many intellectuals back to the church in the middle of the twentieth century.

In sum, in order correctly to ascertain the action of social factors on practice, it is not sufficient to state that certain social groups practise and certain other groups do not. Questions must be asked on the quality of practice and on the meaning which the faithful themselves attribute to it. There can be a purely traditionalist practice that considers Christianity to be only a necessary decoration, assuring a certain stability of morals and a certain social dignity: the very high incidence of religious practice among the upper classes perhaps is nothing more than one element of a way of life, one aspect of social standing. Among the managerial circles of industry in Alsace (especially Bas Rhin), Protestantism has easily been absorbed, to the point where the key positions have passed from Protestantism to Catholicism. Perhaps this has happened because Catholicism seems to offer greater social potential than Protestantism. There can also be an element of superstition present, which, in the accomplishment of certain supposedly salutary acts, seeks a guarantee both of a long and happy life and of an easy passage into a comfortable beyond.

It is just such things which attract people towards a church institution guaranteeing with juridical precision the conditions for access to salvation, and which turn people away from a church that is content to proclaim the promise of salvation. Underneath the continued existence of certain forms of practice can be hidden an alteration of the very meaning of practice. In a survey made among French and Spanish families living in furnished apartments in the Parisian area, Andrée Michel concludes that the sacraments have been desacralized. The people have recourse to them sometimes, but only in giving them new meaning.

The person [she writes] no longer does his religious works in order thereby to forget himself; rather, he thinks that they are done for him. Thus we see communion serving to satisfy needs relative to a promotion of age, religious marriage serving to satisfy the festive need, and Christian burial serving as the means of rendering homage to the body.[43]

Discrimination among these types of practice is difficult to make by way of sociological inquiry. It is not impossible, but the survey must bear on more personal factors of practice than simply the attendance at offices, or participation in the sacraments, or confession. The survey must also bear on giving, on religious activities having a less official character, on Bible reading, on theological and religious works, on religious publishing, on the secular activity of members, the risks they take, their everyday involvements.

Naturally, certain periods of history are especially favourable for measuring the authentic religious vitality of a community: the period in which practice is held in low esteem by the powers that be, or in which the faithful are uneasy or even persecuted for their faith, or in which the church is reduced to a sort of clandestine existence. The astonishing vitality shown by Orthodox Christianity in the USSR seems, indeed, to be a very favourable indication. Yet it is necessary to wait until the generations which have been best assimilated by the régime (20 to 45 years of age at present) have given way to the following generation, in order to see if this vitality is maintained despite the ideological pressure that has been exercised on the level of education.

The alteration of the religious life is shown by the fact that the practices of daily piety are debased much more rapidly than the solemn practices (among which must be placed the sacraments which have become social rites of passage and of initiation). Baptism, marriage, religious burial continue to be celebrated, although no living faith continues to animate the families which demand them. Chélini estimates that at least four-fifths of the children born today in cities of Latin Europe of almost unanimous Catholic tradition are baptized.[44]

Marriage undoubtedly is the most affected of the sacraments. Funerals are still religious, but the use of last rites is clearly declining. The same remarks can be made of Protestant countries. In Sweden, which is 95 per cent Lutheran, only 250,000 persons regularly participate in worship (3·3 per cent of the population), although 86 per cent of the children are baptized and 91 per cent of the marriages are religious. Dechristianization rarely is marked by a decline in church membership: from 1952 to 1958 there were only 28,369 demissions, which represents less than ½ per cent of the population.[45]

Further inquiry would be necessary, namely, to study the role of social and economic factors in so far as they favour or thwart the return to religious practice. We have already emphasized how individuals who are subjected to strong pressure from a homogeneous social class with a well-defined ideology, encounter difficulties in returning to a faith and a practice which the group disapproves of. The suspicion that surrounds the church and priests in certain worker circles means that individuals cannot return to the church and the faith without betraying their class. The abortive attempt of the worker priests did not aim at direct evangelization (the priests in question were unanimous in recognizing that their evangelizing action was insignificant); its primary purpose was to raise, by their very presence, the interdiction which rested upon the church. The worker priests wanted to reaccustom worker circles to simple contact with the church, so that in following generations the decision of personal faith would be possible.

It is no less certain that the purely material conditions of life can make conversion impossible. Evangelization is possible only where one can reach or call forth a free person, that is, a person whose behaviour is not at each instant controlled by the group. In the worker cities, in the worker barracks, such is not always possible: "There are interdictions which one cannot overcome," writes Marcel Ducos, "either because the whole worker community would feel it to be a challenge, or because it just isn't done."[46] Moreover, as Ducos notes, those who live in a worker community or barracks feel ostracized. They put up with their isolation, but end by desiring it. They are not like the others and consequently do not wish to rejoin them. The too great promiscuity in the family lodging and the impossibility of isolation mean that the action of the priest or pastor, or of the militant member of a secular movement, cannot be exercised freely on a given member of the family who might be more receptive. This is why the problem initially is one of isolating the individual from his milieu. In this regard, youth movements take on significance precisely to the degree that they succeed in enabling the young person to live for a certain time in a milieu where the constraint of the immediate group no longer plays a part.

Practice cannot be isolated from concrete reality, from the social context in which a man lives. Thus practice is not conceived in Christianity as an abstract activity of man, but as a worship in which he offers his whole person, his body in living sacrifice, holy and acceptable to God (Romans 12.1).

NOTES

1. Cf. M. Leenhardt, *Do Kamo.*

2. In regard to Protestantism, we do not think that it is possible to follow the schema proposed by Le Bras: "worship – behaviour – belief" ("Nuances régionales du catholicisme en France", *Revue de psychologie des peuples*, 8th Year, 1953, no. 1). The adoption of such a schema rests on a theological option that is precisely not that of Protestantism, for which worship is structured by the Word – the personal and doctrinal revelation of God – through the events of history. Thus belief is not essentially an intellectual transcription of cultic and ethical behaviours.

3. Cf. R. H. Esnault, *Luther et le monachisme d'aujourd'hui* (Geneva: Labor et Fides, 1964).

4. G. Le Bras, *Etudes de sociologie religieuses* (Paris: PUF, 2 vols., 1955 and 1956), p. 302.

5. G. Le Bras, "La vitalité religieuse dans l'Eglise de France", in *Revue de l'histoire de l'Eglise de France*, vol. 31, 1945, p. 280.

6. G. Le Bras, "Secteurs et aspects nouveaux de la sociologie religieuse", in *CIS*, vol. 1, 1946, p. 43.

7. Vol. 3/2, col. 2404 (article by A. Chollet).

8. R. Will, *Le culte* (Paris: Alcan, 1929), vol. 2, p. 34.

9. ibid., pp. 36–37.

10. G. van der Leeuw, *La religion dans son essence et ses manifestations*, French edition revised and translated by the author with the collaboration of J. Marty (Paris: Payot, 1948), p. 411. The author intended to give a general description of religious worship. In fact, however, he has a tendency to interpret all religious phenomena through Christianity (cf. pp. 364–365).

11. On this point, again, the celebrated controversy of the *manducatio impiorum* shows that Protestant piety often courts the risk of not being faithful to itself.

12. H. Desroche, "Domaine et méthode de la sociologie religieuse dans l'oeuvre de G. Le Bras", *RHPR*, 34th Year, 1954/2.

13. See the article "Messe" in the *Weltkirchenlexikon* (Stuttgart: Kreuz-Verlag, 1960), col. 907.

14. This notion of contemporaneity is not foreign to Protestantism. It animates the whole theology and piety of Kierkegaard. But it is corrected and limited by the meaning of the commemoration of an event accomplished once for all. On this subject, see the book by Oscar Cullmann, *Christ and Time.*

15. V. Lossky, *Essai sur la théologie mystique de l'Eglise d'Orient* (Paris: Aubier, 1944), p. 7.

16. J. Meyendorff, *L'Eglise orthodoxe hier et aujourd'hui* (Paris: Editions du Seuil, 1960), p. 172.

17. Ambigva, *Patrologie grecque*, vol. 91, col. 1076 BC, quoted by J. Meyendorff, op. cit.

18. Vatican II took up this problem and tried to redistribute the monarchical power of the pope both by the doctrine of the collegiality of bishops and by the definition of the authority proper to the local community.

19. The very problem of the definition of the Protestant (which is a difficult problem for the sociologist, since the limits of the church in Protestantism are necessarily indistinct) can be resolved only by the criterion of membership in a parish. This makes possible a classification of various types of Protestants according to their degree of integration into the local parish and according to the responsibilities that they assume or do not assume in the parish. The classification is not according to practice in the sense that Le Bras uses the term. See Chapter 3.

20. Pin, *Pratique religieuse et classes sociales dans une paroisse urbaine, Saint-Pothin à Lyon* (Paris: SPES, 1952).

21. See E. G. Léonard, *Le protestant français* (Paris: PUF, 1953), pp. 42 ff.

22. Data from *Actualité religieuse dans le monde*, no. 6, June 15, 1953.

23. Jacques Petit, "Structure sociale et vie religieuse d'une paroisse parisienne", *ASR*, no. 1, January–June 1956.

24. A complete account up to 1957 is given in Jacques Maistre, "Les dénombrements de catholiques pratiquants en France", *ASR*, no. 3, January–June 1957.

25. H. Godin and Y. Daniel, *La France, pays de Mission?* (Paris: Editions du Cerf, 1943), pp. 45–46.

26. See the newspaper *Le Monde* of September 3, 1952.

27. Canon Boulard, whose estimates are somewhat optimistic, estimated in 1953 that 94 per cent of French citizens were baptized.

28. J. Chélini, op. cit., p. 103.

29. Among the results of surveys now published, we would mention especially Edmond Perret, *La pratique du culte à Genève* (Geneva: Centre protestant d'études, no date).

30. E. R. Wickham, *Church and People in an Industrial Society* (London: Lutterworth Press, 1957), p. 14. On the same question, see also Richard Taylor, *Christians in an Industrial Society* (London: SCM Press, 1961); *The Church and Industry* (British Council of Churches, 1958): *The Task of the Church in Relation to Industry* (Church Information Office, 1959); Clifford Cleal, *The Minister in an Industrial Community* (Baptist and Congregational Unions, 1959).

31. F. G. Dreyfus, "Le protestantisme alsacien", *ASR*, no. 3, January–June 1957.

32. Pierre Bolle, "Un essai d'étude socio-religieuse: la paroisse réformée de Grenoble", *CS*, 66th Year, April–May 1956, no. 4–5.

33. Francis Andrieux, *L'Eglise réformée d'Alsace-Lorraine telle qu'elle apparaît dans la vie des différentes communautés*. Thesis for the *Doctorat ès sciences religieuses* of the Faculty of Protestant Theology of the University of Strasbourg (mimeographed).

34. Cf. F. G. Dreyfus, "Milieux sociaux et édification ecclésiastique", *CS*, 66th Year, no. 4–5, April–May 1958.

35. See the study, already cited, of Maurice Montuclard, "Aux origines de la démocratie chrétienne".

36. These figures are taken from the book by J. Labbens, *L'Eglise et les centres urbains* (Paris: SPES, 1959). One should refer also to the following works: J. Chélini, "Les facteurs généraux d'influence sur la pratique religieuse urbaine", *Chronique sociale de la France*, 1955, no. 1; Joseph Folliet, "Les effets de la grande ville sur la vie religieuse", *Chronique sociale de la France*, 1953, no. 6; F. G. Dreyfus, "Villes, campagnes et chrétienté", *Studium Generale*, 16th Year, no. 12, 1963; Joseph H. Fichter, *Social Relations in the Urban Parish* (Chicago: University of Chicago Press, 1954); William

Stringfellow, *A Private and Public Faith* (Grand Rapids: William B. Eerdmans Publishing Company, 1962): Gibson Winter, *The Suburban Captivity of the Churches* (New York: Doubleday and Co., 1961) and *The New Creation as Metropolis* (New York: The Macmillan Co., 1963 and London: Collier-Macmillan, 1965); Robert Lee, *Cities and Churches* (Philadelphia: The Westminster Press, 1962).

37. In his book, *Essai sur le déclin du clergé français* (Paris: 1950).

38. Quoted by J. Chélini, op. cit., p. 76.

39. *Pratique religieuse et classes sociales.*

40. Master's thesis (mimeographed), Faculty of Protestant Theology, University of Strasbourg, France, 1958: *Le recrutement du corps pastoral dans les Eglises d'Alsace et de Lorraine de 1918 à 1957.*

41. L. J. Lebret, *La France en transition* (Paris: Economie et humanisme, Les Editions Ouvrières, 1957), p. 168; see also J. Lew, *Journal d'une mission ouvrière* (Paris: Editions du Cerf, 1959).

42. G. Le Bras, in the preface to the above-mentioned work by J. Chélini.

43. Andrée Michel, *Famille, industrialisation, logement* (Paris: Editions du CNRS, 1959).

44. J. Chléini, op. cit., p. 230.

45. *Statistique de l'Eglise luthérienne de Suède*, 1959.

46. Marcel Ducos, *Action missionaire en quartier ouvrier* (Paris: Editions du Cerf), pp. 160–165.

VII

The Development of Religious Structures

Christianity, being by nature a religion which calls communities into existence and which is lived in the midst of communities, is characterized by original social structures. These structures appear more in their specific nature to the degree that Christian communities are differentiated from the civil community and to the degree that a certain distance is established between the global society and the religious society. In the constructing of their organization, the Christian churches find themselves caught between two contradictory exigences. On the one hand, their existence is tied to the free action of the Holy Spirit and to the charisms which the Spirit gives and calls forth. In order to preserve this freedom of the Spirit, the churches must not harden their structures. The Confession of La Rochelle (article XXXI) affirms that "no one should obtrude, on his own authority, in the governing of the church; this should be done by election" (the Confession of Augsburg speaks of ministries *recte vocati*), yet then adds this reservation: ". . . it has been necessary . . . that God call forth men in an extraordinary way to reform the church."

On the other hand, since the churches must take shape under a social form that must, to some degree, be homogeneous with the surrounding society (the homogeneity is often imposed by the society), they will tend to establish rigid constitutions which will sometimes be more democratic and sometimes more hierarchical according to the social models presented to them.

Religious structures are structures of slow development. This is easy to understand, if we remember that Christianity, like most religions, has a traditionalist nature. Since religious structures are designed to permit the *conservation* of the *depositum fidei* and its transmission from generation to generation, they are necessarily conservative. Even the great religious reformations and revolutions do not always affect them. Anglicanism separated from Rome without at all touching religious structures, and the same can be said for Scandinavian Lutheranism. Yet as a whole, the Reformation rather profoundly modified the religious structures of the past, especially in those places where the Reformation did not achieve total victory and had to establish new churches over against the Roman church. Thus the church saw the birth of a more democratic structure, of which the presbyterian synodal form is the most typical.

But differently from civil and political societies, whose primary end is to regulate a *social order*, ecclesial societies are not primarily concerned with establishing well-defined structures from the very beginning. This is especially true of Protestant societies. They are more concerned with proclaiming a truth, with gathering about a message, with assuring a spiritual communion, than with defining a power-structure, a hierarchy, or a set of laws for the faithful. The preoccupation with structures appears only when the church is established, when it has found a sociological foundation, and when it feels the need to differentiate itself in relation to other groups or rival religions. This is confirmed by the history of primitive Christianity. The structures of the early church were flexible and created in an empirical way; the authority rested less on an installed hierarchy than on the personal influence of the apostle, who had been qualified as such not by an institutional consecration but by a spiritual event. It is also confirmed by the history of the beginnings of the Reformation, especially under its Lutheran form. The concern with organization appeared only later, with the preoccupation of assuring catechetical teaching for the faithful. It would quickly be abandoned to the prince or to the civil authority. Thus Luther clearly indicated the secondary nature of the organization of structures.

1. *The First Christian Communities*

The primitive Christian communities showed great diversity in their organization. But one important fact characterized all of them: it was the local community which played a preponderant role. The whole reality of the church was manifested in the local community; this is why Paul could speak of the church of God which is at Corinth. However, we should make a distinction between the churches of the Jerusalemite type and the churches of the Pauline type. In the Pauline type, there is no Mother Church. All the communities were on exactly the same footing. They were distinguished only by their more or less great fidelity to the apostolic teaching, their more or less great spirit of union and of peace, or perhaps their strategic importance (the importance of the Letter to the Romans seems to indicate that Paul considered Rome as a key church, without it having for that reason any hierarchical privilege whatever).

As for the Jerusalemite churches, on the contrary, one can scarcely speak of them in the plural. As Hans Lietzmann points out:

> In the thought of the first Christians, there was only one community of "disciples" of the Lord; the seat of this community was the city of Jerusalem, until the Parousia of the Son of Man, when the new Jerusalem would descend from the sky and become the abode of the elect. Those who lived outside the walls of Jerusalem belonged no less to the community: the other communities were, in a sense, the extensions of this parent-cell. They all were subject to a single authority, that of the apostles to whom the Lord himself had given the right of making final decisions on all questions of cultic order. In practice, this meant that Peter, the only apostle who had had any real activity in the area of mission, possessed supreme authority over the ensemble of filial communities. He was the foundation on whom, during the initial period, the church was built; the admission of new communities into the body of the church depended upon him.[1]

These filial communities appeared in Judea, in Galilee, in Samaria, especially under the influence of the Hellenists (Philip, in particular). Wherever these communities appeared, there also appeared "representatives of the Jerusalem community, who were responsible for examining the conduct of the new brothers and of setting up the conditions for relationships with them".[2] Thus we see the outline of a hierarchical system, which Catholicism took over by transferring the seat of the Mother Church to Rome. But it should be pointed out that the hierarchical principle in the early church was not valid by itself: it was in relation to the eschatological expectation of the heavenly Jerusalem.

The Jerusalem community provides another lesson for us: the church differentiated itself only very slowly from the Jewish community. It did not initially seek to provide original structures for itself. The first Christians frequented the temple, and regularly met in Solomon's Portico.

> The Jerusalemite community . . . divided its cultic life between the temple and the house-church meetings, which took the place of synagogal meetings.[3]

The ritual precepts, Sabbath, and liturgical cycle of the Jewish feasts were observed. The custom of fasting, which was practised by the disciples of John, seems to have been adopted by the primitive community (cf. Mark 2.18–20). The Book of Acts (21.20–26) presents the baptized Jews as "zealous for the law". What brought about the clearest differentiation between the two communities was also an event of spiritual nature, namely, the juxtapositioning of the Sabbath with Sunday. Sunday, as the day of the Lord's resurrection, was, by way of consequence, the day on which the Lord's return would take place. It was for this reason that the Lord's Supper, with its messianic and eschatological invocation *Maranatha*, was celebrated on Sunday. The hostility of the synagogue and the necessity of combating certain forms of Jewish Christianity could have contributed to adding Sunday to the Sabbath, and then of substituting it for the Sabbath. But it seems that the theological motive necessitated this modification of structure, which has been so important for the later history of the church.

The internal organization of the church was not at all uniform. In the Palestinian church, authority belonged to the Council of the Twelve (in which the personalities of Peter, John, and James asserted themselves). Where did they get their authority? As Simon observes, it has a

historical nature: they had been the intimates of Jesus. They had been chosen by him, and they were the first to see him after the Resurrection.[4]

Later, the necessity of filling vacancies brought a sort of dynastic principle to the forefront. James, the brother of Jesus, took on considerable authority in the council after Peter abandoned the direction of the church in favour of missionary activity.[5]

The organization of the Pauline churches seemed to be much more flexible. Authority did not have a historical nature, but a charismatic one. Only the call of the Spirit or of the Lord qualified a person to exercise authority. Paul himself was an example of this freedom with which the Lord called to his service. In the various communities there was a spontaneous manifesting of charismatic gifts, and it is certain that the life of the community was founded on these gifts. The problem was not one of raising such gifts, but of circumscribing them. Paul set himself to this problem and attempted to regulate these gifts in relation to their common utility, that is, to the building up of the church (I Cor. 14). Three categories of permanent-type ministries gradually came out of this attempt to put things in order:

And God has appointed in the church first apostles, second prophets, third teachers (I Cor. 12.28).

The Spirit designates those who are to exercise these permanent ministries; the authority of the apostle consists in recognizing these gifts. All of these functions are relative to teaching, which is not distinct from mission. It is worth noting that the aim of these initial structures was the exercise of a doctrinal magisterium. Alongside these basic ministries, but without

there being any fixed institutional delineation, the bishops, deacons, pres-
byters, and elders exercised functions (primarily administrative) to which
they acceded both by charismatic designation and by the choice of the
community. The ritual of the laying on of hands, which was inherited
from Judaism, consecrated them in their function (laying on of hands was
also used for other purposes, e.g., baptism and the healing of the sick).
Laying on of hands was destined to play an essential role after the charismatic age had come to an end: it would assure the continuity of the
exercise of the ministry, and would become, in Catholicism, the sacrament
of the apostolic succession. But during several centuries, it would not be
sufficient by itself; it would be only the ratification of a designation by the
community. The end of the charismatic age began during the period of
the Pastoral Epistles, and the community became increasingly important
in the designation of the ministries of the church. Catholic theologians
have too much of a tendency to project the light of later development back
onto this history, and to bring out the existence of a hierarchical principle
in the primitive church. It is certain that a hierarchy existed, but precisely
not as a principle. It was the Spirit alone which qualified a person; when
this spiritual designation no longer had the obvious character that it had
at the beginning, then it was that the reality of a divine qualification was
recognized by the community in prayer and by the laying on of hands.

It was the Pauline structure that won out over the Jerusalemite structure
in the history of primitive Christianity. This came about not only by
reason of external factors (the destruction of Jerusalem and the dispersion
of the community), but because the dynastic direction of the church risked
stifling both the role devolving on the Spirit and that devolving on the
community.

Authority is manifested in the cultic, doctrinal, and moral realms. But
in developing this point, we must be careful not to fall victim to a modern
point of view, in which the different sectors of existence are partitioned.
In reality, the sectors mentioned crowned the whole of existence. Authority
extended in particular into the realm of mutual assistance. This is the
source of the importance of the collection which Paul organized for the
poor of Jerusalem. This is also the source of the concern to tolerate neither
indigents nor parasites. Finally, it is the source of the support which the
communities provided for those who proclaimed the gospel to them.

This quick glance shows us that the religious structures of Christianity
from the very beginning had nothing of a juridical nature, were constituted
very progressively and empirically, were related to spiritual needs and the
growth of the communities, and were obedient to the concern of respecting

the freedom of the Spirit. Furthermore, although these structures made a place for the community, it was because the community was the receptacle of the Spirit and as a consequence became capable of recognizing the gifts of the Spirit and of honouring them. The authority of the apostles was not the authority of princes of the church, but the authority of founder-witnesses. Moreover, the opposition between Paul and the Twelve of Jerusalem made it clear that there was nothing rigid in the qualification of apostle. Neither familiarity with Jesus during his earthly ministry, nor membership in his family, nor descent from his family guaranteed any privilege. The disappearance of the apostolate with the death of the witnesses of the Resurrection indicates the exceptional, transitory nature of the apostle, which was valid only for the foundation period. The New Testament contains no trace of any apostolic designation of new apostles to succeed the original ones.

2. *The Structures of Modern Christianity*

Primitive Christianity, which constituted a dispersed minority in the ancient world, presents structures that are variable, unstable, and designed primarily to manifest a charismatic authority and to permit the realization of a true communion among the faithful. Modern Christianity, which represents more than a third of the world's population, which still lives in rather compact groups (at least in Europe and in North America), and which, under various juridical modalities, has become an official power maintaining numerous relations with other social authorities, obviously has a more structured organization. Moreover, concern with these structures, by which Christianity aims to enclose its faithful, to assure a theological and moral discipline among them as well as to assure the liaison with social authorities, and to insert the ecclesial institution into the social institution, has become a major preoccupation of the various churches. This fact is manifest in the Catholic church, where councils and popes, especially in the modern age, have been primarily concerned with the establishing of ecclesiastical structures and with their adaptation to a secularized society, and where ecclesiology is both doctrinal teaching on the nature of the church and a determining of the respective rights of the different ecclesiastical authorities. The development is no less clear in Protestantism, although it takes a different form: while proclaiming that the church is defined by only two marks, the preaching of the gospel and the administration of the sacraments, the Reformation was no less preoccupied with defining a "form of the church", and with indicating the conditions by which one could recognize an "upright church". Although this concern initially was less clear among the Lutherans than among the Reformed, the Lutherans later became trapped in the same preoccupation; constitutional problems play a very important role in all the churches of the Reformation, to the point that Faith and Constitution, doctrine and institution, are terms which often go together and are placed on the same plane.[6] In short, the insertion of the churches into a society which undoubtedly is secularized but which generally accords them a rather wide field and at least an honorific consideration, is expressed by the churches themselves by a development that often gives advantage to the society over the communion.

Every church lives this permanent tension between an organized (and consequently hierarchical) society and the communion of persons, which is suited to more freedom. Within it, because of its very nature, is manifested a process of objectivization which Berdyaev saw as being part of all of society: "The organization of society," he wrote, "is an objectivization of human existence and an oppression of the human person."[7] But what is true of all society is *a fortiori* true of the church, with one qualification: organization, objectivization seeks not to oppress, but to assume, to make a community of persons live. It is in seeking to assume it that organization makes the community sterile. Thus the need for renewal of the forms of organization arises. Thus arises the necessity of the piety of individuals and of small groups to maintain a permanent protest against what is oppressive in every structure, especially when it bears a heavy weight of tradition. The movements of religious reform which have been witnessed in all of the churches are, sociologically speaking, the expression of these protest movements against the "institutional ghetto". They are born within the institution, but sometimes, when the institutional sclerosis has become too great, they develop outside the institution. They reconstitute themselves in new institutions, which are imagined to be ideal but which eventually manifest their weightiness. Thus every church develops from pneumatological liberty to organization. This does not mean that organization necessarily kills freedom. It does, however, constitute a trap for freedom. This trap is necessary, for without it freedom would move towards anarchical and individualistic forms which would kill communion. In other words, the church is first communion before being society, but the communion is protected against centrifugal forces at work in it only by the organization of a society which, in turn, threatens the communion by the fixing of precise canonical rules. Certain religious communities have claimed to renounce all structured organization and even an organized pastoral ministry. This is the case with numerous sects, but this renunciation is seen to be purely verbal: pastors are replaced by preachers, who differ from the former only in that they do not exercise a full-time ministry.

The *koinonia* and the institution, as a World Council of Churches report[8] observed, are both inseparable and distinct. Moreover, the institution is not considered as a purely sociological reality added from without the *koinonia*, but as an instrument given to the latter by divine grace in order to bring it to fullness. But flagrant contradictions appear in the churches among the institutional models to which they are attached and the ends which they claim to serve. Structures often seem to be an obstacle to the realization of intentions which are affirmed by the churches. This is manifest concerning unity. The comparative study of the Swedish Baptist Union and the Pentecostal Movement in Sweden, between which a rupture took place, shows that the break had institutional causes: the Baptist Union had become an increasingly institutionalized church by the very fact of its growth and by a modern organization of society; the Pentecostalists, on the other hand, were more ingrown, more isolated within the social body, and reacted vigorously against all "impersonal" institutionalization. Philip Selznick, one of the authors of the report, observes that the "institutional paradox" consists in the fact that the ends of the community can be practically annihilated by the organization which has been developed to attain these ends.[9]

Let us also point out that the numerical growth of a church or of a religious movement involves a movement towards structural and hierarchical organization, even if such organization had not been initially desired. A typical example is seen in the mendicant orders. At first, these orders intended to be truly mendicant, living from day to day on public generosity; but to the degree that their membership increased, they had to become structured and organized. The *de facto* catholicity of the Catholic church explains the necessity of a more hierarchical, more monarchical, more juridical structure; the division of Protestantism into small, independent churches, on the other hand, has permitted the maintaining of a more democratic constitution and facilitates the relative absence of juridical spirit.

In the Christian churches, concerned as they are to preserve the reality of the *koinonia* and of the intersubjective relationship, the parish has become the cell *par excellence*. In Protestantism, in particular, there is a latent congregationalism (which is seen, for example, in the limitations imposed on the central government of the church in the choice of pastors and the respecting of local traditions). This is so because the parish is the society which, by its smaller dimensions and by a certain social homogeneity, permits personal relationships to prevail over structures and rules. In Protestantism, the essential counterweight to hyper-organization is found in the maintenance of the rights of the parochial community, the respect for the base, the obligatory consultation of this base, which is the source of all delegation of authority. In Catholicism, hierarchical centralization has had a freer hand precisely because up to the present time there was little preoccupation with the rights of the local community (a question which figured in the programme of Vatican II). For a Protestant, the church is first of all the parish and secondly the more abstract and more juridical national organization. For a Catholic, the church is first of all the Roman see, from whence emanates all initiative.

The Roman Catholic church, much more so than the Orthodox church (which recognizes the autocephalous nature of territorial churches as a sort of dogma), offers us the example of a perfectly hierarchical religious society. In this society, initiatives coming from the base are certainly not impossible, but they must attain considerable magnitude before they affect the decisions of the Holy See, which alone can give them authority: the cult of the Virgin as well as the biblical movement are examples (antithetical) of this process. These movements coming from the base have seen their action restrained by two factors. First, there was the gradual substitution of papal authority for the authority of councils. Secondly, beginning in the fourteenth century, there was the designation of bishops by the pope. Up to that time, the bishop was chosen by election (which could be called popular election, since the electoral body at first was composed of neighbouring bishops, the clergy of the cathedral, the most eminent scholars of the diocese, inhabitants of the city, and representatives of the civil power). From the tenth to the twelfth centuries, laymen had even become all-powerful in the election of bishops. Beginning in the twelfth century, the electoral body became solely clerical. Finally, designation by the pope, with or without consultation of the civil power, won out. By derogation, the pope could provisionally and revocably concede his powers to an electoral college, which is still the case for some twenty bishoprics in Switzerland, Germany, and Austria.[10]

The pope, elected for life by the assembly of cardinals (who are themselves designated by the pope), is the supreme head of all the bishops, of all the clergy, and of all the faithful. As the visible representative of Christ and holding his power only from God, the pope has a power of absolute jurisdiction in questions of doctrine, of morals, and in generally in whatever touches the lives of the faithful and of the parishes. The acts which he carries out with the fullness of his apostolic power have the nature of infallibility (Vatican Council, 1870). These acts must aim to "define doctrine in what concerns faith and morals". To be sure, these monarchical powers do not mean that the pope absorbs all these functions. An important central administration has developed. But at the head of the principal congregations, offices (including the Secretariat of State), and tribunals, there is a cardinal, and the nomination and number of cardinals depends on the sole pontifical power. Formerly, centralization was primarily carried out by means of archbishops or provincial heads, but their function has developed in an administrative direction, as the sovereign Pontiff wanted to exercise a direct action over the bishops. The episcopal organization is the essential relay system of pontifical authority, with the bishops acting only under the authority of the Sovereign Pontiff. Within their dioceses, however, all secondary powers (chapters and diocesan dignitaries) have been left open to the course of evolution. Theoretically, the powers of the bishop are considerable; in fact, however, these powers are very restricted. A distinction is made between the powers of order which are related primarily to the administration of the sacraments (sacraments of confirmation and ordination, excommunication, blessing of monks and nuns, consecration of elected bishops and of kings), and the powers of government which consist primarily in the application of the decisions of the Sovereign Pontiff, and of the Roman curia, in the nomination of priests, and in the control of the clergy. In these activities, a large initiative naturally is left to the bishops, initiatives which concern especially the weighing of cases and judgments made on men. Their role is also pastoral: teaching of the faithful, of the youth, etc. The bishops are veritable counsellors of the pope, who consults them and is informed by them of the difficulties and desires of priests and faithful. But their collective influence on the government of the church is tied to the authority of the council. The decline of the latter between 1870 and 1961 has obviously diminished the importance of the episcopal structure of the Roman Catholic Church. Theoretically, the pope was only the *primus inter pares* in the body of bishops, a status which reflected his function and dignity as bishop of the diocese of Rome; in fact, the episcopal power was effaced before the monarchical power of the Bishop of Rome.

Although *vis-à-vis* Rome, the powers of the bishop have diminished within his diocese, they have grown, due to the fact that the chapters have diminished in number (formerly there were cathedral chapters and collegial chapters, secular chapters and regular chapters). These chapters, moreover, no longer participate in the designation of the bishop, but are confined to the administration of the diocese and of the cathedral (especially in the administration of ecclesiatical possessions, the revenues from which return to the canons in the form of prebend).

The dioceses are grouped in ecclesiastical provinces under the direction of an archbishop or metropolitan. The latter exercises episcopal functions in his own diocese. Secondly, he has jurisdiction in certain affairs which cannot be resolved on the diocesan level. He has an appellate function in all sentences rendered by episcopal justice. But he has no function of order and no spiritual role of his own, except the possibility of celebrating pontifical mass in all the churches (and cathedrals) of his archdiocese, of having the cross carried before him, and of blessing the people. Thus the archbishop constitutes a link between the Holy See and the bishop, and functions as a court of appeal. But he is not a characteristic element of the Roman ecclesiastical structure. Archepiscopal councils and assemblies, formerly convoked by the pope, have lost their importance.

The parish appeared in the West between the fifth and seventh centuries, as a geographical subdivision of the diocese. It is essentially a sociological phenomenon, the fruit of the territorial regrouping of the population and of its growth. For a long time, the choice of the clergy responsible for directing the parish belonged to the proprietor, employer, or lord who owned the ecclesiastical building. But beginning in the eleventh century, the papacy undertook a major struggle to wrest the parish from the authority of the lay proprietors. Today, except in rare instances, the nomination of the parish priest and of his vicars is made by the bishop. Apart from his administrative functions, the parish priest must regularly celebrate the divine office and administer the sacraments, teach the faithful, provide catechism for the children, give last rites, baptize, assist at marriages, preside at funerals, take the eucharist to the sick, hear confession, and make absolution. The select vestry has no ecclesiastical authority, but is an administrative body in charge of curial possessions.

The regular clergy, grouped in various orders and with a certain autonomy and hierarchy, is directly attached to the pontifical authority. The pope has sole authority in instituting a congregation. The congregations form a militia within the church that is responsible for assuring the unity of the church and of taking care of educational deficiencies in the parishes. They constitute a supplementary armour of the church and at the same time often participate in its renewal, since they are less encumbered than the hierarchical organization.

Pacaut characterizes the ensemble of this hierarchical structure as follows:

One cannot help but admire the perfection of its organization, the detail of its administration, and the majesty of the entire edifice. As the result of nearly twenty centuries of history, the fruit of long searches and always knowing how to draw the lesson from events, the Catholic church appears as the most imposing body of the contemporary world, solid on its base, difficult to disorganize or to impair, quick to ripost. At the same time, it is a body that sometimes seems out-of-date. Its conservatism, immobility, and inflexibility can be criticized. Yet, although the magnitude of it justly slows down all of the movements, the search for a more supple, more rapid, and more independent system, by threatening to undermine the hierarchy, can also lead to a dislocation of dogma. It can lead especially to assaults on the Unity of the Church under the all-powerfulness of the pope, which is one of the foundations of catholic beliefs.[11]

With a slightly different emphasis, we can subscribe to this general analysis. The Catholic church is, in fact, one of the few world-wide hierarchical organizations having effective power. One can find its counterpart only in the Communist party and in the great financial trusts.

Certain sociological traits can be remarked in this organization. It rests entirely on the hierarchy, the sole dispenser of the sacraments which guarantee salvation. Thus the Roman Catholic church presents itself as an institution that guarantees salvation. Certainly that does not impede it from being missionary; it has even provided a more supple transitional organization for mission territories which lessens the gap between the mission and the papacy (apostolic vicars named by the Holy See and apostolic prefects named by the Congregation for the Propagation of the Faith). But the object is to make the new converts enter as rapidly as possible into the ordinary frameworks of the institution of salvation, a movement which has been accentuated by the rapid development of formerly colonized peoples. This organization expresses the concern to constitute a *de facto* universal Christendom under one sole rule. Centralization indeed seems to be one of the essential views of Roman policy.

However, this system finds itself confronted by the movement of secularization and dechristianization, which makes it obvious that Christendom no longer exists, not even in the West, and that entry into the church is no longer made by virtue of one sole magisterium or the prestige of the church. The Catholic church has taken account of the importance in each socio-professional group of the witness and outreach of laymen as well as its missionary value. It has understood the importance of the involvement of lay catholics in all forms of social combat, especially among militant unionists from social classes over which the Catholic church, by itself, has no influence. This explains the methodically pursued effort to support Catholic Action movements, as well as Christian unions and Catholic political parties. In an apostolic letter of January 18, 1939, Pope Pius XI recalled the relative independence on the technical level of Catholic socio-economic organizations, but he added:

As we have said on other occasions, in continuing to draw their inspiration from the principles of love and justice taught by the church and to follow the directives given by ecclesiastical authority in such a delicate matter, these organizations not only truly assist in the amelioration of the moral and material situation of the workers, but also prepare the way for the apostolate of Catholic Action in worker circles.[12]

The church, in other words, has been led from the necessity of social action to the apostolate of laymen by reason of the very evolution of the industrialized world. But a basic question arises if an apostolate is entrusted to the laity. The structure of the church provides no place for laymen; it rests on the fundamental distinction between priest and layman, on the opposition between a clergy which is the sole dispenser of the means of grace and a people which can only receive these means of grace passively. The question is whether this structure can be maintained integrally. Take, for example, the various crises of Catholic Action, of the Catholic youth movements, or of the geographically more limited movements of worker-priests: do not these crises show that an effort has begun to close the gap between clergy and laity? Do they not evidence a desire on the part of the laity to share in the apostolic ministry? Theoretically, and in terms of canon law, nothing has changed and there is no indication of an imminent change. At most, it should be pointed out that Vatican II undertook to restore the order of deacon, which can now be conferred on married laymen. But it is none the less certain that a basic inquietude exists and that Catholicism, from the very fact that it finds itself in the presence of a problem of evangelization in a secularized world, is led to consider the problem of the part of the laity in the apostolate and in the government of the church. The idea of the priesthood, upon which rests the whole structural edifice, has been covertly or overtly called into question. Father M. D. Chenu has written, in regard to the worker-priests, that although the priesthood is defined as

a profession bearing essential functions: the worship of prayer, the celebration of the sacrifice of the mass, the ministry of the sacraments, catechetical and pastoral teaching . . . it is quite clear that the priesthood of worker-priests is a diminished priesthood . . . But we do not believe this to be the case, and a total theology of the priesthood and of its role would give another view of the problem.[13]

The constituent functions of the priesthood which Chenu mentions presuppose that the faith is uniquely "present and proclaimed" – that is, a state of Christendom. Once a "human collectivity exists outside of the faith and the mystery of Christ, the primary function of the priesthood is precisely to bear witness to the non-Christian world" of this faith and mystery. Father Chenu concludes that it is necessary to return to "A missionary status of the priesthood".

Such preoccupations show how the missionary task can bring the priesthood out of its canonical isolation, and consequently can allow the laity to participate more widely in this ministry. If such a movement, which is not restricted to a few persons, were to become more widespread – as the situation of Christianity in the world seems to call for – the whole immutable structure of the church would be shaken.

Certain political facts can also have an effect on the structure of the Roman church. The great incision made by the iron curtain has increased the difficulty of maintaining the absolute sovereignty of Rome over certain parts of Catholic Christendom. There is a Chinese Catholicism which lives in separation from Rome. Forms of national Catholicism threaten to appear, which Rome will not be able to disclaim, even if international relations become easier. It is doubtful that churches which find themselves in countries of communist control can re-establish, in the foreseeable future, ties as close with Rome as in the past. Perhaps they would not even want to. And yet Rome could not exclude them from catholicity without losing the advantage of a secular missionary action. Will it not be necessary, in these conditions, to relax the structure of the whole and develop towards a more federal and less monarchical form? Do not the reforms brought by the Vatican Council also have the intention of making possible a catholic communion in a world where ideological barriers no longer permit the existence of an absolute centralization, which the existence of national churches has already severely shaken? The present structure of the church corresponds to the sociological bases of Christendom. These bases no longer exist and have little chance of being reborn. Are we not then on the eve of a great revision of the structures of the Roman Catholic Church, a revision begun by the Second Vatican Council (regional conferences of bishops, increased powers of bishops, collegiality, definition of the ministry proper to bishops, by which they appear less as simple delegates of the Sovereign Pontiff)?

The structures of *Protestantism* offer a remarkable contrast to those of Rome. They cannot be said to have a definitive character. Protestantism, being contemporaneous with the formation of the great modern nations and sovereign states, was cast in the political frameworks that were available. It has sometimes reinforced these frameworks by the support which it gave to national languages and cultures. Its contemporary partitioning is far from being simply the expression of its doctrinal divisions alone, but in fact expresses the dividing up of Europe into nations, and its establishment in Africa and in Asia preceded the awakening of the indigenous nations by only a century. In the face of the thrust of this new nationalism, the young churches, not wanting to appear as importations of the colonial powers, have supported calls for independence. The result is that we are witnessing the germination of national churches which are independent from one another, but which are much more concerned than their western predecessors not to enclose themselves in absolute national frameworks. At present, movements are being formed which express the desire not to stifle the missionary impetus by a nationalistic-type fragmentation. Black Africa, in particular, is seeking common ecclesiastical institutions, which explains the increasing number of pan-African conferences. In the same way, the permanent conference of churches of South-East Asia, which was instigated by missionary interest, is evidence of a concern for transnational unity. To the degree that these churches are minorities in the midst of Islamic, Buddhist, or fetichist nations, they undoubtedly will experience less difficulty than the churches of the West in overcoming national divisions which have less of an existential interest for them.

The types of Protestant structures are diverse, and their diversity is a result of the different nature taken by the Reformation in the various countries. In those places where the Reformation was a clear break with Rome and where only one part of the population went over to the Reformation, the new churches show a distinct difference in their organization compared to Rome. In those places where the Reformation penetrated more slowly after a conflict had already broken out with Rome (England) and where the whole population was won by the new ideas (Scandinavia), the structures changed very little: only the content of preaching and teaching showed any change. This fact obviously does not mean that the Reformation did not have its own ecclesiological principles. But these principles are compatible with extremely diverse structures, which the symbolical writings of the sixteenth century always affirmed.

Obviously, the general socio-political evolution exercises an influence over the formation of ecclesiastical structures in Protestantism as well as in Catholicism. The presbyterian synodal regime of the Reformed churches bears the mark of the democratic evolution of the western countries. The example of the German protestant churches is of some interest. At the time of their formation, during the period of the Reformation, the government passed to the sovereign and to the prince, who showed themselves to be the juridical heirs of the episcopacy:

From the fact that the doctrine of the Reformation had rejected the Catholic conception of the clergy, a state willed by God and designed for the government of the church, each was called to the service of God according to his gifts and his possibilities. Thus it was quite normal that those to whom God had entrusted the government of the city should put their gifts and the means at their disposal to the service of the church, in order to establish and maintain order.[14]

Thus the prince would be the *summus episcopus*, but developments would progressively take away a part of his spiritual power and leave him only the power of order. However, with the revolution of 1848 and the political development towards a liberal and constitutional regime, the *Landeskirchen* saw the appearance of constitutions of presbyterian synodal type. In Joseph Hoffmann's words:

The characteristic of these constitutions was that they organized the churches in the image of the constitutional monarchies that were the political catchword of the day: thus the constitutions expressed the principle of the separation of powers (legislative organs which counterbalanced the executive power of ecclesiastical administrations) and the principle of a constitutional law of churches guaranteeing the right of the faithful and of communities in the face of arbitrary initiatives of the ecclesiastical bureaucracy.[15]

Thus these constitutions were characterized by a juridical thought animated by political liberalism. A democratic ideal appeared in the synods. Undoubtedly, this ideal was related to the progress of the democratic idea which had already introduced parliaments into the civil governments. The political upheavals of 1919, in depriving the churches of "outside bishops" (the princes), upset the juridical and administrative power of order within the church, which from then on would exercise both the spiritual power and the power of order, without the duality of these two orders being totally effaced.

Another example of a similar development is furnished by the institutions of the Lutheran churches of North America:

... the different synodal organisms developed along with the development of the American Republic, and in a conscious dependence in regard to its organic forms. This meant the adoption of a radical congregationalism, the form of government the best adapted to the American outlook. The power exercised by the synods and by the national ecclesiastical bodies was only that which the local congregations wanted to delegate to them. Franklin Clark Fry was led to declare that as president of the Lutheran Church of America he had to preside over his national conference every two years, and that his duties evidently stopped there. Even if this statement is a bit of an exaggeration, it is obvious that for Lutherans the power of the national church is still very slight. The development towards a more centralized ecclesiastical administration, which is clearly visible in the organisms of the churches newly united since 1960, is parallel to the growing power of the federal government in American politics.[16]

Numerous other examples could be cited: those of the Swiss cantonal churches and of the purely federal tie which unites them, the replica of the provisions of the constitution of the Helvetic Federation; the bourgeois imprint given to the constitution of the Protestant churches of France by the regime inaugurated by the Organic Articles of 1802; the transformation into associations of these same churches, which was brought about by the law of separation of 1905.

In general, one can distinguish three types of Protestant ecclesiastical structures:

1. *The episcopal type* is represented by Anglicanism and, with certain variations, by the Lutheran Church of Sweden. Both refer to the idea of a hierarchy in continuity with the apostles. For the Anglicans this succession has a dogmatic value and assures the validity of sacramental acts; for the Swedish, it is a historical fact without dogmatic significance. The Church of England resembles the Roman church in the sense that it is theoretically a church directed by one sole hierarchy, under the authority of two archbishops, one being primate. Each province contains an assembly (Convocation) which can make canonical decisions and which is composed only of representatives of the clergy. The supreme head of the church is the sovereign, but this is a situation which Catholicism knew for several centuries also. The laity does exercise a power (which does not extend to the realm of doctrine) through the Church Assembly,[17] created in 1921 and sitting at least once a year. Moreover, the decisions made by the hierarchy concerning doctrine (for example, Prayer Book reform) must be agreed to by parliament and ratified by the sovereign. Thus we are in the presence of a very empirical system, in which the Roman hierarchical principle is tempered by the intervention of a reputedly Christian parliament and by a veritable synodal assembly. Furthermore, since 1919 each diocese has had a diocesan conference, in which laymen are represented. This conference assists the bishop. It should also be noted that the vicar-general who assists each archbishop and each bishop is a layman. Anglicanism goes beyond the bounds of England and even of the Commonwealth; outside the Commonwealth, the Anglican Church goes by

the title of Episcopalian. And beyond the limits of the Commonwealth, Protestantism properly so-called is more clearly influential on Episcopalianism. There is no organic tie between these churches, except the conference of bishops and archbishops (Lambeth Conference) which meets every ten years. The Lambeth Conference has no jurisdictional authority, but it does have considerable moral authority. All the churches are in communion, that is, there is a unity of ministry and a sacramental unity between them. This communion does not constitute a juridical state; it must be confirmed according to the circumstances. Take, for example, the united Church of South India, in which Anglicans are united with Presbyterians, Methodists, and Congregationalists (preliminary talks with the Lutherans are in progress). The 1947 constitution of this church initially stirred up the water: in effect, all pastors active in the member churches in 1947 had to be integrated into the new union without conditions and thus without new ordination. Many pastors, consequently, were not beneficiaries of the apostolic succession, but this was not made the object of any dogmatic explication. It is considered as a historical fact. At the end of thirty years' experience, the new church will define its own structure. Despite a feeble opposition on the part of the extreme right, the convocations of 1955 recognized the Church of South India and intercommunion with it. In the long run, this fact may signify a development of all Anglicanism towards structures in which the episcopacy would no longer have such a clear dogmatic significance.

Thus Anglicanism would come more into line with Swedish Lutheranism, in relation to which other Lutheran, Reformed, and Methodist forms of churches that have maintained or restored the episcopacy constitute less distinct types of episcopalianism. The apostolic succession is not really present in them. These churches attach no doctrinal significance to the episcopacy. They feel that it belongs to the *esse* and not to the *bene esse* of the church. The episcopacy is primarily a structure which maintains the principle of autonomy in the church and removes it from the movements of governments of assemblies. But with rare exceptions (for example, the Lutheran Church of Denmark), the episcopal government is doubled by a synodal organization, often, as in Germany, with a lay presidency. The particular elements of the position of bishop are that he is not dependent on these assemblies or councils, that most often he is elected for life, that he is *de facto* a member of the councils of the church, and that he possesses a certain number of prerogatives which these councils and assemblies cannot call into question. Like the Catholic bishop, he assures not only oversight of the pastoral corps, but he is also the one who presides at pastoral ordinations. This system constitutes a sort of transition towards the presbyterian synodal regime.

2. *The Presbyterian synodal type*, generally of Reformed tradition, is characterized by the fact that the organization is constituted of a hierarchy of assemblies and councils, which rests on the base of the parish. The parish is the basic cell of the church, being the concrete community in which the word of God is proclaimed and in which the sacraments are administered. It is the gathered church. The parish is administered by a presbyterian council which often has the prerogative, if not of naming the pastor, at least of choosing him and recommending his nomination. However, this pastor, who often is *de facto* president of the council, plays a role in the presbyterian synodal system that the bishop plays in the episcopal system. Above the parish there are elected national and regional consistorial assemblies, composed of both laymen and clergy. During the times when they are not in session, these assemblies delegate their powers to a council or executive committee, which have the additional duty of putting into effect the decisions made by the synodal assemblies. This regime has been called democratic and anti-episcopalian. It is democratic in the sense that it rests on the people, the members of the parishes, which originates all delegations and all mandates. But it originates them only, for to the degree that a person rises in the hierarchy, the pressure from the base is diminished and the highest officials have a real independence *vis-à-vis* the parishes. Furthermore – and this is the anti-episcopalian principle – the presidents of the various executive councils are elected for terms, and are presidents only in their councils, which is to say that they do not have an intrinsic authority. They are only mandatories of their councils. But an internal development has taken place; initially, the presidency of these councils fell, by statute ordinarily, to a minister; this minister had a spiritual authority over his colleagues. In relation to them he had a power of initiative. This power presupposed that he come into personal contact with parishes and pastors, that he settled quarrels, that he intervened as mediator. Also, he often was responsible for the installation of pastors and even of presiding at their ordinations. The very instability of the social body of the church, the need to adapt resources in men and money to changing situations, the necessity of establishing a missionary strategy, of placing pastors according to the requirements of this strategy or even of modifying the ecclesiastical map, all this joined in giving the presidents their own authority and of transforming the councils themselves. Whereas the episcopal system became more flexible by the intervention of synodal

assemblies, the presbyterian synodal system tends to take a step towards the episcopal system.[18]

3. *The Congregationalist type* certainly is a rather late product which expresses a very strong individualism. Nevertheless, it also expresses one of the components of Reformed ecclesiology, in the sense that it accentuates the single local congregation, which in its eyes expresses the whole reality of the church. It is the church and consequently it will be autonomous. Its ties with other parishes will have the nature of a free contractual tie. The church is expressed only imperfectly at the level of its superstructures.

Congregationalism, generally speaking, has been discarded by the churches coming directly from the Reformation (although the Reformed have adopted the principle of absolute equality among parishes and among pastors). It is present, however, in Baptist churches and in many Congregationalist churches in the United States, England, and Commonwealth countries. Yet it is a system that essentially is not adapted to present circumstances. It is a system that is valid only in a bygone type of society. Thus we see the Baptists themselves seeking a world-wide organization and the Congregationalist churches are approaching and sometimes joining with Presbyterians.

In regard to the general problem of authority in the churches of the Reformation, it should be pointed out that in fact this authority is twofold. On the one hand, there is the authority proper of the Word of God. This is expressed in the pastoral ministry. Essentially, it is the power of proclaiming, with all the implications of such a proclamation, the forgiveness of sins, the blessing of God, salvation in Christ. This authority is closely tied to preaching and consequently to the ministries which are responsible for preaching. But, on the other hand, there is also a disciplinary authority that belongs to the church as a body (drawing up and applying a discipline). This authority belongs neither to the individual pastor nor to the body of pastors, who belong in a general way to the various processes of church government (consistories, synods, synodal councils). To be sure, the pastor, as president of the presbyterial council (and he does not always fulfil this role), does take a hand in this second authority. However, he is not the immediate agent of it. It should also be emphasized that the disciplinary power is worked out, in principle, in submission to the Word of God and to the confessions of faith in which the Word of God is summarized. It is nevertheless true that at the level of structures there is a duality, which appears all the more clearly to the degree that the territorial extension and the size of the churches are substantial.[19]

In general, the organization of Protestant churches is characterized by the concern that the leadership of the church be assumed from a common agreement of laymen and pastors, that this government have a collegial form. That is, it makes appeal, by means of elections, to the whole people of the faithful. This is not done by virtue of a properly democratic principle (in the political sense of the word), but by virtue of the religious idea that the Word of God is intelligible to all and that consequently the people of the faithful should be able to decide by reason of its understanding of the Word. This is the norm of the priesthood of all believers, which does not signify the repudiation of all authority nor a confusing of functions, but the fact that every believer can and should take part in the building of the church (and consequently, in its government).

Yet a difficulty quickly arises: how does one recognize the true believers, the mature Christians? Catholicism has a very clear juridical principle: submission to the hierarchy of the church. A religion like Protestantism, which describes membership in the church by faith, obviously could not make use of such a principle. This explains why the churches of the Reformation continue to have the problem of how to define the member of the church. Theoretically, it is resolved in two completely different ways in which two ecclesiastical structures can be distinguished that partially include the ones which we have been analysing: episcopalianism and the presbyterian synodal system, on the one hand, and congregationalism, on the other. It is a matter of the duality between multitudinist churches and professing churches.

The multitudinist churches consider all baptized persons to be members of the church. This means, sociologically, all those who by filiation and family tradition belong to the church, have received a baptism demanded by their social milieu, whether they be true believers or unfaithful members. It is clear that this type of *Volkskirche* is rooted in an age in which Christendom was an uncontested regime and in which the certificate of baptism had the value of civil act of state.

The professing churches, while making baptism a condition of membership in the church, require that their members make a personal profession of their faith (oral or written) and therefore subscribe to an engagement. Moreover, they tend to reject infant baptism in favour of adult baptism only.

In actual fact, in the present sociological development, the two systems interpenetrate. On the one hand, the multitudinist churches include a great number of members who are professing Christians, or proselytes, or men who have personally ratified the promises made for them on the day of their baptism. Many of them inscribe on their electoral lists only those members who personally request it and, in an age of secularization, we can be permitted to think that the majority of such members request it for good reasons. Finally, the practice of confirmation (at age sixteen in most churches; 18 to 20 in some, for instance, the Presbyterian Church of Scotland) presupposes a long catechumenate. This is somewhat equivalent to a personal commitment, to a true public profession of faith. The professing churches, on the other hand, could not avoid the formation of family traditions of practice. This means that they recruit their members primarily from among the children of professing parents and that a certain automaticity of adherence to the church will become current. It should be pointed out that the professing churches were born in an age of the dissolution of Christendom, whereas the multitudinist churches were formed during an age in which Christendom still had solid foundations.

The present dechristianization, the fact that in any case membership in the church is sought more as a source of social prestige, have produced and will continue to produce a sort of natural decantation among the members of the multitudinist churches: the lukewarm will move to the periphery of the church and will end by leaving it. In the young churches born from the mission in pagan lands, membership in the church, with all its accompanying sociological ruptures, is not an easy thing. Consequently, the majority of their members are professing Christians. In the countries where a degree of religious persecution reigns (the German Democratic Republic, for example), the only ones who remain members of the church and who accept the risk of a confirmation are those who have serious and deep reasons for doing so. The principle of the professing church thus seems to have the best chance of winning out, unless it is subjected to severe and, from the perspective of Reformed theology, quite ambiguous questions which accompanied it in the history of the original professing churches.

It is difficult to give even a summary view of the structures of the Orthodox churches. First of all, a great diversity is covered by their nature as *autocephalous* churches in communion with one another without juridical ties. Secondly, they tend to reject the entire juridicism of the western world. Finally, they give infinitely more importance to the living tradition of the church, symbolized in the divine liturgy, than to the virtues of organization to assure their continuity. Although they consider the doctrines of the first seven councils to be the dogmatic foundation of all true faith, they take an attitude of very great liberty towards canon law. "The canons," writes Paul Evdokimof, "are the external, visible, historical, and

mobile expression of what is immutable of the doctrines."[20] Three elements characterize Orthodox structures. They are hierarchical churches
and attach basic doctrinal significance, as Catholicism does, to the episcopacy and to the apostolic succession on which it is grounded. The formulation of doctrine, as the indispensable rule of faith and life, belongs
exclusively to the episcopacy, especially when it assembles in council. But
Orthodoxy refuses to push this hierarchy to its limit and end up in a
monarchism. All bishops have the same power. They all are bishops of the
Church of Christ. Evdokimof writes in regard to their equality and to their
collegiality:

Always the trinitarian principle replaces the principle of power with that of
accord. The fundamental principle of ecclesial structure sanctions the appoint-
ment of *one sole bishop* at the head of *one sole church* on *one sole territory*. The only
difference among bishops is that of honour, of precedence.[21]

The patriarch of Constantinople certainly holds a primacy of honour, tied
to the glorious history of his see. But he does not hold a primacy of jurisdiction. And Orthodoxy sees in the Roman pope only the bishop of Rome,
to whom Orthodoxy is disposed to recognize a primacy of honour (for the
same reasons that it does for the patriarch). In fact, however, the patriarch
of Constantinople does hold a certain right of initiative, as is seen in the
convocation of pan-Orthodox conferences, of pre-synods, and perhaps one
day of synods.

Secondly, the Orthodox churches attach a great importance to the
conciliar idea, to the gathering of all bishops who are in the apostolic
succession. Since the schism, this gathering has not been possible. No
present-day council can claim to be ecumenical. But this idea still retains
a decisive importance. It expresses a fundamental aspiration of Orthodoxy:
only a church realizing the total communion of the episcopal corps is in a
position to formulate the truth. Just as Roman juridicism is foreign to the
Orthodox spirit, so does Orthodoxy think that it is in the communion of
the church represented by its bishops that the Holy Spirit acts with freedom and power over the body of the church. Although Roman structures
are manifestly repugnant to Orthodoxy, although Orthodoxy has a completely different sociological organization, it is not only because its ecclesiology differs from Catholicism on the question of the primacy of the
pope – it is because its whole ecclesiology is pervaded by pneumatology.

Here, in abridged form, is how Olivier Clément describes this ecclesiology:

After the Ascension, the glorified body of the Lord, this body clothed with our
flesh and with the whole flesh of the world, was present in the very midst of the

Trinity. After Pentecost, *this glorified Body which already was the new heaven and the new earth, came to us in the "mysteries" of the church and in the church as mystery*; the Holy Spirit manifested it in the midst of the eucharistic congregation, and, making us *con-corporal* to this *body of God, elevates our community to heaven* (Gregory of Palamas).[22]

Although one can assert that all churches have a sociology that is largely the reflection of their ecclesiology, this truth can be affirmed particularly for Orthodoxy. And this undoubtedly is the reason why it succeeds, despite the persecutions which it has experienced, in maintaining its existence in the most diverse and the most hostile political and social regimes.

Thirdly, the communal nature is very accentuated. The church essentially is the eucharistic community prolonged and perpetuated. There where the sacraments are distributed, even if done clandestinely and not in public assembly, there is the church. The relatively modern idea of *sobornost* expresses for Orthodoxy this reality of a eucharistic institution. One can say that the Orthodox church is one of the cells in which, from a sociological point of view, the communion prevails over the association, the mystical tie over the social tie.[23]

NOTES

1. H. Lietzmann, *Histoire de l'Eglise ancienne*, vol. 1, French trans. by A. Jundt (Paris: Payot, 1936), pp. 73–74.

2. ibid., p. 73.

3. Marcel Simon, *Les premiers chrétiens* (Paris: PUF, 1952), p. 88.

4. ibid., p. 84.

5. Cf. O. Cullmann, *Peter: Disciple, Apostle, Martyr*, trans. by F. V. Filson (2nd rev. ed.; Philadelphia: The Westminster Press, 1962, and London: SCM Press, 1966).

6. The book by J. L. Leuba, *Institution et événement* (Neuchâtel and Paris: Delachaux et Niestlé, 1950) can be considered as a sort of theological justification of the correlation of doctrine and church constitution, if not of their alignment on the same level.

7. N. Berdyaev, *Essai de métaphysique*, French trans. (Paris: Aubier, 1948), p. 241.

8. The report "Institutionalism" of the Division of Studies of the World Council of Churches, published in *Bulletin de la Division*, 1960, no. 1 (6th Year).

9. This contradiction is clearly seen in the following example brought out by Henri Hatzfeld ("Mythe et mystère d'Israël", *FV*, September–October 1949, pp. 437–438): Contrary to ancient Israel, the Christian church wanted to be a spiritual Israel, founded not on the bodily paternity of Abraham but on personal faith – of which Abraham was also the archetype. But an institution of ancient Israel reappeared with the baptism of infants by the church. To be sure, the church gave it a new meaning, the primacy of prevenient grace. But "this sacrament of infancy in fact involves the renewal of the church and familial continuity". In any case, it is possible that this institution entails a

warping of the nature of the church, as is seen in the countries of Christendom. As Le Bras emphasizes (in a lecture given on November 8, 1947), there is a constant dialectic, one that must be maintained, between the structures of the church and its mission: "The transformations of structures exercise a direct influence on life and life gives rise to new structures. For example, the creation of parishes can light new fires of Christian life and, conversely, the demands of the Christian life unceasingly modify the forms of orders and congregations."

10. Cf. Marcel Pacaut, *Les institutions religieuses* (Paris: PUF, 1951).

11. Pacaut, op. cit., p. 73.

12. Text quoted by J. Y. Calvez and J. Perrin, *Eglise et société économique* (Paris: Aubier, 1959), p. 91.

13. In an article in *La vie intellectuelle*, February 1954.

14. H. Liermann, *Deutsches Evangelisches Kirchenrecht*, p, 151.

15. Joseph Hoffmann, "Les Etats (Laender) et les Eglises évangéliques dans l'Allemagne contemporaine", *Istina*, 1963, no. 1, 9th Year, January–March. The material utilized is taken from Hoffmann's work.

16. George W. Forell, "L'influence de l'Amérique sur le luthéranisme", *CS*, 71st Year, no. 9–12, September–December 1963.

17. To be sure, the Church Assembly has a purely consultative power. But an evolution is taking place that is tending to bring about a combination between the episcopal form and the Presbyterian synodal form of the Reformed Churches. Indeed, in 1964 the Archbishops of Canterbury and York designated a committee of sixteen members charged with the task of examining proposals made for giving a synodal government to the Church of England. The causes of this evolution undoubtedly are many. Among them should be mentioned the crisis of religious indifference throughout England and the fact that ultimately it will become impossible to maintain a purely hierarchical government of the church in a country in which all other institutions are democratic.

18. An illustration of this evolution can be found in the very cautious reforms introduced into the discipline of the Reformed Church of France in 1964. These reforms concerned the status of the presidents of regional councils. It is correct that their authority is a pastoral authority: consequently, they are not simply representatives of their elders. For the pastoral authority, in the Presbyterian churches, is the only vestige of episcopalianism. The pastor has an authority that is his own, which he derives not from his election but from the Word of God and from the symbolic texts of his church. He is responsible for preserving the pure doctrine. This responsibility, theoretically, cannot be subjected to the control of assemblies, if they were to deviate from the pure doctrine. Although he thus has his own authority (pastoral), the president of the regional council is nevertheless elected and his charge has the same duration as the mandate of the council.

19. In this regard, see the articles by Pierre Lestringant in *FV*, 1946, pp. 137–140, and in *ETR*, 1949, no. 2, p. 75.

20. Paul Evdokimov, *L'Orthodoxie* (Neuchâtel: Delachaux et Niestlé, 1959), p. 186.

21. Evdokimov, op. cit., p. 131.

22. Olivier Clément, *L'Eglise orthodoxe* (Paris: PUF, 1961), p. 44.

23. A very helpful book in this regard is Jean Meyendorff, *The Orthodox Church: Its Past and Its Role in the World Today*. Trans. by J. Chapin (London: Darton, Longman & Todd, 1965).

VIII

Sociology of Missions[1]

The characteristic of the sociology of missions is that it constitutes virgin territory. It has at its disposal certain valuable documents, the many histories of missions which have been written during the last fifty years, the reports of missionary societies, the monographs from the mission fields. But these documents rarely have been utilized from the sociological point of view. In the French language, the sole works which have opened the way are the works of Raoul Allier.[2] Although Allier was interested primarily in psychological problems, he locates these problems in the context of cultural groups – and therefore in the context of sociology. Elsewhere, Roger Bastide in his article "Sociologie des Missions protestantes",[3] sketches a very helpful outline of the tasks that should occupy such a discipline. Thus we will not go much beyond the programmatic level in this chapter. The subject can be divided into three basic sections:

1. Mission as sociological phenomenon.
2. Sociological problems posed by mission.
3. Sociological problems born from the contact between mission and indigenous religions.

1. Mission as Sociological Phenomenon

It is justified to look at mission as a sociological phenomenon for the simple reason that mission is a well-dated historical phenomenon. It is true, as the ecumenical movement has not stopped repeating, that mission is part of the essence of the church, that there is only missionary church, that since the gospel is not a doctrine for initiates but a good news to proclaim to the ends of the earth, a non-missionary Christianity is a contradiction in terms. It is a fact also that Christianity, from its beginnings, has been missionary and that the diffusion of Christianity throughout the ancient world cannot be explained without this profound dynamism of the gospel. But at the same time, it is also a fact that the church, once established, sometimes ceases to be missionary, and for long periods. It is a fact that when a western Christendom was established, protected by the political power, it was more preoccupied with shoring up the outer walls to protect itself from the Infidels (the Turks, as they said in the sixteenth century) than with being missionary. In particular, although the Reformation has not lost sight of the idea of an apostolate,[4] it was not at all missionary; it was content with evangelizing, with winning to the religion of the "pure gospel" . . . Christians. The only missionary fact that can be cited from the sixteenth century was the ill-fated attempt of fourteen Calvinists who went from Geneva, with the support of Calvin and Admiral de Coligny, to the Topinambous of Brazil (1556–1558).[5] Even this enterprise had a rather ambiguous missionary nature, for although it was designed to convert the Topinambous, it was even more designed to create a Brazilian refuge for the persecuted French Reformed. Whereas Catholicism showed signs of great missionary vitality, especially in China, Protestant missions did not really begin until two centuries after the Reformation. But then it came about as a sort of explosion. Missionary societies multiplied at an accelerated pace:

1792   Baptist Missionary Society (England)
1795   London Missionary Society
1797   Netherlands Missionary Society
1800   Anglican missions
1810   American Board of Commissioners for Foreign Missions (Congregationalist)
1813   Wesleyan Methodist Missionary Society
1814   American Baptist Mission (Boston)
1815   Basel missions
1822   Paris Society of Protestant Missions

The list could be extended indefinitely, for throughout the nineteenth century there was such an expansion of Protestant missions that Protestant missionaries were present throughout the world, overtaking and even outstripping Catholic missionaries. What does this fact mean? What is its sociological import?

1. In what concerns the development of the church, it means that alongside, on the margins of the established churches, there began to form groups and movements which were strongly tainted with pietism and individualism, but which were still restricted by the boundaries and frontiers, in which the official churches had let themselves be inserted.

The missionary movement began before the churches had commenced their process of disestablishment. The churches were still tied tightly to the states, to the policies and interests of western civilization. In regard to the situation of the German church, Ernst Troeltsch has shown that the tie between the civil power and the religious power was such that missionary enterprise was an impossibility. Furthermore, these churches were paralysed by their dogmatic uncertainties and their liberalism:

Mission would have meaning only if these churches, by enlarging, would go beyond the territory occupied by the German States and would permit themselves to make encroachments on foreign soil.[6]

Merchants and officials were irreducibly opposed to missions, since they felt that missions did not always sustain the interests of the colonizing people. Yet there already existed signs of a greater freedom and a greater mobility of the churches. There was a great contrast between German Lutheranism, riveted to the states and closed in upon itself, and Anglo-American Protestantism with its more attractive aspect. Thus the principal missionary enterprises initially were of Anglo-Saxon origin. Furthermore, Free Churches existed on the old continent. The missionary effort also came from them (Moravian Brethren in Germany). Finally, within the established churches themselves there already existed small revivalist and pietist circles which took missionary work in charge (this was the case in France and Germany). Thus the missionary work itself was contemporaneous with those signs of disintegration which showed up here and there in a Christendom which continued to align itself with the civilization and politics of the western states. As these signs multiplied, missionary work expanded. But for a long time, missions appeared as *private* enterprises and not as a function that the churches as such assumed and in which they recognized a basic requirement of their vocation. It was only during the years 1930–1940 that a radical change of perspective took place. This history explains the formation of those bodies independent of the churches, and sometimes in conflict with them, which are the mission societies.

2. In regard to the general evolution of society, it is necessary to mention that missionary expansion was contemporaneous with *colonial* expansion. To be sure, colonization goes back further in history, but beginning at the end of the eighteenth century it took a new form: the colonial powers no longer were content to establish commercial settlements on the coasts; they began to want to exploit colonial territories in depth. This is the source of the penetration of the interior of the African continent which characterized the nineteenth century. This was a materially favourable

circumstance for mission. The missionary appeared in the wake of the colonialist, merchant, or soldier. He profited from the routes opened by the colonialist, from the zones of security created by him. He borrowed his boats. He established his posts in the proximity of administrative and commercial centres. Thus a *de facto* solidarity was established between colonization and mission. It is necessary to emphasize that this solidarity was not consciously desired by mission. Indeed, there are numerous facts that attest to the existence of conflicts between colonization and mission. Many times the missionary went ahead alone, far away from the colonialist, without any protection (think of Livingstone going up the Zambezi). But the problem is not at all one of knowing if in fact the missions benefited from the security which the colonial enterprises procured. It is a problem of knowing if a sort of more or less conscious pact was not made between colonization and mission. It should be pointed out, first of all, that although the colonial powers saw the birth of important missionary societies (England, the Netherlands, France), the countries which remained more removed from the colonial enterprise (Germany) or even totally foreign to them (America, Switzerland, the Scandinavian countries) participated very strongly in the missionary enterprise: from 1832 to 1880, Germany gave birth to ten missionary societies and the Scandinavian countries to four. These facts, however, have only relative importance. Everything depends on the way in which they are interpreted in the collective consciousness of the people in foreign lands. Now, the missionary is a white. Often he is present at the same time as the colonial administrator, with whom he shares (an even more important fact) the same mode of life. He necessarily maintains, in the sight and hearing of all, many relationships with the colonial administration. The latter frequently confers certain official duties on him in the educational or medico-social realms. There is no doubt that for the indigene, the two causes are linked. Indeed, since the mission treats and understands him better than the colonial administration does, the indigene will make use of the missionary as a sort of intermediary between him and the administration. The White presents himself to the indigene with a very clear awareness of his own superiority (which is undeniably true in the technical realm). But the missionary also, in his own activity, presents Christianity as a religion superior to pagan religions. Missionary preaching places pagan religion in the ranks of superstitions, and relegates it to the "times of ignorance". And it is inevitable that Christianity often appears to the indigene to be one of the forms of White superiority. In case of danger, the missionary naturally seeks refuge with the colonial administration. Moreover, certain purely external and non-indispensable aspects of missionary life help to create confusion. An inspector of the Basel Mission observes:

the permanent installation of white messengers in the mission field and their sedentary position as indispensable heads of mission stations are in no way based on apostolic methods. Rather, they are borrowed from the methods of colonization.[7]

Whatever be the diverse intentions of the colonialist and of the missionary, the confusion of their activities is assuredly possible.

It is even more possible to confuse their activities in what concerns Protestant missions because the latter rarely have an international character. Sometimes, in fact, they have a tendency to present themselves as missions of the colonial power. The indigenes often witnessed conflicts between missions. These conflicts undoubtedly were often of confessional or purely human nature, but in the eyes of the indigene they could not miss having a political significance. French colonial expansion almost regularly was accompanied by Catholic missionaries and France, even during its most secular period of history, appeared overseas to be a Catholic country and its domination as a Catholic domination. In Leenhardt's words:

Around 1843, the Catholic mission of the Company of Mary (the Marists) was transported by the French navy to Caledonia. With the aid of the navymen, the mission was established and inaugurated its ministry with a mass for the armed seamen. Later a Catholic society, both commercial and religious designed to trade with the island under the auspices of the mission, sent merchandise to stock the stores of the mission station.[8]

After France annexed the island, the collusion continued. Now, almost everywhere, French Catholic missionaries found foreign Protestant missionaries (English, American, Norwegians) already installed, which they attempted to dislodge. It was this crisis which led the Paris Mission Society to intervene in order to protect, reinforce, and sometimes replace foreign Protestant missions. This was the case in Tahiti in 1865, then in the Leeward Islands, in the Ogoue Valley in Gabon beginning in 1888, on the Isle of Maré in 1897, finally in Madagascar shortly after the occupation of Tananarive. After the First World War, it was once again the Paris Mission Society that was called to replace the German missions in the Cameroons and in Togo.[9]

The political parallel is clear; it was normal, for example, for the French missions to intervene in order to protect and relieve foreign missionaries in areas where the French flag waved and where the French churches had to feel their responsibility especially engaged. But the other side of the operation appeared: the mission and work of the church became partitioned and fragmented according to national boundaries. It seems to have a sort of dependence in relation to the political work of nations. The missions themselves felt this danger. The Paris Mission Society provides a good example of the re-evaluation of practices which was necessary in order to assert the original nature of the missionary work. At the beginning of French colonial expansion, it had been tempted to limit its apostolic action to those territories where the French presence was asserted. Taking it elsewhere has been the source of many administrative difficulties and many political complications. The first French missionaries trained by the Paris Mission Society quite naturally seemed destined for the Algeria of 1830 where France had just installed itself. But the French government closed North Africa to all Christian missionaries, Protestant as well as Catholic. This was due to the policy of "Mohammedan accommodations"[10] practised by the French in Algeria. Later, at the time when Black Africa opened vast territories to France, the Paris Mission Society was on the verge of abandoning the territories of Lessouto, where it had gone in 1833, to the Swiss missions. In considering this move, the Society was responding to a sort of national appeal to devote itself exclusively to French territories. But the courageous work of François Coillard and the doctrine formulated by Alfred Boegner set aside this temptation. In 1884, the French government, in order to oust the English missionaries in Madagascar, requested the Society "immediately to put at the disposal of the government pastors who would be sent throughout the possessions". The Society, then under the leadership of Alfred Boegner, refused to share these views and supported the Anglo-Saxon missionaries.

A confusion between colonializing nation and mission was often possible, even more so because the utilization of the mission by the colonial power for political ends was often observed: the first Dutch missionaries from the end of the seventeenth century were practically without ties with their church. They were dependent on the state and on the Indies Company, and consequently had to follow their directives. In the New Hebrides, before the French and the English signed the Convention of 1888, some English slaveships, disguised as missionaries' ships and with a sailor on board disguised as a clergyman, attracted natives on board and sailed out to sea. The population of Aroe and of Eromango partially disappeared from this massive traffic in people. In the fight for influence between the French and the English, the French government subsidized the small Marist mission (1896) in an attempt to eliminate, by religious bias, the English opposition. Generally speaking, the history of the New

Hebrides was long that of an Anglo-French rivalry taking the form of a rivalry between Catholic mission (considered as a French affair) and Presbyterian mission (considered as an English affair). The missions thus were in danger of becoming the camouflage for a political operation in the midst of international competition.[11] Facts of this type abound in missionary history and they counterbalance numerous other facts witnessing to a real independence of mission in relation to politics.

The severing of the ties between politics and mission has been facilitated in many cases by the attitude of neutrality, even hostility, taken by western government in regard to Christianity and the churches and by the progressive secularization of politics. It has also been facilitated by the interest that missions have been quick to give, especially in the last few decades, to the struggle for autonomy of the colonized countries. In doing so, to be sure, they evidence a political interest, but their attitude has been totally free of self-centred political motivations. It is for ethical and religious reasons that they have chosen this attitude, and often they have had difficulty in making it understood in their country of origin. Thus, after the Second World War, Dutch missionaries who campaigned in their own country for the independence of Indonesia did so at considerable risk. In a general way, the missions that had developed an educational, social, and even economic work in their mission fields have been well-prepared to understand the development of the peoples in mission countries, to comprehend their call for independence and the rediscovery of their national culture.

Nevertheless, even if one admits that Christian missions have succeeded in disengaging themselves from ties with colonial policy, which risk producing a confusion between colonization and mission, at least in the collective consciousness of people in missions countries, another risk, perhaps more profound and more subtle, continues to exist: the risk of a confusion between missionary work and the work of civilization, between Christianity and western culture.

Indeed, the Christianity brought by the missionaries was and could only have been the Christianity of the missionary people, a Christianity strongly westernized and tied, since Constantine, to the destiny of western civilization. The two are linked not only for political reasons, but more profoundly, for intellectual and cultural reasons. However foreign was the Christian message to Hellenized thought, it was still in the world of this thought that Christianity had to formulate and express its doctrinal convictions. From the second Christian generation, from the entry of pagan philosophers into the church, a development began which seemed to be irreversible: the alliance of Christian theology with the conceptual apparatus perfected in the Mediterranean world. Many theological quarrels and the majority of problems dealt with by the councils were rooted in the forms of thought inherited from Greek civilization. As we have already emphasized, Christian theology was elaborated by utilizing all the non-biblical ideas of being, substance, modes, attributes, and accidents. The penetration of Aristotelianism into Christian thought in the Middle Ages was the most striking and most fecund example of this symbiosis, since it led to that majestic Thomist synthesis which still has normative value in the Catholic church. Certainly, the Reformation marks a breaking-point in this development. The protest of the Reformers in favour of the "pure gospel" must also be understood as a protest against the synthesis of Christianity and Aristotelian thought. But no break with a deeply rooted culture is total, because such culture is eminently formative. In fact, in its polemic with Catholicism, the Reformation necessarily had to take up theological problems in the terms in which they had been posed by the Pagan-Christian tradition. One could not create in one fell swoop a new language, new forms of thought, a new feeling. The thought of Luther is marked by Aristotelianism and Occamism, that of Calvin by Platonism. It necessarily had to happen in the destiny of Christianity that, having lost none of its dynamism, it would profoundly mark all these elements of civilization and culture which had initially been its modes of expression. The time had to come when the marriage between Christianity and civilization would become so intimate that it would be impossible to dissociate that which came from civilization and that which came from faith. This time was the age of Christendom, when Christian doctrine put on its classic forms, under which it was taught from generation to generation, with so much facility that this civilization impregnated with Christian values seemed to be one body with the *depositum fidei*.

This process of interpenetration of civilization and Christianity was made even easier by the fact that the diffusion of Christianity for a long time was restricted to the western world itself. It became provincial in becoming romanized, in inserting itself quite exactly into the framework of the Roman Empire. This romanization of Christianity undoubtedly had, among others, the consequence of the abandoning of Africa. From the time of Saint Augustine, African Christianity was cut off from Rome and driven back to heresy. It soon disappeared, and beginning in the seventh century the barrier of Islam was interposed between western Christianity and Africa. Islam did not even have to destroy the Christian church, for it had disappeared long before[12] and this Islam now constituted the most imposing force able to oppose the Christian penetration of black Africa.

This westernization of Christianity directed its entire history. In the sixth century, when Christendom experienced its first great division in the monophysite affair, the break was exactly along the historical frontier between the Roman empire and the Parthian or Persian East. Whatever were the theological motives at play, this division corresponded to the line of separation of two civilizations. The crisis did not bring about the disappearance of eastern Christianity, but it slowed considerably its progress towards Asia and consequently enclosed it in its western boundaries.

This constant process of westernization became especially evident from the sixteenth century on, when the Jesuits, after having followed the Portuguese caravels in the Indian Ocean, abandoned the political and commercial wake of Portugal and engaged alone in a vast epic journey through India and China. It was then that they experienced the impossibility of implanting there the Christianity of which they were the representatives:

... suddenly the problem was posed of the incarnation of the church in these civilizations which were radically foreign to the theology of the day. The world of India or of China did not permit a simple transposition of the western church with its specific forms. The Jesuits were all the more aware of this, since they arrived in countries by means of a lay subterfuge. They became acclimatized and were accepted by putting themselves in service as physicians or teachers. They did so well that sometimes they became counsellors or officials of princes and received indigenous names. At the very least, brahmans or mandarins, here were the missionaries concerned with presenting Christian truths in the language and categories of native thought. They started with supports which they believed they discerned in local philosophies in order to build the church.[13]

The problem of a dewesternization of Christianity was thus posed. Father Nobili and his followers went very far in this direction, moulding the organization of the church on the caste system, creating a new rite (Malabar Rite). But the difficulty was not resolved, for the specific nature of Christianity was thereby compromised and in the eighteenth century the Roman authorities condemned the Malabar rite and the Chinese rite and finally the Society of Jesus itself. This failure shows to what degree Christianity was westernized, since it seemed impossible to dewesternize it without alienating it. This is an important point: western culture and the western mode of life have furnished Christianity not only with its concepts, its intellectual armature, its modes of argumentation, and its vision of history, but has also penetrated its symbols and rituals, that is to say, the realities which it is hardest to transform. The eucharistic rites, the species of bread and wine have an immediate signification for every westerner. Indeed, bread and wine are a basic nourishment in the whole West. They possess an emotional charge and a sort of sacred aura. Their link with human life is immediately perceived. What will they become when presented to men for whom rice and tea constitute the provisions *par excellence* of life?

It is easy to see that the problem which mission poses to Christianity is a sort of challenge: can Christianity stand the test of its catholicity, of its universality? Or will it appear increasingly as an ideology of the West, tied to the destiny of its civilization? Mission at the moment is undergoing a basic reflection and certain "rending revisions" because, in great part, its initial insertion was in a sociological context of which it has often been prisoner. It must be aware of its sociological conditioning, not with the pretension of escaping from all sociological context or of somehow disincarnating itself, but of making a critique of its context.

2. *The Sociological Problems Posed by Mission*

Mission, in the very exercise of its activity, causes a certain number of sociological problems in the mission field, by reason of its profound and subtle ties with western civilization and with the colonialist movement which is one of the expressions of this civilization. It could be added that even shorn of these ties, it would still give rise to sociological problems in the societies which it evangelizes. Indeed, whether it is a question of pagan fetichist or islamized societies, Christian mission finds itself confronted by groups in which religion and magic are intimately linked in the social structure which they partially define. In seeking to bring a new faith and to dethrone the indigenous religions, Christian mission will thus contribute to the destruction of social frameworks, of customs, and of traditions, at the risk of leaving the individual without social supports. To be sure, although missions have had spectacular results and have converted entire tribes *en masse*, they could, ideally, have rebuilt a new society, supposing that they could eliminate the powerful remnants which continue to act on the spirit of the converts. But these massive conversions were the exceptions and, moreover, they were suspect from the religious point of view. In order to avoid the problems raised by the breaking of social ties at the time of conversion, mission has sometimes been tempted, especially when it was of pietistic and individualistic inspiration, to withdraw the converts from their native social world and to erect veritable Christian islands or villages around the mission post. Beginning in the nineteenth century, the German mission of Hermannsburg stopped sending isolated missionaries and began to establish entire colonies, a sort of missionary village, which would give the pagans a view of Christian life and would integrate the new converts. Some Christian villages were indeed constructed in certain mission fields. They declined rapidly. It is not possible, in fact, to segregate the converted pagans from their fellow countrymen. It is not possible artificially to create new social groups. At a time when the nationalism of formerly colonized peoples is so strong, and when there are even the beginnings of pan-African movements, the risk of this segregation would be even greater. By withdrawing the converts from their original social milieu, Christianity would immediately become sectarian and would demonstrate its incapacity to be a universal religion.

Generally speaking, we can say that Christian mission has not always been very attentive to the social disturbance which it introduced, by the very fact of its evangelical action, among the peoples of foreign lands. It should also be indicated why it has not been attentive. The Christianity which engaged in missionary action beginning in the eighteenth century was the Christianity of an already profoundly secularized society, that is to say, of a society where the churches had become societies differentiated in relation to the global society. They certainly exercised a large influence over this society, but the principal structures of this society were in the process of secularization. It was already possible to live in these societies without being Christian. Denominational membership had become a private affair or was on the way to becoming it. The pietist overtones of many missionary societies were precisely a reflection of this situation, which can be characterized by a sort of dichotomy: on the one hand, existence in the global society, and on the other hand, more or less free and willing membership in a church. The whole of technical, economic, political, and social evolution was produced, especially in the nineteenth century, outside the influence of the churches. A common morality existed, undoubtedly impregnated with Christianity but distinct from it. It was this situation which led the Christian missions to think through their apostolic action. They went to foreign lands to preach the gospel, to convert souls to the Lord. They could not measure the sociological repercussions of their action.

Christian missions went out to confront completely different civilizations. These were sacralized, non-secularized civilizations in which religion was not at all a private affair but rather the foundation of all the social customs and traditions. The rites of initiation were and still are related to religious beliefs, but they were also the foundation of the whole social body. To attack the religion through the preaching of the gospel was, consequently, to call into question the whole social structure. To convert to Jesus Christ was at the same time to uproot the individual from his social milieu. Thus it was important to have a policy of social re-rooting of the individual converts. But the missions, because of their western point of view and because of the embryonic state of sociological reflection, could not have had such a policy.

In particular, the missions, with their own view of what the Christian *family* should be, with their morality in the sexual realm, could not understand that by attacking these sectors they menaced a whole social structure. The Christian idea of family as a conjugal community founded on free choice and on a certain equality of the partners, and also based on a relative independence of the couple in relation to the larger family, presupposes two things: that the conjoints are considered by society to be adults, and the emancipation of the female. But none of these conditions is generally present. This idea of the family presupposes monogamy, but often mission confronted polygamous societies. And by polygamous society, we do not mean societies where polygamy is an accident of social organization, a detachable part of the social organization, but rather a sort of keystone of the organization. How can one make Christians in these conditions without depriving them of all social roots? Every human being shows and needs to show a certain pride in regard to his past, has need of linking himself to a tradition, to a line of ancestors. But he finds precisely that this past was paganism, that this tradition also was a pagan religious tradition, and that these ancestors were the object of pagan worship. Without renouncing its apostolic action, how could mission respect all that? Georges Balandier summarizes as follows his observations concerning the Lebou people, a tribe of present-day Senegal who live in an area south of Dakar:

... the retreat of initiation (imposed on the youths) involves strict rules and a teaching, a veritable civic instruction, glorifying the history and specific characters of the Lebou people. It is the ensemble of these positive effects which fall to the degree that ritual declines. It tends continuously to create a state of disengagement for the individual and a void in the heart of institutions, for no replacement rule is yet in force. Such a degradation, reinforced by the action of the Christian missionary, has already progressed in central Africa (as I have been able to observe in Gabon and in the southern part of the Cameroons). In no way do I have the intention of defending black conservatism, but of showing the dangers of this collapse of ancient frameworks in societies where an incontestable primitive "state planning" intervened. It brought for a short time only an illusory liberation of the individuals.[14]

Here we are at the heart of the problem: the tradition of the African peoples, which is both social and religious, is expressed in a veritable state control. This control assures the individual of social frameworks and a true security, for his future is laid out in advance by these rules. To be sure, one can say that Christianity brings a rule of life, a personal discipline that can advantageously replace the primitive control. But that proves true only for exceptional personalities, for men in whom Christianity has sufficiently penetrated to fashion a new personality capable of living without the support of ancient social structures. It is not true for the recent converts who remain in their former lives during apprenticeships and catechumenates. Christian missions have had a hard lesson about this in regard to polygamy; how many baptized Christians have "reverted" to polygamy and for this reason been more or less excluded from the church. It is likely that missionaries often interpreted these reversions as it was normal to interpret them in the West, that is, as personal moral faults, whereas in reality it was a question of quite another thing, of an obscure desire for social re-rooting.

Balandier, following C. Levi-Strauss, notes that in African societies "the circulation of beings rather than that of goods composes the fabric of human relations",[15] for the goods circulate only on the occasion of the circulation of persons – which is normal in a society where the techniques of production are elementary. This is the explanation of the very precise and very strict rules which have been established by tradition in regard to the circulation of women, that is to say, the policy of marriages and the practices relative to the dowry. Whatever be the amorous and sexual freedom enjoyed by the woman up to the time of her entry into marriage, that is to say, of her entry into a system, that freedom will cease. Whereas an adultery in the West is an event of only limited effect and creates a disturbance only in the narrow circle of the conjugal family and in the emotional life of the parties concerned, in African societies it becomes an affair of state in the proper sense of the word. To attack the rules concerning kindred relationships, even if it is in regard to a system which confers all authority on the maternal uncle (as is the case among the Lebou people) is to destroy a whole social and moral edifice. Undoubtedly, Christianity could not give its assent to all sorts of taboos and interdicts in the sexual realm, to a sexual "directorate" which would devalue love. Yet at the same time, it must be attentive to the fact that in attacking this "socialized sexuality" (or ritualized sexuality), the way is opened to a "libidinous sexuality" (to use an expression of Roger Bastide). The problem is not altogether new for Christianity, since it has encountered it from the very beginning. We see that Paul's preaching against the religion of the Law, that is, against the socio-religious foundations of Jewish society, had as consequence a libertinage, an irregularity which the apostle sought strenuously to root out. But the task undoubtedly was easier than in mission countries, because a common denominator existed between Judaism and Christianity on the ethical level, and Jewish Christians were perfectly capable of understanding that the unchaste would not inherit the kingdom.

Mission faces the same difficulties in regard to the problem of the dowry.[16] Although it is opposed, for excellent reasons, to this veritable purchasing of a wife, which is what the system of the dowry constitutes (and the price, given the present-day economic development, is more and more indexed on a price schedule), Christianity did not succeed in assuring that proven Christians would not pay the price secretly or even that the Christian solidarity of the community would not be shown in the help given the marriage candidate in securing the sum for the dowry. Why this resistance? The reason is that the system of the dowry is tied to the whole economic structure. It represents a mode of circulation of goods and of appropriation of wealth in societies where work and production do not always permit this accumulation of riches and especially the monetary species whose need is exacerbated by contact with western civilization. If the fiancé does not hesitate to act without the knowledge of his church, it is because he knows perfectly well that in wanting to throw off customs, he will expose himself to extremely serious sanctions – he will not find a wife. Balandier described the veritable anguish of a young Gabonese Fang who kept a diary to which he confided his uneasiness in seeing recede the moment, not when he would experience sex but when he would accede to the dignity of father, of the creator of a line. The number of young Africans who cannot take a wife because of the rising price of the dowry is considerable.

It is quite certain that reforms are necessary and that the Christian church is seeking to promote them. There is no reason to cast doubt on the spiritual grounds of its demands. But the church must see that many of the reforms risk creating a social void, a breakdown of the structure of social protection, without a new order having been set in place.

The problem is all the more acute in that these structures and the traditions which support them are not, obviously, called into question only by missionary action, which to a certain degree can integrate new converts into parochial communities. The decisive shock comes from the contact between civilizations and economic necessities. The circulation of goods will bear on the circulation of beings. Economic exchange will impose not only a transformation of the techniques of production, but of the social structures themselves. Given the rapidity and brusqueness of the transformations, the social void will be frightening. The Shanty-towns surrounding great population areas, in which are found individuals from quite diverse peoples who have escaped all traditional and ritual control as well as the salutary disciplines of the tribe, have not known the rituals of initiation and yet have not succeeded in being integrated because they constitute a sub-proletariat, a new society. This is why the libidinous sexuality, the alcoholism, and sometimes the membership in certain political parties constitute the sole recourses of these individuals.

No doubt the young Africans themselves feel the need to invent new social models. Witness the young Lebou men of Dakar who, being pre-occupied with the problem of marriage and the dowry, have undertaken a campaign with the goal of a new "matrimonial pact" in which the recent power of money will be limited. But Balandier, who reports the fact,[17] adds the following remarks:

Yet the Lebou men have had the framework superimposed over their own traditions by Islam, and this framework has also been upset. The situation seems most serious in the regions where Christianity has been diffused sufficiently for it to attempt an attack on old rules, but too superficially to impose its own system of values. The situation seems even more critical since the areas of Christianity often coincide with those of the greatest economic development. Such is the case in central Africa.

Bishop Stephen Neill gives a succinct summary of what we have just stated when he says that the missionaries have rarely succeeded in implanting Christianity without destroying existing civilizations to the benefit of an imitation of European civilization.[18] Even if this statement is too radical for the simple reason that other infinitely more powerful forces than Christian missions (industrialization, technical civilization, etc.) have brought about this dissociation of indigenous cultures, it remains true in the field of activity proper to mission.

For more than a century, mission has often been limited to transplanting cultic and liturgical practices and styles of western origin into the life of the indigenous church. A good observer describes as follows the errors of the Christian mission in Australia among the aborigines:

First of all, the missionaries have been too anxious to erase the culture of the aborigines. They have condemned all their customs and all their ideas as being satanic, instead of trying to bring about a progressive change and of using already-existent traditions whenever possible. The result has been that each conversion has been surrounded by anxiety and conflict, and has created useless opposition between converted members and the non-converted members of the same family or of the same tribe.

Secondly, the missionaries have gratuitously identified Christianity with the English middle-class style of living, precisely as though the salvation of the soul depended upon the fact that one drank tea, took showers, and lived in stone houses. The conditions of life that were imposed on them rendered the aborigines quite vulnerable to tuberculosis and deprived them of the resistance they previously had to pneumonia. The situation was such that two missions had to cease their activity for the simple reason that their members were dead.[19]

Such examples, though they are not caricatures, should not be generalized, the more so because, in this case, the civilization was extremely primitive and the missionaries thought with good cause that it was condemned. But in a general way, experts on mission insist on the fact that mission has not been attentive enough to the autochthonous civilizations which it encountered, that it considered them to be obstacles to its action and not at all as the normal framework in which it should insert the Christian church.

To be sure, this insertion of Christianity into civilizations formed by paganism is a difficult work. It is not brought about by a pure and simple adoption of certain indigenous customs and traditions or institutions. It presupposes a very precise theological effort in order to avoid any doctrinal syncretism favouring this adoption of institutions and of customs. It presupposes a sort of Christian baptism of these realities.

The most important task to fulfil in India [writes Ernst Benz] if Christianity is to be felt there in a proper way is to try to create a positive link between the gospel message and the spiritual content of the great traditions of Asiatic India, as the primitive church did between the gospel and pre-Christian Greek philosophy. Thus it is necessary, especially for the theology of the young churches, to discover the positive link between the development of the religious consciousness of the high asiatic non-Christian religions and the Christian message, in other words, to understand the religious development of the high asiatic non-Christian religions as a soteriological event, as an element of the history of salvation.[20]

We quote this text purposely to show that the problem is far from being a simple one. A culture is a homogeneous whole. It is difficult to extract certain elements (institutions, customs) and to integrate them into a spirituality oriented in a completely different way. What is in danger of happening is that these elements drain off with them something of their original spirituality, and thus a breach is opened to syncretism. Indeed, the thought of Ernst Benz seems not to be totally exempt from it, since he goes so far as to consider the "high asiatic religions" as a moment of the history of salvation.

An African pastor expressed it more prudently when he writes:

The revision of mission policy will be that of the method and means by which the gospel must be presented to the people and will not involve the transformation of Christianity. It is not a matter of adapting the Christian religion to the customs of the people, but of adapting the customs to the Christian religion, of purifying them through the gospel without destroying that which is good about them. Some missions have done this. They have given a Christian character to the rite of initiation through the ceremony of baptism. Such an approach elicits the co-operation of autochthonous leaders who are better acquainted with the mores of their peoples and who, through Christian education, can help to transform those aspects of their mores which are incompatible with the Christian faith. In this way, they can aid in giving Christianity an African form.[21]

The author of the above lines obviously could point to what happened at the time of the christianization of Europe, when the church took over and baptized many prechristian practices and even beliefs, or, on another level, when the church integrated hellenistic philosophical concepts. But the history of western Christianity shows that these operations, however cautious, were not without danger to the Christian faith. This movement resulted in the constitution of local pieties which could not easily be called Christian and to doctrinal syntheses which appeared to the Reformers to be incompatible with the gospel. The risks of such operations must be pointed out.

The first conference of all Africa churches which was held at Ibadan (Nigeria) in January, 1958, devoted a great part of its work to the question of the Christian attitude in the face of African customs. Emphasis was laid on the promising beginnings in adapting indigenous music and dance to the forms of Christian worship. The conference brought out that the rich heritage of African customs must not be rejected out of hand by westerners, as if it constituted nothing but a crude superstition. African culture has sufficient resources to give the life of the Christian churches in Africa forms of expression proper to them.

It will be noticed, however, that this conference approached the problem of the indigenization of Christianity by the easiest possible way: that of the forms of cultic expression. Specifically aesthetic elements are sufficiently uprooted from their original terrain, especially nowadays, easily to support this type of transplantation. In the same respect, the style of buildings of worship can easily be inspired by indigenous architectural models. The problem becomes complicated, as we have seen, when one deals with practices and traditions which have a precise meaning in the framework of the indigenous religions tied to certain social structures. One can even wonder if the preliminary dislocation of socio-religious ensembles under the action of economic transformations, of urbanization, of the mixing of populations does not constitute a sort of necessary preliminary for the liberation of these cultural and traditional elements and their insertion and re-employment in a Christian context.

In any case, mission is placed before the sociological problem of acculturation. This is not true in general, but on a particular point. Roger Bastide formulates the rule of this research:

It is placed in the context of studies on acculturation or of studies on the *changes* of social structures, viz., on the passage from tribal solidarities to ecclesiastical solidarity.[22]

In fact, the integration into the life of the Christian church of cultural and mythic elements which have developed on the soil of paganism will be successful only if those who are members of the church have found the church to be a more decisive place of rooting than the tribe. Ecclesiastical solidarity must prevail over tribal solidarity. Otherwise, these cultural elements, which at the same time are cultic elements, will preserve their primitive religious affective potential and will reintroduce their religious background.

The heart of the problem, then, is to constitute parishes structured differently than they are in the west, parishes which can be true communities for the indigenous members. Despite dechristianization, the parish in the west can still count somewhat on the educative and formative action of the family and even of the school, which develop values that are integrated quite easily into the Christian world. The indigenous parish can do this only in rare cases. The type of community which it develops is, in effect, totally different from that of the surrounding communities.

What is involved [writes Roger Bastide] is a type of grouping which is not founded on lineage or alliance, nor on kinship or economic trade – but on faith. To be sure, pagan religious confraternities can exist, more or less detached from lineages, but the tie then rests on the communion, in myths and rites, and not in a history and doctrines; not in the awareness of sin, but in taboos; not in a cultivation of affectivity, but in the search for ecstasy.[23]

Protestantism, Bastide continues, is based on the doctrine of the cross. In order to create a new man and a new society, the break with the old man and the old civilization must be total. No doubt care must be taken that this new society – the church – does not become isolated from the global community. Various forms of co-operation must be set up between it and pagan society (and this is why it is essential that mission develop a programme involving schools, hospitals, hygiene, even economic action where necessary). Otherwise the indigenous people will run all the risks of uprooting to which we referred previously. The church will then play only the role of a temporary refuge. The young churches indeed feel this necessity of building communities which are truly Christian, and consequently distinct from other local communities, yet at the same time are not cut off from the local communities. As an example, among many other documents, witness the report drawn up by the Christian Conference of East Asia as a result of numerous regional consultations. It states that *de facto* contacts are increasing between Christianity and other more and more active beliefs. It asks (a sign of uneasiness) that the relationship between Christianity and these beliefs be rethought theologically, in order that belonging to the people of God does not isolate the Christian from common tasks or break his solidarity with the history of the nation.[24]

Do we need to add that although the problem is felt, it is far from being resolved? It is much more difficult to resolve for Protestantism than for Roman Catholicism. Protestantism, since its beginnings, has presented itself as a form of Christianity that accentuates the breaks between faith and doctrine on the one hand, and beliefs, traditions, and rites on the other hand. Catholicism starts from the fact that every human truth is Christian *ipso facto* and can be integrated into the church. Thus Catholicism is more adroit in the working out of syntheses and more easily shelters certain forms of syncretism than does Protestantism.

Protestant mission sometimes encounters a clear desire to work out this acculturation, if not these syntheses, between national traditions and Christianity. This seems to be the case in Asia and especially in India among the indigenes. (In particular, Indian Christianity often has only a moderate respect for the Old Testament and judges that the Old Testament revelation can be usefully replaced by the ancient and venerable religions of India; as with Catholicism, Indian Protestants often think that one easily can take up again in a Christian setting institutions such as the Ashram or Saduk monachism.) But it also happens, especially in Africa, that the converted peoples are very much concerned to break undiscerningly with *all* their past.[25] Consequently, they are hostile to any elaboration of forms of civilization which would be attached to their past, to all teaching which would not be European Christian teaching. Acculturation is, indeed, a complex phenomenon which operates in several ways. Sometimes the autochthonous culture tends to penetrate, to surround the Christian community on all sides, to establish bridges between the old belief and the new. Sometimes, on the contrary, adherence to the new faith is accompanied by an effort to rid oneself of all traces of the past.

In any event, a successful acculturation, one made with discernment, could succeed only through a collaboration on equal footing between representatives of the two cultural patrimonies. During the course of the last hundred-and-fifty years the problem of the indigenization of Christianity has made little progress. This is undoubtedly because the western missionaries have carried alone the responsibility of their work. They have not been able or have not known how to surround themselves with indigenous collaborators who would share with them not only the direction of the work of evangelization properly speaking, but who would think through with them the sociological problems raised by missionary action. It is possible, furthermore, that a rapid change will take place in the course of the next few years. In fact, in all Christian denominations one notices, on the one hand, the formation of an indigenous clergy and even of an indigenous high clergy. The first missionary conference of Edinburgh in 1910 included only a few indigenous representatives among the thirteen hundred delegates; in 1928 the Conference of Jerusalem was truly mixed; in 1938, the Conference of Tambaram (Madras) included as many indigenous delegates as whites. Since then, indigenous delegates have had a clear majority. The situation has completely changed. The recent conference of the whole of Africa was a conference organized and directed by responsible indigenous leaders; whites played only the role of speakers.[26]

On the other hand, during the past two decades the young churches that have acquired a certain numerical strength and a certain majority have rapidly acceded to total independence. This should act in the same direction, that is, a more intimate knowledge of local traditions and institutions should favour the discernment of elements which could usefully be integrated into the Christian community, in conformity with the wishes expressed by the Conference of African Churches at Ibadan. The conference clearly affirmed that:

1. the abandonment of certain customary practices, if it is not compensated for by suitable practices of replacement, can produce a rupture of the social body;
2. some elements of tribal custom can accord perfectly with Christianity and consequently can be preserved.[27]

But it is evident from this statement that what is involved are elements of tribal customs, which means that the context of these customs will previously have been dissociated.

The dissolution of forms of community and of ancient social structures, which is conditioned by technical and economic development as well as by missionary action, is a sociological risk. In the face of this risk, the spiritual duty of the churches obviously is to constitute solid communities, where the individual can take root anew. But this rule does not exhaust the task of the church, which is infinitely more complex. In offering the individual a new community, the church must not isolate him from the human

community to which he belongs. It must not denationalize him in christianizing him, any more than the church in the West which attempts to
evangelize the working-classes should make bourgeois those whom it
converts. That is to say, the church must try to avoid being a community
closed in upon itself, which isolates its members and prepares a refuge for
them that shelters them from all social, political, and cultural problems.
On the contrary, it must prepare men who are ready to assume their
responsibilities in the building of a new civilization and of social structures
which no longer can be hierarchical, paternalistic tribal structures. But it
must not reproduce the elementary structure of the western proletarianized
masses either. In short, the Christians of Africa and of Asia must be men
who know how to discern in dissolving archaic societies all the structures
and values that are capable of being preserved and integrated into a new
context. The church will aid its members much more effectively in building this new society, in assuring these transitions if it has known how to
make a place for these structures and values in its own life, in its cultic
organization as well as in its family ethic.

We have just spoken of a spiritual duty of the church. Apparently we
have left the level of sociological analysis. But this is only apparent, for this
spiritual duty is also a sociological condition of the success of its action.

3. *The Sociological Problems Born of the Contact between Christian Mission and Indigenous Religions*

Christian missionary action has the goal of driving back the various forms
of paganism, of destroying them in so far as they appear to be forms of
idolatry. We have seen that this action has often had an unexpected result:
the destruction of social and ethical frameworks too closely tied to this
paganism to be able to subsist without it. We must now point out another
equally unexpected consequence: the appearance of new religions, which
are modifications of more ancient beliefs and which integrate certain
elements of Christianity (which, in this case, could better be called the
religion of the white man, for it often is difficult to figure out if this phenomenon of religious acculturation is produced under the influence of
Christianity properly so-called or under the influence of the prestige of the
reputedly Christian white man).

First, let us give some examples: Take, for instance, the "Malombo"
cult of possession. For half a century it has spread from the north with an
astonishing rapidity among the Bantus of the southeast.[28] There is nothing
particularly new in the foundation of this cult. It is based on the idea that

certain unfortunate dead people are obligated to wander the earth, seeking to become manifest through the living, of whom they take possession by rendering them ill. A specialist is then called, the "witch doctor", but he does not practise exorcism in the traditional sense of the word. Rather, he seeks only to appease the spirit, to render him favourable, to oblige him to state his name. When he is appeased, the sick person is healed. But he remains in a special relationship with this spirit Shilombo (singular of Malombo). He follows his period of initiation with the witch doctor. After having paid, he enters a confraternity of the possessed which is directed by the witch doctor. He then ceases to belong to his family and becomes a member of the witch doctor's "family". This new cult has entered into competition with ancestor worship and supplants it in important ceremonies. J. Eberhardt writes:

We would suggest that one of the elements which is most important in the recent growth and rapid spread of this worship of Malombo spirits is contact with western societies. The latter involve a breaking up of traditional systems and necessarily introduce, through the mode of life which it imposes on the Bantus, an element of individualization in worship which traditionally was collective.

Whereas ancestor worship was the affair of the whole clan,

the worship of Malombo spirits offers the possibility of an individual worship, with the *possessed* establishing a personal link with his Shilombo spirit. One can see confirmation of the suggested hypothesis in the fact that often the possessed and the witch doctors are women, unhappy in married life, sterile, unbalanced by the fact of social disaggregation, who find in this worship a means of freeing themselves from their condition of submission in regard to men and of acquiring a social prestige.

The influence of Christianity is tenuous and quite indirect here, but it is not non-existent. The western civilization which has informed and oriented this new cult carries values of Christian origin: personal relationship of the faithful with his God, emancipation of every individual and especially of the woman.

Another example would be the "Cargo Ship" cult in New Guinea, the "Naked" cult of the John Frum movement in the New Hebrides.[29] Beginning in 1940–1941, the movement of John Frum developed in the New Hebrides. It was political, economic, and religious all at the same time. The programme can be summarized as follows: kill or drive out all white men, bring in natives from other regions, get rid of European money, and give renewed honour to ancient customs. The movement was directed both against the Christian mission (Presbyterian in this case) and against the authorities. It was presented as the fulfilment of the predictions of the prophets. Soon well-known American Negroes would come, they would liberate the island, and would bring a new money. The so-called "Ticka" movement is a less violent variation and does not end in upheaval like the preceding movement. It is organized around a mysterious personage living in the bush, called Ticka, who will soon be considered as a prophet. He commends the rejection of all clothing and ornamentation (hence the name of the "Naked" cult), the destruction of old buildings and the construction of new houses (an eschatological sign), the abandoning of everything that has been introduced by the Europeans (especially money), and the expectation of the imminent arrival of a cargo coming from America which will bring wealth. A myth unites these diverse movements: the myth of this fabulous cargo which will come from America, but which also is sent by the ancestors. The fantastic wealth will more than replace the white man's presence. These are the religious forms born of the desire to appropriate the white man's riches through magico-religious means.

These movements [writes P. Martin] are part of a process of economic and social adaptation, still incomplete and unfulfilled, to new conditions born from contact with western civilization.[30]

These cults are imprints of a "symbolic Europeanism". It is certain that what we face here is a complex attempt of rejection and at the same time of appropriation of western civilization. It is typical that these cults are often directed against the Christian mission, the symbol of the spiritual power of western civilization. Nor is it impossible that the Christian preaching of the Kingdom has nourished this infantile eschatology fixated on the expectation of the coming of the cargo, but one cannot say this with certainty. Acculturation is at work here more on the level of economic aspirations than of religious aspirations.[31]

On the other hand, southern Africa provides examples of religious movements which have been directly brought about by missionary action, movements which sometimes appear to be schisms of the Christian church but which push their roots into the soil of African beliefs.[32] These movements expand and recruit their numerous adherents even within the ranks of Christian churches. They present themselves as prophetic churches. Their characteristic traits can be summarized as follows:

At the heart of most of them we find *faith-healing* and the *casting out of demons*. They have a river or a pool, their Jordan or their pool of Bethsaida, where they carry out baptisms and purifications. *Spirit possession is decisive*. The Holy Spirit is manifested through speaking in tongues or – as in the Congo – through convulsions and wild leaps. *Music, drums, and rhythmic movements* are part of the worship ceremonies. Often, but not always, the preaching of the

Word passes into the background. The prophet called by a vision or a dream is the inspirer. The figure of John the Baptist is very important in these churches. Often it seems that there is an identification between him and the prophet. But the latter is also Moses who leads his people from the house of bondage to the promised land. This is why it is very important ... to possess a piece of land where a new Zion, or Moriah, or Jerusalem can be built. The adherents can attend the great feasts and healings there and thus see what paradise is. The Lord's Supper frequently must give up first place to rites of purification, for example, the foot washing ceremony in the Shembe Church.[33]

These prophetic movements often are paired with messianic movements: the prophet is also the messiah. It is quite clear in the case of the Zulu prophet Jessia Shembe. He is aware that he himself is more than a prophet: he is the Servant, the liberator, the promised one. In 1911 he founded the Nazareth Baptist Church. In the 1930s his followers announced that Shembe is the God of the Blacks, whereas Jesus Christ is the God of the Whites. A hymn composed by Shembe himself shows that he has taken the place of Christ. One prays to the God of Shembe instead of the Father of Jesus Christ. Bishop Sundkler marks well the messianism of this church:

... the unfulfilled royal mythology of the Zulus is, in a way, baptized in the living waters of the Zulu Jordan. Shembe is a sort of reincarnation both of the ancient Zulu kings and of Jesus of Nazareth.[34]

One might think that we are in the presence of the sectarian phenomenon here, for we know that a compensation for a social frustration often is operative in sectarian doctrine. In this case the frustration could be political, social, and cultural at one and the same time. The similarity cannot be contested, but a basic difference must also be noted, namely, the invading of belief by myth, the mythic interpretation of the whole Christian revelation. Jerusalem, Zion, Moriah are no longer geographical places; they are mythic places which can be transported without difficulty to the land of the Zulus. Shembe can be both a Zulu king and Christ, for both have become mythical personages. The consciousness of the historical nature of the Christian revelation is effaced. Christ, although sometimes his name is still invoked, is no longer the one who was crucified in the time of Pontius Pilate. It is even typical that the historical person of Christ is so embarrassing that it disappears, since the confession of faith of the Church of the Nazireans of Shembe declares: "I believe in the Father and in the Holy Spirit and in the Communion of Nazirean Saints." The meditation of the myth makes it possible to retrieve a whole fund of politico-religious beliefs, of rooting the new religion in political-national aspirations.

But all that would not have been possible without Christian preaching, without missionary action. We can see how difficult it is for the mission to exercise its ministry. In the West, the church's preaching elicits faith or unbelief or indifference. In mission-lands there is another possible result. Missionary preaching, in confronting religions (frequently rather poorly structured) which witness to the disintegration of old social structures, can facilitate the synthesis of these scattered mythical, prophetic, and messianic elements. Thus it will also give rise to new cults, where one will find certain Christian themes promoted to the rank of myths but grafted onto a completely different inspiration.

This is to say that mission can result in unexpected consequences, especially when it operates in areas where it contributes to the dissociation of social and religious structures without having the chance to create a community sufficiently vast and structured to keep the old myths from being operative and from annexing some odds and ends of Christian teaching through a sort of selective acculturation.

To be sure, the undeniable specific nature of Christianity should protect it, theoretically, from the danger of syncretism. In fact, such is not the case. Even in Europe syncretisms have appeared, not so much between Christianity and other religions as between Christianity and a culture of Hellenic origin. It is all the more understandable, therefore, that in mission countries these syntheses or rather simple amalgamations between the elementary forms of paganism and a poorly assimilated Christianity should be born so easily. As A. Metraux reports,[35] in Haiti there exists in the same souls, in perfect harmony, Catholicism and the Voodoo religion, which was imported from Africa by slaves from Dahomey and from Nigeria. Devotion to Voodooism which is always acquiring new divinities, is accompanied by a respectful submission to the Catholic church and to its hierarchy. To convert to Protestantism (rather frequently the case) is often to abandon both the Catholic church and Voodoo.

But Protestantism itself does not necessarily destroy this syncretism since conversion to Protestantism, for many Haitians, represents only an entrance into a particular magic circle where the ancient gods lose their power.

Conversion then becomes a sort of magic precaution against the wrath of the gods. Protestantism fills the role of a retrenchment, or rather of a magic circle, where the individual in the grasp of misfortune can take refuge in the hope of putting an end to his misfortune.

In case of misfortune or of sickness which resists the efforts of the witch doctor, "the sick person has only one recourse: to become Protestant".

And often the new converts maintain an implicit faith in the spirit of the Voodoo, but now it is called Satan.[36]

The great danger run by Christian mission is, indeed, superficial christianization. This danger is greater than it has been in the West, where Christianity had the chance to see a civilization develop with it which it could, in large part, control and inspire. From this fact, it has succeeded in extinguishing many of the urges to syncretism.

NOTES

1. The first part of this chapter is based on analyses already presented in our work *Décolonisation et Missions protestantes* (Paris: Société des Missions évangéliques, 1964).

2. R. Allier, *La psychologie de la conversion chez les peuples non civilisés* (Paris: Payot, 1925), and *Le non-civilisé et nous, différence irréductible ou identité foncière?* (Paris: Payot, 1927).

3. *ASR*, no. 8, July–December 1959.

4. Cf. G. F. Dankbaar, "L'apostolat selon Calvin", *RHPR*, 41st Year, 1961/4.

5. See Olivier Reverdin, *Quatorze calvinistes chez les Topinambous; Histoire d'une mission genevoise au Brésil* (Geneva and Paris: E. Droz et Minard, 1957).

6. E. Vermeil, "Ernst Troeltsch et le problème des Missions chrétiennes", *MNC*, October–December 1953, no. 28.

7. H. Witschi, "Vers l'autonomie de l'Eglise indigène", in the collective volume *La Lumière des nations* (Neuchâtel: Delachaux et Niestlé, 1944), p. 47.

8. Maurice Leenhardt, "De la gangue tribale à la conscience morale", *MNC*, no. 66, April–June 1963.

9. Jean Bianquis, *L'Evangile et le monde*, Congrès des Missions protestantes, 1931 (Paris: Société des Missions, 1931).

10. Cf. M. Leenhardt, "Les Missions protestantes françaises", in the collective work *Protestantisme français* (Paris: Plon, 1945), p. 378.

11. Cf. M. Leenhardt, "L'expérience hébridaise", *MNC*, 1951, no. 19.

12. Cf. Louis Joubert, "La prise de contact entre l'Afrique et la Mission chrétienne", *MNC*, no. 14, April–June 1950.

13. Louis Joubert, "Les caractéristiques de la Mission chrétienne en Asie", *ETR*, 30th Year, 1955, no. 1.

14. Georges Balandier, *Afrique ambiguë* (Paris: Plon, 1957), p. 30.

15. ibid., p. 27.

16. G. Balandier ("Actualité du problème de la dot en Afrique Noire", *MNC*, no. 21, January–March 1951) has emphasized the whole social importance of the dowry in a clan society. He shows that the suppression of the dowry is followed by a certain number of consequences that are disastrous for social structures and social equilibrium, yet this measure nevertheless is called for, in the name of ethical and religious principles, both by the more advanced Africans and by the Christian missions. One can see the complexity of the relationship between Christianity and social structures.

17. ibid., p. 33.

18. Stephen Neill, "Une école des Beaux-Arts en Ouganda", *MNC*, no. 18, April–June 1951.

19. Bengt Danielsson, *Expédition Boumerang* (Paris: Albin Michel, 1960).

20. Ernst Benz, "Manilal Parekh, le Gandhi chrétien", *MNC*, no. 55–56, July–December 1960.

21. Josuhé Danho, "Rencontre entre chrétiens et non-chrétiens", *MNC*, no. 43–44, July–December 1957.

22. R. Bastide, "Sociologie des Missions protestantes".

23. ibid.

24. See this report in the *Bulletin* of the Division of Studies of the World Council of Churches (1961/1) under the title "Rencontre chrétienne avec des hommes de religions différentes".

25. Stephen Neill, art. cit.

26. The same movement is seen in the Catholic Church. In 1957, for twenty million Black Christians in Africa there were twenty Black bishops as opposed to eleven white bishops. But there were only 1784 indigenous priests as against 10,796 foreign priests. The indigenous Catholics still constituted the mass of the lower clergy, or 50,000 catechists (*Nouvelle revue théologique*, 1957, pp. 636–641).

27. See the brochure *Ibadan: Conférence des Eglises d'Afrique, 1958* (Paris: Société des Missions évangéliques, 1959).

28. It has been described in an article by Jacqueline Eberhardt, "Note sur l'acculturation et le culte de possession 'Malombo' chez les Bantous du Sud-Est", *MNC*, no. 43–44, July–December, 1957.

29. Cf. Jean Guiart, "Forerunners of Melanesian Nationalism", *Oceania*, 22, December 2, 1951; Pierre Martin, "Les mouvements de John Frum et de Ticka. Deux faits sociaux totaux aux Nouvelles-Hébrides", *MNC*, no. 43–44, July–December 1957 [cf. also, Peter Worsley, *The Trumpet Shall Sound; A Study of the "Cargo" Cults in Melanesia* (New York: Schocken Books, Inc., 1967)].

30. Martin, art. cit.

31. This is particularly those forms of messianism (as we see already in the Old Testament) that integrate socio-political aspirations and the fragments of revelation into a difficult-to-analyse whole. These syntheses take on considerable power at the time of liberation crises: "The subjugated peoples, whose cultures and beliefs were crushed by the invaders, tend to transform their nostalgia of a happy past into dynamic dreams oriented towards a future which will restore their initial glory and confound their enemies. Such emotional crises have been often repeated among primitive peoples crushed by white civilization, and have often had extremely serious political consequences. The history of the North American Indians provides many examples of mystical movements, the expression of the intense melancholy of a moribund culture and the expression of its desperate desire to affirm itself, even through the most fantastic dreams." This phenomenon often takes the following form: "The thaumaturge who has gained fame as a healer of the sick and who is presented as saviour, preaching resistance to the foreigners and promising his followers immunity to bullets" (A. Métraux, "Les Messies de l'Amérique du Sud", *ASR*, no. 4, July–December 1957). These facts should be compared with the analyses of H. Desroches on the messianism of sects.

32. See Marie-Louise Martin, "Face aux mouvements prophétiques et messianiques en Afrique méridionale", *MNC*, no. 64, October–December 1962.

33. ibid., pp. 235–236.

34. B. Sundkler, *Bantu Prophets in South Africa* (2nd ed.; New York and Oxford: Oxford University Press, 1961), p. 282, quoted by M.-L. Martin.

35. A. Métraux, "Vadou et protestantisme", *Revue de l'histoire des religions*, vol. 144, October–December 1953, no. 2.

36. See also, on this subject, the study by Roger Bastide, "Le Folklore brésilien" *Revue de psychologie des peuples*, 1950, no. 4.

IX

Sociology of Ecumenism

1. *Characteristics*

For more than half a century, the ecumenical movement has penetrated deeper and deeper into the life of all of the churches, and has led them to seek, by various paths, the unity of the church. This *movement* takes concrete form in a certain number of *institutions*, which can both render it effective or paralyse it. We shall have to consider ecumenism both as movement (organized movements as well as the more diffuse aspirations) and as institutions (World Council of Churches, world-wide confessional alliances, Pan-Orthodox Conference, Roman Secretariat for Unity, Second Vatican Council).

The historical point of departure of the ecumenical movement can be located at the end of the nineteenth and the beginning of the twentieth centuries. Of course, this statement can be contested by alleging that the search for unity has never been totally abandoned in Christianity. One could list numerous conferences and reunions which in the sixteenth century, for example, attempted either to reunite Protestants and Catholics, or to prevent the disintegration of Protestantism. One could mention the often precise and concrete ecumenical discussions that took place in the seventeenth century between men like Bossuet and Leibniz. To be sure, all of these facts, considered in their *value*, have ecumenical significance. But, firstly, all of these phenomena involve only a certain number of individuals (usually individuals having an ecclesiastical authority or social prestige); and, secondly, they aim to repair a breach, ultimately by the pure and simple reduction of heresy (cf., for example, the Council of Florence, 1439). They are not motivated by the idea of a manifestation of the unity of the Christian church throughout the inhabited earth. They look backwards to an already existing institution, which must be restored to a lost unity. Certainly, the present ecumenical movement also presents this aspect. It gives preference to discussions aiming at the reunion of separated churches. During the past forty years, it has recorded a considerable number of successes (United Church of Canada, Reformed Church of France, Church of South India, etc). But this aim remains secondary, included as it is in a higher, more complete goal: the church united through the geographical and sociological diversity of the world. The Roman Catholic Church entered into the ecumenical dialogue a number of years ago, through a certain number of quite spectacular acts and gestures. One can say that, despite these acts and gestures, the entry of the Catholic church is still timid and hesitant. But this is because the Catholic church continues to think more of *reunion* of the churches (generally under the form of a great return) than of ecumenism properly so-called, which calls it into question as institution. Similar remarks can be made regarding Orthodoxy. Certainly, Orthodoxy does not envisage so much the absorption of other confessions into itself (its division into autocephalous churches, which are only in communion with one another, forbids such an aim). Rather, it envisages a common march of all the Christian churches towards not an absolutely new and unknown form of the church, but towards the past, towards a return to the undivided church of the first seven ecumenical councils. Of course, these diverse ideas do not constitute an absolute impediment to ecumenism. The power of the movement is seen from the fact that it acts like a magnet and draws the various Christian groups together. Yet it remains, none the less, that in its origin the ecumenical movement was more of a Protestant phenomenon because the Protestant churches, from the fact of their ecclesiology, were more disposed than others to attempt the ecumenical adventure. (Thus the Encyclical *Mortalium Animos* of 1928 was not entirely wrong in qualifying it as a panProtestant movement, although this term greatly over-emphasizes the aspect of reunion of the separated denominations.)

2. *How to View the Ecumenical Movement from a Sociological Point of View*

The motivations of the ecumenical movement are essentially religious and theological. The search for unity is presented as obedience to the command of the Lord and as conforming to his prayer. These motivations are the basis of the awareness of the scandal of division. That it is not a matter of subsidiary motivations, of an ideological superstructure reflecting a quite different natural process, is proven by the very policy of ecumenical institutions. One thinks, as example, of the World Council of Churches, which readily eliminated from its decisions anything that would seem to make ecumenism appear as an attempt to create a common front against an external enemy (communism, materialism[1]). The reason that the Roman Catholic Church has remained apart from the ecumenical movement (aside from dogmatic reasons) is that it has been very open to the idea of a common anti-materialistic front and long has nurtured the nostalgia of the reconstruction of a *Christendom* of the medieval type. The ecumenical movement, precisely to the degree that it looks ahead, has undoubtedly underlined the importance, for unity itself, of mission and evangelization, of witness borne to those outside.[2] But this mission and evangelization are the complete opposite of an action of defence, of a strategic operation of reducing an adversary. Numerous official texts of the World Council of Churches recall the fact that Christianity is not bound to any form of civilization, to any particular type of political and social organization. And, although the World Council takes up the defence of freedom wherever it is threatened, it has never formulated, as Rome has, a condemnation concerning collectivist regimes as such. Of course, the work of the former Life and Work movement, as well as that of the present "Church and Society" department of the World Council, attempt to show the perils run by freedom and human dignity in collectivist regimes. But capitalistic and liberal society is submitted to the same criticisms.

These very brief remarks are intended solely to emphasize the difficulty of our undertaking: a sociological approach to the ecumenical movement. Is not such an approach in itself distorting? Let us say again what we have said of all ecclesial sociology: it does not claim to reduce the spiritual to the social, it does not claim to trim back theological motivations to the rank of more or less illusory ideological superstructures. It seeks only to understand the social conditioning of an event. This conditioning does not exhaust the essence of it, but it manifests the sociological situation in which a movement is born.

In one of the rare sociological studies devoted to the ecumenical movement, Mario Miegge correctly points out two types of sociological research capable of clarifying it. On the one hand, one can directly consider the ecumenical movement and the churches which compose it, and ask what type of threat the church feels that constitutes the ecumenical movement as a *response* or a reaction. What crisis situation started the churches on the ecumenical road? On the other hand, in an indirect fashion, the point of departure is taken in the evolution of the global society. The question then is whether or not this society, in the process of economic, cultural, and social unification, has exercised pressure or a certain attraction on the churches. Has it not led them to seek a greater unity of religious forms, has it not been the occasion for them to ask themselves the question of their unity? True, in this perspective, one considers these differentiated societies that are the churches as a function of the general social process. But it would be useless to want to pretend that the churches pursue their existence completely on the margin of this social process and without paying it any attention.[3]

Although this study inspires us, we will follow a slightly different approach.

3. *The Sociological Conditioning of Ecumenism*

First of all, we should point out that for the phenomenon of missionary expansion as well as for ecumenism as we have defined it, the beginning and development came at a particular moment in history. The precise moment was when it became evident that the secularization of society would finally result in a real dechristianization and that this dechristianization was expressed in the fact that reputedly Christian peoples no longer felt that the churches assumed an indispensable function. Religion was considered to be a private affair and, even more, as an affair exclusively concerning certain social classes, as an affair serving to provide the dominant classes with ethical decorum (after long serving to assure their prestige). This view was justified by the formation and growth, in the nineteenth century, of an important working-class, which developed outside all contact with the churches and most often with hostility regarding the ecclesiastical powers. Did not Marxism, which came to serve as the cultural armature of this working-class, teach that religion is one of the forms of human alienation, that although Christianity and especially the Reformation had had revolutionary meaning, this meaning had long since been lost? According to Marx, it would be fruitless to want to attack religion as the cause of all human evils:

To demand that the people renounce the illusions of their situation is to demand that they renounce a situation that has need of illusions.

Now Marxism justly claims to call man to a situation in which, fully master of his destiny and disposing of the fruits of his work, he will no longer have need of illusions, that is to say, of those fantastic projections which serve as compensation for his humiliated condition. The communist revolution was under way. The working-class had become aware of its real situation and of the power which it held to transform this situation. And because of it, the world of religious and spiritualist illusions was collapsing. The churches are losing their social function and are condemned to disappear. Although at the time of the Reformation, certain marginal movements (like the Anabaptism of Thomas Münzer and the various forms of prophetism) had been able to get in step with social progress and to bring about profound changes, this time was past. Since the French Revolution, we have been in a period of the liquidation of religion, in a period in which the idea of God had no place, in which Christianity could neither be reborn nor renewed nor even leave a place for a new religion.[4] Despite these marxist analyses and predictions, the nineteenth century certainly experienced all sorts of movements of religious revival and renaissance, Protestant as well as Catholic. But since such movements scarcely affected the working-class, Marx and Engels took no account of them. Since Marxism did not remain an academic doctrine, but effectively became the ideology of the world-wide proletariat, it is easy to understand how it was able to make the churches feel their total isolation in a social evolution which abandoned them on the sidelines.

The working-classes' dislike and disinterest regarding the church and Christianity (despite the religious and even Christian flavour of certain forms of non-Marxist socialism which, however, were progressively eliminated by the Marxist tendency) was not compensated by any strengthening from the other social classes. From the eighteenth century, the peasant class was characterized by the existence of zones of religious practice and zones of indifference. Peasant traditionalism assured the continuation of these zones without much change. The cultured classes, liberal and middle-class, were quite variegated. However, a great many of them, heirs of the philosophy of the Enlightenment of the eighteenth century and of the positivism and scientism of the nineteenth century, had long been alienated not only from all religious practice, but from all real faith. They retained only a vague deism and considered that religion was good for maintaining the lower classes in submission. This was the source of the often very clerical politics of the managerial and bourgeois classes, a political view which denounced the different movements of the so-called Social Gospel (whose very existence attested to the gravity of the situation). The bourgeois class thought that religion was necessary for the masses, at the precise moment in history when these classes had long been detached from the churches. The bourgeoisie could not see that the ideas it professed went along the very same lines that Marxist teaching did, namely, that religion is an illusory compensation (Marx's opium) for the oppressed classes.

At the same time, despite the undeniable successes of missions, the non-Christian religions were not ready to admit defeat. During the twentieth century there has incessantly been both a renaissance of ancient asiatic religions and a movement of conquest in North Africa on the part of Islam. As long as the Asiatic and African peoples remained under the domination of the West, this situation caused no particular alarm to western Christendom. However, the political events between the world wars and especially after the Second World War led to rapid decolonization, the access to independence of Asian and African peoples, and their entrance on to the stage of history. Since the matter involves human masses of great fecundity, Christianity has had to take account of the fact that time is not on its side and that it will find itself in a minority position in the world.

Crespy asks a pertinent question in this regard:

Would ecumenism be possible if all the churches were not in the process of realizing that they are in the same boat, that each, for its own part, no longer is in its own heritage, with nothing to face the contemporary situation? The hope for unity arises out of a common distress. When churches proudly think that they hold a truth which puts them out of reach of all difficulty, there is no ecumenism (this is the case for the fundamentalists; not long ago it was still the case for the Roman church).[5]

A crisis situation which has become fully obvious: such, undoubtedly, is one of the aspects of this awakening without which the ecumenical enterprise would not have been born at the precise moment that it was. But this awareness of an internal crisis could have led to a simple league of defence of the Christian churches in the face of the renaissance and initial missionary efforts of the great pagan religions (Buddhism, Islam) and the growth of substitutionary ideologies. It could have led only to a more accentuated movement of introversion, as was often the case during the period of Christendom when the Moslem threat arose. Something else was necessary for this awareness to give rise to something more than a league of defence against the godless, or to the futile attempts to resurrect a Christendom. (It is possible that the Roman church long envisaged things in such a perspective and that it saw a means of building an effective dike in NATO or in a Europe united under the direction of Catholic governments: Schumann, de Gasperi, Adenauer.) Something more was necessary than a movement of the Moral Rearmament type, or a movement of pietist withdrawal (as was the case in the eighteenth and nineteenth centuries). It was necessary that this awareness expand to the dimensions of the world. The Christian churches had to measure their responsibilities regarding the world viewed in its totality. The reason that they had long accepted the divisions and partitionings imposed on them by the political world is that they felt that their responsibility was involved only in very limited sectors. While maintaining the idea of a universal jurisdiction, the Catholic church itself had not been able to impede the *de facto* (sociologically) formation of national ecclesiastical entities. Nor could it do much about the fact that missionary movements did not take the form of a prolongation of national churches. It has only been in the past few decades that Rome has taken measures to internationalize missionary action. The victory of ultramontanism at the end of the nineteenth century was never a total victory over all the forms of Gallicanism, Josephism, and religious Nationalism.

Now, at the present time, the Christian churches are faced with a new and irreversible fact which ideological and political divisions, no matter how strong, cannot succeed in hiding. This fact is the birth of a *world civilization* and the correlative birth of a human community. This world civilization is obviously the product of technology. Particular societies owe their existence to the great diversity of technology and to the beliefs which support and reinforce it. Although science has been universal for centuries, the awareness of this universality was the possession of a few élites, which, moreover, were concentrated in a very limited part of the world. Technology, on the contrary, has given birth to the means of its own universalization. By creating extremely rapid modes of transportation and communication, by giving birth to techniques of information that permit every man always to be the contemporary of all his fellow men, technology has opened paths of penetration through the diversity of cultures. The progressive urbanization of the world effaces differences in style of living, brings about a uniformization of beliefs, and creates a common language among men. Nothing resembles a large city more than another large city. There are the same modes of housing, of comfort, of clothing, of alimentation, the same types of leisure activities, the same types of work everywhere. Everywhere are manifested the same cultural needs, in terms of the technical possibilities put at our disposal. Civilization is in the process of becoming a *planetary* phenomenon. To be sure, this "planetarization" is not a uniformization. The ethnic and cultural particularities continue to exist. But whereas previously these particularities were dominant factors serving to partition humanity, now they are superadded to a common fund.

This planetarization of civilization has aided the Christian churches in rediscovering their ecumenical vocation, their sense of Christian universality.[6] To the degree that they have preserved the memory of a period in which they themselves represented the most concrete forms of human universalism, they could not observe with indifference the formation of a universality which has a completely different foundation. For the first time in human history, the creation of a united humanity appears as a possibility. This nostalgia of a unity of mankind and of Christian universality has already been expressed in the missionary movement. But as the missionary movement was extended to non-western continents, the divisions of occidental Christendom could not constitute a satisfactory response. Nevertheless, it is understandable that it was not by chance that the aspiration for Christianity came precisely from the missionary societies and that the birth of the ecumenical movement is dated precisely from the first world missionary conference (Edinburgh, 1910), that the first ecumenical institution was the International Missionary Conference (1921), that from its birth the World Council of Churches established ties of co-operation with the International Missionary Council (creation in 1946 of a common commission of international affairs), and finally, a fusion as a result of this co-operation (New Delhi, 1961). More profoundly, it is understandable that the search for unity has always been presented as tied to reordering of the mission of the churches, to the remodelling of their structures in a missionary direction and, finally, that until recently it has been the missionary churches (Protestant and Anglican) which have been the most active agents of the ecumenical enterprise, whereas the majority of orthodox churches live in hope or follow the movement rather than determine it.

Yet, this planetary unification by means of a technological civilization leaves intact certain basic contradictions or even aggravates them. The fact is that a civilization in the process of universalization produces equally universal conflicts. War, which in the pre-industrial era was limited to conflicts between neighbouring states or occasionally between power *blocs*, has become world war. These conflicts, which a technological civilization is incapable of regulating by itself, are schematized by Denis de Rougement in the following way:

Political and economic conflict between the totalitarian state and the rights of man. Moral conflict between aggressive collectivism and anarchizing individualism. Ideological and religious conflict between imposed unity and thoughtless division, between rigid centralization and random dispersion.[7]

In this perspective, it is not without importance to note that the ecumenical movement took shape on the occasion of the First World War, initially under the form of a World Alliance for International Friendship through the Churches (1915), then under the form of the Life and Work

Movement (1918–1919), and that one of the tasks set for the latter was precisely to unite the churches in a common action for peace, social justice, racial equality, and international co-operation.[8] What was involved, then, was for the churches to respond to this challenge presented by a world civilization that was incapable of overcoming its own contradictions by itself. In fact, even after doctrinal problems took an important and even central place in the ecumenical movement, after a *rapprochement* was established between Life and Work and Faith and Order, and after the World Council was instituted from the latter two movements (the idea was born in 1938 and realized in 1948), the element of so-called practical Christianity maintained an important place in all the activities of the World Council. Evidence of this is seen in the initiatives of the Church and Society Department and of the Division of Interchurch Service. The World Council feels that it should assist the churches in promoting a new ethic of social relationships, a new consideration of the relations between politics and economics, between public life and private life, a new reflection on the relationships between industrialized nations and underdeveloped nations, on personal responsibility in a socialized world (cf. the works of the World Council on the nature and the implications of a "responsible society"). It feels this way because it considers that the search for ecclesiastical unity is not unrelated to the development of this planetary civilization. It considers that Christian unity does not only have meaning in itself, as the fulfilment of the command of the Lord of the church, but also that it can aid the world in resolving conflicts which the world cannot resolve or can resolve only by modifying the terms of the alternatives which de Rougement has outlined.

It is historically exact that the social and practical tendency in Christianity has often been in the forefront of the ecumenical movement. Part of the reason for this is that the reigning theology of 1920–1925 taught that doctrinal division is both insurmountable and secondary, that doctrine will always divide for no good reason, but that common action presents increasingly stronger possibilities of unity. But this fact should not obscure another, even more decisive fact, namely, the awareness of a tie between the necessary unity of the churches and the fact of the appearance of a world-wide human community. Theological thought itself has taken up the study of this tie. We see developing in ecumenical circumstances a reflection on the meaning of the catholicity of the church, on the lordship of Christ over the church and the world, on the relationships between Christian hope and the hopes tied to the world civilization (the theme of the Assembly of Evanston, 1954), on Jesus Christ, the fulfilment of history in the century of the universal.[9] These preoccupations clearly witness to the desire not to seek solely a union of separated churches, but to make the churches become aware that they must unite not as a means of common defence but in order to help the planetary civilization move beyond its own contradictions.[10]

Although the ecumenical movement was born and grew up from a certain sociological context in which a sort of challenge to Christendom was present, and although the ecumenical movement found one of its reasons for being in this challenge, it is none the less true that its birth was also tied to negative sociological conditions. Paradoxically, it was necessary first of all to bring about the complete rupture of Christendom as a homogeneous society with geographical unity. To the degree that Christianity was expressed in a Christendom of this genre, it found the very base of its unity in sociologically given foundations. Even the rupture of the sixteenth century, although it introduced a differentiation between Protestant peoples and Catholic peoples, did not completely unsettle this western Christian consciousness, which was convinced of its basic unity in the face of the Turks and of the Moslem world. What was necessary was for this break-up of Christendom to be far enough along for the Christian missions to cross the ancient borders of Christendom; for the disintegrating Christendom to set about integrating individuals from all peoples and all races; and thus, for Christendom to cease being bordered by pagan peoples. Once spread out through all the peoples and deprived of its homogeneous socio-geographic base, Christianity posed the specific and new question of the unity of a dispersed church. Ecumenical unity is not an expansion of homogeneous Christendom; it is a form of existence of the church corresponding to the annihilation of its socio-geographic unity. As the church finds its base less in pre-existent sociological unities, the more will it be obliged to forge a unity which will indeed be its own.

This truth can be expressed in another way. The church has modelled and has continued to inspire the civilization in which it exists, even though this civilization has integrated elements from a completely different provenance. It is necessary that the church cease receiving the image of its unity from this civilization. It is necessary that this civilization cease to return to the church the image of what it felt to be the normal form of its unity. Only then will the church be able to undertake a quest for a unity in that civilization where the church has not been or no longer is present. Ecumenism of bygone days saw itself as an extension of Christian civilization; thus it was tied to the pre-eminence of the Christian West in the world. The ecumenism of the twentieth century is tied precisely to the

decline of the West, to the end or to the questioning of Christian civilization. Ecumenism is a typical manifestation of the church in a secularized
world.

Finally, the appearance of modern ecumenism is tied to the presence
of the unbeliever, a presence which no longer is sporadic but massive,
no longer on the fringes of zones of Christendom but in the societies
of former Christendom.[11] This irreducible presence of the unbeliever
reminds the churches that they are not homogeneous societies which
could be modelled on the frameworks of a pre-existent society, that they
no longer are multitudinist, popular churches, but "small flocks" lost in
the midst of a mass of indifferent people. These indifferent people are even
within the church, since sociological surveys show the existence of an
increasingly large fringe of men who have only an attenuated awareness
of their membership in a church. They are only "seasonally" aware of
their integration in the church. All at once the churches are discovering
that their universality is no longer a fact, not even within the bounds of
ancient Christendom. They are discovering that their universality can only
be a missionary universality in the world. But the *sine qua non* of this
universality of missionary presence is the visible manifestation of the unity
of the churches. Denominational missionary presence no longer has any
meaning. It even goes counter to the sought-after witness. This denominational presence only witnesses to a renunciation of universality. Here again
we find that missionary component of the ecumenical movement, that
indissoluble tie between mission and the search for unity. The unbeliever
has come to unbelief under the pressure of modes of thought (rationalism,
science) that have provided him with a demonstration of their universal
validity. He has considered that the universality asserted by Christianity
is without foundation, that Christianity was only the ideology proper to
the white western world at the height of its glory, or even simply the
ideology of a dominant class in the midst of this western world. He records
the decline of Christianity, which is incapable of asserting its universality
in a world-wide civilization. Thus the Christian churches find themselves
driven by the unbeliever to a sort of challenge: to demonstrate that Christianity retains all its value for new peoples, that it can root itself in peoples
foreign to the cultural heritage of the West. Thus ecumenism will be an
attempt to show the universality of Christianity. This universality is
symbolized in its unity, and this unity in turn is symbolized in the fact
that the young churches do not remain dependent on the churches of the
West but collaborate with them, in full equality, in the midst of the
ecumenical movement.

The unbeliever is sensitive to Christian preaching only if it can be presented to him with marks of universality. One of Léon Brunschvicg's tasks as a philosopher has been to oppose the effective universality of rational thought to Christianity, which, according to him, has been incapable of opting frankly for the universal. And he notes with avowed interest and sympathy the new perspectives opened by the ecumenical conferences of Oxford and Edinburgh (1937):

There scarcely could be a happier event . . . the separation and ingrownness of the churches which proclaim the same Christ are even more bitterly felt when one is oneself a stranger to the particularism of the symbols and of the rites by which the agreement of kindred confessions is so often thwarted. Is not the appearance of absoluteness which each group of believers confers on its confession of faith, and which it acrimoniously maintains, the most certain sign of its relativity?[12]

The churches cannot ignore this witness of the unbeliever. The ecumenical movement has a stake in attempting to respond to this challenge, without alienating Christian fidelity.

But it is quite evident that the churches cannot seek this response without presupposing certain of the values represented by the unbeliever. One of these values, the first which has been set out in bold relief, is freedom of conscience, the right that every conscience has of giving its adherence only to the truths which it recognizes obviously as such. Christianity long has rejected such a value because it seemed to imperil another value: the objectivity of truth, the universality of truth. Now, at the precise moment when the churches want to restore, in their missionary effort, the universal validity of Christian truth, they find themselves up against the requirement of freedom of conscience which contests precisely the objectivity of the gospel message. For a long time, Christian thought has been able to believe that the unbeliever was mad and that it was possible to heal him by administering to him the proof of the truth of Christianity. From Anselm of Canterbury to Descartes (and even in a certain degree to Pascal), this was the avowed project of all Christian thinkers and of the apologetic which they constructed. The churches were grasped with the belief, in the face of the growth of unbelief, that perhaps the unbeliever was not simply a madman but indeed a man of bad faith. The spiritual and intellectual climate of Christendom had long justified this attitude: as long as an almost homogeneous Christian civilization existed, one covering all domains of thought, activity, and human affectivity, theology benefited from a climate of obviousness. What it taught could be and indeed was contested, but it was at least held to be intelligible. Even the rupture of the Reformation

did not alter this community of language and truth. Of course, the denominations submitted the concepts of theology to a critique and a purifying.
But they were still the same concepts. The brother enemies spoke the same
language. The dissolution of Christian civilization, to the degree that it was
pervaded by the thought of the natural sciences, broke the charm: from
that time on, the idea of creation was less obvious than that of evolution,
the notion of sin retreated before that of moral fault, the idea of redemption seemed much less necessary to thought than that of progress. The
whole of the Christian message left the zone of common truths or at least
only covered it partially. It was inevitable that in these circumstances the
unbeliever would refuse to consider Christianity as belonging to common
knowledge. Thus he contested its place in cultural instruction and in all
institutions exercising a power of constraint over the entire collectivity
(State, school). He called for freedom of conscience over against the teaching of the churches and proclaimed that religion is a private affair. Science
benefited from this truth which was denied to religion.

It is understandable why the churches long reacted negatively to this
claim to freedom of conscience, since it was the validity, objectivity, and
universality of their doctrines which were in question. Thus they reacted
by stating that error could not have the same rights as truth. This proposition was also maintained by their adversaries, but the term truth no longer
had the same meaning for both parties. Pope Pius IX in the encyclical
Quanta Cura and the *Syllabus* which was annexed to it (1864) expressed
in particularly clear fashion this reaction of Christianity:

There are not lacking today men who apply to civil society the impious and
absurd principle of *Naturalism*, as they call it. They dare to teach that the perfection of governments and civil progress absolutely require that human society
be constituted and governed without any longer taking account of religion as if
it did not exist or at least without making any difference between the true religion
and the false ones (Encyclical).

And the Syllabus condemns as false, under no. 15, the following proposition:

Every man is free to embrace and profess the religion which he will have
deemed true according to the light of reason.

The terms used are highly significant: human society must not tolerate
error; it cannot be ignorant of the existence of the true religion, which is
part of the common human patrimony. Thus what is needed is that the
privilege of a total objectivity be claimed for Christianity which will give
it a place and, if possible, a preponderant place in the world of truths which
constitute culture.

It is well known that this struggle of the Catholic church was doomed to failure. And it was doomed for a sociological reason: a human culture was constituted which in no way included religious truths. Religion became a possible option, nothing more. The battle waged by Pius IX was, in fact, a simple delaying action. Moreover, the Catholic church was alone in waging it. The other churches no longer were involved in this rearguard action.

This conflict did not hinder the churches from orienting themselves in a completely different direction. The Catholic church became involved in the conflict very late, but the cause of religious freedom is theoretically won, and Roman theologians are trying to root it in a soil other than that of relativism and scepticism.[13]

Now, it is remarkable that the ecumenical movement, from its beginning, has espoused the cause of religious freedom. Undoubtedly, it can be maintained that it did so because it gathered together churches having suffered persecution. But this was not the only reason: the ecumenical movement could not have been constituted without taking seriously the demands of the unbeliever, without unhesitatingly assuming the need for religious freedom. If it had not done so, it would have given the impression of wanting to reconstitute a Christendom. This is why the World Council of Churches formed a Secretariat for religious freedom. This department was charged with the task of following the course of the question of religious liberty throughout the world, of preparing the Council's interventions in favour of religious freedom, of seeing to it that the constitutions of the states inscribe religious freedom among the basic rights of man; but the department was also charged with the responsibility of giving this idea, born on a non-Christian soil, a theological foundation. It is no less remarkable that the Roman Catholic Church, at the moment when it engaged in an ecumenical dialogue, immediately confronted the problem of religious freedom. (Vatican II provided a chapter on this question in the schema on ecumenism.)

The breaking-up of Christendom, the dissolution of Christian civilization, the presence of the unbeliever: such seems to us to be some of the sociological conditions that have made possible the ecumenical movement and have oriented its works.

When one considers the ensemble of positive and negative factors that constitute the sociological background of the ecumenical movement, one obviously can call into question the specifically Christian nature of this movement. This, indeed, has been done by Jacques Ellul:

The ecumenical bent? Is it through pure faithfulness to the will of Christ to gather his church that the ecumenical movement is developing? If this were happening in the seventeenth century, for example, I would not hesitate to reply yes. But today? How many subsidiary and purely sociological motives can be discovered! Christianity is in retreat everywhere. It has been attacked in most countries of the world, submerged by new religions (Communism), by old expanding religions (Islam), by secularization. But it is the tendency of all groups threatened by an external enemy to gather together, to hush up internal divisions. The national unity in a country in time of war is of the same order! In the same way, we at the moment are witnessing a general, almost universal, tendency to form racial or political *blocs*: western and eastern *blocs*, Moslem *bloc*, Black African *bloc*, the creation of Europe, etc. Are not the churches following the same movement in forming their own *bloc* as all the major unities of the world are doing?[14]

One can subscribe to such assertions only if they are not over-emphasized. Ellul's error is in confusing a certain type of exclusive causality with sociological conditioning. To say that the ecumenical movement is born in a given sociological context, to say that its birth and development have been favoured, influenced, and oriented by such and such sociological facts, is in no way to make a statement about the significance of this movement. The act by which a movement assumes the conditions of its birth permits it to avoid both disregarding this conditioning and being imprisoned by it. Here we should recall the rule of sociological interpretation as Joachim Wach formulated it:

Even if one could prove that the general economic or social conditions of a society gave rise to a desire for salvation, the promises of redemption that could involve a religious message are not invalidated by studies of their social understructure, provided that the correlation is not conceived in deterministic terms but rather interpreted as a functional relation . . .[15]

The error of Jacques Ellul consists in throwing a suspicion of inauthenticity on a movement under the pretext that it was born in a certain sociological context and is dependent on it – as if the birth of Christianity itself, and its spreading out through the Mediterranean basin, in urban centres, and along trade routes, had been independent of all sociological conditioning.

4. *Ecumenism and Protestantism*

The Protestant churches are the ones in which the ecumenical hope has been most strongly manifested, they are the ones that have played a pre-eminent role in the organization of the movement, and they still constitute the driving force of the movement. It is therefore no wonder that Catholic writers, at least until the massive entry of the Orthodox in 1961, have readily pointed out the Protestant character, Protestant inspiration, and Protestant style of the initiatives and declarations emanating from the World Council of Churches. Nor is it any wonder that until 1961, the Orthodox churches showed a certain reserve in regard to the World Council.[16] Why this more marked ecumenical interest in Protestantism than elsewhere? Why have the Protestant churches felt the ecumenical call to concern them especially? Are there factors in the sociological situation of the Protestant churches that have influenced this orientation?

First of all, we should ask whether the *internal* situation of the Protestant churches made this recourse to ecumenism particularly desirable. The response to this question is affirmative: Protestantism is geographically cut up, more affected by political boundaries than other confessions, fringed by sectarian movements, and has experienced increasingly numerous schisms during its brief history. It has been tempted to blame these divisions for its relative stagnation since the blaze of the sixteenth century. Moreover, its denominational divisions do not seem to be very decisive: the passage from one denomination to another was and is still made without serious crisis and often for reasons of pure convenience. Assuredly, there is a *de facto* relativization of their doctrinal divisions for churches of the Reformation, that is to say, these divisions are not felt and lived in a general way by the mass of the faithful. The faithful are more aware of the unity of a style of piety and of the unity of preaching than of doctrinal conflicts. All of a sudden such conflicts appear to be more like scholarly problems than the basis for legitimate ecclesiastical divisions. The fact that western Protestantism always finds itself confronting Catholicism betrays the feeling of Protestant unity *vis-à-vis* Rome. Furthermore, we should not forget that the Protestantism of the nineteenth century was pervaded by religious and theological currents (orthodoxy, liberalism, pietism) that affected it without regard for official ecclesiastical divisions. Each denomination has its orthodox, its liberals, and its pietists. The same will be true for the twentieth century: biblical renewal, liturgical renewal, dialectical theology, denominationalism itself, the Social Gospel movement, all have been general movements that have touched the majority of Protestant churches and have become rooted without denominational differences providing anything more than a superficial colouring or sometimes a certain resistance.[17] Finally, the youth movements of the various Protestant churches are nearly all covered by international and interdenominational organizations (the Scout movement, Student Christian Movement, etc.) and it is well known that these youth movements have generally played a decisive role in the birth of the ecumenical movement. The same is true of the Protestant missionary societies. Although they have not all been interdenominational, they have often recruited their missionaries and their support from various denominations (this is especially the case for the Basel and Paris Mission Societies).

All these facts thus prepared Protestantism to play an active role in the ecumenical movement.

But beyond these obvious facts, there undoubtedly exist more profound and less conscious motives that lead to the ecumenical movement having appeared in Protestantism as a response to its own questions, and even to its own unsettled crises. Protestantism is particularly tied up with western civilization through which it is expressed and which it has helped model. On this point, the analysis of Mario Miegge is especially suggestive:

The Reformation of the sixteenth century accentuated, from its beginnings, *the involvement of the Christian life in society*. In effect, the Reformation called into question and transformed the type of relations between church and society that had been established during the course of the middle ages and that was cemented by a *compromise* consecrated by Roman ecclesiology. This compromise involved the *division* of the Christian people into two sectors. On the one hand, there were those Christians who lived in the "world" (in a world which remained under the reign of disorder and violence). To these Christians, the Church in its sacramental work administered the "treasures of the merits of Christ and the saints". On the other hand, there were the "regular" Christians who, in the *sui generis* and separated society of the cloister and of the orders, tried to accomplish the perfection of the Christian life.

The new style introduced by the Reformation was manifested in the destruction of these separated orders. The rejection of the cloister and of the cenobitic life was not, as some tend to assert nowadays, an unfortunate accident of Reformation history. It springs from a new vision of the relations between church and society, from a new conception of Christian life in the world. The Christian must live in the world in order to accomplish there his Christian service. Work and profession must therefore be considered as *vocations*. This point is so important that a work as central as the Augsburg Confession gave it special emphasis. In article XVI the Confession states that

it is right for Christians to bear civil office, to sit as judges, to judge matters by the Imperial and other existing laws, to award just punishments, to engage in just wars, to serve as soldiers, to make legal contracts, to hold property, to make oath when required by the magistrates, to marry a wife, to be given in marriage.

And in order to leave no doubt, the article continues:

They [the churches of the Augsburg Confession] condemn also those who do not place evangelical perfection in the fear of God and in faith, but in forsaking civil offices; for the Gospel teaches an eternal righteousness of the heart. Meanwhile, it does not destroy the state or the family, but very much requires that they be preserved as ordinances of God, and that charity be practised in such ordinances. Therefore, Christians are necessarily bound to obey their own magistrates and laws, save only when commanded to sin; for then they ought to obey God rather than men.[18]

The important word is ordinances (Stände). It is found throughout Luther's writings, and connotes a new conception of Christian ethics: the Christian life is a life lived in the temporal, in the diversity of states that constitute the social life. Each state should be considered as given by God in order that one's Christian vocation can be exercised therein. Max Weber rightly characterized this ethic as a "Protestant secular asceticism". It is ascetic because the individual does not consider his state as a source of benefit and enjoyment; it is secular because it involves a Christian involvement in temporal existence. The Calvinist view is undoubtedly less individualist, but is animated by the same concern: Calvin considered society as a whole rather than as a juxtaposition of states. Nor did he consider that the state could be substituted for the church: although the state was responsible for observing respect for the two tablets of the law, it did not exercise a spiritual magisterium. But a collaboration must be established between the civil authorities and the ecclesiastical authorities (this is what he tried to set up at Geneva, and not at all a theocracy),[19] so that an order would be established in the city conforming to the will and glory of God. And the Christian ministry of the layman consists in assuming his share of responsibility in this order.

This ethic has not remained a simple theory: it was an ethic perfectly adapted to the needs of the new classes in ascendance, to the commercially controlling bourgeoisie which, conscious of its responsibilities, developed in the cities and sustained the Reformation. The Protestant ethic provided these new élites with the feeling of being in place in the business and civic worlds. They were no longer treated as minors. Although the Reformation gave a new impetus to the growth of capitalism, it was not because it had invented capitalism nor because there is a profound link between justification by faith and the capitalistic enterprise. Rather, it was because the Reformation promoted the worth of secular existence, of existence in the world. Thus there was a solidarity between

Protestant values and the behavioural models of the western bourgeoisie (free enterprise and the rational conduct of economic life) (Miegge).

Under the influence of the Enlightenment, the bourgeoisie became detached from the church. But when this happened, the pact was not broken with Protestant values. This detachment of traditional formulas and institutions was simply a new step in the same secularization of existence. Thus a Protestantism was formed outside the church, a liberal Protestantism linked with bourgeois liberalism. The movement that had brought the triumph of the Reformation in the cities of the bankers and merchants now extended up the social and political ladder of the bourgeoisie. To be sure, this bourgeoisie was no longer attached to the doctrinal content of the Reformation. It was more characterized by rationalist deism or the religion of Jean-Jacques Rousseau. Yet it had preserved all the values of the Protestant ethic which favoured the freedom and worth of man as the producer and accumulator of wealth in society. This ethic, up to the present time, has found its best field of expression in North America, where the formation of a religion of the American Way of Life found its first model in "the external forms of Protestantism", in a secularized Protestantism. It is this Protestantism which has been the cradle in which, from the beginning, was formed that Americanism, which is a sort of religion encompassing all confessions. It is an a-theological, a-liturgical, but ethical and activist religion whose credo includes the affirmation of a God-Providence, human freedom, human dignity, democracy, and free enterprise.[20] Now, this western bourgeois and liberal society is in a period of crisis. It has been put on the defensive. It has suffered the blow of the melting away of western power in the world, of the calling into question of capitalism by communism and socialism, of the birth of an organized proletariat. Although still prosperous, this liberal bourgeoisie knows that it has lost its power of expansion and conquest. Its ethic, increasingly detached from its religious premises and increasingly secularized, poorly resists the attacks of Marxism and of the radical ideologies of our times. This crisis of western liberalism must necessarily reflect on the Protestantism which had given birth to it. The end of the First World War marked the decline of the liberal West. By a coincidence, which was not fortuitous, it was also the moment at which the long theological tradition of Protestant liberalism was called into question. It is not incorrect to consider, from a sociological point of view, the first theology of Earth as a theology of crisis. Protestantism thus turned towards ecumenism and initially emphasized the effort towards rethinking the relationship between the church and the world, between the church and society, between the church and the social and economic disorder (themes that run through the whole ecumenical quest from Stockholm to Amsterdam). But is this not precisely because it felt the need of a new ethic, because it realized with dismay that its original ethic was the captive of a previously expanding social class, and now followed the irreversible decline of this same social class? But it was aware that, in a world in which the West had lost its primacy and in which it itself was losing speed, it no longer was able to attach a new ethic to its faith. It was aware that the task was beyond its means, that it was necessary to formulate an ethic on the world's scale, that it could no longer envisage a social ethic without the co-operation of Christians throughout the world, especially those who live in nations undergoing rapid social change. And this is why it involved itself with fervour and dynamism in the ecumenical venture which could give it a world-wide vision of Christian existence.

It had all the more need of this renewal since it saw the breakup of the unity between church and people which had been the ideal of the Reformation and which Calvin had tried to incarnate in the city of Geneva. This profound insertion of the church in the people, this *Volkskirche* had been dislocated both by the dechristianization of the élites and by the formation of a massive proletariat on the margin of both the church and the city. Of course, Protestantism tried to react by attempting itself a critique of the multitudinous church, by denouncing its hypocrisy, by seeking to form small groups of the pure in the interior of the church (*ecclesiola in Ecclesia*), by insisting on the inner life, on piety alone, by letting go all other forms of human life in a devalued secular realm, in the domain of the prince of this world. This individualist, pietist, revivalist movement, whatever be its results, was also the face of defeat, a declaration of impotence. It could not hide the fact that man's life was increasingly involved in this world which was declared lost. It would have been necessary for these Christian élites of pietism actually to retire from the world, but they retired from it only to devote themselves to exercises of piety in fervent conventicles. Otherwise they were quite good at business in the world. Consequently, this solution was not really a solution, since it did not result in the reconstitution of a people of God, since it established no link between the preaching of the church and the daily life of men. This reaction, writes Miegge, which consists in "hiding the rupture of the unity of church and people" is the "spectacle of a twilight Protestantism". The call to unity, to the visible manifestation of the unity of the church thus appeared as the means of giving the church its influence in the world. It appeared as the means to procure a new respectability which would permit preaching to flood into the world and reach the people where they were. It is not by chance that evangelization was to take such an important place in the ecumenical movement and institutions. In all ecumenical studies there is much emphasis placed on the fact that we live in a post-Christian civilization and that this fact implies a new way of understanding evangelization. It implies the necessity, if evangelization is again to become a movement of the church, of leaving the "institutional ghetto" (Visser 't Hooft) of the church. It means that the church must truly respond to the questions which man raises in his professional life, in the midst of a secularized world dominated by technology. The churches can no longer act as if their social environment were a Christianized world, as if there still existed a Christian people.

One cannot help but be struck by the fact that the ecumenical movement is in search of a *new ethic*. Conferences organized by the World Council of Churches place great emphasis on the idea of *responsible society*, that is, society in which each individual has the possibility of exercising his responsibility and knows that his actions are accountable before man and God. This emphasis indicates that here indeed is a permanent theme of ecumenism and that this theme leads it to re-evaluate all forms of human relationships – in the sphere of work, of co-operation between men and women, in the interior of the family as well as in the mingling of nations and races. This search for a new ethic has not remained solely theoretical. It is leading the World Council not only to intensify its mutual aid efforts, to prod the countries of the West to feel responsible for the development of the Third World, to make the churches feel that their overseas missions cannot be detached from the phenomena tied to the rapid transformation of societies, but, even more, to attempt some experiments on the scene, e.g., putting teams of technicians at the disposal of young countries, concrete manifestations of solidarity (reafforestation projects in Algeria), and participating in the educational work which provides the conditions for a real emancipation of women, and so on. When one considers the structure of the Genevan organization, one sees that the place given to the search for doctrinal unity is relatively small. *Faith and Order* makes up only one department of a vast Division of Studies, where the problems of ethics and of relationship between church and society have a predominant place. Catholic observers have often pointed to the danger that doctrinal research will find itself rather stifled in such a vast body. Everything happens as if the Life and Work Movement had won out in this symbiosis of two movements which constitutes the World Council of Churches. It is no less striking that a development of the same genre was evident at the Second Vatican Council. There was less concern with the defining of new doctrines and the sketching of a new theological orientation than with giving the church a new look, with making laymen aware of their social and ethical responsibilities, and with making the church a church of the poor, etc.

Why this profound orientation towards ethics if not because the churches feel that the evolution of civilization not only calls into question the traditional ethic that Christianity had in large part shaped, but also brings forth new values that Christianity did not have a chance to consider or evaluate. On this point, the suggestions of Miegge are worth considering.

He emphasizes the fact that despite the growing dechristianization tied to the "demographic explosion" of the non-Christian and to western secularization, all the bridges have not been burned between the West and Christianity. It is in the West that Christianity maintains its directive centres, the centres where decisions of universal import are worked out: Geneva and Rome. The western perspective in Christian reflection remains predominant. Christian values start with the West in seeking to become universalized and to adapt to a profound transformation of the world. Despite the considerable efforts made by the World Council to dewesternize its perspectives (a particularly eloquent symbol of which was the organization of the Third World Assembly at New Delhi in 1961), one can wonder if the ethical crisis of the West is not continuing to play a major role in the whole developing ecumenical ethic. The question becomes even more pertinent when one considers the important role played by the churches of the Anglo-Saxon world in the directive bodies of the World Council.

What are these ethical changes which are taking place in the western world and which affect the development of ecumenical thought? Miegge asserts that they are changes characteristic of a "mature capitalism".

1. All the elements of social life are subordinated to the exigencies of industrial production. Salaried work has gained access to spheres where it had not previously been. It has become widespread in agriculture. Middle and upper level technicians occupy a privileged position. Links are being established between science (the University) and industry, in such a way that the scholar is less and less a free worker. It is industry that proposes problems to him, offers him laboratories, mobilizes him as expert.

2. An effort is being undertaken to reduce the distance between underdeveloped regions and long-industrialized areas. This effort has resulted in a massive displacement of manpower from agricultural and poor zones towards the industrialized zones (the World Council is increasingly preoccupied by the worker migrations and in 1963 organized a major conference on migrant populations).

3. This industrial extension presupposes a concentration of the power of economic decision. No particular industry can any longer make its decisions without submitting to the directives from the top, and this top has become both political and economic. Mature capitalism, or neo-capitalism as it is sometimes called, is increasingly characterized by the *de facto* abandonment of the doctrine of free enterprise and by its receptivity to the idea of planning – which it had long repudiated as being collectivist. The construction of European unity has taken the form of an immense enterprise of industrial planning, which presupposes very strong ties between industry and states or groups of states. Moreover, this planning has an authoritarian character rather than a democratic one. The authority, however, belongs less to the owners of capital than to the technological leaders, to the technocrats. The result of this is a level of social cleavage within capitalistic society. One of the themes of socialism is very nearly fulfilled, namely, the rationalization of the production, subordination of the interests of capital to productivity, the submission of production to a co-ordinating authority. But the other aspect of socialism, namely, the democratization of industrial work, has not been realized.

The whole problem of democracy [writes André Philip] is that, under extremely diverse forms, of the organization of a dialogue between those in a group making decisions and those who are obliged to submit to the decisions of others. Democracy is a dialogue following a prescribed procedure.[21]

Now, this problem, on the level of industrial organization, does not yet have a solution nor even an outline of a solution. Quite the contrary, the opposition within industry between the centres of decision and the mass of those who carry out the decisions tends, rather, to be reinforced, from the fact that the problems of decision completely escape the understanding of the executants.

4. This course of industrialization is reinforced, on the one hand, by the exigencies of the defence of the West *vis-à-vis* the ideologically opposed *bloc*. It is reinforced, on the other hand, by the exigencies of competition with the countries of the Soviet *bloc* (and tomorrow the Chinese *bloc*) in regard to the conquest of Asian and African markets. Just as in the time of colonization, the western economy in the era of decolonization cannot conceive of itself outside its relation with the Third World.

5. Although economic unification is not accompanied by a political unification (a great diversity is found in the West: dictatorships exist alongside traditional democracies and authoritarian regimes of a presidential type), at least social policies tend to become standardized. They are dominated by the necessity of letting the greatest number participate in

abundance, the necessity of a redistribution of revenues, the necessity of assuring uniform welfare, of compensating the inequality of incomes by social supplements to salary, the necessity, finally, required by technology itself, of assuring a rapid social promotion. This last necessity arises from the fact that the role of unskilled and even skilled labour is tending to diminish.

This evolution of the western world naturally has ethical repercussions: new institutions develop new values, a new conception of human destiny. The creation of a social security develops a new anthropology, to the degree that it erases certain secular attitudes either of needy prudence or of resignation regarding life. A new type of man undoubtedly is in process of being developed. Morals will be much less marked by religious over-tones than in the past. The traditional differences between Catholic mentality and Protestant mentality are tending to become blurred. One can wonder in these conditions if religious attitudes and behaviour are not going to undergo some sort of modification.

Miegge raises the question of the relation between the old religious truths and the truths now presented by the surrounding civilization.

Traditional Catholicism (at least in Latin countries) is prevalently characterized by a type of relation to the religious object which one could call the *relation to the immediately visible and tangible sacred* (it has its culminating point in the sacrament of the altar, in the sacrifice of the mass with its *real presence* of the Lord). But this type of relation no longer corresponds to the usual mode of perception in an industrial society. In fact, in an industrial society the relation to objects (on the level of production as well as of consumption) is increasingly *indirect, reflected, mediated by systems of conventional and abstract symbols* (such as the setting up of indexes on numerical scales which, in any mechanical machine, condition the work of a worker as well as the leisure of a motorist, etc.).

One can wonder if Miegge, in comparing such different human demeanours, does not establish relationships which are too artificial. We do not think so. Indeed, it must be understood that in each historical epoch, when civilization has attained a certain degree of systematization, of homogeneity, of integration of various elements, it sets up a world of common truths that are encountered in all corners. The apparitions of saints were perfectly plausible in a world where the sacred occupied reserved spots in social space; the miracle was common currency in a world where each sickness was the sign of an intervention of celestial powers, where the physician was, if not a being of charismatic powers, at least a clergyman. In a civilization where the perceptible element was the more important, where writing and printing played a more background role, the Catholic church could multiply the visible signs where the divine abounded. It could utilize symbols in a realist sense as the equivalents of the thing signified. The Reformation threw discredit on the objects of piety, on images and statues. It devalued material practices and the adoration of relics. It incessantly emphasized that God is a hidden God, that the movement of faith is secret, and that Christianity is a religion of inwardness. In doing so, the Reformation, whatever its theological motivations were, gave evidence of a profound accord with the new civilization that was being born. This new civilization was one of the signs of printed matter, of the book. It is beyond doubt that one of the elements of the success of the Reformation, even if it was an occasional and a-theological element, was its adaptation to the new world of culture. This is why the Reformation, although it touched all classes of the population, was also selectively a movement deeply affecting the cultivated classes. This is why the fight against superstition and magic went hand in hand with the progress of culture.

Now, we are observing at the present time a profound, still-nascent development in Catholic piety. This development is manifested in the decline of certain devotions, in the purifying of sanctuaries, in the simplification of the liturgy, in the place given to preaching, in the insistence on the Word of God more than on the sacred. These developments which condition the entrance of the Roman Catholic Church into the ecumenical dialogue represent a victory of the form of feeling and piety that can be called Protestant.

The Catholic church manifests a lively interest in Protestantism. The interest is not so much for Protestant doctrine, which the Catholic church continues to consider as incomplete and impoverished, but precisely for Protestant forms of piety, for the Protestant conception of faith. And is this not because Catholicism has been led to this point by the fact that its own style is less and less adapted to the world of common truths, to the style of life and the mode of perception of our civilization? It certainly asserts that in undertaking to give itself a new visage, in rendering itself more accessible to modern man, in re-examining doctrinal formulations (in a process that will be long and that it has the wisdom not to hurry), it in no way intends to call into question the substance of dogma itself. Every church is by nature a conservative society. But the link between the substance of dogma and its cultural trappings is more profound than a simple tie between content and container. In attacking theological formulations, it is our apprehension of the content itself that can be transformed. One can wonder if after having eliminated the most elemental forms of the sacred localized in images, statues, and shrines, the Catholic church will not be led to call its sacramentalism into question, and especially the foundation of this sacramentalism, namely, the doctrine of transubstantiation. Will it not be led to seek another way of giving account of the real presence? And if it starts on this path, it is the whole doctrine of the priesthood which it will be led to re-examine. For the priest is priest only by reason of his role in the administration of the sacraments. The idea that the layman can preach the Word of God is not foreign to the Catholic church, and it is at the moment pursuing experiments in this area. It is possible that the Catholic church will stop half-way in its development, that it will be content – as the Reformation undoubtedly intended – to reform certain abuses. Nevertheless, it will have unleashed a movement that calls for it to go further.

But supposing that the development does not proceed further. Will not the Catholic church in any case be constrained to re-examine the social relations as they have been organized within Catholicism? The industrial society in which we live is certainly a hierarchical society and tends to subordinate the mass of executants to increasingly distant centres of direction. Yet it nevertheless introduces a new type of *authority*. This new authority is far different from that which existed in an agricultural society with the master working his realm with his servants. The relationships between master and servant had a semi-feudal, personal character; the servants depended on the will of the master and passively accepted his orders. The situation is completely different in an industrial society. This is so, first of all, because the executants have a juridically defined status (their condition increasingly approaches that of the civil servant). The relationships with management no longer have the nature of personal allegiance; their relations are purely functional. The executant is gaining greater freedom in everything touching his private life. Moreover, because of technological progress, the orders that the executant receives from the top are presented as directives under the form of a work-plan: the technician, the skilled labourer have the possibility of executing these directives in more or less variable circumstances:

With a more or less extended margin of secondary decisions which cannot be forecast in a rigid fashion and which, moreover, are indispensable to the overall functioning of the mechanism of production (Miegge).

This is precisely why an industrial society is so attentive to the promotion of workers: it wants to make them fit for these secondary decisions. But the worker can make decisions only if he has some understanding of the general process of production. Trade unionism, in spite of the conflicts that it has unleashed, has become an indispensable institution of the industrial world, even in the eyes of the managerial centres which have often been sorely tried by the unions. The reason unionism has become indispensable is that it co-operates in this personal advancement of the worker. It does so by giving him a vision of the totality of the enterprise and of modern production, and by increasing his responsibility and his capacity for personal decision. In this way industrial society (and not only in the western world) has given value again to a certain number of ethical attitudes (self-discipline, the exercise of personal responsibility) which Protestantism had encouraged from the time of the Reformation.

Is it possible, under these circumstances, for the Catholic church to maintain its members in a situation of minority and dependence in regard to the priest when, in their professional life, they are given adult responsibility? Can it continue to prescribe an attitude of unconditional submission? The Second Vatican Council has given a public and official outlet for a demand that has already been voiced for several decades: the demand of the laity to share in the priesthood, to have a part in the evangelization of the world, and even in a certain way, in the government of the church. It is symptomatic, according to Miegge, that this demand of the laity has come from the social classes most directly related to the world of industrial production, the class most conscious of their social responsibility, from the worker branches of Catholic Action. And we would add, from the most developed branches of agricultural movements. It is notable that one of the major themes of Vatican II was the status of the laity, that complaints were voiced because laymen had not been involved in the preparation of the council, and that a place (purely symbolic, however) was made for them among the guests of the Council. If this movement develops to the point of exercising sufficient pressure on the authorities of the church, the latter will be constrained to modify its hierarchical structures in a direction that will bring it closer to Protestantism, or at least closer to Anglicanism (where the same development has been going on since the end of the First World War, with quasi-synodal Conferences co-existing with ecclesiastical convocations).

But this *rapprochement* with Protestantism is not univocal. Although Catholicism perceives the necessity of re-evaluating the relations between the laity and the church hierarchy and is becoming more protestant, it maintains no less fervently the need for a central power of decision. This is the case even though the revaluing process of councils and the rediscovery of collegiality tends to diminish the monarchical nature of this power. On this point, Protestantism, to a certain degree, is moving more in the direction of Catholicism. Congregationalism is losing pace in Protestantism; many churches have restored an episcopacy (which is functional rather than ceremonious); the centralization of the government of the church is being accomplished both intra-nationally and internationally; the Reformation doctrine of the equality of all ministers is turning out to be incompatible with an effective government. Undoubtedly the world-wide confessional alliances and the World Council of Churches itself still have only a minor authority, a moral and not institutional authority. But can one be certain of remaining at this level?

Here, again, the parallel with industrial society is inescapable: the degree of initiative and of decision left to the executants does not at all place in question the idea of social hierarchy. Self-discipline and responsibility on the part of the executants are parts of a system in which the supreme centres of decision must guard all their authority and are not responsible to inferior bodies. Yet the supreme power has ceased to be monarchical; the monarchical boss is a figure that has disappeared in the age of mature capitalism. Management now cannot be effective unless it is collegial, unless it is gathered in a team which is well-structured with diverse proficiencies. Authority in the industrial society is held not by individuals but by boards.

The same development of industrial society involving a development of social relations and of forms of authority thus involves both Catholicism's adoption of Protestant values and Protestantism's adoption of Catholic values. We are not saying that this twofold process is not guided by an internal development, that it does not find its justification in a parallel theological investigation. We are saying simply that this process mirrors the evolution of industrial society itself; that it manifests the impossibility of making men live simultaneously in societies between which exists no homogeneity, to say nothing of societies which hold to diametrically opposed conceptions of man. The feudal lord and the peasant were at home in the hierarchical church. The boss of capitalistic industry long tried to preserve the feudal type and to treat the worker as a servant, as a domestic. Once this was no longer possible, once it was necessary to bring economic society into harmony with the democratic models of political society, the purely hierarchical and non-democratic ecclesiastical society was called into question. This happened less than a century after the initial tremors which hit economic society, less than two centuries after the shaking of political society.

But if the layman is no longer treated entirely like a minor in the church, if his demands are being taken into account, if a council has been convoked for the first time in history to respond to the needs formulated by the laymen of the church, then how could that church continue to maintain certain values? How, for instance, could it maintain intolerance, which laymen saw decline in civil society long before and which they struggled to eliminate in industrial society? After political democracy guaranteed freedom of opinion and of thought to all people, and after unionism assured this same freedom within the industrial world, how could the Catholic church still maintain its intransigence? The latter was manifested one last time with the *Syllabus* (1864), the very year that French workers obtained the right to organize. Then slowly but surely it was toned down in most western countries. How could the Catholic church not have been led to do what the Reformation had not led it to do but which social development now imposes on it, namely, openly to proclaim religious liberty and freedom of conscience (thus again acquiring a Protestant value)? It is obvious that Catholicism does so hesitantly, for the introduction of such a value can involve even more transformations. At least the question was openly raised before a council.

Ecumenism has sometimes been defined as a common march, a pool of Christian values. This pool is coming to reality before our eyes. In the western world, the denominations are increasingly less characterized by the possession of ethical values that are specifically their own, values that are confessional as well as ethical. For this ethical compartmentalizing is incompatible with a society which is both democratic and industrial. There is no doubt that specifically religious motivations act on this common quest, enrich it, and help it to avoid obstacles. But they nevertheless find a certain point of support in the fact that the global society has already introduced a certain number of ethical attitudes and behaviour into human life that lack only what the churches can supply, namely, a basis and a justification.

Protestantism is especially interested in the ecumenical adventure because the latter offers Protestantism the means of extending the field of application of values which it discovered previously, and the means of correcting some perspectives which arose from its internal compartmentalizing and from its relative isolation.

NOTES

1. On this point, see the book by W. A. Visser 't Hooft, *No Other Name; the choice between syncretism and Christian universalism* (Philadelphia: The Westminster Press,

1963; London: SCM Press), especially chapter four, which deals with the rediscovery of Christian universalism in the ecumenical movement.

2. There is an extremely complex relationship between the mission phenomenon and the ecumenism phenomenon. On the one hand, one of the strongest impetuses for the ecumenical movement has come from mission, from the scandal that the division of the Christian churches caused in mission lands. Historically, the whole ecumenical movement came from the first World Missionary Conference (Edinburgh, 1910). On the other hand, after having been one of the causes of the search for unity, mission has become one of the objectives of the ecumenical movement: the church has a chance of finding the path of unity only if it rediscovers its missionary dynamism. This is one of the most important meanings of the integration of the International Missionary Council and the World Council of Churches (New Delhi, 1961). Finally, in many regards the missionary federations have served as models for the work of the churches in their quest of unity. In Leenhardt's words, "The churches were juxtaposed, opposed, partitioned in the old countries. But they founded missions. Now human groups are finding their personality and seeking, beyond dictatorial prestige, to become federated. But missions, in advance of these other groups, have already brought about this federation. Despite appearances, an order is found within them" (Maurice Leenhardt, "Découverte des Eglises et de l'Eglise aux territoires d'outre-Mer", MNC, no. 18, April–June 1951).

3. Cf. Mario Miegge, "L'oecuménisme est-il un phénomène culturel plutôt que théologique?", CS, 72nd Year, March–April 1964.

4. On this point, see Henri Desroche, Marxisme et religion (Paris: PUF, 1962).

5. G. Crespy, "Le protestantisme a-t-il un avenir?", CS, 70th Year, No. 9–10, 1962.

6. Significant, among many others, is this statement by Mgr Charrière, Bishop of Lausanne, Geneva, and Fribourg (the place where the statement was made undoubtedly makes it even more symptomatic): "In an age where daring pioneers are shot into space in the impassioned adventure of the exploration of the cosmos, it is no longer possible for us to judge our past quarrels from the perspective of a narrow provincialism. From now on, we must relate them to world-wide dimensions. We must judge them with the expansiveness suggested to us by the exploration of the cosmos. And this expansiveness will give them their true value in our eyes. It will restore them to their proper perspective. At the same time, a holy spiritual rivalry will set us on the path, not of forgetting our differences, but of passionately seeking the solutions that we should find for them" (in a speech given at Moscow on the occasion of the jubilee of the Patriarch Alexis in July 1963, quoted in the bulletin Vers l'unité chrétienne, 16th Year, November–December 1963, no. 9–10). One of the sociological roots of ecumenism is surely the collective awareness that a church cannot claim universality by remaining provincialized in the age of planetary perspective.

7. In an article published in 1941, "Fédéralisme et Oecuménisme", published in FV, 44th Year, No. 6, 1945.

8. On the history and beginnings of the ecumenical movement, see G. Thils, Histoire doctrinale du Mouvement oecuménique (Louvain: Em. Warny, 1955).

9. This was the study theme set by the New Delhi Assembly (1961) for the five or six years following.

10. It is evident that the meaning of the ecumenical movement is not necessarily univocal. It could be nothing more than a vast and general movement of retreat following secularization. In such a case, the churches would try to join in a coherent and closed unity, sheltered from the attacks of the world and finding even a certain security in this unity. Confronting a unified world, the churches would seek to form a vast, equally unified ghetto. It does not appear that this is the intention of the World Council of Churches. The latter refuses to become involved in a centralized institutionalization (which is forbidden by its statutes). On the contrary, the World Council, in taking up

the whole social ethic of *Life and Work* in a new theological context, centres its studies on the problem of Church and Society and on mission.

11. It can no doubt be maintained that the presence of the unbeliever is not a new fact, that the roots of dechristianization go back to the eighteenth century and even beyond. The existence of practical indifference, of intellectual scepticism is one thing. Public and avowed unbelief is another thing. What we now have is unbelief that presents itself as natural and valid and wants to be recognized as such, which demands and receives juridical guarantees of *freedom of conscience* and is no longer satisfied with simple *tolerance*.

12. L. Brunschvicg, *La raison et la religion* (Paris: Alcan, 1939), p. 10.

13. See, in particular, the collective volume *Tolérance et communauté humaine; chrétiens dans un monde divisé* (Tournai and Paris: Casterman, 1952, especially the study of Canon Roger Aubert, "L'enseignement du magistère ecclésiastique au XIXᵉ siècle et le libéralisme".

14. J. Ellul, *Fausse présence au monde moderne* (Paris: Librarie Protestante, 1963), p. 72.

15. Joachim Wach, "Sociologie de la religion", art. cit., p. 427.

16. This reserve is manifested in the practice of separate declarations from the Orthodox Churches and in the sending of lay delegates (thus engaging the hierarchy of the church to a lesser degree).

17. This was notably the case for the dialectical theology of the Barthian type. Since 1945 the Lutheran churches of Germany and of Scandinavia have mounted growing resistance to dialectical theology, yet their theological output has not been able to avoid being marked by Barthianism.

18. *The Augsburg Confession* (St. Louis: Concordia Publishing House), article XVI.

19. See F. Wendel, *Calvin* (New York: Harper and Row, Publishers, 1963; London: William Collins).

20. Cf. W. Herberg, *Protestant-Catholic-Jew* (Garden City, N.Y.: Doubleday Anchor Books, 1960), p. 81 et seq.

21. André Philip, "Le chrétien, la société et l'Etat", *CS*, 71st Year, no. 34, March–April 1963.

X

Sociology of the Sect

1. *The Problem of the Sociological Definition of the Sect*

The term "sect" and especially its related adjective "sectarian" have a pejorative connotation in popular usage and opinion. Christendom, in its concern for universality and despite its confessional divisions, has always considered the sect to be one of the gravest dangers facing the church. Consequently, the sect is regarded as something bad. The result of this is that when a division arises in the church, those who separate themselves are considered as sectarians by those who maintain the continuity of the ecclesiastical tradition. Thus the Roman Catholic Church has long qualified as sects those churches born from the Reformation. Indeed, in countries with Roman Catholic majorities, "protestant" and "sectarian" have become synonymous. In fact, the label "protestant" has been affixed to each new sect that has appeared in the course of history. This is true even when the new sect has no real contact with the churches of the Reformation and when it is impossible to establish a tie of historical filiation between the particular sect and the churches. In Roman Catholic countries, the Jehovah's Witnesses and even the Mormons are considered as Protestant sects, even when their members are recruited primarily from among believers of Roman Catholic origin.

Several responsible works by Roman Catholic authors have begun a reaction against this tendency. On the theological level, one of the principal initiators of this reaction was Bossuet, who emphasized the generality of the sectarian phenomenon. In the same vein, Jean Séguy has stated that the sectarian phenomenon

in no way characterizes Protestantism, despite the magnitude it has assumed there. Catholicism also has known schisms of similar nature, especially during the Middle Ages.[1]

Once freed of the value judgments that a majority church levels against it, the sect appears as a "denomination, section, or group of believers separated from the main church".[2] There is undoubtedly an element of truth in this definition: the origin of the sect is always traced back to a schism, to a separation. Yet the act of separation and divorce is seldom unilateral. Often it is difficult to say who has separated and who has maintained the continuity, i.e., who merits the appellation "sectarian". The Reformers, in attempting to reform the church in its body and in its hierarchy, simply resumed an enterprise that had already been attempted many times before. They had no schismatic intention in doing so. Circumstances forced them to form new churches, with a disciplinary organization and administrative structures. But, as the sixteenth-century confessions attest, they firmly believed that they were remaining within the universal church, in historical continuity with the church of all ages. This continuity was manifested by fidelity to the ecumenical creeds and confessions. In short, they refused to be sectarians. Quite to the contrary, they tended to qualify the Roman church as a sect by calling it the Papist church. Often in later history we see the Protestants treating the Roman Catholic Church as the Roman sect.

The same observation can be made regarding the relationship between the Eastern Orthodox Church and the Roman Catholic Church. In this case, the question of knowing who separated from whom is even more intractable. The Orthodox consider the pope to be simply the Bishop of Rome and Patriarch of the West, who has broken communion with the patriarchs of the East.

The idea of separation is quite relative and when we try to make it more precise, we almost inevitably bring in specifically theological criteria bearing on the nature of orthodoxy. Thus we move from a historical appraisal to a doctrinal one. We find ourselves then on the level of doctrinal controversy and not on the sociological level.

It should also be added that schism and secession are not always apparent in the birth of sects. A sect can have a spontaneous birth. This is the case, for instance, with the genesis of that sect which naturally has taken the least sectarian name there is, the Universal Christian Church, founded by the self-styled Christ de Montfavet. During the ages of Christendom, when everyone was a Christian and almost obligatorily belonged to an organized church, the only possibility open to religious innovators or reformers was to create a schism. But in an age of dechristianization, where there exists a large floating mass of individuals who are not attached to any definite religious community yet who nevertheless have unsatisfied religious needs, it becomes possible for religious movements to arise with the sole purpose of responding to these needs. These movements are not secessions in the exact sense of the term; they simply content themselves with waging a polemic against the major existing religions. Such movements are sectarian only in so far as they base themselves on a common Christian fund (to which they often hold quite tenaciously) while at the same time differentiating themselves from all other Christian churches. But they do not grow out of a schism in its precise meaning as an historical event produced within a constituted religion (for example, Methodism is related in its genesis to the internal history of Anglicanism, the Reformation to the internal history of Catholicism).

Could we say, then, that the only objective criterion that would permit us to qualify a religious grouping as a sect would be a purely quantitative criterion, namely, that of numbers? Custom seems to have sanctified this way of looking at the matter: the sect is small, or it is in the minority. But here again we are in the realm of the relative: who would say at what minimum number the sect begins? In the United States there are many Protestant churches which live together, deal with each other as churches, are considered churches by public opinion, and join together in the National Council of Churches. Yet their membership numbers are extremely variable, ranging from some tens of thousands to several millions. Wherein lies the difference between a small church and a sect? Moreover, there is a question of scale: in Europe, Methodist and Baptist groups often are considered as sects; in the United States, where these groups number millions of members, no one would dare consider them as sects. Yet the Baptists and Methodists of Europe are quite similar in doctrine and organization to the Baptists and Methodists of the United States. They belong to the same world-wide organizations. Could it be said, then, that a religious group should be considered as a church or as a sect according to its particular religious environment? That would be to say that the concept of sect has no real consistency and that it escapes any scientific determining. The concept would then fall prey to completely arbitrary use. Indeed, such arbitrariness of use appears in many works.[3]

Thus it seems impossible to base oneself on statistics in order to classify religions as churches or sects. There also seems to be no minimum below which a church would become a sect. But can we not at least retain the idea that the sect is situated and defined in relation to dominant religious groups and that it is often the dominant religious group which imposes both the name and the effective behaviour of a sect on the minority group? Sometimes the sect is born from the injury done to it by the majority church. This dominance should be understood both in the religious sense (a strongly entrenched church, supported by a long tradition, and exercising an effective authority over the people) and in the social sense (the predominance in the church of a social élite). As Henri Desroche writes:

The classification of a religious group as *sect* tends to reflect the points of view of a socially dominant religious perspective. Every *church* recognized as such has been, more or less, *sect*; and every *sect* designated as such tends to designate itself as *church*. Many scholars have pointed to this. Thus the vocabulary tends to develop in relation to historical and social forces.[4]

These comments are illustrated quite well by the birth of Christianity. Primitive Christianity was limited to a few small communities scattered along the periphery of the Mediterranean. It was composed primarily of lower class people belonging to the Jewish diaspora and to the ranks of Jewish proselytes, to whom were added some pagans who had previously been more or less infected by the mystery religions. Yet the Roman power considered Christianity to be a Jewish sect, and the Jews had the same point of view. But beginning with the second half of the second century, Christian recruitment became more widely inclusive and a good part of the pagan intelligentsia were converted to Christianity. At this time, the sect became church, in the sociological meaning of the term. It was a social reality which had to be taken into account, to such a degree that Constantine made it the religion of the state. Although Protestantism, in Catholic countries, is treated as a sect and counts among its members the social and intellectual élite (persecution is the lot reserved for the sect), in Protestant countries the situation is reversed: Protestantism makes Catholicism feel as if it were only a sect, and takes irritating measures against it (as has been seen in England, in the Netherlands, in Sweden, and even in Switzerland). On the other hand, in countries where there is a balance of confessions, we see the two partners treating each other as churches. Their relationships are on an equal footing and, although it is doctrinally and canonically forbidden, Catholicism does not hesitate to apply to Protestantism the title of church.

Thus there is a relativity in the idea of sect. This relativity is related to the variable relations of interacting social and religious forces.

However, we cannot be content with this relativity. To be sure, we should not disregard the changing relation of social and religious forces, the consequence of which is that the term "sect" is sometimes applied to the left, sometimes to the right. Yet neither must we forget that in a given situation, the sect has an original genesis and that sectarian behaviour also has its own originality. Inside the churches themselves there are individuals and groups which have a sectarian comportment and sectarian aspirations. All sorts of means are tried in order to realize these aspirations within the church, even at the risk of leaving the church if they do not succeed in their aims.[5]

It was the feeling of this religious originality of sectarianism which Ernst Troeltsch was describing when he characterized sects of all times in the following manner:

Compared with this institutional principle of an objective organism, however, the sect is a voluntary community whose members join it of their own free will ... An individual is not born into a sect; he enters it on the basis of conscious conversion.[6]

Even when the sect is not born of a schism in the precise sense as a datable event, it always represents a kind of protest against the instituted and established church, against that institutionalism and establishment which appears to it as the very symbol of treason and of compromise with the world. The sect sees itself as a movement more than as an institution. This is why it is so often characterized, at least in the beginning, by a fluid, embryonic, and spontaneous organization, and by the abandoning of the pastoral ministry as a professional activity. It refers itself frequently to the model of the primitive church, which it feels (not completely incorrectly, moreover) was not at all institutional, As with the primitive church, the sect attempts to make charisma prevail over function, spontaneity over organization, the prophet over the priest, inspiration over doctrine. It is "enthusiastic" in the proper sense of the term. Luther hit the mark when he characterized the Anabaptists as *Schwärmer*, and Calvin was no further off when he qualified them as *fantastiques*. Whether or not it is born of a rupture with a church, the sect is qualified first and foremost as an "anti-church", to use the apt expression of Henri Desroche.[7] Thus we see the sects waging a particularly lively battle against the churches, lumping them all under the same censure and rediscovering over the centuries the same expressions to qualify every church: the great church, the great Babylon, the great prostitute. This anti-ecclesiastical attitude of the sects is manifested in two ways: either they assert the general apostasy of all the churches, or they assert that the churches have long since completely disappeared. Thus the sect represents the rebirth of the church, or even its true birth: in this way, for example, the Neo-Apostolic Church dates the disappearance of the church with the disappearance of the apostles. As there were no longer apostles, so there could no longer be any church. Not less significant is the attitude of Pentecostalism: the very name which it has chosen expresses the claim of being – in a permanent way – the true nascent church. Nothing is more foreign to the sect than the idea of continuity and tradition which is so characteristic of Catholicism. It is to the degree that the Reformation also was a movement of separation, of a return to the sources in an effort to recover the dynamism and simplicity of the primitive church, that a certain relationship is established between the sects and the churches of the Reformation. Although sects ordinarily refuse to associate themselves with churches in common councils, there are examples of associations of this type in mission areas. The entry of two South American Pentecostal churches into the World Council of Churches (at New Delhi in 1961) was a spectacular and unexpected event. It should be pointed out, however, that the Pentecostalism of the churches is of ancient implantation in South America. It is more sedate and closer to the Baptist position than to the original and effervescent Pentecostalism.

The insistence of the sects on spontaneity and their anti-institutional character explain why they also insist on the necessity of a conversion and of a free, personal adherence. The anti-institutionalism results in a very accentuated personalism. In certain sects, whoever wishes to become a member must make a personal confession of faith, which is examined by the community or by the elders of the community. But in general, there is no need to repeat a formal, official confession of faith. It is not doctrinal strictness which is important; rather, it is much more the personal fervour of the candidate. In this regard, the working hypothesis proposed by J. Séguy seems correct:

Our inquiry has led us to observe that the sect is not a dissidence of a theological or doctrinal order, but of an essentially spiritual order. The dissident does not seek to resolve problems of an intellectual nature, but of the interior life.[8]

The Christian sects are so partial to comparing themselves to the primitive church because they see in it also a church into which one entered by personal conversion and by a profession of faith in the lordship of Christ. Undoubtedly, there are professing churches which exist alongside the multitudinous churches. But the sectarian tendency of the former is often manifest, and in any case, it is such churches which entertain a greater number of relations with the sects. The difficulty which the sect experiences in remaining a sect comes from the fact that what has a history also has its traditions and gives rise to family traditions. There are sectarian families: one becomes a sectarian by tradition from father to son. The sect is led to react against this weight of sociological traditions which would turn it into an institution. This is why the sect generally is hostile to infant baptism and baptizes only adults who request it; it also does not hesitate to rebaptize members coming to it from a church. Baptism is tied to various obligations, and becomes less a sacrament than a ceremony similar to that which Protestant churches call confirmation. Sometimes there is also a distinction made between baptism by water and baptism by the spirit, the former being declared insufficient. Only the baptism by the spirit, which confers personal charismas, is considered valid.

By these various precautions, the sect attempts to achieve a community of the pure or the perfect; thus the sect is the heir of gnostic traditions. Sometimes it includes a slightly larger periphery of "second zone" Christians who go through a kind of probationary period before being received fully into the community; sometimes, also, it includes only the elect, only the saved. It often happens from this that the sect has an agitated history: in the domain of perfection and absolute purity, the suspicion of impurity is easily born. He who had been considered as one of the perfect today, tomorrow disappoints and backslides. The number of the elect is necessarily limited. A pure one always finds a purer one who purges him. Such seems to be the law of the sect; and this explains the many crises, the numerous purges, and often even schisms. Many important members of a sect, sometimes the founders, came from another sect and sometimes even passed through several sects. The Jehovah's Witnesses are a schism of Adventism, and the Friends of Man are a schism of the Jehovah's Witnesses.

Thus the sect is an anti-church, not simply because it is treated as such, driven outside the church by the dominant religious and social forces, but because it considers itself anti-church. It develops within itself all the potentialities which have not been able to blossom in the churches, which have been severely controlled and rejected in the churches. Every moment of rupture (and the Reformation was one without seeking it) is waylaid by the slide towards the sect. Indeed, the Reformation had to defend itself against this slide. The violence of the Reformers against the Anabaptists and other movements attests that they were combating a kind of enemy within. In fact, the Reformation was always accompanied by a sectarian fringe. This is explained by the fact that it also had been led to carry on a vigorous criticism of the established church, of the church as institution, and that it had sought to recover a church as pure as in its first days.

But the sect (and here we take up the second part of Desroche's formula to which we have referred) is also an *anti-world*. The moral strictness, the asceticism of the sects, the absolute value given to certain interdictions (refusal of alcohol, tobacco, dancing; vegetarianism; indeed, the interdiction of sexual relations even in marriage) are all quite clear signs of this refusal of the world. The world is evil – thus it is necessary to flee from it. How to flee from it if not to isolate oneself from it or to seek refuge in that part of the world which, according to the old myth, is considered to be the least soiled, namely, the country? Thus it is that the descendants of the Anabaptists, the Mennonites, have long shunned the cities and that even today the Mennonites are still primarily farmers. For a long time, they refused to send their children to city schools and to permit them to engage in professions other than those of the peasantry. If America has become a preferred land of the sects, it should not be forgotten that the myth of the New World has played in its favour; that is to say, the myth of the land where humanity can begin anew. It is undoubtedly this myth which is manifested in the doctrine of the Mormons: the Book of Mormon is claimed to have been composed by a prophet, Mormon, on the order of God; in this book Mormon condensed the annals of the prophets who taught on the American continent six hundred years before Christ, when a Jewish colony from Palestine settled there and became a numerous people (the ancestors of the American Indian). After his resurrection, Christ came to visit these tribes, set up his church among them, and ordained twelve apostles having the same authority as the Twelve of Jerusalem. This church did not continue, but in 1830 it reappeared – with the Mormons. It is organized on the model of ancient times, and is pure and spotless; it has nothing in common with the world, for it descended from heaven.[9]

Sometimes this rupture with the world is marked physically by an exodus: the saints with their families withdraw from the cities and come to settle in a virgin land. Once again, the Mormons provide a good example of this, for in 1846, after the murder of their founder Joseph Smith, they began an exodus towards the west which lasted several months. They entered the valley of the Great Salt Lake and founded Salt Lake City there, where some 65,000 Mormons came to settle between 1847 and 1869.

There are abundant examples of these exoduses of sects through the desert towards a holy city which will be as isolated as possible from the world. They are related to a period in history when the New World offered the possibility of this type of adventure and exercised through its very prestige as New World a sort of attraction that was not only economic but religious as well. One of the most spectacular attempts was that of the American Shakers, which has been analysed by Henri Desroche.[10] This sect was born in England, in the general milieu of Methodism. Its founder was a Manchester factory-worker named Ann Lee, who in 1774 embarked for America with eight companions. In the wilderness around Albany, she organized a type of cenobitic retreat, a sort of forest underground which equipped itself to live by its own means without having to ask anything of the world. As Desroche points out,[11] the Shaker organization consisted of building a church outside the church and a world outside the world. That the New World exercised a mysterious attraction over this millenarian sect is seen from the fact that all the dates concerning the last events are related to American history, which was considered as the sole cradle of religious liberty.[12] The desire of the Shakers to have nothing in common with the world was translated into the refusal of the fundamental laws of creation, as, for example, procreation. This sect, which was to include several thousand adherents and would survive up to the beginning of the twentieth century (with an apogee around 1830), maintained the prohibition of all sexual relations and recruited new members only by its influence. The development of several sects (notably the Shakers) in the direction of a socialist and even communist regime, in which Engels saw one of the *Vorläufer* of Marxism, should not be interpreted as a form of practical wisdom and of compromise with the world: their regime is so new, viewed as so utopian, that it is in contradiction to the organization of the civilized world. Their socialism was a form of anti-world.

Should this opposition to the world be explained by social causes, by the popular recruitment of these sects (Ann Lee had suffered at Manchester the harshness of the great nascent industrial regimes)? Are we in the presence of a movement of social demands, of proletariat revolution which cloaks itself in religious overtones? Is the religious aspect of sects simply a sort of epiphenomenon, as Marx and Engels tried to show in regard to the birth of Christianity and of the movements of the Reformation? As concerns Shakerism, for example, Desroche shows its close connection with Methodism (which was also sectarian at that time), and then asserts that the two sects were responding to the same needs, namely, those of the first industrial proletariat. He further maintains that the two diverged because Methodism had chosen the way of reform, in the framework of liberal economy as in the framework of moralization through popular education, whereas Shakerism evidenced a radical dualism which led it

to the denunciation of all compromise with the world, with the church and state: the world coalition of churches and states. And the logical conclusion was drawn: begin the world afresh on the basis of a new type of human relationships.[13]

This relationship of the message of the sect and a historical social situation is undeniable. But sociological causality is multifarious. The sects do not constitute an anti-world solely in order to respond to the social needs of an age and to yield to the pressure of their members who often belong to the poor and disenfranchised classes. This refusal of the world is rooted more profoundly in a millenarist religious experience, which is older than Christianity itself. The sect is the heir of a long tradition (which becomes radical in the sect), and the source of this tradition undoubtedly is the opposition between the sacred and the profane. This protest against the world will take the *form* of a protest against an economic and social system whenever history makes the wickedness of the world appear under the economic and social form of alienation.

In short, we can characterize the sect as a closed religious group which is constituted by opposition to the established institutional churches and by opposition to the world. The sect is nourished on this double opposition, which often is manifested against it by a double persecution, that of the churches and that of the states. The churches denounce the sects as dangerous fanatics who imperil the unity of the church and its authority; the states see the sects either as feared revolutionaries or as a-social.

A sociology of the sect certainly can also take account of doctrinal motifs in the birth of the sect. The sect represents a *heresy*, but since sociology does not stand on any confessional orthodoxy, it will give only relative meaning to this term: it is the orthodoxy of the great churches which qualifies the doctrine of the sects as heretical. Nevertheless, in this relative context, in relation to the orthodoxy of the churches, it is possible to sort out the basic traits of heresy. Moreover, these traits are contradictory. On the one hand, the sect chooses from the doctrine of the church from which it has come (directly or indirectly) certain points which it holds dear. To these doctrinal items, the sect attributes great, indeed decisive value for the salvation of men: the observance of the sabbath among Seventh Day Adventists; food proscriptions in nearly all the sects (here the relation to the doctrine of the Christian churches is further removed, since the churches recommend only a certain sobriety, which pushed to its absolute limit becomes sectarian abstention); adult baptism among the Mennonites, Baptists, etc.; the exclusive emphasis on the role of faith and of personal conversion. On the other hand, the sects add new doctrines to the received doctrines. The origin of these new doctrines is found in a supplementary revelation made to new prophets (The Book of Mormon, the prophetism of the Pentecostals and others). But in these additions, which seem so obviously to be the contrary of the previously mentioned selection, there is none the less an exaggeration of an element with which the churches are well acquainted: the role of the Holy Spirit who governs the church, who leads the disciples into all truth.

Does this basic nature of the sect, i.e., to be anti-church and anti-world, appear in the mechanism by which the sect engenders heresy? Assuredly, yes. It is because the church has become apostate that it is a dead church or a false church – indeed, the church of the Antichrist – that it has dimmed or forgotten certain elements of doctrine which the sect wants to emphasize. The church has settled in the world, has made compromises with it, has conformed itself to the order of the world. It is for this reason that it has preached universal salvation, has not discriminated between true believers and hypocrites, has said nothing about the number of elect: the sect, therefore, for its part, emphasizes and precisely calculates the number of elect (for the Jehovah's Witnesses, there are 144,000 of the elect). Here again, the sect proceeds by accentuating the Christian doctrine of election or predestination. It is in order truly to condemn the world in a definitive fashion that the sect accentuates certain aspects of Christian doctrine: for example, detachment from the world, non-conformity. Moreover, the sectarian heresies have the objective of releasing the member from the grip of worldly considerations: for example, they ignore completely the teaching of Romans 13, and throw into bold relief the thirteenth chapter of Revelation.

The states (for the Jehovah's Witnesses) are . . . satanic, as is all that is of the world. The duty of the Jehovah's Witness is to hold himself apart from all encounter with them. Divine law makes it his duty to guard himself against the contamination of the world: thus he does not participate in local, national, or international elections, and for even stronger reason refuses all civil or military service and will not salute the flag (it is contrary to the first two commandments of the Decalogue). First the League of Nations, and now the United Nations are the beasts predicted by the Apocalypse.[14]

There are a few modifications of this position in the thinking of the Adventists, Mennonites, etc., who call only for a refusal to obey laws which are contrary to the laws of God. One could even formulate a rule in this respect: a sect is so much the less sectarian and moves closer to becoming a church when (1) it agrees to collaborate with other churches, and thereby relativizes its own heresy; and (2) does not forbid its members from obeying the state and the civil laws.

But it is obvious that the doctrinal selection which the sect makes, despite the diversity of forms which this selection can take, is not done haphazardly: this selection always has the purpose of accentuating the anti-church and anti-world aspect of the sect.

2. *The Social Composition of Sects*

A sociology of sects, a sociological interpretation of the sectarian phenomenon, would require a precise knowledge of their recruitment and of their
social composition. Furthermore, it would require a comparison of these
data with the social composition of the churches and with the distribution
of social classes within the global society in which the sects exist. Unfor-
tunately, such studies have not yet been made; indeed, they have scarcely
been begun for the churches. And for the sects, there are particular problems, from the fact that their "clientèle" is not always stable, that the
children of sectarians do not always follow their parents, that the adults
readily pass from one sect to another and, above all, from the fact that the
sects are loath to keep statistics, that they put little importance on the
social origins of their members (that would be a concession to the world),
and that they are even more loath to give information on their members
to outsiders.[15] Yet we are not entirely without information on the social
composition of the sects, but this information comes from general impres-
sions gathered by those who have frequented sectarian assemblies. Thus
they are essentially subjective and should be used cautiously.

Father Chéry, whose purely French documentation comes in great part
from surveys undertaken by the Catholic League of the Gospel, gives the
following information:[16]

Adventists: generally from the populace, but also includes persons from
the middle class (tradespeople, skilled craftsmen, small businessmen).
Religious origin: some deserters from the Reformed churches, but the
great majority comes from Catholicism.

Jehovah's Witnesses: success in the industrial and especially in the mining
regions (the northern basin of France, Belgium, Saint-Etienne, Car-
maux, Lorraine) and especially among immigrants (Polish and others).

Friends of Man: minor craftsmen, minor officials, domestic servants,
retired people, rural folk, some workers. Religious origin: mainly
Catholic.

Darbyites: rural families of Drôme, Ardèche, and Haute-Loire, of Protestant origin (we would add: some industrial workers from the Mulhouse
area).

Mennonites: same social recruitment.

Neo-Apostolics: Chéry does not furnish information. Dagon,[17] however,
states that they have a popular, agricultural, and industrial recruitment.

Salvation Army (is this properly speaking a sect?): it works exclusively in the underprivileged sections of the large cities, but it is difficult to say if they recruit many members there.

Pentecostalism: a quite varied recruitment, but predominantly popular. Pentecostalism reaches especially those common people who are also the clientèle of faith-healers and spiritualists.

Antoinistes: the preceding tendency is even more marked, but the number of members is quite limited.

Christian Science: it draws, on the contrary, from "genteel society, especially feminine and of Anglo-American sympathy".

Disciples of George de Montfavet: a rather unusual clientèle. Chéry says that its members come from restless intellectual circles, yes, but it should be added that it is a question of minor intellectuals.

Mormons: clientèle solely of imported Anglo-Saxons.

Small Church: modest families of rural origin, some urban elements at Lyons.

Is it possible to draw some provisional conclusions from these vague and fragmentary data? Yes, it is in *certain* circles of the common people, primarily, that the sects recruit their members. But these circles are only rarely the working-classes properly speaking. Rather, it is a case either of the sub-proletariat or of the middle classes (minor businessmen, etc.) who, because of the growing secularization, are no longer guided by the Catholic church but who are not yet proletarianized to the point that they are taken in charge by the labour unions and by the political parties of the extreme left. Socially and religiously, these individuals constitute a floating mass. Perhaps it is not without interest to emphasize that it was in a similar social milieu that *Poujadisme*, a movement both demanding and reactionary and expressing an impotent frustration, recruited its adherents. Thus the sect would quite frequently represent a type of compensation for individuals who do not belong to the powerful or rising classes (capitalist bourgeoisie, working-class) and feel irrelevant, and who are not integrated into a church with which they have only transitory contacts. The double phenomenon of the proliferation of sects and of their relative lack of success is explained in the following way: their adherents represent social classes which suffer from social and religious frustration, but which are classes without a future; they live on the margin of history, and from this fact, they are tormented by an anxiety which renders them vulnerable to the most fantastic promises of the future. Moreover, it should be noted that with the sects which are closest to the church (Mennonites, Pentecostalists, and even the Darbyites), the more their social composition becomes diversified, the more the frustration-complexes are attenuated, and the more also the sect sobers down. Furthermore, the composition of these sects gives evidence of a greater stability: the recruitment of the Mennonites is primarily familial; or else its members come in a direct line from Protestant churches (e.g., for the Pentecostalists and Darbyites) without having passed beforehand through a religious no-man's-land. When the adherents of a sect come in a direct line from a church, their adherence to the sect must be seen as a movement of religious protest against a church which they feel has become muscle bound, incapable of revival or of profound reformation. But the cause of this hardening of their church of origin can at the same time appear to them to be social: the established church is also the bourgeois church, the church with the money, the one which builds splendid sanctuaries and pays fat salaries to its pastors, or even the church which receives subsidies from the bourgeois state. Thus religious frustration appears tied up with social frustration, and it is impossible to figure out the part played by these different factors. All that one can say is that the determining and conscious reason for the adherence to the sect is felt by the individual to be religious.

For those sectarians who belonged only nominally to a church, or who came from religious indifferentism or even from atheism, their adherence to a sect is evidence of the presence in them of non-satisfied and often long-repressed religious needs. One cannot dismiss the hypothesis that through their adherence to a sect (often to a strange sect which cuts itself off completely from the official churches), they are manifesting in an aggressive fashion their need for personal and social identification. They view themselves as strangers to all religious communities, and perceive that in the face of certain situations (sickness, suffering, death, rejoicing) they are deprived of spiritual underpinnings. They perceive that they have nothing, in comparison to those people who differentiate themselves from one another and who mutually identify by means of their religious belonging. But since they belong to social classes without prestige, they cannot compensate for this type of social poverty by some other form of social integration. Yet, at the same time, integration into a large church, where they would be submerged in the mass of members, would not provide them with any singularity or with a sufficient relief. Thus they seek the small sect, the strangest possible, that which has no common denominator with the other churches, a group in which their originality would at least be safeguarded. This interpretation which we propose in no way tends to discredit the authentically religious motivations that can inspire sectarians. It is intended only to explain the form which their religious commitment takes. It rests on the hypothesis that the majority of sectarians belong to social classes which are poorly enough defined, which have no particularly acute self-awareness, social classes which do not succeed in situating themselves in relation to the dominant social classes, marginal and often futureless social classes which consequently do not give their members sufficient means of forming a social personality.

It is not the great mass of these social classes who move towards the sects; the masses are too apathetic for a decision of this type. Rather, it is often the best, the strongest personalities who are attracted to the sects, because they alone are capable of becoming aware of what it is that they lack. These facts provide a basis for understanding the pride, indeed the conceit, of the sectarian and his intransigent attitude regarding the churches. This pride means that nothing in the world can make him renounce what has effectively become the foundation of his social personality.

3. *The Behaviour and Beliefs of the Sect*

If there is indeed an essence of the sect, then every sect, despite its particular characteristics, must share in a common fund which belongs to all. This common fund involves both doctrinal beliefs and practices. However, in theory, it could be posited that the common fund of practices is more important than that of beliefs, since practices, as the visible, objective expression of faith, constitute something more basic than an intellectual expression.

This hypothesis could be verified if it were possible to show the community or identity of certain themes in, for example, sects born in the modern era and sects that arose very rapidly on the margin of early Christianity. In other terms, have the Gnostic, Manichean, Montanist, and Millenarian heresies been continued in the modern sects? It seems to us that there is no doubt about the answer.

Gnosticism may be defined as a heresy which maintains that, beside and beyond the biblical revelation, there are hidden revelations. Sometimes these are buried in the literal text of the Scriptures, sometimes they are received by illumination. In any case, they are accessible only to certain faithful, to those who have progressed sufficiently in the faith, who have succeeded in passing from earthly faith to knowledge. Now, it is well known that modern sects represent a tendency in the direction of gnostic religion, in that they limit the number of saints or elect, insist on a certain doctrinal esoterism, and put emphasis on direct illuminations of the Holy

Spirit (Pentecostalism) or on special revelations of the Holy Spirit (Mormons). The difference is that there no longer is any effort to arrive at a refined knowledge, which would be something that their popular recruitment would prohibit.

Manicheeism attributes the creation of matter to an evil god, and opposes this god to the good God of redemption and the Gospel. Thus it introduces the most radical dualism into the very principle of being. And by dissociating creation from redemption, it dissociates the Old Testament from the New Testament. Present sectarian transpositions undoubtedly present notable differences: the dualism remains, but it is no longer located on the level of God, although the accentuation of the personality of Satan or of Lucifer[18] (for example, among the Jehovah's Witnesses) almost becomes the equivalent of a duality of gods. However, the dualism is located primarily on the level of men. Sects often accentuate the radical distinction between the elect and the damned. Far from this distinction remaining God's secret, they want to make it visible and manifest right now: this damnation of certain individuals is no longer a possibility or a threat, it is a fact. And the number of elect can be known now. The emphasis on eternal punishment in preaching (among the Darbyites especially) arises from the same dualism.

Montanism is characterized by a rejection of the hierarchy of the official church, the development of prophetism, moral strictness and asceticism, the proclamation of the imminent return of Christ, and the role of the Paraclete ascribed to the founder Montanus. Here again, we find in nearly all present sects, some characteristics that are a reviviscence of Montanism. The inspired prophets are found once again in Cévenol prophetism, among American Shakers, in Pentecostalism. Moral strictness, asceticism, and the rejection of military service are characteristic of many sects, with the prohibitions bearing on all actions that are thought to be forms of submission to the world and its vanity. The imminent coming of the kingdom and the precise calculation of the date of the event are important elements of the doctrine of the Jehovah's Witnesses (according to whom the kingdom of God has been established on earth since 1914), for the Friends of Man (for whom the kingdom will soon be proclaimed), and for the Adventists, who think that the nearly total fulfilment of the various predictions contained in the Book of Daniel and in the Revelation of John is proof of the nearness of Christ's return.

Millenarian speculations, finally, are frequent in the sects, and are combined with a gnosticism which enables the sect to give a precise description of the millennium. Thus, for the Adventists, the just will pass the millennium in heaven, then the Holy City with the elect will descend to earth. At that time, Satan will lead the damned, who have been raised, in a battle against the just. But heaven's fire will destroy this army and purify the earth, which, returned to its Eden beauty, will be the eternal abode of the just.

Thus, despite certain interruptions, the entire history of sects shows a permanence of the major sectarian themes. Moreover, it would be of interest to show how these themes have been variously coloured or accentuated according to the civilization in which the sect develops. The situations of social misery produced by industry in the eighteenth and nineteenth centuries have certainly contributed to the revival and accentuation of the prophetic, messianic, and millenarian aspects of the sects, while at the same time, these situations also pushed the sects in the direction of charitable, humanitarian action and inspired them to efforts of social revolution.

We shall study sectarian comportment by approaching it from two different perspectives: sectarian comportment as reaction against the established church and sectarian comportment as reaction against the forms of civilization.

A. The development of the churches is characterized by their institutionalization, which is marked not only by the establishment of a clergy, by a sacerdotal hierarchy, and by a canon law, but also by the adoption of fixed cultic and liturgical forms, by the creation of a prescribed style of piety, and by a doctrinal orthodoxy (recorded in the creeds). The sect reacts precisely against all forms of this institutionalization. Séguy shows this quite plainly in his study of the historical origins of sects, or at least of nonconformist movements, in England:

The first sects were born of the *revolt of popular religious sentiment* against the liturgical piety of Anglicanism. Or, more generally speaking, it was the revolt of enthusiasm, of sentimentalism, of individualism – with all that these imply of good and bad – against the regimentation, barrenness, and abstruseness of the elaborate liturgies.[19]

The mark of this is the frequent appeal to the Holy Spirit as the power that overturns things. Against the very idea of a clergy, the sect would brandish that of the equality of all, of the universality of the priesthood.[20] To be sure, this rule is not absolute, but it is generally true. (An exception would be, for example, the Community of Christians, founded by a Lutheran minister, a disciple of Rudolf Steiner; this sect has a learned hierarchy of priests: the founder is the Conductor or Patriarch, and under him are chief conductors, superior conductors, and patriarchs.) On the other hand, the disappearance of any idea of sacerdotal hierarchy is compensated for by the role attributed to the founder, who is considered as a kind of saint. The smaller the sect, the more decisive the role played by the founder. Certain sects sometimes teach what are essentially the ideas of the founder, or of one of his successors, or of a contemporary prophet.[21] As the role of the founder begins to be effaced, the sect begins to approach more closely to the church-type: for example, the role of Wesley among Methodists, or of Menno Simons among the Mennonites, is nothing more than the role of the reformers among the churches of the Reformation. This sectarian insistence on the person of the founder witnesses to the desire to restore a *charismatic* power in place of an *institutional* power; charisma has more religious authenticity than the institutionalized function and offers the member the possibility of a more direct link with the divine source of inspiration. The sociological trait of sects is the claim to build a church without sociological foundations, where the vertical line of communion with God outweighs any horizontal line of historical and institutional continuity. The best way to arrive at this is by suppressing the horizontal dimension.

This same comportment is seen in the quite common rejection of any hierarchical organization on the part of the sect; local communities are to be independent from each other, each one obeying the inspiration of the Spirit. The Baptists and Congregationalists brought this principle into the very heart of the churches of the Reformation, which were already aware of it, since they themselves had to free themselves from the Roman hierarchical centralization.

In the second place, the sectarian attempt at renewal will bear on the *structure of worship*. It will manifest itself in an anti-liturgicalism, to the degree at least that the liturgy claims to give a fixed, objective aspect to worship, and to the degree that personal feelings of the present moment are unceasingly controlled and limited in their expression. The sectarian worship, on the contrary, is characterized by a very great freedom of form and by the large place given to subjectivity (due to its quality as receiver of the inspiration).[22] Sectarian worship is particularly remarkable for the warm atmosphere of emotion and fellowship in which it unfolds, and for the enthusaism that it engenders (sometimes under the cover of very elementary and mechanical processes, whose deterministic character escapes the participants: the sentimental nature of long and often repetitious chants, which have the same effect as certain modern songs; the very vigorous haranguing of the congregation by the preacher; long sermons overloaded with superlatives and exclamations; calls to repentance, which are followed by an immediate response on the part of some members of the group, whose penitence then spreads contagiously among the rest).

Moreover, all barriers between clergy and laity are abolished: each person can get up to give his personal testimony. It is not so much a matter of preaching a doctrine as of recounting a personal experience, in which it becomes clear that God has acted with power in respect to the person involved. To be sure, the doctrinal element is not always absent, but it needs a sort of experiential verification in the life of the subjects. This is, moreover, the source of the high degree of certainty that characterizes the faith of sectarians. They do not know doubt, they are not open to rational argument: their whole faith is based on a personal experience that receives its value from revelation.

In regard to the freedom of forms, it has often been pointed out that there is a certain similarity between the worship of sects and worship in the early church. This similarity is not fortuitous. The sect is a church which wants to begin at zero or, if you will, at year one of the church. This is not only because the churches have failed in their mission over the centuries and have betrayed their message, but because it is necessary in any case to suppress any temporal development which would take us further away from the source. In other words, it is a matter of becoming contemporary with the salvation event. This is why the sects reduce the role of the Bible, almost to the point of rendering it insignificant. This follows a logic inherent in their piety: the Bible which recounts to us a past history is only a troublesome intermediary, and must yield precedence to direct inspiration.

Yet many sects, far from putting the Bible aside, are characterized by a very marked fundamentalism. No doubt, such comportment is radically opposed in form to the preceding. But it serves the same function. As with inspiration, direct contact with God is guaranteed by the fact that each word of Scripture is the word of God without human intermediary and that each letter and each mark is traced by the very hand of God. The book itself is dropped from heaven; it is a sort of fragment of God at our disposition in a permanent way.

Furthermore, the two types of comportment can be combined: direct inspiration brings the light that opens up the true meaning of the Scripture, since the latter, the divine book, is necessarily a book of mysteries. It was thus that William Miller discovered that the essential point of the Gospel was the imminent return of Christ and that from this intuition everything became clear: the Bible enabled one to date this return. If the facts belie the calculation, the facts are wrong: the return has really come, but in the invisible world. With William Miller, the part played by personal intuition was restrained; he drew his inspiration from the visions of Daniel. But Joseph Smith, for his part, received personal revelations, thanks to which he discovered a third testament that enabled one to interpret the other two testaments correctly. It was on the basis of a personal vision that Ellen Gould White constrained the Adventists to observe the sabbath, which, of course, has scriptural roots.

Whether the sect develops in the direction of personal revelation or in the direction of biblical literalism, it is the same basic need that seeks to be satisfied, namely, the need for an unassailable certitude. Modern sects have been born in an age in which scientific progress, on the one hand, and the democratic rejection of institutional authority, on the other hand, have shaken the traditional certitudes, that is to say, the authoritarian ministry of the church and the Bible as the book of God's revelation. The sects react over against this threat; they respond to the challenge of the age. Some consider that one is lost as soon as historical criticism is given its part in the interpretation of Scripture, for the certitude attached to the Holy Book will be progressively encroached upon; in the eyes of the sect, fundamentalism is the sole bulwark possible against these insidious attacks. Consequently, the Bible is considered in its very materiality to be a book coming from God. There could be no question of taking a critical attitude towards it, not even in the least detail. Either certitude is total, or it is not. Such an attitude naturally reinforces the sectarian nature of the sect, for it can maintain itself only if the members are preserved in their whole existence from the attacks of modernism. Thus it is necessary that the sect be constituted as a closed society, that it exercise a rigid control over its members, that it exclude the lukewarm, and that it keep a careful watch over the development of morals, for moral contamination could have consequences of an intellectual nature. Modernism is considered to be a global phenomenon influencing, at one and the same time, both morals and mind. Thus the fundamentalist sect will avoid any contact and even any collaboration with non-fundamentalist churches. The refusal of some fundamentalist churches in America to become members of the World Council of Churches is an indication of the development of these churches towards the condition of sects.

The confidence placed in revelations is another method of defence against the same danger: to a certain degree, one defends oneself against science with the weapons of science. In effect, revelation is an *experience* and science teaches us that all certitude has its source in experience. In the face of experience, one can do nothing. To be sure, in this case it is an unverifiable experience and gains credence only by the prestige of the religious personality who experiences it. But this authority is itself recognized and tested experientially. In the same way, healings are experiential. The reason why so many sects develop a ministry of healing (and so many testimonies in the meetings and services of sects are the recounting of a healing) is that here again certitude comes from experience. The truth defended by the sect becomes unassailable because of the healings, just as one cannot attack the science of the uncertified healer who has had spectacular results.

Previously we have felt it necessary to emphasize that the modern sects continue certain themes and doctrines that appeared during the early history of the church. Now we must call attention to the fact that modern sects have their own forms of behaviour, since they are responses to certain challenges which were unknown to the first centuries, the challenges of science and of experience as the source of certitude. The churches have also faced these same challenges, but they have tried to respond to them by giving a more considerable place to tradition; they have also tried, not without success, to respond to these challenges by giving an important place to critical science while at the same time preserving the central kerygma of Scripture. Sometimes the churches have also become involved in an experiential theology (from the end of the nineteenth century), but this theology has been nothing other than a mode of comprehension of the revealed deposit.[23] The sects manifest more freedom in regard to tradition precisely because they claim to be a new beginning of Christianity, because they postulate that the churches have been wrong or that the church has long since disappeared. This is why the sects permit themselves to innovate or to adapt the traditional faith to their innovations. This does not come about without a certain naïveté (precisely the naïveté of innovators), and after a period of tumultuous innovations one frequently sees the sects proceeding along much more traditional lines.

B. The sect is a church which sees itself particularly besieged and menaced by the world. Thus it reacts with simplicity and with solidarity towards these dangers; what is more, the term "world" has a uniquely pejorative meaning in sectarian language. It has lost the ambiguous sense that it has in the gospel, where it designates both the creation disfigured by evil, flesh, the principle of evil, as well as that reality which God has so loved. The gospel maintains the equivocal character of the world, whereas the sect gives it a univocal sense. The insistence on judgment, on eternal punishment, on the destruction of the world by violence are just so many ways for the sect to indicate the fundamental wickedness of the world.

This is why *mission* assumes a particular significance in the sect. The sects often are very strongly missionary, and the rather spectacular evangelization of the South American continent must be credited to them much more than to the churches of the Lutheran or Reformed traditions.[24] But sectarian mission, which quite often makes no distinctions between true pagans and the members (even faithful) of the churches, has the goal precisely of taking those people out of the world who can be taken out: the entry of these people into the sect will prove exactly that they belong to the number of the elect. The object of the sect's missionary preaching is to point out this basic distinction between the elect and the damned. It retains the idea according to which the Word of God is also judgment of God, according to which this judgment signifies that one will be taken and the other left; but the characteristic of sectarian mission is that it claims to be able, through its preaching, to manifest visibly this great division between the elect and the damned. And this claim goes hand in hand with the affirmation, on the part of many sects, that the kingdom of God is already realized, that the end of the world has already arrived. The eschatological theme is always tied to the Christian mission. When the eschatological dimension of the faith is weakened, there is always a weakening and indeed a disappearance of the missionary activity of the church (as was seen, in particular, at the time of the Reformation). But the eschatological theme may be interpreted in various ways: the sect insists either on the temporal imminence of the end or on the effective arrival of the kingdom. Moreover, it is possible that this interpretation is tied up with the desire for an immediate compensation for a state of social frustration. But in any case, in relation to this visibly present end, the human attitude can no longer be other than a definitive and irrevocable decision. The goal of sectarian mission is to provoke this decision. If the decision does not come, all hope of salvation must be abandoned. The time of forbearance is at an end.

This very conception of mission explains the *exclusivism* of the sect. Whoever is not for it is against it and against the kingdom. Only militants are admitted within the interior of the sect. This, moreover, helps to explain the aggressive dynamism of some of the sects. But this exclusivism is also expressed in the exclusion of all those members of the sect who are deviationists on one point or another. Generally speaking, the sect wields the weapon of excommunication much more promptly and severely than the churches. This exclusivism is tied to the nature of the sect. In effect, the nature of the sect results sociologically from the breaking up, from the disintegration of the global ecclesiastical society. In this way, it is related to the dissolution of the idea of *Christendom*, that is, of the coincidence between the church and the whole of society. The churches retain something of the idea of Christendom: they are multitudinous, grouping together believers, the unattached, the peripheral, even the indifferent. Canonically the Catholic church considers that all the inhabitants of a diocese belong to its jurisdiction, even if the people themselves have ceased to consider themselves as Catholics or are members of another confession.[25] Far from practising an exclusivism, it practises an inclusivism. Whenever possible, it fights to be recognized as the official religion, indeed as the religion of the state. The churches of the Reformation do not put forward such claims, but they also are churches of multitudes. They carry over the universalist claim from the juridical or canonical level to the moral level, that is to say, they consider themselves to be responsible for the whole of the population. The sect, on the contrary, weeds out. It considers the era of Christendom to be totally superseded. In its fashion, the sect takes on the new situation, it knows itself and wants itself to be the small flock. It even takes some pride in this, being assured that the small number of its members is the sign of their election.

Christendom was still characterized by the existence of a tie between church and state, by a division of powers mutually agreed by church and state, and by their co-operation. This epoch is today no longer with us. The concordats of the nineteenth century already represented something quite different from harmonious co-operation between church and state. They were compromises arduously hammered out. The sect, following the free churches, denounced every alliance with the state, every concordat, as sin itself, as a form of prostitution, as an intrusion of the lost world into the bosom of the community of the redeemed. The refusal of some sects to participate in political life comes from the same spirit. This general comportment towards the state explains why numerous writers have wanted to define the sect as a church separated from the state. But this is an insufficient characteristic, since it is only a particular aspect of behaviour going back to the essence of the sect. The rejection of any tie with the state results from sectarian exclusivism.

The exclusivism proper to the sect, of Protestant origin, is also related to a profound *individualism*. Sectarian individualism excludes all the impure, all those whom the church tolerates as a kind of sociological burden. The sect rejects this burden. Certainly it wants to be a community, but a community of equals, of men equally pure, who submit to a collective discipline that sometimes is very strict. As a manifestation of individualism, the sect is bound up with the spiritual origins of the Reformation, which, considered as a sociological movement, was indeed a protest of individual conscience against the tyranny of ecclesiastical power. This kindredship of individualist spirit between the sects and the Reformation justifies Troeltsch's opinion that the sect represents one of the possibilities of primitive Christianity and, consequently, of the Reformation (which wanted to be the resumption of primitive Christianity). Primitive Christianity contained the twofold possibility of the institutional church and the sect.[26] This twofold possibility expresses the ferment of individualism which both the Reformation and primitive Christianity contained and which was directed against all purely sociological religious forms. What should be remarked against Troeltsch is that the ecclesiology of primitive Christianity and of the Reformation contained an important corrective to this individualism. Agreed, the doctrine of salvation among the reformers places the individual man in the sole presence of his Saviour and rejects all ecclesiastical mediation in regard to justification and salvation. And the reformers reject even the Catholic idea of the spiritual maternity of the church. (Although this rejection is not unanimous: one remembers Calvin's famous formula that the church is the mother of all those of whom God is the father.) Yet on the level of Christian life and of sanctification, the church plays a decisive role. It is symptomatic, for example, that in the *Confessio Gallicana*, all doctrine of grace, of justification, and even of the Holy Spirit is set forth without reference to the church (in order to emphasize that the spiritual adventure is something between each man and the God of love), but that the article on the doctrine of the church (Article XXVI) is introduced by these words:

We believe, therefore, that no one should withdraw separately and be content with his own person, but that all together should guard and foster the unity of the church. . . .

In the same way, it should be remarked that the very definition of the church unanimously given by the Reformation is inspired by a nominalist and individualist conception. The church has no ontological substance: it is solely

the company of the faithful who agree to follow the Word of God and the pure religion which depends on it (*Confessio Gallicana*, Article XXVII)

or, according to the Augsburg Confession (Article VII), it is

the congregation (*congregatio*) of saints (thus the church does not engender believers: they are believers by the act of the Lord, not by the action of the church), in which the Gospel is rightly preached and the Sacraments are rightly administered.

There is no doubt that the ecclesiology of the Reformation corrected absolute individualism and recovered some of the authority of the church, but it also integrated this individualism into its very definition of the church. If there are more sects issuing from Protestantism than from Catholicism, it is thus precisely because a certain individualism is authorized more widely by Protestantism than by Catholicism.

This individualism is manifested in the sect by the rejection of an organization that is too hierarchical and distant, by the defiance towards any institutionalism which would resemble that of the world, and by an anti-sacramental attitude (although this is not absolutely the case). In regard to the latter point, the Salvation Army, born in spiritual proximity to Methodism, has a reserved attitude towards the sacraments (an attitude that becomes negative among the Quakers). And, of course, many sects reject infant baptism precisely because such a practice does not give any place to the faith of the individual.

This individualism explains above all the limited development of the sects. The sects were born in an epoch in which individualism was all the more exacerbated because it was contemporaneous with the formation of a civilization that was giving increasing importance to the collective over against the individual and was submitting the individual to collective disciplines. In this situation, individualism seemed to be a sort of last leap before humanity entered into a mass civilization. In relation to this civilization, the sect was a bit out of place. It is easy to think that the sect, better than the churches, constituted a remedy and a corrective to the dangers of this civilization. In fact, however, the sect is primarily a refuge for those beings who have been particularly maltreated by this civilization, for those who have not known how to adapt to it, and who have adopted only a negative attitude of protest against it. For this reason also, it would be interesting to have socio-professional statistics on the composition of sects, in order to see if their members occupy dominant functions in the sectors of active life or if they stick to more or less ephemeral forms of activity and to minor occupations.[27] In any case, whereas the member churches of the World Council of Churches are increasingly conscious of their responsibilities to the civilization as it is, of the problem of the development of under-developed peoples, of the problems of industrial and urban civilization, and of the humanization of technology, the sects feel that they do not have to participate in this effort, which they regard as a religious rationalization, a politicization of the church, and ultimately a form of infidelity. The individualism of the sects is seen in the fact that they give a restrictive interpretation to the idea of sanctification, that they aim at the formation of a totally interior, individual, and familial piety, and that they are more or less insensible to the appeals of the world.

Nevertheless, we have no right to forget that *social messianism* is, along with individualism, one of the aspects of sectarian comportment. Many sects were born in the eighteenth century, at least partially from a protest against pauperism and social exploitation. But ordinarily – and here is where social messianism is not a socialism – it is not a question of transforming the world; on the contrary, it is a question of building a refuge of social peace in the midst of this lost world. And this refuge would be a kind of prefiguration either of the kingdom or of the millennium. The elect and the elect only thus would live there according to a law which is not that of this world. Once again, among the economic activities which would be authorized in this sort of paradise, the sect rarely chooses activities which would lead in the direction of economic and technical progress. The case of the Shakers is typical: they were suspicious of industrial production and, on the contrary, built at their community at Albany a very efficient, communist-based system of rural and artisan production sustained by an ethic of work, saving and asceticism.[28] To be sure, the Shakers wanted to set their system up as a global society, and their criticism of slavery, of agrarian capitalism, and of wage-earning classes has a universal bearing in their thought. But this social prophetism which was accentuated during the course of the nineteenth century (especially in the teaching of Evans) came about precisely at the time when the sect was in its decline, when the recruitment of members fell off, and thus when it was in the process of failing as a sectarian community. As Henri Desroche writes:

> Decline thus overtook the Shakers when they attempted to define the tasks of a political progressivism in terms of religious prophetism. Perhaps we can assume that this mixture of genres was part of the process of decline.[29]

When a sect opens itself to a worldly task, it destroys itself as a sect. Its social prophetism and its social accomplishments permit it to continue to exist only to the degree that these items are of internal usage.[30]

The sect succeeds (where the church has nearly always failed) in maintaining a relationship between three terms that one would think are antithetical: the sect itself, as closed society, eschatological messianism, and socialism. The idea of *purity* is the hinge which maintains this tripartite relationship: it is necessary that the sect remain a sect in order to include only the pure (doctrinal and ethical purity), and it is the concern for this purity that has led the sect to break with the great church and to want deliberately to be only a small flock. That this purity must be maintained at all costs is due to the nearness of the coming of the kingdom. The desire to be found pure leads the sectarians to the concern with austerity and asceticism; sectarian socialism is in no way the indication of a desire to create a society of abundance or an expanding society.[31] It is in a sense against themselves, just like the Puritans, that they create economic prosperity. Sometimes, indeed, this prosperity is very disturbing to them. Evans, in the nineteenth century, quite clearly became concerned about the extension of the property owned by the Shakers, an extension which led them to bring in personnel from outside the sect and thus to re-establish a wage-earning class. The triad of sect, eschatological messianism, and socialism can be maintained only to the degree that the sect remains grounded in an incessant will of purity, which roots it in sectarian individualism. The Anabaptists of the Reformation as well as the American Shakers witness to the fragility of this triad. In order for a sect to be the bearer of a true socialism and for it to propose to the world a formula of this socialism, rather than realizing it in a closed society, the sect must itself agree to be present in the world, to exist for the world and not to be separate from it. It must view itself not as a microcosm of the pure, but as a leaven in the midst of the world. But for that, the sect undoubtedly would also have to modify its conception of the coming of the kingdom, which remains apocalyptic and millenarist, which signifies destruction much more than the manifestation of the hidden meaning of human history.

4. *From Sect to Church*

Troeltsch has summarized as follows the basic characteristics of the sect and of sectarian behaviour:

Lay Christianity, personal achievement in ethics and in religion, the radical fellowship of love, religious equality and brotherly love, indifference towards the authority of the state and the ruling classes, dislike of technical law and of the oath, the separation of the religious life from the economic struggle by means of the ideal of poverty and frugality, or occasionally in a charity which becomes communism, the directness of the personal religious relationship, criticism of official spiritual guides and theologians, the appeal to the New Testament and to the Primitive church.[32]

The proportioning of these different elements can vary, and certain elements can become dimmed to the point of disappearing and be replaced by contrary elements (the strict sacerdotal hierarchy being substituted for the equality of the brethren). It is nevertheless true that this composite table of characteristics has a unity and that on nearly every point one sees the sect deviating in relation to the historical line followed by the churches. The latter are characterized by clericalism and hierarchy, they have given importance to the institution and to discipline over against the free expression of feelings; as churches of the multitudes they have not always given adequate attention to the importance and quality of personal relationships. On the other hand, they have sought very attentively to define (usually in a positive way, although sometimes negatively) their relations with the state; they have sought to establish themselves solidly in the higher social and cultural classes; they have made major compromises with the civilization of the present age; although they have sometimes encouraged a spirit of poverty, they have not condemned wealth; sometimes, indeed, as with the Protestantism of the seventeenth century, they have played a certain role in capitalistic, industrial, and financial expansion; in general, they have honoured theology, and have encouraged theological science; and, although they have not ceased to keep alive the archetype of the primitive church, they have not at all sought to erect a servile copy of it, since they feel that one should be attentive to the difference of the times.

Whatever be the common doctrinal basis which unites a large number of sects and churches, this difference of style has sufficed to create an extremely deep gulf between them. The breach is so serious that the churches bitterly defend themselves against the propaganda of the sects, and the sects, often insensible to the call to missionary activity in pagan lands, carry on their evangelization among the members of the churches, recruiting their members from among the malcontents, disturbed, and unsatisfied of these churches. Each time that a new sect appears, it reproduces some of the traits mentioned by Troeltsch. For example, in the nineteenth century a sect called the Hinchists appeared in a very circumscribed and well-defined geographical region (the region of Sète and Nîmes).[33] This sect is characterized by the importance attached to visions and personal revelations, by a fundamental Manicheanism (it being well understood that the official churches are the incarnation of the spirit of evil), by a protest against traditional dogmas (in particular, against the dogma of the two natures of Christ: Christ could not have been a man, since the flesh is evil), by a social messianism which is shown in important charitable foundations (The Evangelical Establishment of Sea-side Spas for the

Poor; Evangelical Shelters of Nîmes for Abandoned Girls), by pacifism and conscientious objection. This sect differs sociologically from other sects in that it recruits its members from among the middle class of the business world.[34] Yet in these other respects, this minuscule sect reproduces the perennial characteristics of the sect with astonishing fidelity, without one being able to speak of an influence of another sect or of a filiation in relation to another sect. Even more remarkable is the fact that the founder was, like Ann Lee for the Shakers, a very young girl having no historical culture from which she could consciously draw pre-existent models.

In the face of this astonishing antithetical parallelism of church and sect, we should undoubtedly accept Troeltsch's contention that the sect is as foreign to Protestantism as it is to Catholicism:

> In the last resort, however, the sect is a phenomenon which differs equally from the ecclesiastical spirit of Protestantism and of Catholicism. It is an independent branch of Christian thought; it is the complement of the church-type . . .[35]

It would still be necessary, however, to explain why the sect is created on the periphery of Protestantism rather than of Catholicism. In saying this, we should not lose sight of the fact that there are numerous Catholic sects: the Old Catholic Church, the French Catholic Church (of Gallican inspiration), the Gnostic Apostolic Church, the Primitive Catholic Church, the Catholic Church of the Mariavites (founded in 1906 on special revelation by a Polish nun), the Catholic Apostolic Church of France, the Holy Apostolic Church, the Celtic Apostolic Church, the Ancient Catholic Church, the Small Church, the Catholic Apostolic Orthodox Church of France, the Autocephalous Gallican Catholic Church, the Liberal Catholic Church, etc. All of these groups were born of a split with the Roman Catholic Church and claim to conserve the essential part of Catholic doctrine. But one can say that from the point of view of their extension, these sects have not known the same success as sects of Protestant origin (e.g., Adventism and, especially, Pentecostalism). We can affirm that the sectarian phenomenon encounters on Protestant terrain a greater ease of becoming recognized and even of rejoining the family of churches of the Reformation. Witness, for example, the cases of Methodism, of the Baptists, of Congregationalism, and of other free churches. Reformation ecclesiology is less opposed than the ecclesiology of Rome to the birth of new communities, since it admits in any case a freedom in the institutional, ceremonial, and disciplinary domains. Where this ecclesiology insists on a doctrinal unity, the latter can only be by mutual consent and is not at all guaranteed by a doctrinal magisterium which defines an orthodoxy.

This observation should not make us forget, however, that the sect responds to religious needs and sociological situations that are also found in Protestantism as well as Catholicism. Although from the point of view of their structures the Protestant sect and the Catholic religious order are fundamentally distinct, this does not exclude the possibility that they fulfil the same function. Although it is true that many Protestant churches have been revived and renewed by the sects (as witness, the Awakenings in France during the nineteenth century; these revivals were raised and carried forward by the Darbyists and the Methodists, and reached a large part of the church), it is equally true that the Catholic religious orders have raised revivals of piety and even reform in the Roman Church. The orders, like the sects, serve as refuges for restless and unsatisfied souls. In both the order and the sect, there is the development of the idea of a perfect Christian life, one submitted to a certain number of prohibitions and abstinences. Even the monastic vow of chastity has found its parallel in certain sects (Shakers). Many sects have developed the same ideal of community life, of the giving up of all individual appropriation of goods, that is found in the religious orders. The person of the founder plays a role in the orders analogous to that which it plays in the sects. Quite often the sect constitutes an anti-world, if only by its style of life and its discipline. As with the sect, the order extends itself not only in charitable institutions but sometimes in economic enterprises, especially of an agricultural nature. To be sure, it is never an anti-church, since it is under the authority of the pope and since its aim is to be of service to the church. Its members co-operate in the ordinary ministry of the church, and increasingly the orders seem to be a kind of shock troops which fulfil some particular form of ministry which the parish itself has not been able to fulfil, and sometimes the orders set up special "missions" in the parishes. Nevertheless, it should be observed that the orders maintain, sometimes jealously, a certain autonomy in the church; they elect their own generals, and by and large escape the jurisdiction of the bishops. Thus it does not seem invalid to think, with Troeltsch, that the Catholic church has been wise enough to contain sectarian protests within the structure of religious orders and congregations. Such protests in Protestantism, on the other hand, run headlong into a rigid institution of local scope, and generally find no other outlet except secession and the formation of a separate group. That the Catholic medium has not always proved sufficient to channel this sectarian protest is seen in the appearance of sects in Catholicism

(Troeltsch held to the false idea that sect had disappeared in Catholicism from the time of the Middle Ages[36]).

The Catholic sects ordinarily experience a rapid decline. Sects issuing from Protestantism, on the contrary, often experience a fruitful expansion and a long history. In this history there is frequently a development that leads them towards the status of church: Baptists and Methodists, both born as sects, became churches. It is not impossible that Pentecostalism will become a church. To be sure, this development presupposes first of all a numerical growth of the sect, an extension in space which gives it the sense of the ecumenical dimension. The sect which would remain withdrawn into itself, contenting itself with being an island-refuge, quite probably will remain a sect. After a period it would experience a decline, since it cannot find any source of renewal within its own space and since it has broken all ties with a tradition which has moved beyond it. Every sociological development is tied to certain conditions of social morphology. Baptists and Methodists, after having experienced a remarkable development in the United States, undertook a world-wide extension. They outdistanced the older churches in the movement towards the frontier, and recruited their members from truly popular levels of society.

Two signs of this development, which also sometimes play a causal role, should be emphasized:

1. A sect progresses towards the status of church when it becomes missionary. Obviously, every sect seeks to recruit new members by means of a certain propaganda. But this recruiting action should be distinguished from mission properly so called. Mission addresses itself to non-Christians, and from this fact it does not consider its essential task to be one of entering into competition with other churches. It considers that its common task with other churches is to make the gospel known, however much it be under a slightly particular form. The sect which becomes missionary recognizes that the propagation of the gospel constitutes a more fundamental task than polemic and competition with other Christian churches. Thus it complies with the understanding of the church, if it is true that the essence of the church is to be missionary. Baptists, Methodists and, more recently, Pentecostals have been remarkably missionary churches (one need only think of the missionary work of Pentecostalism in South America). Quite often they have reawakened the missionary zeal of the older churches.

2. A sect progresses towards the status of church when it agrees to collaborate with other churches. This second point is tied to the first. The

community that exists in the fulfilment of the same apostolic work ordinarily leads to certain *rapprochements*, especially in pagan lands: in the face
of paganism, confessional differences necessarily grow dim. In general, it
has not been in Europe or in North America where co-operation between
sects and churches has been sketched out. Such co-operation first began
to become evident in mission countries, in the common missionary councils. Then it began to spread out towards the territories of ancient Christendom. It was by means of the International Missionary Council (founded in
1921) that many sectarian churches have drawn nearer to the ecumenical
community.

Whereas the Catholic sects ultimately have no other possibilities except
to disappear or to lose themselves in small, ingrown groups, the Protestant
sects, in so far as they conserve solid ties with Scripture, can follow the
course of a progressive *rapprochement* with the churches. This very
rapprochement assists them in transforming themselves into churches.

It is true that not all sects follow such a development. Some sects, on
the contrary, accentuate their sectarian character. The reason for this very
different development probably resides in the fact that it takes place in
sects having a positive message, bringing a useful corrective to the teaching
or the piety of the churches (for example, the emphasis on the role of the
Holy Spirit in the conduct of life and of the church, the spontaneity of the
spiritual life over against too liturgical forms of piety, etc.). Once the
bitterness of the split is overcome, these sects will find the way of *rapprochement* with the church, indeed even the way of reunification.[37] Other sects,
of course, are simply a permanent protest against the mother church, a
denunciation of its apostasy – and are content to remain so. They have
need of this opposition in order to survive, and one can be assured that
their sectarianism will not be modified.[38] There is also the inverse process, that is, the development of a church in the direction of the status of
sect. But in order to observe this phenomenon, one must put aside all
dogmatic *a priori*. The Catholic church teaches that any schism in respect
to it can only be sectarian. Thus it has long asserted that Protestantism
could only become fragmented into more and more numerous sects. In
the face of the present ecumenical regrouping and of the reunion of certain
Protestant denominations, the Catholic church has been constrained to
revise its opinion.

But it is possible to determine objectively the conditions of the movement of a church towards the sect. A good example is provided by the
Free Churches of France. This ecclesiastical organization was born in 1849
from a split with the Reformed churches. This was based on a rejection of

the Napoleonic Concordat, and called for a total liberty of the church in regard to the state. Moreover, the free churches were not the only ones to call for such a separation: in 1848 the separation of church and state was called for by a great many people. Due to a rather liberal application of the Concordat, French Protestantism at the end of the Restoration[39] and during the July Monarchy experienced a certain prosperity (both the increase of pastoral posts and a fairly large demographic growth are evidence of this). Yet in many respects Protestantism suffered from the interference of the state, which hindered all synodical life and intervened in theological conflicts. The current in favour of the separation of church and state was only accentuated during the course of the century, and, despite the rather difficult conditions, the Protestants welcomed with satisfaction the separation that came in 1905. From that time, the motif that had brought the dissidence of the free churches disappeared. However, the latter continued to exist. It is true that these churches, at once both pietist and orthodox, could argue from the fact that a strong liberal current existed in the Reformed church (which led in 1872 to a new division in the Reformed church). But whereas these theological oppositions were sufficiently resolved for the reconstitution of a united Reformed church to become possible in 1938, a part of the free churches refused to join the movement. These churches formed a separate union which exists today with two to three thousand members and twenty-three ministerial posts. Its sectarian characteristics have become accentuated: at first it was affiliated with the Protestant Federation of France, where it played a relatively minor role and remained constantly on the defensive; it refused all participation in theological debate, abstained from taking part in any vote having political or social relevance (the sect is an anti-world), and rejected *a fortiori* any contact with the World Council of Churches. In 1963 the Union proclaimed its disaffiliation from the Protestant Federation. The reasons for this act are especially illuminating: the Union of Free Churches refuses to ratify the new statutes of the Federation because they make provision for a reinforcement of structures and a collaboration of churches in the framework of specialized departments. Thus it is primarily a matter of a refusal to co-operate with other churches, which are seen as being more or less unfaithful. This is typical sectarian behaviour, to which every church is exposed whose demographic bases are very precarious and whose only perspective for the future lies in considering itself as a "small flock", compensating for its isolation by a concern for its purity. As a general rule, a church that separates itself from another, and whose schism outlasts the reasons that caused it, is engaged in the

way of sectarianism. The maintenance of the institution in its autonomy
and in opposition to other institutions is its justification.

The movement from church to sect is easy, due to the fact that the
boundary between the two realities is blurred and sometimes undefined.
Church and sect possess a large number of distinctive characteristics. But
it is precisely this large number which hinders their reunion, which makes
it inevitable that the church will have the seeds of certain ecclesiastical
characteristics. According to the circumstances (among which the size of
the given community plays a primary role), these seeds can be developed
and become decisive. The chance of the sectarian seeds developing is
considerably reinforced by the state of division of the churches, by their
oppositions: it is quite true that every division in the church increases the
possibilities of sectarianism. For each branch which separates becomes an
anti-church in relation to the church. And to the degree that the divided
churches, preoccupied with safeguarding their particularities, isolate
themselves from the world and are no longer ready to assume responsibilities benefiting the whole of the global society, they also become anti-
worlds.

NOTES

1. Jean Séguy, *Les sectes protestantes dans la France contemporaine* (Paris: Beau-
chesne et ses Fils, 1956), p. 6.
2. E. Royston Pike, *Dictionnaire des religions*, French adaptation by Serge Hutin
(Paris: PUF, 1954), p. 283.
3. See the otherwise quite useful book of Gérard Dagon, *Les sectes en France*
(Strasbourg, 1958), where the division between churches and sects is perfectly arbitrary
and most frequently is based on the titles claimed by the religious communities themselves.
4. H. Desroche, "Approches du non-conformisme français", *ASR*, July–December
1956, no. 2, p. 48.
5. A good example is furnished by the movement of *Gemeinschaften*, which, for over
a century, have existed among Alsatian Protestantism, especially in the north of Alsace.
6. E. Troeltsch, *Social Teaching*, p. 339.
7. H. Desroche, *Les Shakers américains; D'un néo-christianisme à un présocialisme?*
(Paris: Editions de Minuit, 1955), p. 12.
8. J. Séguy, op. cit., p. 6.
9. Cf. G. Dagon, *Petites Eglises et grandes sectes en France, aujourd'hui* (Paris: SCE,
n.d.), pp. 66 et seq.
10. Henri Desroche, *Les Shakers américains*, pp. 84 et seq.
11. ibid., p. 109
12. ibid., p. 77.
13. ibid., pp. 44–45.

14. H. Ch. Chéry, *L'offensive des sectes*, "Rencontres" (Paris: Editions du Cerf, 2nd ed., 1954), pp. 180–181.

15. This is what partially explains the divergences among authors in regard to membership totals of sects. Chéry, for example, estimates that there are between 115,000 and 120,000 members of sects of Protestant origin in France, whereas Séguy, op. cit., p. 10, takes issue with this estimate and sets the figure at 30,260.

16. Chéry, op. cit., pp. 416–418.

17. Dagon, op. cit., p. 58.

18. Lucifer, among the Jehovah's Witnesses, is only the leader of the angelic armies. Having conceived in his heart the desire to become God's equal and having won over the angels to his side, he succeeded, after the fall of Adam and Eve, in making God's name forgotten. Lucifer became Prince of this world, so that the sovereignty of God on this earth in fact disappeared (cf. Séguy, op. cit., p. 122).

19. Séguy, op. cit.

20. There even exists a sect whose essential theme is anticlericalism. It is called the Secret Catholic Anticlerical Society (see Dagon, *Les sectes en France*, p. 36).

21. Cf. Dagon, *Petites Eglises et grandes sectes*, pp. 5–6.

22. Chéry, *L'offensive des sectes*, pp. 387 et seq., gives a good description of a Pentecostal worship service.

23. The Catholic church, cautiously and guardedly, also has tried to give apparitions (notably those of the Virgin) and healings a certain role in the support of Catholic truth. The scientific precautions taken at Lourdes in the confirmation of healings is evidence of this concern to win the support and prestige of science to the profit of Catholic doctrine.

24. See E. G. Léonard, *L'illuminisme dans un protestantisme de constitution récente* (*Brésil*) (Paris: PUF, 1953).

25. Chéry, op. cit., p. 37, even proposes to call "church" any religious group that claims to comprehend all members of society.

26. Troeltsch, *Social Teaching*.

27. It all depends, however, on the social context. Léonard, op. cit., p. 73, has shown that in Brazil, whereas Catholicism recruits its members from among the poorer section of the population, Pentecostalism has largely helped the social promotion of its members.

28. See H. Desroche, op. cit., pp. 220 et seq.

29. ibid., p. 231.

30. It is obvious that this analysis remains true only in so far as the sect remains a sect. The co-existence of sects and churches in the same country can produce phenomena of osmosis. It even happens that sects have attitudes towards social problems that are more determined than those of official churches: "According to the work of the sociologist E. G. Campbell, during the school integration crisis of 1957 at Little Rock, Arkansas, the ministers of small sects were generally segregationists and openly expressed their opinion, whereas the ministers of well-established denominations were generally integrationists and remained silent." Campbell writes: "Ministers who, during the crisis, would not defend the moral imperative that their conscience dictated to them . . . defended values and beliefs centred solely around their professional obligations. This had the result of calming all doubts that otherwise might have been raised in their minds" (*Social Forces*, March 34, 1961). Report made by Samuel S. Hill, Jr., "Le protestantisme dans le Sud et l'intégration raciale", *CS*, 71st Year, no. 9–12, September–December 1963.

31. We freely summarize here an article by H. Desroche, "Essor et déclin du Shakerisme", in *MNC*, no. 26, June 1953.

32. Troeltsch, *Social Teaching*, p. 336.

33. The sect is named after its founder Coraly Hinsch, who was born at Sète in 1801, daughter of Danish Lutherans, raised in the Reformed Church of France. The Evangelical Hinchist Church was officially founded in 1831. It continues to exist and numbers about 250 members scattered throughout France, Algeria, Great Britain, and Switzerland. The Hinchist doctrine was formulated in its entirety in 1919.

34. Cf. E. Appolis, "Dans le monde des affaires au XIXe siècle: le mysticisme hétérodoxe à Sète", *Annales*, April–June 1957, no. 2.

35. Troeltsch, op. cit., p. 701.

36. Jean Séguy has analysed the formation of a small modern sect born in Catholic terrain and strongly apocalyptic, namely the sect of the Giuridavidici founded by David Lazaretti in Italy in the nineteenth century (see Séguy's article in *ASR*, January–June, 1958, no. 5). Séguy notes that similar cases abound in the nineteenth century. It seems, however, that the Catholic sect is destined to a quick death.

37. This reunification is, in fact, envisaged between Anglicans and Methodists in Great Britain. After six years of conversations, a relatively optimistic report was submitted in 1963.

38. This is suggested by Kurt Hutten in his study "Die Kirche und die Sekten", in the collective volume *Die Einheit der Kirche und die Sekten* (Zollikon: Evangelischer Verlag, 1957).

39. Cf. Daniel Robert, *Les Eglises réformées en France (1800–1830)* (Paris: PUF, 1961).

XI

The Sociology of the Minority Church

Although the sect quite often represents a numerical minority and a socio-logical minority, it should not be confused with the minority church. To be sure, a minority church can eventually develop in the direction of the sect, but this development is not inevitable, to the degree that the given religious group conserves the consciousness of its ties with the larger community of which it is only one family. It views its minority nature as a relative thing, attributing it to historical and political contingencies. This is the case with French Protestantism, which remains persuaded, rightly or wrongly, that if its spirit had not been broken by the political persecution which began in 1560, the whole kingdom would have become Protestant. The minority church considers the international community to which it is spiritually connected to be a sort of reference group,[1] whose extensiveness, power, and universality helps keep the minority church from becoming a sect, from feeling itself to be a sect, from sectarian behaviour. Minority and dominance often alternate from country to country, as is notably the case in Europe concerning Protestantism and Catholicism.

The sociology of minority churches takes on a particular importance for Christianity as a whole; due to the advanced secularization of the West and to the missionary diffusion of Christianity into almost all non-Christian regions of the globe, Christianity tends everywhere to have a minority character.

Numerical minority does not necessarily coincide with sociological minority. A numerical minority that is only slightly accentuated does not of necessity lead to the constitution of a sociological minority group: one could not say that in Germany or in the Netherlands, at the present time, Catholics and Protestants constitute minority groups over against each other. Nor does every religious diaspora constitute a minority in the sociological sense of the term: when a diaspora is too diluted in the body of a nation, there is no possibility of its arriving at any group consciousness. In such a case, the confessional appurtenance of the individuals of this diaspora becomes a simple individual characteristic which, most frequently, escapes the attention of the society at large.

In order for there to be a minority group it is necessary that it be recognized as such by public opinion. And this recognition often is manifested, or at least has been manifested in the past, within the structures of a particular legal status. This status, of course, means that the members of the minority confession are second-class citizens. Spanish Protestantism offers us a typical example of this situation. Thus the minority church lives a segregated existence: its members do not have the same juridical capacities and the same political rights possessed by the members of the dominant religion, who benefit, *de facto* or *de jure*, from a sort of privileged position. But although the existence of a particular statute provides the point of departure for the minority-group consciousness, this consciousness can continue to exist even when the legal status has disappeared and even if the numerical relation of the confessions has been inverted. A case of the latter is seen today in the Netherlands: the Catholics, who are on the way to becoming the dominant group numerically, still retain the minority-group consciousness and continue to feel themselves threatened. The disappearance in France (some time ago) and in Italy (much more recently) of all legal discriminations against Protestants has not stopped them from feeling like minorities and from being treated as such by public opinion.

However, the religious minority can retain, beyond the disappearance of its legal status, a very lively consciousness of its unity, of its originality, even of its particular mission. This consciousness is rooted in its own religious convictions as much as in the style of life of the communities which constitute it.

How does this consciousness defend itself against all the factors that act in favour of a more complete integration of the civil community? What are the reactions of the minority church in regard to the ensemble of the national population and in regard to the dominant church? (It sometimes is the case that these two realities are more or less the same, for example in the Scandinavian countries where 95 per cent of the population belongs at least nominally to the Lutheran Church.)

In relation to the civil community, the minority church normally seeks to show that it is constituted of citizens who belong to the whole, that is, of citizens who are exactly like others or who perhaps even are distinguished by a particularly pronounced sense of civic duty. The example of the French Huguenots is significant: even during the time of worst persecution, even during the War of the Camisards, the Huguenots never ceased to proclaim their loyalty to the monarchy and to participate, whenever possible, in national obligations. When French Protestants were given legal existence by the Edict of Tolerance (1787) and by the Organic Articles (1802), they were anxious not to remain aloof from national enterprises. This undoubtedly is one of the reasons why the Protestant minority in France has given the nation such a disproportionate number of higher-level functionaries and even important officials of the state. This is all the more remarkable in that there are persistent currents of thought in public opinion (*Action française* is the clearest illustration) which tend to represent Protestants as non-French, that is, as representatives of a foreign ideology.

In many respects, this situation can be compared to that of the Christian churches in Communist countries: in regard to the official doctrine of the state and of society, they are in a minority situation. However, they do not accept being considered as groups foreign to the community. This is why, especially in Hungary and in Czechoslovakia, there is an effort to go as far as possible in co-operation with the Communist society, in the economic realm, in social and cultural works, in the defence of peace. There is no doubt that this attitude can be and often is justified on theological grounds. Yet it is none the less also a typical sociological reaction of minority churches to the civil society from which it in no wise wants to be excluded.

One can qualify this attitude as a process of integration. This process is all the more laborious and requires all the more efforts at imaginative response when the minority community intends to safeguard what is essential of its own originality and convictions. By choosing to go along as far as possible with the Communist society, the churches behind the Iron Curtain certainly run a risk, the risk that some of their members (in particular, those of the younger generations) will no longer grasp the reasons for putting certain limits to this co-operation with the Communist society and will be agreeable to allowing themselves to be completely assimilated by the society. Moreover, this risk can take other forms: in wanting to show that it can be fully integrated into a society which does not share its essential convictions, a minority church can give its members the impression that the religious conviction is a strictly *individual* affair, that it has no bearing on social and civic behaviour. It also happens, sometimes, that the minority church will be tempted by a sort of pietism, which is manifested by a very fervent, very warm, very demanding interior community life and by the absence of any spreading out into the surrounding society. This, of course, is a certain type of dualism. However, the minority church generally views itself as a missionary church, as P. Diemel[2] has observed regarding some German Baptist communities. But sometimes the minority church has a tendency to confuse missionary action and proselytism. It attracts certain malcontents to it who are dissatisfied with the over-official, institutionalized, even muscle-bound nature of the dominant churches, but it hardly makes a dent in the secularized society. In the communities studied by Diemel, forty-two per cent of the members were originally from other churches. The great majority of members were traditionally Baptists. In intention, the minority church wants to be a *Missionskirche*; in actuality, it quite often remains, like the other churches, a *Nachwuchskirche*.

This remark brings us to an examination of minority behaviour regarding the dominant church. This behaviour is far from being uniform.

It can be the case that the number of members of the minority church is so small that the dominant church exercises a veritable attraction over it. Such an attraction is quite understandable, for when the number of members falls below a certain figure it becomes difficult to organize a real parish life: "the greater the dispersion, the more the danger of a diminished parish integration."[3] Our civilization, characterized as it is by a considerable network of communications, is not really favourable to the maintaining of very small closed units. Moreover, the extreme dispersion opposes the attempt to constitute such units. The policy of yoking parishes which is practised in Protestant regions that were in the process of depopulating has not resulted in the formation of homogeneous parishes, but simply in the juxtapositioning of parochial sections which become weaker and eventually disappear. Young men and women in regions of great dispersion find it difficult indeed to start households within their denomination. Thus mixed marriages are a necessity, and rarely do they turn to the advantage of a declining community. Such marriages are even more facilitated due to the fact that the differences between the minority and the majority are less marked and are relative to ancient traditions and historical causes which are no longer understood by the new generations. Thus it is that in French Protestantism in the southern part of France, the small independent evangelical, Methodist, and free church groups are incessantly cut into by mixed marriages, to the profit of the Reformed Church of France.

But even when adequately structured minority groups conserve their substance, they cannot avoid coming under the influence of the majority church. This influence is manifested by the adoption of practices belonging to the dominant group. Thus Diemel, in his study of the German Baptist communities, noted two facts which are related to a process of assimilation. On the one hand, the major Christian feasts, against which the Baptist movement (following the example of the ancient church) nourished a certain mistrust, are celebrated with fervour (the chapels are much fuller on these feast days than on ordinary Sundays). On the other hand, the ceremony of confirmation, which originally was characteristic of the churches which practise infant baptism, has appeared under a different name in the Baptist groups. A similar alignment could be drawn between the pastoral function in the small communities and the same function in the dominant church: often the pastors receive the same education as their colleagues of the dominant church, in the same seminaries. Many of the church unions of the past thirty years, especially in the United States (between Lutherans of diverse denominations, between Presbyterians, Congregationalists, Evangelicals) are undoubtedly explained by their participation in the ecumenical movement; but they also express a sociological process of assimilation. To be sure, such a process can take place only where there is already a common denominator, so that the assimilation is experienced by the members of the minority not as an infidelity but as an ordering of the house and even a form of fidelity of the highest order.

Although one can reasonably assume that this process of assimilation will continue within Protestantism, with its increasing ecumenical concern, it is also necessary to realize that assimilation is not the first reaction of the minority churches. They have first of all the tendency to fight to maintain their particularism. Every minority group is inclined to emphasize and even to exaggerate its exclusive originality. To do this, it often refuses any contact with the dominant church. As a general rule (although there are exceptions), the ecumenical dialogue between Catholics and Protestants is effected more easily in those countries where a certain numerical balance exists between the two confessions (the United States, Germany, the Netherlands, Switzerland). The dialogue is difficult in those countries where one of the confessions is in a minority situation (Italy, Spain, Belgium for Protestants; the Scandinavian countries for Catholics).[4] This process of increasing inflexibility and exaggeration of the minority churches in relation to the dominant church can easily be observed within Protestantism. A good example is furnished by the Evangelical Reformed Churches of France. These churches refused in 1938 to enter the reconstituted unity of the Reformed Church of France because they felt that all of the seeds of liberalism had not been extirpated. From that date these churches have accentuated their literalistic biblicism and theological fundamentalism, when in reality these things were much less emphasized in the evangelical communities whose heirs the Evangelical Reformed Churches claim to be. A similar example is found in the French-speaking sections of Switzerland: certain sectors of the free church communities, to the degree that a union with the national churches has been imposed on them, have experienced a fervent renewal of free church principles, despite concessions made by the dominant national churches. Finally, the preliminary discussions concerning union between Anglicans and Methodists in the United Kingdom have had the side-effect of giving rise to a Methodist minority which is very firmly decided unconditionally to maintain its heritage.

The criticisms of the majority church which are developed by the minority denomination are astonishingly stereotyped and this indicates clearly that there is a specific minority comportment (sometimes paralleling sectarian comportment). The great church is always denounced as too hierarchical, too worldly, too institutionalized, too much a prisoner of its attachments to the surrounding society. It is reproached for not defending strongly enough its own principles. It is seen as a victim of the seductions of the Constantinian era. In short, it appears to the minorities as deeply secularized, which is expressed in Protestantism as an abandonment of exclusive fidelity to Scripture and an abandonment of the apostolic tradition. The stereotyped nature of these arguments is not surprising, for quite often the arguments have been proven. Like labour unions within a capitalist society, the minority churches fulfil the function of a permanent critique in regard to the dominant and more or less established church. Quite frequently there is no profound doctrinal difference between the minority church and the majority church. Sometimes, indeed, both hold to the same confession of faith. But their opposition comes from their style of life: latitudinarian on one side, suspicious strictness on the other. The dominant church appears to the minority church as a lukewarm church. If, on the other hand, major doctrinal divergences exist, the great church is denounced by the minority as a false church, as the great Babylon, the great prostitute. Thus it is not difficult to find sectarian language among the minority churches. Moreover, the dominant church has a tendency to treat the minority as a sect.

But the minority church is not content to denounce the lukewarmness or the heresy of the dominant church. It follows an inner effort *sui generis* that is expressed on the organizational plane and on the level of piety.

The communal and familial nature of the religious minorities, when they are not too dispersed, is often remarkable. All the members know one another, help one another, and welcome and integrate newcomers. Yet not just anyone is integrated into the community. Signs of a true conversion must be given. The minority churches tend to be professing churches, and reject the multitudinist principle which is a heritage of the Constantinian era. Following the same logic, they generally repudiate infant baptism and subordinate the administration of baptism to a dedication or to a profession of faith. Although the integration thus obtained is stronger, there is an accentuating of the closed society nature of the community. Yet within this closed society the democratic character of the organization is more marked; the pastor is elected by the community and is not appointed by a central organization. The congregational structure prevails over the hierarchical structure (It should be noted that the Baptists reserve the term "church" only for the local congregation). The parish is characterized both by a very warm atmosphere and by a high level of practice; quite regular atten- dance at Sunday worship, worship often celebrated on Sunday morning and Sunday afternoon, a considerable financial effort,[5] a multiplicity of religious associations and works. W. Goddijn indicates that for the Catho- lic minority of Friesland only two per cent do not attend Easter mass and that the 35,000 Frisian Catholics provided 221 priests living in 1951.

Precisely because the minority church scorns the secularized society and considers the dominant church to have allowed itself to be conquered by this secularization, it seeks to be sufficient unto itself and not to utilize the social institutions of the civic society: it creates its own schools, its own hospitals, its own social services.[6] In Switzerland, in Germany, in France (Alsace), the small Methodist or Methodist-like groups have created and sustained very important deaconess houses. The 35,000 Frisian Catholics already mentioned have organized 772 religious and social associations. An active and widespread press assures communication between the various parishes.[7] When the minority is not too widely dispersed and when it attains a high enough numerical level, it seeks even to have its own political organization; in the Netherlands, for instance, the Gereformed Kerk quite openly secures the recruitment for a political party.

Certain characteristics of the minority churches, especially the intensity of religious practice, is found in parishes belonging to majority churches but which are located geographically in a minority situation. Exhaustive surveys and investigations have enabled Dr Luckmann to show that the most developed religious life is found in dispersed parishes. He points out further that although half of the members in the large rural parishes of northern Germany still practise by tradition, the proportion of members truly committed and assuming precise responsibilities is infinitely weaker there than in the parishes of the worker quarters of a large city.[8]

The minority attitude is not tied to a certain type of church. It is found wherever the parish finds itself in a minority situation. This is readily understandable. Obliged by the surrounding milieu to become more aware of its particularity and of the specific nature of its message, and faced with the threat of absorption, the minority community reacts both with a certain aggressiveness regarding the majority groups and with a constant effort of inner renewal and conquest. It is not without reason that the Protestant missionary movement in the nineteenth century was taken up initially by small minority communities, whereas the great churches regarded this missionary thrust with a certain suspicion.

The specific comportment of the minority churches is explained by their sociological condition. They live under the pressure and sometimes under the threat of the majority church and often also under the pressure and threat of the state (clerical or atheistic) and of the secular society. They tend to form closed and isolated spiritual families, often reserving their missionary efforts for far-off lands rather than the immediate environment. They incline towards a sectarianism which is sometimes the price of their religious fervour. But this sociological conditioning does not represent a strict determinism. Many minority churches react vigorously against their sociological conditioning. The World Council of Churches, which witnesses to a desire for universality, is constituted at least for a a third of its members by minority churches. Attempts at co-operation among minority churches, especially in the Latin countries, have been developed under the inspiration of the World Council. It is quite possible that an ethic particular to the minority churches will be developed. An essay on this subject can be found in W. A. Visser 't Hooft's study, *Misère et grandeur des Eglises minoritaires*.[9]

NOTES

1. H. Carrier defines the reference group as follows: "The reference group designates any group to which the individual is psychologically tied, either because of the fact that he is already a member of it or because he wants to be a member of it on the level of projection. The reference group polarizes the psychology and the practical interest of the individual. It can be a group of actual belonging, such as our family, our professional or religious group. But it can also be a group to which one aspires without belonging, such as a given social group or a given association that has prestige in our

eyes" ("Le rôle des groupes de référence dans l'intégration des attitudes religieuses", *Social Compass*, 1960, 7/2). We feel that this idea of reference group is valid not only for individuals but for the groups themselves. It is particularly applicable in the sociology of Protestantism, for the splitting up of the latter into national and regional groups has left it with the nostalgia of an ideal and universal Protestant community. This nostalgia has been partially satisfied by the appearance of world-wide ecumenical and denominational institutions.

2. "Minorität und Dominanz in der deutschen Kirchensoziologie", *RHPR*, 41st Year, 1961, no. 3.

3. W. Goddijn, "Le concept sociologique de minorité et son application à la relation entre catholiques et protestants", ibid. In the same way, Boulard emphasizes that in the French countryside the smallness of certain parishes brings about a decline in parochial life. He mentions in particular that a small parish with a curé serving it and it alone tends to be self-centred and automatically impedes the formation of open and active members (*Paroisses urbaines. Paroisses rurales*, Actes de la Vᵉ conférence de sociologie religieuse, vol. 2 [Tournai and Paris: Casterman, 1958]). The danger is undoubtedly less great on the Protestant side, where the principle of the priesthood of all believers often receives greater application in the regions of the diaspora than in the well-equipped and well-organized larger parishes.

4. France is an exception in this respect. However, it should be noted that the dialogue between Protestants and Catholics is very fragile, and often non-existent, in the old Protestant territories of the country.

5. The free churches of France, with between 2,000 and 3,000 members, are able to support 23 pastors or evangelists.

6. Minority churches in Germany are called *Freikirche* as opposed to *Volkskirche*. This indicates their desire to be in no way tributaries of the organization of the civil society.

7. See P. Diemel, art. cit., p. 286.

8. See D. Goldschmidt, F. Greiner, H. Schelsky, et al., *Soziologie der Kirchengemeinde* (Stuttgart: F. Enke Verlag, 1960).

9. *FV*, 49th Year, July 1951, no. 4. A sketch of an ethic of the same type is found in the declaration on the minority churches, religious liberty, and mutual aid among churches made at the Assembly of the World Reformed Alliance (Frankfurt, 1964). In regard to the evangelizing power of the minority churches, see Samuel Mours, *Un siècle d'évangelisation en France* (1815-1914) 2 vols.: (Flavion: Editions de la Librairie des éclaireurs unionistes, 1963 and 1964).

XII

Protestants and Politics

1. *The Sociological Interest of the Question*

The participation of the members of a religious group in the political life of their country constitutes one possible measure of the religious vitality of that group. This assertion, although often made in contemporary studies, is not self-evident. It rests on two postulates:

1. The first postulate is that a complete and conscientious religious faith of itself should necessarily find an expression in political activity, as it finds expression in ethical action. This has not been self-evident in all ages, it is far from being self-evident in contemporary Eastern Orthodoxy, and is a contested proposition even in Protestantism. In any case, it has become a reasonable proposition only in a more or less democratic political context. It is quite evident that in the primitive church the question of a political involvement of the Christian did not come up and was not raised. The only question posed was that of submission, of obedience of Christians to the political authority. Later, the question of military service arose, with all that it involved (recourse to violence, the oath to Caesar: it is difficult to ascertain which problem was the more troublesome to the Christian conscience[1]). But military service itself was only a rather minor form of political involvement. Later, beginning in the third century and especially in the fourth century, the problem of military service was resolved in a very positive fashion by Christian conscience. Indeed, Christians were considered to be soldiers *par excellence*. But it cannot be said that this concern for the defence of civilization which guaranteed the peace of the church represented a general involvement of Christians in political service. The Christian prince who, beginning in the Middle Ages and up to the French Revolution, would dominate the political scene, represented only a *very symbolic* participation of the Christian in the political life. Undoubtedly, Calvinism had emphasized the Christian's

responsibility in the political realm, whereas Lutheranism only posed – and resolved affirmatively – the question of whether it was proper for a Christian to fill the post of magistrate in the city. But the question of the positive duty of the involvement of every Christian in a political service could not be raised in a general way except in a democratized political world, where civic duty is included among the general exigences of ethics. In order for the ethical interest of politics and the responsibility that each of us assumes in politics to appear in clearer fashion, political power had to become more extended, and instead of concerning itself only with the general order of society and with juridical relations, it had to penetrate to the very heart of individual and familial existence. At the present time, the theme of the political involvement of Christians is the subject of many theological publications and is at the centre of deliberations in ecclesiastical meetings This is because politics has been brought to our attention as one of the major components of our ethical situation. It has become justifiable to think that if the church and Christians show a certain indifference in the political sphere and reduce the exercise of their civic rights and duties to a minimum, it is effectively a negative sign of the vitality of the particular religious group. One can diagnose not a weakening of faith in the absolute, but at least a weakening of the sense of the concrete manifestations of faith. In any case, this diagnosis is valid for Protestantism, that is to say, for a form of Christianity that theoretically has not considered the temporal world as a neutral reality, or as a reality to flee from, but on the contrary, has extolled a "lay Christian asceticism" (Weber). Yet this diagnosis should be tempered according to the particular Protestant group being considered. When it is a matter of a church having a long pietist tradition behind it, it is evident that the use of the criterion of political involvement will become more problematical, and a thousand other factors can intervene to temper the use of this criterion, for example the minority nature of the group considered. For, in such a case, the members can be discouraged in their political witness (whether rightly or wrongly) by the awareness of its ineffectiveness. It is likely that their involvement will have little appreciable influence on the political evolution of their country and the witness that they would want to give would pass unnoticed. It must also be taken into account, if one wants validly to use this criterion, that the classic forms of political action (voting, elective mandates, the role played in political parties, etc.) do not represent the whole of the political service which a Christian can accomplish as a consequence of his faith. An inquiry seeking to measure the vitality of a confession through the political role of its members must also take into consideration the involvement of the members in public office, in the major civic administrations, in the teaching function, etc. This criterion is even more important when we are dealing with a religious minority for which acceptance of responsibility in public life represents an easier and more effective mode of political involvement than participation in electoral campaigns. French Protestantism is a good example of this situation: it furnishes the state with infinitely more officials of rather high rank, and even of major rank, than deputies, general councillors, and mayors. In countries of either Catholic majority or secularist majority, the Protestant finds himself in a situation little favourable to starting political conflict. In the eyes of Catholics, he is a heretic (sometimes considered dangerous), and he must be kept from representative functions. To the secularists, he is, as a Protestant, the representative of a superannuated religious tradition.

Finally, it must also be noted, always in the perspective of a proper use of the political criterion, that modern political life does not only take place on the level of electoral consultations and the winning of powers. It also takes place, in a less obvious but sometimes more effective way, in trade union action, in all the semi-spontaneous, semi-official groupings that play a consultative role in the politics of a country: Parent-Teacher Associations, family groups, committees for economic expansion and for preservation of natural resources, offices of construction, and finally in all the official bodies issuing from what is called social welfare (social security, family benefits, etc.). All these data must be retained if we want to attempt an evaluation of the vitality of a religious community in its outreach in the city. Politics must not be understood in the narrow sense of the term. All that a church undertakes to favour the education of militants in these various domains (evangelical academies, lay centres of information), to give the various sectors of public life competent men who are conscious of their responsibility and concerned to link their action to the ethical demands of their faith, must be entered to the political credit of the outreach of the given church.

2. The second postulate is that there is really, and not simply theoretically, a link between religious convictions and political involvement, that the latter can be concretely attached to the ensemble of beliefs and practices of the given church. It can happen that a political involvement or abstention on the part of church members has causes other than religious causes. Theoretically, it can even be posited that there is more than one cause. But religious sociology is interested in the problem only to the degree in which the religious factor effectively plays a role in the taking of political positions. Sometimes it is the case that the memberships'

political behaviour is better explained by the social composition of the church than by the religious factor. But it can also be the case that this social composition is not unrelated to the religious situation of the given group. Take the example of the Third Republic of France. Although the republican character of the regime was still far from assured, French Protestants joined the republican camp with remarkable unanimity and formed a common front against the monarchists and Bonapartists. They did so because they felt that only a republican regime, by its confessional neutrality and its independence from the Catholic hierarchy, could guarantee the liberty and security of the Protestant churches. The slogan was born during this time that the Protestant is a leftist. He was a leftist undoubtedly less by a political conviction clearly linked to his faith than by the necessity of assuring the survival and development of Protestantism in the country. Black Americans, the majority of whom are Protestants, generally vote as a *bloc* in favour of the Democratic candidate. Their expectation is that the Democratic candidate, more than the Republican candidate, will pursue a more energetic policy of desegregation (especially if he is from the North). Undoubtedly this policy can be justified by religious motives. But it is also conditioned by the social situation of Negroes in the United States. These examples show that it often is very difficult to separate things, to see to what degree membership in a religious group effectively conditions political choices.[2]

This difficulty has become particularly evident at the present time, and for two reasons:

1. The solidarity between religious problems and political problems is no longer quite as strong. Basic political options (between capitalism and socialism, between economic freedom and planning, between parliamentary democracy and the personalization of power) do not have an immediately obvious tie with the content of religious faith. Despite propaganda made in German Protestant circles coming from the old *Bekennende Kirche*, a propaganda tending to show that the acceptance of German rearmament and atomic armament is to repudiate the three articles of the Apostles' Creed, it does not seem that this tie has been perfectly obvious in the eyes of most German Protestants. Generally speaking, the attempts made by Christian pacifist movements to demonstrate that only the attitudes of absolute pacifism and conscientious objection are compatible with the Christian faith have not received very wide approval. The political problems with their social and economic implications tend in our time to constitute themselves in autonomous sectors, and the options which they require do not find their responses or their motivations in one sole religious

faith. We live in a society where the difference between Christians and non-Christians is much more marked than in the past, where the churches constitute differentiated and sometimes clearly delineated societies in relation to the global society. These delineations do not mean, however, that it is impossible to establish political and social consensus beyond the walls of partition. Politics thus has a tendency to become a domain largely independent of religious convictions. Obviously it was not always so. During the epochs when religious allegiance raised passionate and even violent oppositions, it also governed clearly differentiated political options. But the fate of religious confessions was clearly involved in each of these political options. In an age of religious tolerance, in which the churches for the most part no longer hold a share of direct power in the state and no longer control its functioning, religious convictions become questions of private order. It is more difficult to see what role they play in political debates. In short, we can say that the secularizing of politics has resulted in an effacement of the religious impact in politics. Indeed, it is often possible to observe that in such countries where the churches are almost in balance, the votes of the different confessions are split up in almost the same fashion. Thus in Germany the Christian Democrats and Liberals share the Protestant votes and the Catholic votes in somewhat similar proportions. The only interesting fact is that the Social Democrats undoubtedly receive many more Protestant electors than Catholic electors. Only a certain limited number of political problems can bring about a confessional cleavage. Among them are the problems of the status of the schools and of the legal status of the family. We certainly would not claim that faith is not interested in the solution to political problems other than these. We would never claim that the problems of the form of the state, of the relationships of capital and of labour, of wages, etc., are not related to the Christian ethic. We observe simply that in fact these problems are regulated by individuals and groups outside all conscious reference to the Christian faith. This regulation is done in the name of ideological options whose link with the religious option is very loose or non-existent, and in the name of technical considerations which are considered spiritually neutral. It has become very difficult to show the existence of conscious religious motivations in political decisions, of a link between confessional membership and political choice.

2. This difficulty is related to a general phenomenon: the secularization of political life, the growing influence of economic and technical factors over the political life. Thus this difficulty is valid for all confessions. But it is even more accentuated in the case of Protestantism, from the very fact

that Protestantism has no doctrinal magisterium which defines, even in general fashion, the bounds within which the Protestant political man, the Protestant citizen, must move.

On the Catholic side, the social encyclicals from Leo XIII to John XXIII have defined these bounds, outside which the Catholic no longer can consider himself to be in line with his church. Obviously, the preciseness of these limits should not be exaggerated. French Catholics before the War of 1939 could proclaim either the reactionary nationalism of *Action Française* or the progressivism of Christian Democracy, and either side was able to find the motivations for its political involvements in the Catholic faith. But even so, these examples show the existence of limits. These limits are attested by the double condemnation, at different times and for different reasons, of *Sillon* and of *Action Française*. This double condemnation did not hinder the formation of a Catholic left and of a Catholic right. It did not stop the *Sillon* of Marc Sanguier and *Action Française* of Maurras from forming a following. At least it turned aside both movements from certain excesses which were condemned in the pontifical doctrine. Undoubtedly the sociologist must pose the question of knowing to what degree these positive indications and these condemnations of the Holy See have a real efficacy in the behaviour of the faithful; to what degree are they obeyed and consequently to what degree does the church play a directive role in politics. But even if these pontifical directives are not scrupulously obeyed, they still have an indicative value for the mass of faithful and define political spaces within which the great mass of practising Catholics will be found.

It is not the same for Protestants, even if their church is not totally silent in the political and social realm. For the teaching which the church gives them through the preaching of its ministers is by resolutions and mandates from its assemblies, and the faithful do not receive this teaching as having constraining power. It remains open to discussion. The fact of not respecting it does not involve canonical sanctions. The divergence between Catholic political comportment and Protestant political comportment is related also to more profound reasons which testify to the divergence of their ecclesiology. Because the Catholic church considers itself as a perfectly structured society, it feels at the same time that it is capable of serving as an infallible guide in the political and economic organization of human societies, which is quite evident from a reading of the Encyclicals.

Because the Protestant church sees itself only as a congregation of forgiven sinners, it does not claim to have the secret of a perfect society.

Society is never perfect and must constantly be remade by a new engagement. This necessarily results in a greater flexibility in the political involvements of Protestants.[3] At the present time we see churches in communist countries which contain within them attitudes ranging from active resistance to the regime to positive collaboration. And between the two extremes are attitudes of pure and simple abstention, or of prudence and vigilance that tries to discern the cases when a Christian must participate in the building of a socialist society and the cases when he must abstain and protest. This great variety of attitudes, which is often explained by non-religious motives, is also connected to the fact that the Protestant churches have never formally condemned communism as a system of social and economic organization. They have condemned it only as an anti-religious ideology – which is equal to allowing the faithful the greatest margin of freedom on all occasions when the future of the Christian church is not in question; it is equal, once again, to recognizing that there is a certain independence of the political and social sector as such.

The considerable independence which Protestants manifest in the political realm as well as in many other areas comes undoubtedly from their very conception of the freedom of the Christian man. It also has a sociological source: individualism is proportional to the level of culture. Culture is opposed to mass movements. Now, for religious reasons the Reformation promoted popular culture in a much more intensive way than Catholicism had done. At the present time in certain countries where denominations are more or less in equal proportion, the cultural superiority of Protestantism is still obvious.[4]

In conclusion, we should point out that the project of measuring the vitality of a church in the political involvement of its members and in the form of this involvement faces a difficulty: politics is less influenced than in the past by the repercussions of denominational cleavage. The motifs of political involvement are much less determined than in the past by membership in a given denomination. Although a long tradition obviously rooted in the Protestant past of the United States, wanted the president of the USA to be Protestant and although Protestant votes preferably incline towards the Protestant candidate, John F. Kennedy, the first Catholic president, received large Protestant support.

In fact, the National Council of Churches warned Protestants against a confessionalization of the political problem. This is indeed a sign, among many others, that in becoming differentiated societies in relation to the global society, the churches no longer can directly inspire their members in regard to political options. It is a sign that they recognize that the political realm is a realm where motivations are at work which are not directly tied to faith and that political judgment is largely influenced by considerations independent of faith.

Does it follow that a sociological study on the political conduct of Protestants is futile? It would be if it were evident that Protestants act politically solely in relation to their membership in a given social class, in a given socio-professional category, in short, if it were evident that their quality of Protestant constitutes a category devoid of any political significance. Now that is not at all evident. The relative slowness with which the resistance was organized against Hitler's National Socialism in the Protestant churches of Germany; the fact that the confessing church, the semi-official parallel organization created when the State imposed a unified direction on the churches (*Reichsbischof, Reichskirchenleitung*), never represented more than a minority; the fact that the confessing church was more active in Reformed and United Church circles than in Lutheran circles: all these facts are not unrelated to Lutheran tradition derived, rightly or wrongly, from the doctrine of the two realms, according to which the church and the state are each autonomous in their domain. Consequently, as long as the state does not attack the essence of the church (preaching of the gospel and administration of the sacraments; cf. article VII of the Augsburg Confession), the faithful must be obedient to the state no matter what the state ordains. Indeed, the church itself must submit to the will of the state, even if this will leads the state to impose an order on the church that is contrary to what the church would have wished. By virtue of this tradition, the church did not protest when the Hitler state suspended all civil liberties and organized the persecution of the Jews and Communists. The historical point of departure for its resistance was the moment when the state wanted to impose the Aryan paragraph on the church, thus making a discrimination among its baptized members and a break in the eucharistic communion. Here we confront a fact which attests that a movement of manifestly political incidence can be rooted in religious convictions and doctrines. So also, at the present time we see that the principal resistance to apartheid legislation in South Africa is located in the Christian churches. It is true that the latter example is not entirely univocal, since the principal Reformed churches of Dutch origin, representing the old colonialist element, try on the contrary to justify this policy. Although they are in a predominant social situation, they also feel threatened by black expansion. Consequently, they have refused to be associated with the anti-segregationist policy of the World Council of Churches and even do not hesitate to leave the World Council because of this very strong anti-racist attitude. The very ambiguity of the example which we have cited should lead us to a qualified attitude in regard to the problem concerning us. One can neither affirm nor deny that confessional membership determines forms of political involvements. Although we stated that this confessional membership is no longer a decisive factor of political cleavage, we must certainly not deny any religious influence in politics. It is a matter now of seeing how and where this influence is exercised, and what new forms it has taken.

2. *New Forms of Influence of Religious Confessions on the Political Life*

What is the situation of the churches in the modern society of the western world? Let us leave aside the few countries like Spain, where the church preserves not only a position of prestige (which would also be the case for the Church of England and for the Lutheran churches of Scandinavia) but a direct role in the political guidance of the country. In most other countries, the churches exercise no direct control through their hierarchy over political life. This is true no matter what their juridical status – free, official, or semi-official. It is sometimes the case that they are consulted by the civil power on a given question which is of direct interest to them. But it is the power itself which fixes the conditions of this consultation and limits the scope of it. On the other hand, the church is often the tributary of the political power when internal reforms are introduced in the church. (The reform of the Prayer Book depends on the English Parliament; the modification of ecclesiastical districts depends on the Swedish Parliament; the King of Denmark is theoretically the *Summus Episcopus* of the Lutheran church; many churches behind the Iron Curtain depend on a department of state for their initiatives.) Of course they can utilize their prestige and the popular support which they enjoy to bring pressure to bear on the decisions of the political power. However, they act then not as official power, but as *pressure groups*, disposing of a power more or less co-extensive with public opinion. The churches play a political role to the degree in which they act on public opinion and contribute, through their teaching, their publications and their social institutions, to the forming of this public opinion. Thus this role is an indirect one.

It is sociologically valid to compare the role of churches to that of trade unions. Both are unlike political parties, which, in accordance with special legislation or even constitutional right, intervene directly in political struggles leading to the conquest of power. Unions, on the other hand, act uniquely on public opinion. To the degree that they succeed in mobilizing public opinion in their favour, they hinder the powers from becoming oriented in a given direction or they obtain the passage of certain laws. It is not rare today to see churches, especially Protestant churches, associating themselves with public opinion campaigns in very varied areas: the fight against the policy of nuclear armament, against rearming (West Germany), in favour of a policy of family and childhood security, against racial segregation. Such behaviour is typically the behaviour of a pressure group. For the Protestant churches it is generally the principal mode of political action. Sometimes it is combined with steps that church authorities initiate in the centres of political power. But these steps have efficacy only if they can find support from a large popular consensus. Consequently, religious minorities find themselves in positions of inferiority and it is quite probable that the small Spanish Protestant group would not have succeeded in obtaining the state's reconsideration of its legal status had not the Protestants been supported from outside by favourable world opinion and by the pressure of the American government.

The sociologist should, therefore, try to study what role a church plays, as a pressure group, in the formation of public opinion. This is a difficult study, for it is not sufficient simply to collate the public declarations of the churches. There must also be an evaluation of the effective influence of such declarations, which is a rather tricky matter: one must ask, for example, what space was given by the press to such declarations, what attention the political parties gave to them; it should be seen if a given theme thrown into the political debate by the churches has been effectively inserted into the programmes of the government and of the parties, and if political organizations have contacted church leaders in order to plan forms of common action. In France, for example, the policy of the outstretched hand appears rather frequently in communist tactics and indicates that the Communist Party takes seriously the political and social demands which Catholicism has asserted in Catholic Action movements. It should also be asked to what degree political and social organizations have called upon religious leaders to occupy posts of leadership. Finally, there should be a measuring of the external influence of the religious press to the extent that it touches on political problems.

But because the churches are politically only pressure groups, they also have another way of acting politically. And it seems obvious, especially since 1945, that the Protestant churches have attached great importance to this way. It consists in the churches forming groups which would be capable of becoming involved, on their own authority, in the diverse sectors of political and social life. Since the nineteenth century, that is, precisely since the era when the churches lost their official position in the state (or saw it diminished), there has been a growth of all sorts of *movements* on the fringe of the official organization of the churches. The object of these movements is the civil, political, and social education of their members, and a call for the churches to become politically aware. This phenomenon is typical of the new situation of the churches in society. They themselves have become differentiated societies, without direct action on the general course of the global society. Moreover, they are anxious to mark out the specific nature of their action. They create or inspire the formation of movements which are designed to serve as intermediaries between the churches and the global society. These movements possess a variable independence in relation to the leadership of the churches. They are not integral parts of the ecclesiastical institution (on this point there is a marked difference between Catholic movements and Protestant movements). They do not officially involve the churches. They shelter the churches from the charge of clericalism. Even when, as is often the case, they do not have much favour among ecclesiastical authorities, they still are, sociologically, annexes of the church. They are appendices pushed in the direction of what the church calls the world. The different movements called christian socialism or social gospel are good examples of this new form of action in the political and social field.

In a secularized world, they attempt to re-establish a link between religious motivation and political involvement. They hinder the churches from drawing one of the possible consequences of secularization, namely, the unreserved acceptance of their status of differentiated and consequently specialized societies. They help the churches to avoid withdrawal into purely spiritual tasks, which in a sociological context would signify purely private tasks concerning only the private existence of the family.[5] It is remarkable that in France, for example, the Law of Separation of 1905 led in that direction: the law considered the churches solely as organizations grouping private persons together with the view of providing for the needs of worship. It did not at all consider them as institutions analogous to trade unions, which could act as a body to push and promote reforms concerning society as a whole. Even social and charitable activities are not considered as possible aspects of the activity of the churches. Of course, members are not forbidden to group themselves into movements in order to engage in activities of this type. But in such a case, it is a question of groups which are not part of the church.[6]

The politico-social oriented movements which have appeared on the fringe of the churches, more or less sustained and inspired by them during the nineteenth century and which have grown considerably since that time, have the following sociological meaning: they give the church itself a group of militants, a commando group designed to remind the church that despite the secularization of society its task is not exhausted in preaching and teaching the gospel to individuals. It awakens in the church the sense of politico-social responsibility.

Has this undertaking been successful? Yes, in large degree. The sign of its success is that during the past few decades we have seen these movements, initially marginal in relation to the church, flow back on themselves. This backward flow came about in two ways:

1. On the one hand, the churches have created organic links with these movements, to the point of according them representation in their directive bodies.

2. On the other hand, the churches have largely come to the relief of these movements by forming various departments within the churches themselves: social action committees, committees on international relations, commissions on special problems like nuclear armament and disarmament. These bodies prepare decisions which the official leaders of the church take up under their own name. In the same way, the churches, especially since 1945, have increased the formation of specialized institutes, which under various names (Evangelical Academies, Christian Information Centres, etc.) have as an objective the educating of members to the knowledge of civic, social, and political problems. The hope is that the members will then be able both to become involved in a personal and valid way in the politico-social world and to provide help to the churches' leaders in the politico-social decisions that they will have to make.

It should also be added that this development has been strongly encouraged by the ecumenical movement itself, which has given the example of such initiatives. The large place given in the work of the World Council of Churches to the old Life and Work Movement, the creation of a department called Church and Society, the numerous educational sessions organized by the Ecumenical Institute of Bossey, all of these phenomena have the same meaning: to help the churches not to be enclosed in the role of differentiated societies which a secularized society attributes to them. In the same way, it is obvious that in their search for unity the churches are not losing sight of the politico-social role which they claim to be able to play. It is equally obvious that all the liaison bodies and all the federated councils which they have created over the past fifty years are assuming the task of making public opinion and governments understand the information, the counsel, and even the demands which the churches consider to be a natural outflow of their *opus proprium*. Such work is being handled by the National Council of Churches of Christ in the United States, the British Council of Churches, the Council of the EKID, the Council of the Protestant Federation of France, the Council of the Federation of Swiss Churches, etc., and the young churches of Africa and Asia are following exactly the same line. The more the churches leave the isolation in which their divisions confine them and the more they become aware of their social and political responsibilities, the more they will feel better armed to respond to the challenge of secularization.

Several times we have used the traditional date of 1945 as a point of reference in this development. However, this date is not completely arbitrary. Indeed, the experience of different forms of fascism and of totalitarian states has made the churches become aware of the dimensions of secularization. They have been able to interpret it by means of the currents of nineteenth-century political liberalism and social reformism as a sort of neutrality in regard to spiritual options which have become private affairs and protected as such by the state. Moreover, the liberal state practised an ethic whose values were borrowed from a civilization strongly marked with the imprint of Christianity, to the degree that the churches felt they could look benevolently on this ethic. The totalitarian state called upon a completely different set of values, which were either totally foreign to the *Weltanschauung* of Christianity, or were even violently anti-Christian.

With the totalitarian state, secularization reached its extreme point and began a movement backwards. That is to say, after having driven back the sacred from public life, society and the state claimed to fill the void by a new sacredness, a sacredness immanent in society or in the state (race, blood, soil, social class, ideology). Thus was born what Raymond Aron has called "secular religions", that is, religions without any transcendence. Secularized society set about producing sacredness for its own use. It was as if society, not being able to stand the void created by secularization, set out to resacralize it.[7] This was the source of the breaking out of open conflict between secularized society and the church, a conflict which the German *Kirchenkampf* of 1932–1945 illustrated in a particularly vivid fashion and which previously had already found its expression in the religious persecutions in Soviet territory. It was this development that resulted in making the churches publicly leave their neutrality in regard to politics (a neutrality which for some of them consisted in according support to the established order or in giving full autonomy to the political power in its domain – *Eigengesetzlichkeit*). The experience of Nazism with all its extensions into territories occupied by Hitler Germany thus served to catalyse the awareness of the Protestant churches in regard to the politico-social sector.

One fact well illustrates the evolution of the attitude of the churches in the first half of the century. In 1925, the first conference on *Life and Work* gathered at Stockholm. It was the emanation of the whole current of social Christianity which already had been in existence for half a century. Now, on the precise point of the politico-social function of the church, the conference was very discreet. It affirmed that

the church is an instrument which God uses to hasten the coming of his Kingdom (and which) must above all assure the return of the individual to God; yet, since all men are brothers, the task of the church is not only to lead *each man* and the *whole man* to find God but to work to assure *all men* of their *right to salvation*.[8]

However, for all that, the conference did not think that the church should take concrete initiatives in the political and social realm:

The Christian Church does not itself need to present plans of reform, but to penetrate them with the spirit that gives life and to co-operate in reform wherever it is necessary . . . It must be a centre of spiritual love and, above all, it must insist on the creative power of love, brotherhood, and justice.[9]

The formula dear to W. Monod, "give a soul to the League of Nations", seems to have characterized well enough the climate of somewhat romantic optimism in which the churches were then living. In fact, the conference of Stockholm, aside from some wise considerations on the family, housing, youth, the relations between the sexes, penal repression, and alcoholism, undertook no criticism of sociological structures. The church was content to be "prophetic".

The climate of the following conference, that of Oxford in 1937, was completely different. The conference took place at the moment when totalitarian fascism had extended its shadow over a great part of Europe. At the Oxford conference there was the clear awareness of a profound link between economics and politics, the clear awareness also that the call for good will and co-operation was not sufficient and that what was needed was a modification of the very structures of the state and of capitalism. Although the conference did not follow the example of some missionary churches (in particular, those of China cited by William Paton) which unhesitatingly filled the functions of the co-operative and mutual assistance society, at least it attempted to call laymen to a militant socio-political action. In its report on "The Church, the Nation, and State in their relations with the economic order", [10] it drafted an outline of a critique of the capitalistic system, of the phenomenon of the concentration of economic power without corresponding responsibility, of the frustration of the sense of Christian vocation from the fact of the forms of work, of economic exploitation, and of the danger of unemployment. Although it did not take sides on the question of free enterprise versus socialism (it was content to denounce parallel dangers), it sketched out a whole Christian teaching relative to the economic and social order – a document that can be said to have been the first of this type for many of the Protestant member churches of the conference. And when the conference envisaged the type of political and social action of the churches, it insisted that the churches be given first-rate means of information and thought, not only for purposes of evaluation but as tools for action as well. Thus it was clear that a major turning-point had been reached. The ensuing work of the World Council of Churches and of the churches themselves was carried out on this initial thrust. The churches thought that they had a concrete message to bring to the socio-political dimension, that they could not avoid a permanent politico-social critique, and that they should arm their members to play an effective role on the political level.

To what degree has this *profound mutation* of the churches been followed by effects? That is, to what degree have Protestants found in the thought of their church the motivations for their personal political involvement? The themes have been discussed unceasingly since Oxford and have been examined thoroughly both on the ecumenical level and on the level of national churches. But to what degree have they had a reverberation on the political conduct of Protestants? Lacking micro-analyses of this conduct, it is difficult to say. It should be one of the tasks of the sociology of Protestantism to undertake such an investigation. The latter should not be limited to seeing how Protestant votes are split among the different traditional political parties, but to try to measure the degree of creativity shown by Protestant citizens.

3. The Political Ethic of the Churches of the Reformation

Since we do not possess the means of evaluating the political behaviour of Protestant citizens and the changes undergone by political behaviour, we must be content to present a general view of some characteristics of the political ethic which can be sorted out from the general behaviour of the churches of the Reformation. The intention of our project resembles that which Ernst Troeltsch effectively completed in a very detailed fashion in his monumental study *Die Soziallehren der Christlichen Kirchen und Gruppen*.[11] Yet this work cannot be considered to be definitive. For one thing, the work is inspired by some theological *a priori* which sometimes warp the interpretation of the facts. In particular Troeltsch minimized the elements in primitive Christianity concerning the organization of the community. He wanted to see in original Christianity only a pure internal renewal of souls and felt that Christianity could be fulfilled in three completely different ways: church, sect, and mysticism. Consequently, Christianity was not tied to an ecclesial form.

On the other hand, Troeltsch's study, which concerns the doctrinal positions of the great theological schools more than the empirical reality of the churches, in fact stopped at the eighteenth century. As the author himself emphasized, completely new phenomena intervened at the beginning of the eighteenth century: the socio-ecclesiastical unity had been broken, modern thought had lost the unity of its objects and was diversified into a multiplicity of autonomous disciplines, the church lived within a bourgeois and capitalistic society and within states of bureaucratic and military organization.[12]

The very stating of these characteristics shows that even if Troeltsch had been able to continue his study beyond the eighteenth century, the world which he would have described is no longer completely our own, and that Christian thought confronts a social universe whose new dimensions could not have been guessed by Troeltsch at the beginning of the twentieth century. Thus it is necessary to take up Troeltsch's project, to pursue his inquiry on entirely new bases. And it must be done with methods of investigation that bear not only on doctrines, but on the effective situation of churches in the present industrial society and in a world where science and technology play a normative role. We can only sketch out the framework of such research.

1. The secularization of modern thought has resulted in giving a large measure of autonomy to political life and to political thought. They are much less attached than in the past to the great philosophical and ethical options. The idea of natural law which inspired much legislation and many political systems has become so uncertain that even those who still refer to it speak of a natural law of variable content. Is the right of property a natural law of man? Pontifical encyclicals continue to assert it, but *Mater et Magister* as well as *Pacem in Terris* do not hesitate, in fact, to qualify this assertion by introducing a necessary socialization of the means of production. This fact is significant. It shows that one can no longer deduce the content of a political doctrine or a political practice from an abstract

conception of man, from a theological or philosophical anthropology. Political doctrine and practice do indeed refer to a certain vision of man and of the world, and there certainly are many differences between political conceptions operative in the western democracies inspired by a certain liberalism and those operative in the people's democracies. But in East as well as West, political practice is shaped by the transformations of technology, by the industrial system which permits massive production and the satisfaction of primary needs as well as a good part of secondary needs. This fact involves, in both East and West, a necessary planning of the economy, which obviously is brought about by various means, depending on the political regimes, which does not attain the same degree of intensity everywhere, which more or less reduces the margin of individual freedom, but which none the less constitutes a sort of common denominator for modern politics. And this fact means that politics involves a greater part of management and administration than in the past. Politics is becoming technologized and the prophecy common to Saint-Simon and Karl Marx is coming to pass, according to which the administration of things is substituted for the government of men. This is a partial fulfilment perhaps, since the ideological conflicts are far from being toned down on the political level and the opposition between the communist world and the free world retains all of its virulence. Nevertheless, one can wonder if these conflicts have as much weight as is attributed to them, if an osmosis of political regimes is not taking place. Whatever may be the case, the impact of technology on politics, and the pre-eminence of economic problems in politics is obvious. The political person could make no decision without relying on expert advisers who are more sensitive to technical problems than to the great ethical options. A major consequence results for the churches; they are out of their element in the world of politics. It is difficult for them to discern the values which are operative in political problems. They are aware that a political message is difficult for them to formulate, that it is not sufficient to recall general principles which do not take hold of political reality. In the past it was easy for the churches to state with authority the qualities which princes and governing officials should demonstrate. They believed themselves capable of defining a just social order. Today they realize that any intervention of the church in the political realm has become difficult and that they risk being reproached for not having taken account of reality. For centuries the church felt capable of defining the limits of what was called the just war, the war in which Christians could participate without qualms of conscience. Today the churches seem much more hesitant. Up to the time of the Ecumenical

Conference of Oxford (1937), although many churches had already begun to be hesitant, they continued to give a place to the idea of the just war. But with the profound mutation of the war which was coming a few years later, and with the entrance of nuclear arms on the scene, the criterion for defining a just war became problematical. Whatever be its initial goals, can a war remain just when it sets going means which precipitate it towards total war in which destruction can no longer be limited, when what is at stake is not only the annihilation of an adversary guilty of unjustified aggression but the annihilation of entire continents? Thus in 1958 the World Council of Churches issued a provisional document on the prevention of war in the atomic age in which the following recommendation is contained:

Christians must never . . . allow the use of nuclear arms for a total and un-limited war. If a total war should break out, Christians should call for an armis-tice, on the enemy's conditions if necessary, and have recourse to non-violent resistance.[13]

This provisional document was never ratified by the churches, but no other document has replaced it. This is a manifest sign of the uncertainty of Christian thought in formulating a political ethic. The churches are dimly aware that they can no longer risk formulating such an ethic without at the same time becoming involved in a patient effort of reflection and information. The Ecumenical Conference of Oxford, in approaching the problem of the churches' action in the social and economic realm, recom-mended that the churches develop means of study and action. It insisted that these means be both theoretically and technically first-rate. This necessity had not escaped the attention of the churches. Indeed, they continue to mobilize commissions and to multiply study groups. This is the cost of the churches' intervention in the politico-social sphere. Their message in this area is still greatly confused, and one of the objectives of the World Council of Churches is precisely to aid the churches in carrying forward their reflection on this subject. This is proof that the tie between the ethical message of which they are the guardians and the politico-social realm is difficult to find. The time is past when the churches could easily find enlightenment in scripture and tradition to clarify the action of politics. The sixteenth-century confessions of faith, which contain a whole teaching on the civil authority and its role, are today completely useless on this point. On the Catholic side, the great social and political encycli-cals indeed try to affirm the maintenance of the traditional teaching of the church. But, in fact, it is evident that this traditional teaching is called into question by the church itself and that the church is oriented in completely new perspectives.

2. This basic uncertainty does not, however, reduce the churches to silence. It is a fact that church leaders are increasingly taking a public stand on political and social questions. Even the churches with a long tradition of indifference to politics, like the Church of England or the German churches, are engaged in this direction. But it is easy to see that the numerous documents coming from the churches generally have a very noticeable topical nature. They are less a positive teaching of the church on the organization of the city and on the permanent problems facing contemporary life than protests on very precise points regarding threats to man, his freedom, his dignity, his private life, his familial existence. The churches have given their political action a warning nature. They exercise a ministry of warning more than a ministry of teaching. They denounce the perils rather than indicating in a prophetic way the paths that should be followed. It is possible that this attitude is precisely related to their present uncertainty: it is easier to denounce an injustice than to propose structural reforms. But it should also be understood that this attitude is related to the social function delegated to the churches in a secularized society. E. Dupréel[14] thinks that the social function of the churches, in an age in which they no longer control nor inspire the creative centres of public life and in which they no longer act directly on the development of civilization, is essentially to ensure the defence of threatened values. Indeed, the technical transformations, mutations of social classes, the mass media, the cross-cultural movements of our world have general repercussions. They are no longer limited by the partitioning of small societies impervious to each other. In such a civilization not only does the number of marginal (because maladjusted) individuals grow, the values discovered at an earlier stage of civilization, and generally bearing on individual life, are totally lost from view. The force of global developments is such that the social mechanisms of compensation are rarely set up in time. Phenomena such as urbanization are so rapid that human masses are gathered together without having the possibility of being inserted into the existing traditions or the possibility of creating a socio-cultural life if they are not assisted. The great amount of leisure time is growing so rapidly that man abandoned to himself no longer knows how to utilize the time. The possibilities of culture are so diverse and so attractive that man, if he is not aided, can no longer make a choice. He receives everything in a passive way and paradoxically gains no culture. Religious bodies are characterized by the concern for the singular destiny of human beings.

Their mode of action puts them into contact not with the masses, but with the individual in his private life. All this particularly qualifies the churches to be inclined to the points where individual man and certain human values are especially threatened. In regard to the Christian churches, it turns out that the vocation assigned to them by the global society happens to coincide with the vocation which basically is their own: concern for the poor. But they will fulfil this task correctly only if they know how to discern the true poor, the new poor, the victims of social progress, which presupposes a renewed reflection by them on socio-political development.

3. This politico-social function of the churches also presupposes that they maintain a certain distance in regard to the movement of civilization which will permit them to make a critical reflection. Whether it be a matter of the positive teaching which they are seeking or a matter of the defence of threatened values, the churches can exercise their political ministry only to the degree that they are not themselves swept along in the general development. In the nineteenth century the Christian churches gave support and moral backing to certain political movements and parties. Today, however, we see the churches much more desirous of keeping their distance.

The awareness of the irremediable collapse of Christendom and the lessons drawn from the missionary experience, have certainly not led the churches to become disinterested in the work of civilization (of which politics is only one aspect). But they have led the Protestant churches, more rapidly than the Catholic church, to want not to tie their destiny to this civilization. The churches have been led to think that they will fulfil their ministry to humanity only to the degree in which they can clearly distinguish between the gospel and the values of civilization. Thus if the faithful must fully involve themselves in the work of civilization (and consequently in politics), the church as a community of universal scope must, on the contrary, preserve a very great freedom in relation to these individual involvements. The church will encourage them to the degree that they give evidence of an awareness of responsibility; it can neither approve of them nor disapprove of them, and in no case can it give support to them. The church must be present in the world through its preaching, which includes critical admonitions, warnings, and directive ideas. But it cannot espouse the cause of the society if it is to guard against the establishing of a confusion between gospel and civilization, gospel and ideology. The church does not give up any idea of influencing civilization and ideology. But it does feel that it should be able to exercise this influence over every type of civilization and within every political regime.

This type of thinking is ideal, for in fact the Protestant churches feel much more at ease in regimes of freedom, even of liberalism, than in regimes where collective disciplines leave less room for flexibility. But in any case, such ideal thinking explains various aspects of Protestant political ethics during fifty or a hundred years.

(a) At the time when the democratic form of government was set up and necessarily led to the formation of *parties* on the political level and of *unions* on the social level, the Protestant churches felt no particular concern to form Protestant or Protestant-inspired parties and unions. This is true even in regions of the world where the Protestant population was sufficient to make it a profitable proposition: the United States, England, Scandinavia, Germany. This attitude is even more remarkable considering that the Catholic church, despite certain disappointments, has never fully given up acting on the political and social world in this oblique way. The openly Protestant political parties are insignificant. They are limited to two relatively minor parties in the Netherlands (the Anti-revolutionary and Historic Christians Parties) and to some parties of purely local importance in a few cantons of the German-speaking part of Switzerland.[15] To be sure, this absence of Protestant parties and unions does not hinder Protestants in certain regions from choosing certain parties by preference. But in the major countries like the United States, England, and Germany, Protestants are equally spread throughout opposing parties. Of course, the liberal and bourgeois parties have often rallied the great part of Protestant voters, but the massive presence of Protestants in worker and socialist parties has been a fact for fifty years. Although the German Social Democrats had hardly any but marginal Protestants and few churchmen before the Second World War, since 1945 it has begun to recruit its members from the ranks of faithful Protestants. It cannot be said that the Protestant churches are very much opposed to this scattering of their members among various parties. Rather, they have encouraged it, to the extent where their teaching, while insisting on the necessity of political involvement and emphasizing at the same time the relativity of political involvement, insists on the necessity of rendering a Christian witness in all milieux.

(b) This spontaneous practice of Protestantism of not tying itself to an ideology and to a political party is tending to become a norm of its political ethic. At Amsterdam (1948), the churches were in agreement in formulating a qualified warning regarding so-called Christian political parties:

> The existence of Christian political parties in several countries poses a problem. The church as such should be identified with no party and should never act as if it were one. In general, the formation of these parties is not unaccom-

panied by danger, for they easily assimilate Christianity to the compromises inherent in politics. They threaten to take Christians from other parties which would have need of Christian leaven, and to reinforce – not only against their party but against Christianity in general – the position of those who do not share their political opinions. Nevertheless, Christians can be led, in certain circumstances, to organize themselves in a political party with precise goals, on the condition that they do not claim to be the only ones who represent the Christian attitude.[16]

This text shows that political reflection in modern Protestantism is oriented towards certain well-defined, although negative attitudes. This rejection of Christian parties does, however, permit a dialogue between the churches and all parties on limited objectives. In regard to these objectives, the churches will consider that Christian witness is involved.

(c) This attitude of neutrality regarding parties has often permitted the Protestant churches to have a more flexible policy than the Roman Catholic Church in areas of communist control, and even to encourage their members to have an attitude of loyalty and co-operation towards the collectivist regimes (East Germany, Hungary, Czechoslovakia, etc.). They have generally outdistanced the Catholic church, which only with Pope John XXIII and the Encyclical *Pacem in Terris* began to sketch out a certain progress by distinguishing between atheistic communist doctrine and the historical movement that communism represents. The churches behind the Iron Curtain have not ceased to protest against all the shackles placed on religious liberty and against the attempts of the state to make atheism an official doctrine obligatorily taught to all. But, on the other hand, they have never brought their criticisms to bear on the principle of a collectivist-type economic organization. They have been content to denounce the excesses or the brutality of the system. In this way they want to affirm that Christian faith as such is not tied to a particular conception of social and economic organization, and that the imperative of social justice which they defend has not found its expression in the capitalistic West either. In 1937, at the time of the Ecumenical Conference of Oxford, the churches were in agreement in "examining the credentials" of the economic system of the West, in order to carry out a critique of the system of private property and in order to propose a certain number of principles of social ethics. This conference gave birth to the first document in which the Protestant churches and the other member churches of the ecumenical movement expressed a group of recommendations which sketched the possible framework of a political and social ethic perfectly independent of the position taken by traditional political parties and by the major ideological divisions.[17]

4. The Protestant churches are distinguished from the Catholic church in their relatively positive analysis of the process of secularization. They do not see the formation of a civil society independent of the churches, a secular culture and a secular state, as absolute catastrophe. Rather, they see it as an opportunity provided for the freedom of Christian preaching. The truths that the Protestant churches are inclined to accept are that the world is profane, that political and social institutions are secular, that civilization cannot be baptized, that Christian baptism has to do only with persons, and that no human order can be declared Christian. Does not the American Constitution, which bears so strongly the imprint of the Protestant spirit, set up the strict separation of church and state? Even in countries where Protestantism is still the official religion, if not the religion of the state, the Protestant churches continue to fight for an independence of the church in relation to the political power. This is true concerning its preaching and teaching as well as its internal organization. Indeed, this movement is inherent in the original doctrine of the Reformation. The Lutheran theory of the two kingdoms, as well as the organization of relations between church and state as it appears in the "Ecclesiastical Ordinances" of Geneva of 1561, contains the beginning of this Protestant acceptance of secularization. The Confession of La Rochelle in article XXVI invites the faithful to maintain the unity of the church and to do so "everywhere where God will have established a true order of the church, no matter what the magistrates and their edicts may require to the contary". Undoubtedly, many Protestant churches have continued until recent date to entrust the responsibilities of governing the church to the political authority and have considered the prince as *summus episcopus*. In the churches of Germany, it was only after the disappearance of the state sovereigns (1918) that the power of self-organization and self-administration was taken over by each church.[18]

In a general way, although the general development of society has strongly contributed, it can be said that the Protestant churches have rather easily accepted the idea of no longer viewing the state as an authority which protects them, assures them of a position of strength and prestige, and intervenes in their administrative functioning. The evolution is more or less rapid, depending on the country, and has not reached the same extent in every country (many Protestant churches have preserved the concordat type). But everywhere the idea is affirmed that the church should call for a complete freedom in relation to the political power and that the "era of Christendom" should not be lamented. Even more, the Protestant churches and the World Council of Churches are attempting to draw the positive consequence from the end of Christendom by calling everywhere – not just when it benefits Protestants when they are in the minority – for full religious freedom, freedom of conscience, freedom to change religion, freedom to propagate one's belief or one's unbelief, and even freedom of atheistic propaganda (decision of the Executive Committee of the World Council of Churches, Odessa, 1964).

5. This concern of freedom for believer as well as unbeliever explains why the socio-political ethic of the Protestant churches, especially up to the present time, has shown its vitality regarding problems where human emancipation was involved. Innumerable are the declarations and actions of the Protestant churches concerning the emancipation of women, racial desegregation, and even the emancipation of colonized peoples, although on this latter point the churches have often been bound up with the colonial countries where they originated.

In sum, the political and social ethic of the Protestant churches undoubtedly is far from being formulated and the actual consensus in this domain has limits that are still quite narrow. The Protestant churches are far from having carried out all the transformations of the concept of social justice which are implied by the industrial age and by the constituting of the working-class. They are seeking such an ethic, as is shown by the whole development of ecumenical thought in this area. Their interventions on the political and social level consequently have an occasional nature and most often are limited to denouncing dangers or abuses. They bear more on the defence of man, of his freedom, of his dignity, of his familial existence, than on the structures of society and of the state, although a critique of the established order is often made. But the Protestant churches, though they vigorously and competently play the role of defender of threatened values, have not recovered the guiding role, the prophetic function, in the politico-social development. They have fulfilled a certain number of conditions that would permit them to play this role, albeit with a certain modesty; they have loosened the ties binding them to reigning ideologies, and have, from this fact, gained a greater degree of freedom. And they do not cling to the vestiges of a bygone age, that of Christendom.

It is obvious that the task which would consist of proposing neither a socio-political system nor doctrine, but simply an ethic of political and social life and of international relations, is a task beyond the capabilities of each individual Protestant church. It is also evident that progress in this area is tied to the progress that the Protestant churches will make in their present search for unity. Progress is also tied to the Protestant penetration into new social classes where the influence of Christianity is exercised only in sporadic fashion. Only a greater presence of the working-class among Protestant communities will be likely to be the catalyst for this search for a politico-social ethic.

NOTES

1. See the book by J. M. Hornus, *Evangile et Labarum, étude sur l'attitude du christianisme primitif devant les problèmes de l'Etat, de la guerre et de la violence* (Geneva: Labor et Fides, 1960).

2. The studies of the colloquy organized at Strasbourg in 1963 by the National Foundation of the Political Sciences and the Institute of Political Studies of Strasbourg seem to have shown a sort of decline of religious factors over the political life (cf. *Forces religieuses et mouvements politiques* [Paris: A. Colin, 1965]). However, there are cases in which one can show the persistence of the political role of confessional membership. The success of the left is ordinarily and regularly linked to industrialization and urbanization. But, although these two phenomena are quite evident in the French departments of the Rhine and of the Moselle, the movement towards the left seems to have been checked. The Catholic party MRP was even able to resist the Gaullist landslide. In the worker milieux as well as in the rural areas, the voters of the CFTC (French Confederation of Christian Workers) vote in great part for the MRP (cf. F. G. Dreyfus, "Jalons pour une sociologie politique de la France de l'Est", *Revue française de science politique*, vol. 10, no. 3, September 1960.

3. Cf. R. Schramm Stuart, "Traditions religieuses et réalités politiques dans le département du Gard", *CS*, 61st Year, no. 4–5, 1953.

4. Witness, for example, the following statistics on confessional percentage in the various school levels in West Germany (1963):

	Protestants	Catholics
Primary Schools	48·2%	50·4%
Middle Schools	61·9%	37·0%
Secondary Schools	54·7%	43·2%
Universities	59·8%	36·3%

5. This view of things is still quite often the view, if not of Protestantism, at least of Protestants. It is expressed in the slogan "Religion and politics don't mix". A considerable divergence can be noted between the attitude of the body of church leaders and that of the members. In the United States, for example, the National Council of Churches and the various denominations do not hesitate to intervene, often quite effectively, in the political realm (racial segregation, nuclear explosions, relationships between West and East, etc.), but the rank and file Protestants are far from giving unanimous approval to such intervention. Samuel S. Hill, Jr., in the article mentioned ("Le protestantisme dans le Sud et l'intégration raciale"), reveals that southern Protestants feel that all moral problems which the church should deal with are individual ones. This fact is explained by sociological factors and by the uncomplex nature of southern society: "People of the South live on farms and in small towns where important problems and sins were essentially individual ones. If southern society had been more complex and interdependent at the dawn of religious development in the South, the churches probably would have better understood the full import of biblical ethics." The same opinion is given by Kenneth Underwood ("Evolution sociale et protestantisme américain", *CS*, 71st Year, no. 9–12, September–December 1963): "The Protestant

ethic – expressed by businessmen as well as by the preaching of the minister – required personal honesty in regard to contractual obligations, the sense of thrift, sobriety, active attention to the production of a quality product, self-confidence resting on the belief that man had less need of the group than the group had need of his creative thought and independent judgment." Such facts, and they could be multiplied, explain why Protestantism has been rather backward in the study of political and social ethics. Such study has increased since the appearance of the World Council of Churches, but it is far from having penetrated deeply into public opinion.

6. The decision of the National Synod of the Reformed Church of France (Mulhouse, 1962) constitutes a protest against this state of fact. Institutions, projects, and movements will have a right to send delegates with deliberative voices to the synods.

7. See our study "La sécularisation de la cité", in *Problémes de la civilisation chrétienne* (Paris: PUF, 1951).

8. Report of the Stockholm Conference (French edition, p. 68).

9. ibid., p. 66.

10. *Les Eglises en face de leure tâche actuelle* (Paris: Editions Je Sers, 1938).

11. German edition, Tübingen: J. C. B. Mohr, 1903.

12. ibid., p. 965.

13. Provisional document: "Christians and the prevention of war in the Atomic Age. Theological discussion", Geneva: World Council of Churches, Division of Studies, 1958.

14. E. Dupréel, *Traité de sociologie générale* (Paris: PUF, 1948).

15. A Protestant political party called "Christian Democratic Party" was formed in Sweden in May 1964, at the instigation of a Lutheran minister and a Pentecostal minister. This creation raised a loud protest in the Protestant press and among church authorities. Attempts of the same type were made in Argentina, but quickly failed. Religious divisions often are exploited in electoral campaigns. Indeed, in Newfoundland this has been done systematically. Attempts have been made there to make the electoral districts coincide with the districts of the various religious denominations (Catholic, Anglican, Methodist, etc.), thus politicizing the denominations. Such attempts, of political rather than ecclesiastical origin, gave rise to numerous abuses (see the study by Gordon O. Rothney, "The Denominational Basis of Representation in the Newfoundland Assembly, 1919–1962", *Canadian Journal of Economics and Political Science*).

16. *La Première Assemblée du Conseil oecumenique des Eglises*, Official Report (Neuchâtel: Delachaux et Niestlé, n.d.), pp. 104–105 (English edition: *The First Assembly of the World Council of Churches*). The final reservation is aimed at certain countries where political parties are confessional (for example, Moslem as in Indonesia) and where it is difficult for Christians to be active in them.

17. See *Les Eglises en face de leur tâche actuelle*, Report of the Oxford Conference, pp. 158 ff. (English edition: *The Churches Face Their Task*).

18. On this development and its different steps, see the studies (already cited) of J. Hoffmann, "Les Etats et les Eglises évangéliques dans l'Allemagne contemporaine".

XIII

Sociology and Pastoralia

Every science, no matter how disinterested it might be (and it should be), gives birth to an applied science and to certain techniques. Thus we should ask in what way a sociology of the church can be useful to the ministry of the church. By the term "pastoralia", at present more widely used in Catholicism than in Protestantism, we mean the ensemble of methods and means by which the ministry of the church is carried out. This ministry, in turn, can be defined as the action by which the church attempts to call forth and nourish faith and to build up communities of believers joined together in the Body of Christ. The church's action takes the form of the preaching of the Word, sacrament, catechetical instruction, and pastoral counselling.

In relation to the finality of this ministry of the church, sociology obviously can play only a secondary role. Sociology cannot be asked for suggestions on how to attain a renewal of the church. But it is a fact that the church, when it centres its attention on such renewal, takes an interest in sociology and seeks its assistance. Two examples demonstrate this in a particularly clear way.

In France, the book by Fathers H. Godin and Y. Daniel, *La France, pays de Mission?* [France, A Mission Country?], has brought Catholicism to a rude awakening in regard to the state of the church and the necessity for a renewal. This work, although it contains many general sociological insights, is not a sociology book. It has given a new thrust to efforts of liturgical, catechetical, and missionary renewal in French Catholicism. It is more prophetic than scientific. Yet it is the missionary effort which it has provoked that has led to the remarkable work of sociological inquiry on the part of Canon Boulard and his colleagues. The Catholic church hardly ever now undertakes important evangelization campaigns without first making a long and thorough sociological survey, which bears not only on parish life and practice but on the social environment as well. In the course of the past ten or fifteen years, the majority of French dioceses have conducted and published systematic sociological surveys, most of which have taken other Christian groups as well as unbelievers into consideration. Thus the missionary concern has been responsible for a detached sociological study. The former would not have given rise to the latter had it not felt the need for it.

In the United States, the remarkable fact is that it has been committed Protestants, quite often ministers, who set up the first studies of religious sociology. They expected this young science to help them understand the new social order in which the church had to exercise its ministry. Albion W. Small, who organized the first department of sociology at the University of Chicago, was a Baptist minister. William Graham Sumner, whose book *Folkways* has become a classic of American sociology, was an Episcopalian rector in New York before becoming the illustrious sociologist of Yale University. The first sociology course at Harvard was given during the academic year 1891–92 by the Rev. Edward Commings, a Congregationalist minister in Boston. Francis G. Peabody, of Harvard Divinity School, and Graham Taylor, of Chicago Theological Seminary, were the chief architects of the new science and of the church's interest in social problems. The influence of Harlan Paul Douglass and his colleagues was decisive for sociological research and investigation among the Protestant churches in the United States.[1]

This need on the part of the churches, which has played such a major role in the birth of present-day religious sociology, undoubtedly has had the advantage of diverting sociologists from over-ambitious and over-theoretical speculations. In a society in perpetual and rapid transformation, affected by the phenomena of industrialization and of urbanization and by the great mixing of populations which results therefrom, the churches have need of quite empirical information in order to be able to meet the situation. The religious sociology of the nineteenth and the beginning of the twentieth centuries, that of Durkheim, of Max Weber, and even of Joachim Wach, no matter how different they might be in their intention and in their inspiration, are of only slight importance to the churches. The churches have need neither of a sociological explanation of religion in general, nor of considerations of the social role of Christianity in the past, nor of a scientific typology of religious communities. They want to know how to adapt to the new situation, how to approach the social classes with which they have lost contact, where to organize new parishes, what modifications the traditional structure of parishes should undergo, what new forms of ministry they should create.

This need of the churches has resulted in directing sociology to inquiries which are much more modest and more empirical than in the past. Indeed, a veritable hiatus has arisen between the great works of religious sociology of the past and the studies of today, which often are purely sociographical. Yet it is necessary that this gulf should not grow wider. For as a science, sociology has as much need of basic research as of empirical surveys. The advantage of empirical surveys is that they lead to practical conclusions which can be immediately utilized. Furthermore, they restrain sociology from becoming speculative too rapidly. But by themselves, they do not lead us to a sociological comprehension of religious communities. Their results must be placed in broader perspective. It does not suffice to note, with statistics and precise figures, the decline of religious practice in certain social classes. It is necessary to understand modern atheism in its sources and in its motivations. It is necessary to understand how the evolution of science engenders new conceptions of the world, which in turn introduce a crisis of transcendence into thought. It is not sufficient to ascertain variations in religious practice according to age, sex, social situation, standard of living. What remains necessary is to consider whether the church must not re-evaluate all of its social functions.

The risk which the need of the churches poses for sociology is that the latter will become purely technical and be absorbed by immediate problems, which it will resolve poorly if the necessary reflection is lacking, if there is no effort to understand a development in its entirety.

Thus, in order to deal with the relations between sociology and pastoral concerns, it should be emphasized first of all that religious sociology is not at the service of the pastoral. Although the pastoral can legitimately and advantageously submit questions to sociology (much like industry to physics), the latter must aim first and foremost to be a disinterested science. It is this very disinterestedness which will permit it to be truly useful to the church. It is not difficult to see that in the United States, for example, where sociologists have been too dependent on the need of the churches, their works have been too exclusively devoted to studies which aim at safeguarding the ecclesiastical institution and with extending the sphere of influence of a given denomination. In being too responsive to the pressures of immediate problems, one risks not having a sufficiently broad and detached perspective on the problems. A sociology oriented towards the pastoral must still be a scientific sociology. As G. Le Bras writes:

Sociology is always a science, whether it has knowledge or action as its object ... (between pure science and applied science there is a difference not of *quality* but of *finality*).[2]

Let us add that this finality should not be felt by the scholar in too pressing a fashion, for otherwise he will risk over-hasty conclusions.

With these preliminaries now stated, in the present state of fragmentary research which we have at our disposal, what services can religious sociology render to the pastoral ministry?

The first thing would be a better knowledge of the *reality of the parish*. To be sure, many pastors arrive at a good understanding of their parish, through many pastoral visits and other means of contact. But how many years does this take? Moreover, by reason of the very nature of the pastoral ministry, this knowledge is much more that of a collection of individuals rather than that of the group as such. In the final analysis, the minister will know primarily, if not exclusively, those who have recourse to the ministry of the church. It is rare, above all in the organization of the multitudinous church, if some of the zones of the parish do not escape the minister completely. Sometimes it is the case that the nucleus of the most committed members will form a screen between the minister and his parish. Furthermore, every parish, especially when it is very old (as most of them are), has gradually developed a tradition. It is by this tradition that it is judged; one parish will be reputed to be liberal, another conservative. Moreover, quite freqently it is a question more of a pastoral tradition than of a parochial tradition.[3] In any case, the parish's traditional view masks its reality rather than reveals it. When sociological surveys of a more exhaustive nature are made in a parish, their results usually call forth astonishment and even scepticism on the part of those who felt that they knew the parish, namely, ministers and church elders. The reason is that their knowledge was purely intuitive or empirical and considerably distorted by certain traditional prejudices. Sociology reveals the true human composition of the parish. It underscores the sometimes abnormal nature of this composition. It calls attention to the fact that often the parish simply mirrors the social milieu which surrounds it.

Alsatian Protestantism is often presented as essentially rural, and this view of things is not without influence on the decisions made by the ecclesiastical authorities. Yet sociological studies have been made which show the heavy urbanization and suburbanization which has taken place during the last few decades. Surveys which are often quite simple can lead to an objective measurement of the religious vitality of a parish. For example, in comparing the average attendance-figures for worship on ordinary Sundays with the average figures for religious holidays, two possible situations can appear: either the gap between the two figures is insignificant, in which case it is valid to conclude that we are dealing with a parish of great vitality, or else the gap is considerable, in which case we may conclude that the majority of the people in the parish are members only by tradition. This tradition exercises a certain compulsion on the occasion of ecclesiastical solemnities.[4] Such findings enable the minister to orient his preaching and his teaching.

In the same way, the figures relative to participation in the Lord's Supper, which indicate whether or not the community that worships on Sunday differs from the eucharistic community, are of such a nature as to enable the minister to see – and we say this without hesitation – into the privacy of souls. If the majority of parishioners withdraw at the time of the celebration of Holy Communion, and if these same members flock to the church when Holy Communion is celebrated on Good Friday, must not one conclude that there is a certain catholicizing misinterpretation among them in regard to the significance which they attribute to the sacrament?

The minister knows quite well those of his parishioners who assume responsibility in the life of the church. He can easily evaluate the relation between the number of responsible members and that of members who must be called passive (this is one indication of vitality). But (and this is another indication of vitality), in a secularized society, does he know the number of his parishioners who assume responsibility in civic affairs (political meetings and parties, unions, civic associations, charitable organizations, etc.)? It is such laymen who are in a position, if they are aided, to actualize the presence of the church in the world, to open new opportunities to the church's witness and to keep the church from becoming a closed society, whereas the whole tendency of secularized society seems to push the church inexorably in that direction. Such a stock-taking is of the greatest importance for preaching, pastoral counselling, and the organizing of parish groups, and at the same time will disclose areas where Christians are not involved. Too often, Christians who accept service in the world have the feeling that the church does not follow them there, is not interested, does not help them to resolve the conflict of conscience with which they inevitably are faced. It is to the degree that such surveys have been made that one sees the churches organizing centres for the instruction of laymen, where a reflection of Christian social ethics has begun.

It is of great importance that every minister know the social composition of the parish and that he take account of the proportion of different social categories represented in the various groups of members.[5] In a survey made in a metropolitan parish (Hamburg), Reinhard Köster[6] has observed that the majority of the members of group A belong to classes which are poorly integrated into modern society. These people are, in reality, marginal beings: women over forty who exercise no profession (and with grown children), widows, unemployed spinsters, etc. On the contrary, the members who are actively engaged in social life and in production fit, for the most part, in groups B and C. The conclusions of such a limited survey should not be generalized. For instance, we think that in our present state of understanding Friedrich Fürstenberg overstates the case when he concludes from the above survey that "the traditional and churchly style of piety has become a marginal phenomenon". Nevertheless, the fact that such parishes can and do exist poses a serious question to pastoral thought and theological reflection: is not the church in danger of losing its capacity for social integration? If the church does in fact group together only those on the fringes of society, how can it continue to be an effective, radiating, and conquering community? Does it not court the risk of being only an *ersatz* society for those who have not found their place in the real society? Thus sociology places before theology, and before those who are charged with governing the church, the whole problem of the church's function in a productive society and in a society oriented towards work.

But the minister, in order to be effective in his ministry, needs more than the data of religious sociology alone. He has need also of the data of sociology in general. As François Houtard[7] has emphasized, the church must be attentive not only to the transformations of the social structure which result in a modification of the implantation of human groups, the relation between work and leisure-time, the conditions of family life, but also to the changes in the index of values which often result from structural modifications. For example, new values emerge, others are forgotten, the culture changes in content at the same time as the sources of cultural information are modified, new types of communities appear, etc. All this is not of purely theoretical importance, but directly concerns preaching. The abstract, irrelevant nature of much preaching comes precisely from the fact that the preacher is ignorant of, or has only a superficial understanding of, ethical life as his parishioners actually live it. Thus, without being aware of it, he helps to establish the idea that the Christian life is a sphere isolated from the rest of human existence. The relevance of Christian preaching derives on the one hand from the exegetical and theological work on which it is based but, on the other hand, from an effective knowledge of the conditions of life and of the values which always are implied (even though they are incompletely defined) in these conditions of life.

Whereas descriptive sociology (sociography) can be used by every minister as a barometer of parish life, comprehensive and interpretative sociology helps to focus the point of impact of preaching. And this is all that is involved. In particular, it is not a matter, as one too often hears, of adapting the biblical message to the *Weltanschauung* of our time or to the evolution of customs. Sociology can help preaching to strike home.

Sociological investigation does not lead only to a more lucid understanding of the reality of the parish. It can lead us to call into question the very form and structures as well as the ministry of parishes and of pastors. One of the most immediate services which sociology can render is to assist the governing bodies of the church to reshape the ecclesiastical map in order to make the ecclesiastical units coincide with the true socio-demographic units. As we all know, the churches are conservative societies of very slow evolution. They have the tendency to maintain their traditional organization throughout the centuries. G. Le Bras has observed regarding French Catholicism:

> Our ecclesiastical divisions ... go back to the Middle Ages. The map of dioceses has scarcely changed over the past six centuries: of 87 dioceses, only four are later than the pontificate of John XXII (died in 1332). The map of rural parishes is even more archaic. In other words, the network of ministry is conceived according to the outlook of the age of Philip the Fair, and perhaps even of Charlemagne. There is no need for sociology to point out this anachronism. But where it is a matter of adapting the districts to the new society, it is indeed a matter involving sociology. When Boulard seeks to demarcate urban zones by taking into account the frameworks of civil society, the courses of population-shifts, and the mood of populations, or when a Dutch institute formulates a prognostic of habitat in order to implant churches, schools, and hospitals, then it seems that sociology is involved.[8]

These remarks can be applied perfectly to Protestantism. Just consider the antiquated nature of some of our ecclesiastical divisions: the cantonal churches of Switzerland, the German *Landeskirchen*, or the Lutheran Inspectorates of Alsace. These latter, for example, radiate out from the centre in Strasbourg and deprive Strasbourgeois Protestantism of any unity. Members are lumped together in the same district who never have occasion to associate in daily life. Such examples could be multiplied *ad infinitum*. We are here once again victims of a perspective that is anterior to secularization, a perspective which has come to us from an age in which the civil society and the religious society coincided naturally. When the powers that be cease to be occupied with the ecclesiastical organization, the ecclesiastical districts tend not to follow the demographic and economic developments which bring about the appearance of new population centres and upset the network of communications. Now the great opportunity of the church, if it wishes to remain missionary, is to encircle the actual units of demographic concentration. A new suburb, a large housing development, or a major shift of population cannot be integrated without further ado into an old urban parish, quite simply because the new inhabitants, because of their origin, mode of living, and sometimes age, lack relationships with the old inhabitants of the urban centre. The creation of new parishes in suburban areas presupposes an exhaustive sociological inquiry which takes account of the network of communication, the places of work, and the places of leisure. The church must set itself to reaching men in the place where their concrete life actually implants them.

An example may be cited here which demonstrates how sociology is able to alert church leaders to a development that affects at one and the same time the civil society, the parishes, and the forms of the church's ministry. This example, from American Protestantism, has been superbly studied by Gibson Winter.[9] His works show that the major Protestant denominations have uninterruptedly constructed new churches and new parishes in the residential suburban areas, which have proliferated since 1870 on the fringes of the great metropolitan centres. In doing so, the church undoubtedly is following a demographic and sociological movement: the American, as he lifts himself up the social ladder and increases his income, flees the large city, which he realizes has been the source of all sorts of traumatic experiences. But he does not return to the country. His ideal is to establish himself as comfortably as possible in these suburbs, which combine the advantages of the city with those of the country, and which create zones of socially homogeneous groupings. The church (primarily the white denominations) has followed this mass exodus, thus abandoning the urban centres. But at the same time those members are lost who do not have the means to move to the suburbs. Thus the church cuts itself off from the lower classes. The result is a complete identification of the major denominations with the middle classes. The underprivileged, those newly arrived from rural areas, Puerto Ricans, and Negroes are abandoned to sects and to the Negro churches.

The first consequence of this is that the church becomes the image or the reflection of the economic and social milieu. Each parish recruits its members in a homogeneous milieu. Instead of being open to all men and making no exceptions among people, it replaces mission with a system of co-optation. It exerts a great effort to bring together families and individuals from an economic and social position comparable to that of the average. In fact, sometimes the congregation will change locations when the social composition of the neighbourhood in which it is located no longer conforms to the congregation's own norms. What is the function of such a church? It is to furnish individuals with a means of social identification. Gibson Winter confirms the analyses of Will Herberg,[10] who explains the astonishing growth of all denominations in America by the fact that the churches become substitutes for the various ethnic groups which have been destroyed by the rapid Americanization of immigrant waves. Furthermore, for these people, who are disconcerted by the rapidity of developments and deprived of their socio-ethnic and cultural identity, the churches provide a means of integration, an opportunity to regain personal identity and prestige.

The second consequence grows out of the first. In order to fulfil these functions, the church must provide each individual not so much with a responsibility as with a role. This explains the phenomenon of the organization church, which multiplies activities, clubs, committees, so that everyone can be given a role. The minister becomes the head of a central administration of activities and committees. The greatest part of his time is absorbed by administrative duties. Traditional American activism is quite suited to all this. The church becomes once again, artificially, what it was during the Middle Ages, namely, a purveyor of leisure-time activities.

To be sure, it remains the church which proclaims the Word of God, and it does so with zeal each Sunday. However, because of its structure and function, the style (not necessarily the objective content) of its preaching is warped. Its members have moved to the residential suburbs in search of a refuge from their professional lives. They have fallen prey to the natural temptation of mass-society man to regain a rustic peace in cosmopolitan comfort, to stem the flow of history and to retire in a garden. Their attention is focused on the values of comfort and privacy, on the values of family. Under these conditions, preaching also will take on the character of inwardness and pietism. It will proclaim salvation as a means of giving meaning to empty lives. It will tend to become one of the elements of spiritual comfort. The preaching of salvation by grace alone is, in fact, contradicted by all the hollow activism of the organization church, which seeks to render the parish more functional and more prosperous, and which nourishes a religion of works. Gibson Winter, with a great deal of severity, characterizes this new, burgeoning parish-form thus:

It represents an island of conformity in the metropolis . . . (it becomes) an end in itself – a collective symbol of the sanctity of middle-class values . . . (it is an) introverted church (which) stresses the church as structure at the expense of the mission and task of the church . . .[11]

Winter further points out that this type of church does not confide true ministries to its laymen, because they wish only to find a means of social identification and to forget their public and professional lives.

In short, it is a church which is perfectly adapted to its sociological conditions. But precisely, it is sociology which furnishes the critical analysis of this "sociologism". By means of this analysis, sociology also suggests the remedies for this situation, as the conclusion of Winter's first book and even more his second book show quite well. It does not furnish the motivations for a rectifying, but it describes the lines of orientation for the theologian who is concerned about the authenticity of the church. The description which it etches out indicates the lines of positive action: let the suburban parish look towards the city from which it flees, let it feel responsible for the poverty-ridden areas, let it cease to mobilize members for its own ends and instead teach them to become messengers in the places where they work, let preaching be oriented towards the social and political responsibility of the church, and so forth. Here we can only refer the reader to the practical suggestions of Gibson Winter. Let it suffice for us simply to point out that these suggestions receive their value and their trenchancy from the sociological analysis which the theologian had at his disposal.

Already, sociological inquiries have led to the attempt to establish new ecclesiastical structures, especially in industrialized and urbanized areas. Several examples of this could be cited. For one, there is the pioneering formation of the East Harlem Protestant Parish, which was an experiment designed to reintroduce the church into the inner city and to overcome its marginal nature. Another example is the Detroit Industrial Mission, which is modelled on the experiment already undertaken in England by Wickham (Sheffield Industrial Mission). The Detroit project seeks to install the church no longer in a geographic framework (which has become artificial), but in the modern factory. The factory represents a self-sufficient complex, with its power plants, transportation systems, restaurants, infirmaries, administration buildings, centres of research and training, and finally, its tradition, its language, its spirit. It goes without saying that this parish, built up in the professional milieu and espousing the rhythms of factory life, creates thus a completely new style in which free dialogue replaces classical preaching.[12]

What can sociology contribute to the pastoral ministry itself? The churches often complain about the insufficiency of ministerial recruitment. This insufficiency can result from many causes. One cause at least is of sociological origin: in a secularized society and in a society of work where

the primary norm is that of production, a devaluing of the pastoral function is produced which is part of a devaluing of all functions related to the
word. In the present system of values, the word has lost its dignity in
relation to direct work on things. As proof of this, it is enough simply to
compare the proportion of national budgets which is allocated to scientific
and technical instruction with the proportion allocated to the humanities.
Homo sapiens has come to a standstill compared with *homo laborans*. Only
the political word, in so far as it brings about a chain of reactions at the
level of action, still retains some prestige. But the pastoral word cannot
benefit from such a prestige. When the communist governments refuse to
consider priests as workers and to guarantee them the privileges which
belong to every worker, they are certainly acting from ideological motives.
But at the same time, they are expressing quite candidly one of the deep-
rooted tendencies of the society of work. The minister is a man who speaks
and not a man who works. The ecclesiastical ceremonies of Protestantism,
for profound theological reasons, are not represented as actions; rather,
they come down to the proclamation of a Word. As long as the church held
a place among official institutions, as long as it was admitted that a human
life could not unfold normally and with dignity without being regulated
by the interventions of ecclesiastical authority, then the pastoral word
retained weight and prestige, at least at the crucial moments of baptism,
confirmation, marriage, and burial. It still does, certainly, in many places
and in many circles, but in the large urban and industrialized centres this
tradition is on the verge of ruin. To the degree that the church no longer
benefits from official subsidies and must depend entirely on the generosity
of members, the financial situation of the minister can sometimes be
critical. This is true especially in regions where the church is in the
minority. Finally, the pastoral ministry scarcely allows of *cursus honorum*,
of the possibility of advancement.

All of these well-known reasons make many parents hesitate to push
their children towards the ministry. In fact, often parents do not look
favourably on a child who shows a preference for such a "career", and
multiply obstacles to the realization of this desire. Many require their
children to pursue other studies first. Such procedure reveals their sus-
picions regarding a profession in which they feel their son will not climb
up the ladder of the social hierarchy. They feel that the pastoral ministry
has become socially marginal. Exhaustive sociological investigations are
not at all necessary to perceive this change in the attitudes of people who
may otherwise be devoted to their church.

But sociology can study with precision the sources of ministerial recruitment, both from the perspective of geography and from the perspective of the appurtenance of the candidates to the various social classes. The establishment of a ratio of ministerial candidates from certain areas will make it possible to ascertain which areas are unproductive and which are more prolific. A detailed study like that made by Jean Pierre Boilloux on the recruitment of ministers in the Protestant churches of Alsace-Lorraine from 1918 to 1957 reveals many unexpected things.[13] It shows clearly that the rate of pastoral recruitment is far from being highest in old Protestant territories, that urban recruitment is consistently higher, that as early as 1945 the percentage of workers' sons at the Faculty of Protestant Theology of Strasbourg was ten times higher than in the rest of the University, and so on. When these observations take a systematic and precise character, when the analysis of data suggests causes, the results of the enquiry permit church authorities to take measures which respond to the situation and permit ministers to orient their preaching.

Quite often sociology will bring no unexpected revelations. It simply confirms certain ideas which present experience suggests to us. In such a case, its value rests in its precision, for action can come through this precision.

Sociology can also bring some light to bear on the form of the ministry in our age. The changes of our society as well as those of the relations between the church and the world must have their after-effects on the very form of the pastoral ministry. Although the content of the ministry does not change, although today as in the past the task is one of proclaiming the gospel of reconciliation, it is obvious that the form in which it is expressed is subject to sociological conditioning. In an age where society was stable and very hierarchical, where the church was a universally recognized and accepted social authority, the pastoral ministry took on of necessity an authoritarian character, quite apart from the personalities of the individuals who assumed the pastoral charge. In the Geneva of Calvin, the Society of Pastors enjoyed many prerogatives, even though there were frequent conflicts between them and the magistracy. The consistory, composed of clergy and laity, could exercise a real oversight of the religious life and of morals, and could subject the entire population to ecclesiastical discipline. If one consults the old discipline of the Reformed Churches of France (1559), in particular the articles which deal with the power of consistories, one will see that these consistories functioned as veritable ecclesiastical tribunals. The principle of the priesthood of all believers had been proclaimed from the time of the Reformation. It had been applied in particular to everything which affected the government of the church.

But in its application, the church underwent an evolution in a much more democratic sense. In a society where everyone is Christian by birthright, where social control coerces the majority of members to attend services, the explicit Christian witness and the teaching of Christian truth become the exclusive business of the ordained minister. It is he who instructs, edifies, consoles, reprimands, and corrects. He can do this precisely because he has all the people gathered before him. His authority is contested by no one. The height of the pulpit from which he speaks is the very symbol of this authority. He fulfils a sociological episcopal function.

Undoubtedly this form of ministry has not entirely disappeared in the countries of ancient Christendom. Sometimes, especially in the rural areas of these countries, the minister remains on a level with the civil authorities, and sometimes better than that, on a level with the central authority. This power is stable (it is not rare to see a ministry exercised in continuous fashion over a period of thirty years or more). The pastor carries out his ministry in paternalistic fashion. He knows perfectly all the inhabitants of the village, and is on familiar terms with many of them. He is up to date on all the projected marriages and on the professional plans of the young people. He is consulted (officially or unofficially) concerning the nomination of the teacher, through whom he controls religious education (and who is also the organist and choirmaster). His influence often is great in electoral matters. This remark also goes *a fortiori* for the parish priest. In France, the Third Republic was so conscious of this *de facto* power exercised over the parish by the parish priest, who was usually unsympathetic to the regime and hostile to the secularization of the state and of the school, that it could not assure its own stability without installing a rival authority into the parish. This rival authority was the teacher. In the same paternalistic fashion, he became the counsellor of the inhabitants, the organizer of their spare-time activities, and the electoral agent of the Republic.[14]

Where examples of this genre still exist, they are nothing more than survivals, and the traditions which support them are crumbling. The action by which the minister can assure his authority is no longer sustained by the sociological dignity of his office (*Amt*). He must win this authority through his personal radiance. During services he no longer has the presence of all the assembled people at his disposal. His ministry becomes one of canvassing, of preliminary contacts. It is up to him to move out to the members, to seek them where they are. The institution of factory chaplains in England and Germany is typical of this new situation.

Since the minister cannot fulfil this task alone, he organizes visitation-

teams. The American institution of stewardship is a good example of this
development. The church-building, which formerly towered above the
city and was the centre of it, is no longer necessarily the meeting-place of
the parishioners. The neighbourhood has become the social reality over
which the pastoral ministry is exercised. The idea of the house-church or
of meetings in homes has already produced promising results. The utilization of the talents of laymen and the confiding of the work of evangelization
to them are undoubtedly exigences of the faith, but these exigences are
reinforced by the sociological situation.[15] Instead of being a parish priest,
the spiritual authority *par excellence*, the person who teaches and who
alone has the power to teach, the ordained minister is tending to become
the animator of multiple teams of various types. He plans programmes
with these teams, discusses the results with them, etc. In connection with
these new teams, the church consistories are coming to life. They are
ceasing to be registry-bureaux and agencies for the administration of
finance and property. Moreover, they are participating in the church's
ministry. A more effective co-operation between ministers and laymen has
begun throughout the governing structure of the church. The various
movements and organizations, which often develop on the margins of
the church, have all at once found it possible to take root in the church.
The isolation of the minister, which is a consequence of the paternalism of
his ministry, diminishes to the degree that the parish ceases to be a closed
society and sends veritable commandos out into the world.

The urban parish lacks social homogeneity. It gathers together in its
meetings men who belong to diverse professional spheres. Geographical
communication is difficult in such a parish, and neighbourhood relationships play only a minimal and incidental role. Thus the urban parish
requires a transformation of the pastoral ministry. As Friedrich Fürstenberg[16] has pointed out, the task of the minister can no longer be one solely
of enlightening the assembled community, for in reality this assembly is
no longer a community. Those who approach the Lord's Table together
do not know one another. They separate without speaking to one another,
and if they do speak, it is no more than common courtesy.

How can the church become concretely a community, the Body of
Christ, if it is lacking that tightly knit fabric of human relationships
between its members which permits the development of mutual assistance,
the fulfilling of tasks in common, intercession? An essential aspect of the
minister's job will be to attempt to formulate various forms of contact and
diverse groups in which a common Christian awareness can develop. The
well-worn technique of church circles, where old friends come pleasantly

together under the pretext of some cause or motive, is no longer sufficient. Such groups must be constituted on the basis of an existential problem of daily life. Instead of preaching being a spiritual clarification of the temporal, the temporal must be the basis for the ordering, through study, of a slow progress towards the spiritual. The multitudinous church will become a congregation without structure or conscience if it is not supported by groups of this type, where an inter-personal communication can be established first.

Thus a modification of parish structures and of the very form of the pastoral ministry is bringing into reality the secular or "religionless Christianity" which Dietrich Bonhoeffer, in a rather ambiguous formula, called for in his desire to respond to the spiritual quest of our time. A sociological reflection can become a critical reflection in the church, through which it can find ways and means of leaving the "institutional ghetto" (Visser 't Hooft) in which secularization has enclosed it and where it often lets itself be enclosed.

The theologian and the pastor can sometimes have the impression that when sociology deals with the ecclesial reality, it tends to forget the special nature of the church. It treats it as an empirical reality, even if, in the fashion of G. Le Bras, it sets aside a particular sphere, namely, that of the relationships of the faithful to "the sacred". Does not this very expression "the sacred" risk "materializing", that is, reducing the person of the living God to the level of objective realities? Consequently, sociological analyses often will be given only limited credence. It will be granted only an external and objectifying approach to reality. This mistrust is perhaps even more instinctive in Protestantism than in Catholicism, for the former has more theological reasons than the latter for rejecting any confusion between event and institution, between the invisible church and the visible church, between the mystery known to God alone which is hailed in faith and the official and empirical Christian community. Of course, sociology, like every science, is objectifying, and theology has the right to remind it of the artificiality and limitations of objectification. But Calvin's teaching should be remembered in this respect. Calvin, without ever confusing the invisible aspect and the visible aspect of the church, nevertheless maintained that only one church existed, both visible and invisible, that it is the nature of this congregation of those whom God has called in Christ to form a visible society, rooted in the world without having its foundation there, engaged in history while awaiting the Kingdom.

Francis Andrieux has written an excellent monograph on the parishes of the Reformed Church of Alsace-Lorraine (Moselle).[17] It shows clearly how a sociological study of parishes which is motivated by a pastoral concern yet completely impartial can lead pastor and theologian to a more lucid understanding of the church's unseen splendour and manifest need as well as the tension which always exists between these two inherent aspects of the Body of Christ. The church certainly has no autonomy. It "receives its life through an act of God which creates it and re-creates it unceasingly". But precisely because of this act of God, which lays hold on men and draws them together, the church is also "that institution which we can analyse, an institution which has its history, and which masks an infinitely complex, developing, social, and human reality".[18]

NOTES

1. See the study by Yoshio Fukuyama, "Groupes religieux et sociologie aux Etats-Unis", *CS*, 71, nos. 9–12 (September–December 1963).

2. G. Le Bras, "Réflexions sur les différences entre sociologie scientifique et sociologie pastorale", *ASR*, 8 (July–December 1959).

3. When one studies the numerous parish monographs which are published on the occasion of some anniversary, it becomes evident that they trace primarily, if not exclusively, the history of the pastorates exercised over the years in the parish. As if the parish were constituted by the succession of ministers who passed that way!

4. This fact has been demonstrated quite well by Jean Pellegrin's *L'Eglise de Marseille* (Marseille, n.d.), which is one of the few parish monographs in our possession to have a sociological approach.

5. A simple classification can be utilized for the groups of members: Group A: regular church-goers; Group B: believers who retain a personal piety, but who have no special attachment to the ecclesiastical institution; Group C: the indifferent.

6. Reinhard Koester, *Die Kirchentreuen; Erfahrungen und Ergebnisse einer soziologischen Untersuchung in einer grosstädtischen evangelischen Kirchengemeinde* (Stuttgart: F. Enke Verlag, 1959); cf. F. Fürstenberg, "Der Strukturwandel protestantischer Frömmigkeit als soziologisches Problem", *ASR*, 8 (July–December 1959) [Trans. note. See also, Joachim Matthes, "The Mission of the Congregation", *Frontier*, 9, no. 2 (Summer 1966), 103–108].

7. François Houtard, *Sociologie et pastorale* (Paris: Fleurus, 1963).

8. G. Le Bras, art. cit., *ASR*, 8.

9. Gibson Winter, *The Suburban Captivity of the Church* (New York: Doubleday and Company, Inc., 1961), and *The New Creation as Metropolis* (New York: The Macmillan Company, 1963). Cf. the article by Daniel Galland, "L'Eglise et la grande ville moderne", *RHPR*, 44, no. 2 (1964).

10. W. Herberg, *Protestant - Catholic - Jew*.

11. *Suburban Captivity*, pp. 102–103.

12. Cf. Lary Shiner, "De nouvelles structures pour l'Eglise dans une société urbanisée", *CS*, 71, nos. 9–12 (September–December 1963).

13. Master's thesis (already cited, *supra*, ch. 6, sect. 3).

14. See the excellent study by Georges Duveau, *Les Instituteurs* (Paris: Editions du Seuil, 1957).

15. It is significant that the World Council of Churches considers one of its essential tasks to be the calling forth in the churches of the witness of laymen, and that its Department on the Laity is playing an increasingly important role.

16. F. Fürstenberg, "Soziologische Strukturprobleme der Kirchengemeinde", *Evangelische Ethik*, 7, no. 4 (July 1963).

17. Francis Andrieux, *L'Eglise réformée d'Alsace-Lorraine telle qu'elle apparaît dans la vie des différentes communautés qui la composent.*

18. ibid., p. 13.

CONCLUSION

The Sociological Problem
of Protestantism

It has not been possible for us, in the course of this study, to isolate
Protestantism from the other Christian confessions. All the churches that
witness to the gospel have a large common denominator, which means that
there will be, of necessity, similar if not identical perspectives in their
approach to mission, organization, and relationships with the global
society. But even more, the churches are confronted by a sociological
situation that is the same for everyone in the West and in the entire world.
Since secularization has produced its extreme effects, and since a civilization of universal scope has been constructed first on the basis of science
and then of technology, Christianity no longer informs and imbues man's
daily life, at least not in a general and uncontested way.

Certainly Christianity has its place in the lives of hundreds of millions
of human beings, but this place is limited. "Religion" becomes a more or
less potent factor in certain of life's events: baptism, marriage, sickness,
burial. It is tied much more to the dramatic moments of human existence,
the religious holidays (the secular civil society has the greatest difficulty
injecting life and enthusiasm into secular holidays), than to daily life with
its technological and economic demands. Christianity only rarely plays a
part in the organization of the structures of existence. It no longer provides
social models. It has withdrawn into a sphere of gratuitousness, and no
longer engages with reality. In many countries, to be sure, the tourist
guidebooks and brochures continue to indicate the times and places of
religious services, but it is symptomatic that this information is placed
alongside indications concerning museums, movies, and theatres. Consequently, such information is addressed to the man with time on his hands
or who is on vacation. Even in countries of long-standing Christian tradition, where there is no anti-religious animosity, public opinion increasingly
classifies the religious life among cultural activities, among leisure-time
concerns.

It is possible, however, that as leisure-time increases, the churches will be beneficiaries of the situation; they have already begun to seek ways to reach man in his leisure-time activities. The opening of centres of worship at the various types of resort areas, the effort made to interest holiday-makers in religious literature and to rewin them by means of concerts of sacred music, etc., is all clear evidence that the churches are conscious of the new situation facing them. But however important be the perspectives opened by a civilization of leisure, it is none the less the case that the real man is *homo laborans*, the citizen, the union member, rather than the man on vacation who seeks only diversion, who seeks to get away from his customary surroundings. And it is *homo laborans* that Christianity must reach if it wants to inform human life and not content itself with bringing man a sort of supplement of spirituality, a spiritual complement for the empty hours.

Also, it is a sociological fact worth noting that the whole thought of the churches, and of Protestantism in particular, at present seems to be dominated by the theme of *presence in the world*. It is this theme which lies in the background of manifold theological publications; it is encountered on all cultural levels; in various forms, it plays a part in the orders of the day of synods, of ecclesiastical assemblies, even of the Vatican Council.[1] This theme of presence in the world has even opened new sectors in theological research that would have astonished classical theologians: theology of the world, theology of work, theology of culture, theology of leisure. The multiplication of such discussions and studies, which often content themselves with presenting the problems, clearly indicates that the churches have entered a new age in which they will have to rediscover their place in society. For this place is no longer prepared for them in advance; indeed, society organizes itself without taking this place into consideration.

These theological reflections do not, moreover, remain academic. They are translated into all manner of innovations and institutions. It should be noted that many of the latter are of a pedagogical nature: the multiplication of lay-training centres, of evangelical academies, is evidence that the churches are conscious of the need for a long preparation before they will be able to take on their new task, or rather, the new forms of presence in the world.

Although the problem of the church's preaching is eminently theological, and although the essential content of this preaching is determined by its object (the biblical revelation), the orientation of this preaching and the accentuation *hic et nunc* of any given one of its elements must equally be determined by the sociological situation in which this preaching resounds. As with the theme of presence in the world, the theme of the relevance of preaching occupies at the moment the attention of ministers, laity, and various church assemblies. In order to define this relevance, especially in a church (e.g., like those of the Reformation) which insists strongly on the social responsibility of the member, various sociological considerations can and must intervene: a consideration of the social *milieux*, of professional interests, of age, of sex. But for several decades, a sociological problem has dominated this reflection, a problem which arises from the very fact of the technical nature of the world civilization that is being elaborated. For such a civilization produces its values and its view of the world. Now, as Max Weber so frequently emphasizes, the view of the world which grows out of an essentially technical, non-magical civilization is a disillusioned view. The world and life are stripped of their mystery. Mankind directs its energies towards the resolution of problems which are problems simply of adapting means to ends, and the ends ultimately are nothing more than means of a higher degree to attain other ends, and so on. Everything happens as if the ends were absorbed and reabsorbed by the means. Anxiety, the basic dimension of being, is at the centre of contemporary philosophical reflection, but for a civilization of work and of that which "works", anxiety ceases to be anything but a pathological symptom belonging to an appropriate category of tranquillizers to alleviate. Thanks to these tranquillizers, the anxious individual will be able to adjust correctly once again to his surroundings and function. And yet the disillusioned world continues to produce a boredom which delivers human-beings to the insidious spread of anxiety. Paul Ricoeur, in analysing the meaning of anxiety, insists on the modern cast of this psychic anxiety [*angoisse*]:

Vital anguish merely varies in intensity from epoch to epoch, following the value given to individual life. But psychic anguish is more conspicuous throughout history by virtue of its very nature. It is indeed striking that it is within the most civilized societies, those best protected against danger and during peacetime, that this endogenous insecurity of the psychism makes its appearance, as if the most fragile of all psychisms were that of the civilized. In addition to the complexity of the psychism, I should like to invoke the role of what might be called the boredom of civilization. There has been no want of descriptions of this boredom that oozes out from societies most endowed with the products of civilization. (I am thinking of E. Mounier's notions on Scandinavia, of Karl Stern's, in *The Pillar of Fire*, on the New World where the Jewish refugee from Germany disembarks, surprised to find, thousands of miles removed from the Nazi hell that he left, that here is a world more fragile psychically than the one that he left.) Not only well-being, but also work, in its piecemeal form, diffuses boredom into industrial societies, as if a more acute psychic evil were taking the place of physical pain. I do not say that boredom is anguish, but it leads to anguish. By creating zones of freedom or at least areas of life organized apart from public order, from political and social security, the growth of civilization leaves man to himself, the prey of boredom; man who is less and less equipped to counter the dangers secreted by his psychism.[2]

It would be easy to multiply *ad infinitum* examples of the type alluded to by Ricoeur: the appearance of gangs of youths engaging in senseless forms of violence, meaningless suicides, all the phenomena that take such alarming proportions in industrialized and secularized societies and which simple police measures cannot seem to check – are not these things symptoms and illustrations of this disillusionment of the world? Even when no pathological manifestation of this boredom of civilization is recorded, it remains the case that industrial societies face a fundamental question concerning their finality. This question often expresses itself in disillusioned formulas such as: "The growth of production, economic expansion, what's the use of it all?" The appearance of more generalized and greater leisure-time will certainly pose even more dramatic problems for human existence. Production and security, which for the two-thirds of underdeveloped humanity are ideals still capable of mobilizing ethical energies, are insufficient ends in the societies of abundance.

If it is true that the gospel gives life and hope, how will the churches respond to this boredom of disillusioned souls? We do not and could not have the intention of replying to such questions. But we should note one thing, as a sociological fact: Protestantism, which for decades was characterized by a moralizing preaching, has rediscovered in the past thirty years the importance of the preaching of the kingdom. The kingdom was seen first as the archetype of social justice (Social Gospel movement; the Ecumenical Conference of Stockholm in 1925), then as eschatological reality, as source of hope. Innumerable theological works have given renewed value to the idea of eschatology, and these works have led to a renewal of preaching.[3]

Obviously, this fact may be interpreted in two different ways: either, in face of this disillusionment of the world, the church finds a kind of alibi or evasion in this hope, thus recapitulating the experience of numerous sects; or the hope of the last things is conceived by the church as the spiritual reality which can give worth and a new flavour to daily life in the societies of abundance and security. In this latter hypothesis, eschatology, rather than being the source of a mythical escapism, becomes the wellspring of an ethic. Such seems to be the way followed by the theological reflection of Protestantism. Whether one considers the theology of Karl

Barth or that of Rudolf Bultmann, however different be their conceptions of eschatology, both establish a very strong tie between eschatological faith and ethical decision.[4]

Thus there is a concomitance between these two phenomena: on the one hand, the disillusioned perspective of the world which is the byproduct of technological and industrial societies; on the other hand, the rediscovery and increased appreciation of the eschatological dimensions of the gospel. This concomitance, in our opinion, needs to be emphasized. The will of the church to be really present in the world is expressed in this concomitance. By attempting to respond to the evils which social mutations introduce into human existence, the church recovers a new social function in this secularized society that had ceased to make anything more than marginal provision for it or had even totally ignored it. This new social function is much less tied to the fulfilment of certain social rites which have been held to be indispensable in the past of Christendom.

Although Christianity as a whole finds itself obliged to face the new situation created by secularization, it is none the less the case that Protestantism has its own sociological problems. The doctrinal particularity of the Reformation is reflected in the communities that it has engendered and gives to them a specific sociological character. As Charles Hauter[5] has so well emphasized, that which the Reformation introduced was a mutation within the religious object itself, within that object about which the community assembles. In the medieval church, on the level of piety, this object was presented in a sort of massive and consistent objectivity. The centre of the Mass was a sacred reality, a redoubtable and worshipped thing which, by its own power, provoked the proper attitudes and behaviour in the faithful, and which engendered a whole ecclesiastical hierarchy that gave the priest his particular status. The priest is the man authorized to approach this sacred thing, to grasp it, and distribute it in conditions such that it will produce a beneficent effect. Statues and images participate in the same virtue as the eucharistic species and produce analogous results. Wherever a sacred reality is thus given, not only does the community gather easily but it necessarily becomes institutionalized. The more the religious object has stability and the more it has the characteristics of the sacred, the more also its handling presupposes precise and meticulous rules. The application of these rules, in turn, presupposes a hierarchical and strongly institutionalized society. The development of the Roman Catholic Church attests to the parallelism of these two phenomena: on the one hand, a sacramentalist objectivism and, on the other hand, a more and more developed institutionalization. The doctrine reflects the objective stability of the sacred; it is congealed in unchangeable definitions issuing from a canonical authority. Respect for this orthodoxy presupposes also a reinforcement of the hierarchy and the formation of a whole juridical apparatus.

The Reformation was indeed iconoclastic in the sense that it devalued all these objective images which solicited piety, and in the sense that it replaced the sacred (under its diverse aspects) with the sole Word of God, a Word which is not a thing, but which is, in preaching and in the sacrament, the actual presence of the living God. Of course, this Word of God has nothing to do with a subjective reality. On the contrary, all human subjectivity finds its condemnation there. But it must be recognized that sociologically it no longer has the massive objectivity of the sacred. It cannot have it, because it is act and event. A religious community obviously has more difficulty gathering together and forming a permanent body around a reality which thus escapes our customary determinations. A religious community is indeed threatened by a subjectivism which was given free rein, especially during the period of romanticism and in certain sects. Subjectivism has not been a threat during all periods nor in all churches born of the Reformation, but it was because it threatened that Protestant orthodoxy sought an objective substitute for the sacred and found it either in Holy Scripture (considered as identical with the Word of God, and consequently surrounded by a respect which is expressed theologically in biblicism, literalism, and fundamentalism), or in the formation of a body of received doctrines which have played the same role in Protestantism that dogmatic definitions have played in the Roman hierarchy.

It is quite true that Protestantism, by putting the Word of God at the centre of faith, piety, and worship, has in no wise forsaken the sacrament. But following an Augustinian tradition, it enclosed the sacrament in the Word of God as *verbum visibile*. It is not a thing, it cannot be the object of worship, and it is perfectly useless to proceed to the reserving of the species. The bread and the wine are, indeed, the body and the blood of the Lord, but they are it by the Word (by the efficacy of the Holy Spirit in Calvinism). In the Larger Catechism, Luther writes these significant words:

As we said of baptism that it is not simply water, so here again, we say of the Sacrament (of the altar) that it is bread and wine, but not simply bread and wine as we would find it on the table: it is comprised in and bound to God's word. The word is that which makes the sacrament and gives it its distinctive character; it is not simply bread and wine, but is and signifies Christ's body and blood.[6]

Thus the sacrament participates in this actualism of the Word. It is not substance. It does not have existence *ex sese*. Thus it cannot constitute, alongside the Word, a second pole for the worship service that would have more of a material and constraining objectivity. In any case, it does not constitute for Protestant piety the indispensable factor which determines salvation and death. It has meaning only in relation to the Word. Thus Protestantism teaches that a worship service can be authentic worship without the sacrament accompanying it. This view, certainly, is contested today by numerous theologians and exegetes. But on the sociological level, it should be remarked that, in fact, in Protestantism (Lutheran as well as Reformed) the Lord's Supper is not necessarily tied to the worship service, although the practice of frequent communion tends to locate it there. In any case, it was in the logic of Protestantism always to subordinate the sacrament to the Word. Thus we should point out that in the Reformation there was indeed a veritable mutation in the structure of the religious object.

The latter was accompanied by a greater relativization of questions of organization, institution, and hierarchy. The fact is particularly clear in original Lutheranism. Luther was in no way preoccupied with giving the church a new constitution and a new hierarchy. It was sufficient for him that the Word of God was preached and the sacraments distributed in conformity to the gospel. He concerned himself with questions of organization only in regard to the development of Christian teaching, and readily left all questions of the temporal (social) jurisdiction of the church to the prince and the magistrate. The essential aspect of the church was not, for Luther, in the organization and the hierarchy, but in the relationship of faith which united the faithful to Christ:

> Bear this well in mind [he wrote in the treatise *On The Papacy* (1920)], Christianity is a spiritual communion of souls by faith, and no one can be considered a Christian by virtue of external signs . . . A non-Christian can possess them, but they will never make him a Christian. Only a true faith makes a Christian. This is why we sing at Pentecost: "We pray to the Holy Spirit to give us above all a true faith." It is in this that Holy Scripture speaks of Christianity and of the Holy Church, and never otherwise.

Only the existence of a ministry seemed essential to the terrestrial life of the church. All organization must be relative to the exercise of this ministry. Calvin undoubtedly had a more sociological view of the church in its visibility. The place which he gave to discipline is more considerable and ecclesiastical ordinances are necessary. But for Calvin as well, the true form of the church is recognized in the fact that the Word of God is preached and the sacraments administered. To be sure, in order for there to be true church order, it is necessary for there to be pastors, superintendents, and deacons (*Confession of La Rochelle*, art. XXIX), but all these functions are subordinated to the service of the Word of God. In order to assure the unity of the church, it is good that it have "superintendents", but as for local organization, one must act "as convenience requires it" (art. XXXII). Of course, the implantation of the church, its mission and tasks of evangelization, the extension of its social services, the need of assuring a unity of action and a true strategy on the regional, national, and international levels, all will determine, in the course of history, an inevitable broadening of the organization and, indeed, of the administrative apparatus. It is none the less true that Protestantism, faithful to its original inspiration, has never ceased to feel that in order for there to be a church and in order to safeguard its basic unity, there needs to be the correct preaching of the Word of God and the administration of the sacraments according to the gospel. Thus Protestantism (with the exception of Anglicanism) has rejected the idea of the necessity of a hierarchy and of a canonico-juridical power. Protestantism generally considers the external form of the church and the existence of an episcopacy as relevant not to the *esse* of the church, but to its *bene esse*. Consequently, such questions are relative, questions which must be asked in the light of circumstances and of common utility.

The mutation which the Reformation brought about in the very interior of the religious object has resulted in primacy being given to the event and, consequently, to interiority and, again as a consequence, to a relativization of the forms of organization and hierarchy. Ernst Troeltsch describes the progress of the Lutheran Reformation thus:

> Religion thus steps out of the material substantial sphere, which was merely accompanied by thought and feeling, and enters into the intellectual, psychological, spiritual sphere ... Religion is now a matter of faith and conviction, instead of one which is bound up with a hierarchical-sacramental system.[7]

Such a formula undoubtedly calls for many reservations: it seems to suggest, as Catholic theologians have often said, that Protestantism is a subjectivism, a fideism, and an individualism. Indeed, these are the categories in which Troeltsch, the theologian, felt the content of Christianity to reside. The language is inadequate, to be sure. It would be more exact to say that the Reformation has replaced one type of objectivity (that of the sacred) with another type of objectivity (that of the act of the living God); one type of community (established, hierarchical, juridical) with another type of community in which the communal element prevailed over the social element. But although the formula is theologically insufficient, although it does not do justice to the consequences of the Reformation, it expresses the specific sociological problem of Protestantism.

Christianity [writes Henry Duméry] is an *established* religion. It can also be said, similarly, that it is an *instituted* religion. Several things are meant by that. It says first of all that Christianity is not an empty religious form, lacking in content. It says that it is not an amorphous religious experience, void of structures. Finally, it says that it is not a subjective view of God, lacking intersubjective expressions (chiefly cultic).[8]

This outline of a phenomenological description of Christianity can certainly be applied to Protestantism. It also is an instituted religion. It also has a piety structured by a doctrine and a confession of faith. It also is pre-eminently expressed in a communal worship. But although it is an instituted, cultic, and social religion, not only by an unfortunate necessity but by its profound movement, although it proceeds from the event to the institution (conceived as the very sign of the seriousness with which the event is received), it is also that form of Christianity (different from Catholicism and Orthodoxy) in which the permanent return to the event always calls into question all forms of the institution – *Ecclesia reformata, semper reformanda*. It is an instituted religion which always attempts to avoid becoming prisoner of its institution. This is what Troeltsch saw quite well. The sociological meaning of the numerous divisions which have been produced within Protestantism (Methodism, Congregationalism, Pentecostalism, etc.) is always one of contesting the institution when it has taken on too much substance and power, and takes itself too seriously. The rejection of the apostolic succession, of the unchangeableness of doctrinal formulas, and of the very idea of doctrinal development (within the institution and nourished by it) has the same sociological meaning. The great controversy between Catholicism and Protestantism, now disengaged from many of its more passionate elements and purified by the very progress of the biblical sciences, is located fundamentally at the ecclesiological level. And the reproach which Catholics direct against Protestants is of not having an ecclesiology, of stopping with Christology. The complaint is very meaningful in its brutality: of course Protestants have an ecclesiology and confess the Holy Catholic Church. But they refuse to give the institutional church a sacral substance; they refuse to identify it with the mystery of the church; they can speak of the body of the church only in speaking of its head.

An inventory of the various forms of Protestant churches and of the diverse theological currents which are present there would undoubtedly

reveal the existence of High Church movements characterized by a sacer-
dotalism, a liturgism, a sense of hierarchy. In the dialectic of event and
institution, it happens that sometimes one feels the need of reinforcing
the institution when the event threatens to engender a pure actualism,
when "angelism" makes the church forget that it is and can only be
instituted, indissolubly invisible and visible. But like a pendulum, these
movements call forth counter-movements. In Protestantism, this dialectic
assumes considerable importance. It always stirs passions and creates
conflict. This is indeed the sign that, in its sociological phenomenology,
Protestantism is that form of Christianity in which the necessary institution is also felt to be the trap of the event.

NOTES

1. The very real originality of the Second Vatican Council has been much emphasized. It is the first time that a Council has not formulated condemnations, and has
applied itself less to defining definitive doctrinal formulas than to seeking a new mode
of insertion of the church in a world of work and in a civilization of work. All of the
concerns are expressed in the important schema on *The Church in the world of today*.
On this important point, the Council is only following the programme of the world
assemblies of the World Council of Churches, which indeed proves the convergence of
the present concerns of all the churches.

2. Paul Ricoeur, *History and Truth*, trans. by C. A. Kelbley (Evanston: North-
western University Press, 1965), pp. 292–293.

3. In choosing "The Christian Hope in Today's World" as its theme for the Second
World Assembly in Evanston (1954), the World Council of Churches both expressed
a latent desire of the churches and promised a new orientation in their preaching. Yet
the fact that this theme encountered the resistance of certain churches, notably of
American Protestantism, shows how slowly this change is taking place.

4. In order to measure the amplitude of theological studies on the relations between eschatology and ethics, it is sufficient to consult the bibliographical analysis
of W. Schweitzer, *Eschatologie und Ethik* (Geneva: World Council of Churches, 1951).
Since that date, the effort has not slowed down.

5. Charles Hauter, *Le problème sociologique du protestantisme* (Paris and Strasbourg:
Istra, 1923).

6. From *Luthers Werke in Auswahl*, edited by Otto Clemen, vol. 4 (Berlin and Leip-
zig: Walter de Gruyter and Co., 1930), p. 90.

7. Troeltsch, *Social Teaching*, vol. 2, p. 469.

8. Henry Duméry, *Phénoménologie et religion* (Paris: PUF, 1958), p. 1.

SELECTED BIBLIOGRAPHY

[Due to the broad scope of *The Sociology of Protestantism*, no attempt has been made to provide an exhaustive bibliography. The following list is meant simply to cover some of the major works in the sociology of religion, or, in a few cases, to provide titles for further study of individual subjects. *Trans.*]

ANDREWS, Edward D. *The People Called Shakers* (New York: Dover Publications, Inc., and London: Constable and Company Limited, 1963).

BERGER, Peter L. *The Noise of Solemn Assemblies* (Garden City, New York: Doubleday and Company, 1961).

— *The Sacred Canopy; Elements of a Sociological Theory of Religion* (p.b. ed.; Garden City, New York: Doubleday and Company, 1969).

CARRIER, Hervé. *The Sociology of Religious Belonging.* Tr. by A. J. Arrieri (New York: Herder and Herder, and London: Darton, Longman and Todd, 1965).

CUTLER, D. R., ed. *The Religious Situation: Nineteen Sixty Nine* (Boston: The Beacon Press, 1969).

HANDY, Robert T., ed. *The Social Gospel in America: Gladden, Ely and Rauschenbusch* (New York: Oxford University Press, 1966).

HERBERG, Will. *Protestant, Catholic, Jew* (rev. ed.; Garden City: Anchor Books, 1955).

KÜNG, Hans. *Structures of the Church.* Tr. by S. Attanasis (p.b. ed.; Notre Dame and London: University of Notre Dame Press, 1968).

LANDIS, BENSON, and others. *Not Many Wise; a Reader on Religion in American Society* (Boston: The Pilgrim Press, 1962).

LENSKI, Gerhard. *The Religious Factor* (rev. ed.; Garden City: Doubleday Anchor Books, and London: W. H. Allen, 1963).

LEEUW, G. van der. *Religion in Essence and Manifestation*, 2 vols. Tr. by J. Turner (Magnolia, Mass.: Peter Smith, Publisher, and London: Allen and Unwin, 1964).

LEEUWEN, A. T. van. *Christianity in World History.* Tr. by H. H. Hoskins (New York: Charles Scribner's Sons, and London: Edinburgh House Press, 1964).

LOSSKY, V. *The Mystical Theology of the Eastern Church* (Naperville, Ill.: Alec R. Allenson, Inc., and London: J. Clarke, 1957).

MARTIN, David. *The Religious and the Secular* (London: Routledge and Kegan Paul, 1969).

— *A Sociology of English Religion* (London: SCM Press, 1967).

— ed. *A Sociological Yearbook of Religion in Britain*, Volumes One and Two (London: SCM Press, 1968 and 1969).

MEHL, Roger. *Images of Man*. Tr. by James H. Farley (Richmond, Va.: John Knox Press, 1964, and London: SPCK, 1966).

— *Society and Love*. Tr. by James H. Farley (Philadelphia: The Westminster Press, 1964, and London: Hodder and Stoughton, 1965).

NIEBUHR, H. Richard. *Social Sources of Denominationalism* (New York: Harper and Row, Inc., "Torch Book").

NIEBUHR, Reinhold. *Faith and Politics*. Ed. by Ronald H. Stone (New York: George Braziller, Inc., 1968).

PAWLEY, Bernard, ed. *The Second Vatican Council; Studies by Eight Anglican Observers* (London and New York: Oxford University Press, 1967).

RAAB, Earl, ed. *Religious Conflict in America* (Garden City: Doubleday Anchor Books, 1964).

SHINN, Roger. *New Directions in Theology Today, Vol. 6, Man: The New Humanism* (Philadelphia: The Westminster Press, and London: Lutterworth Press, 1968).

SMITH, Ronald G. *The Free Man; Studies in Christian Anthropology* (London: William Collins Sons and Co., and Philadelphia: The Westminster Press, 1969).

TAWNEY, Richard H. *Religion and the Rise of Capitalism* (New York: New American Library, Mentor Books, and London: Penguin Books, Inc.).

TROELTSCH, Ernst. *Social Teaching of the Christian Churches*. Tr. by Olive Wyon, 2 vols. (London: Allen and Unwin, 1931, and New York: Harper and Row, Inc., Torch Books).

WACH, Joachim. *The Comparative Study of Religion* (p.b. ed.; New York and London: Columbia University Press, 1961).

— *Sociology of Religion* (Chicago: University of Chicago Press, 1944).

WEBER, Max. *Protestant Ethic and the Spirit of Capitalism*. Tr. by T. Parsons (New York: Charles Scribner's Sons, 1930, and London: Allen and Unwin, 1967).

— *The Sociology of Religion*. Tr. by E. Fischoff (Boston: The Beacon Press, 1964, and London: Methuen and Company, Ltd., 1965).

WILMORE, Gayraud. *Secular Relevance of the Church* (Philadelphia: The Westminster Press, 1962).

WILSON, Bryan. *Religion in Secular Society* (London: C. A. Watts, 1966).

WINTER, Gibson. *New Creation as Metropolis* (New York: The Macmillan Company, 1962, and London: Collier-Macmillan, 1965).

— *Religious Identity* (New York: The Macmillan Company, and London: Collier-Macmillan, 1968).

— *The Suburban Captivity of the Churches* (New York: The Macmillan Company, and London: Collier-Macmillan, 1962).

YINGER, J. Milton. *Sociology Looks at Religion* (New York: The Macmillan Company, and London: Collier-Macmillan, 1963).

INDEX OF NAMES

KING ALFRED'S COLLEGE
LIBRARY